Family EXPLORER

EXPLORER
www.Explorer-Publishing.com

Passionately Publishing...

Family Explorer 2nd Edition

First Published 2001
Second Edition 2004 ISBN 976-8182-34-2

Copyright © Explorer Group Ltd, 2001, 2004
All rights reserved.

Printed and bound by Emirates Printing Press, Dubai, United Arab Emirates.

Explorer Publishing & Distribution LLC
PO Box 34275, Dubai
United Arab Emirates
Phone   (+971 4) 335 3520
Fax   (+971 4) 335 3529
Email   Info@Explorer-Publishing.com
Web   www.Explorer-Publishing.com

Printing Authorisation Number: 001372, 26th October 2004

While every effort and care has been made to ensure the accuracy of the information contained in this publication, the publisher cannot accept responsibility for any errors or omissions it may contain.

No part of this publication may be reproduced, stored in a retrieval system, or transmitted, in any form or by any means, electronic, mechanical, photocopying, recording or otherwise, without the prior permission in writing of the publisher.

EXPLORER
www.Explorer-Publishing.com

Authors
Jane Drury
Elizabeth Fonseca
Joseph Rowland

Publishing
Publisher — Alistair MacKenzie
Alistair@Explorer-Publishing.com
Publishing Manager — Peter D'Onghia
Peter@Explorer-Publishing.com

Editorial/Content
Editors — Claire England
Claire@Explorer-Publishing.com
Jane Roberts
Jane@Explorer-Publishing.com
Contributing Editors — Lena Moosa
Tracey Pitts
Content Manager — Louise Mellodew
Louise@Explorer-Publishing.com
Researchers — Helga Becker
Helga@Explorer-Publishing.com
Tim Binks
Tim@Explorer-Publishing.com
Yolanda Rodrigues
Yolanda@Explorer-Publishing.com

Design
Graphic Designers — Jayde Fernandes
Jayde@Explorer-Publishing.com
Sayed Muhsin
Muhsin@Explorer-Publishing.com
Zainudheen Madathil
Zain@Explorer-Publishing.com

Photography
Photography — Pamela Grist
Pamela@Explorer-Publishing.com
Explorer would like to thank all parents and friends who kindly provided photographs for this book.

Sales & Advertising
Sales & Marketing Manager — Amanda Harkin
Amanda@Explorer-Publishing.com
Media Sales Executive — Alena Hykes
Alena@Explorer-Publishing.com
Sales/PR Administrator — Janice Menezes
Janice@Explorer-Publishing.com

Distribution
Distribution Manager — Ivan Rodrigues
Ivan@Explorer-Publishing.com
Distribution Supervisor — Abdul Gafoor
Gafoor@Explorer-Publishing.com
Distribution Executives — Mannie Lugtu
Mannie@Explorer-Publishing.com
Rafi Jamal
Rafi@Explorer-Publishing.com
Stephen Drilon
Stephen@Explorer-Publishing.com

Administration
Accounts Manager — Kamal Basha
Kamal@Explorer-Publishing.com
Account Assistant — Sohail Anwar
Sohail@Explorer-Publishing.com
Administration Manager — Nadia D'Souza
Nadia@Explorer-Publishing.com

Introduction

Dear Parents,

We at Explorer Publishing are well versed in all the facets of family life and we've got the scars to prove it. It is therefore, with great pleasure, that we are honoured to introduce a new member of our Explorer guidebooks family. Updated, revamped and renamed, the 2nd edition of the **Family Explorer** will take you from birth and beyond.

At Explorer we like to think of ourselves as a family and like a family we had the same... well... squabbles — but the result is a book like no other in the Emirates. We shared the same late nights, temper tantrums and tears at putting the book to bed but most importantly the joys of all things family.

We all know how time consuming kids can be and with that in mind we have spent a lot of time nurturing this book so that you can enjoy the fruits of our labour. Take the **Activities** chapter, packed with as much ammunition as possible to sustain the fight against boredom. In **Going Out** you will discover that sacrificing your social life is far from necessary with a whole host of eateries ready to feed your child's entertainment appetite as well as desire for chicken nuggets. As for **Shopping**, your little ones can outdress Brooklyn and Romeo Beckham with designer threads you'll wish you could squeeze into. With cries of "are we there yet" coming from the back seat we also understand the importance of not getting lost so the extensive **Maps** will keep you on the right track.

The Explorer family tree extended its branches to reach out to the experts – i.e. you – to get the inside track on raising a family in the UAE and to provide us with lovely photos of your little ones. So, with great pride and joy we pass this book down to you and wish you all happy familes!

Explorer Insiders' City Guides

These are no ordinary guidebooks. They are your lifestyle support system, medicine for the bored, ointment for the aimless, available over the counter and prescribed by those in the know. An essential resource for residents, tourists and business people, they cover everything worth knowing about the city and where to do it.

Abu Dhabi Explorer

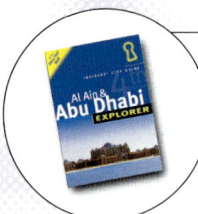

Just when you thought it couldn't get any better! The 4th edition of the **Abu Dhabi Explorer** has been radically revised and revamped, making it the ultimate insiders' guidebook. A lifetime of information is sorted into easy reference sections with recommendations, advice and guidance on every aspect of residing in Abu Dhabi & Al Ain. Written by residents with a zest for life, this book is an essential resource for anyone exploring this beautiful emirate.

ISBN 976-8182-58-X **Retail Price** Dhs.65, €18

Dubai Explorer

The 9th stunning edition of Dubai Explorer has broken the mould in insiders' city guides. A prodigy amongst its peers, and still the best selling in its class, the **Dubai Explorer** has done it again with its newest annual addition.

Full of all of the favourite sections, we bring you even more places to eat, sleep shop and socialise, as well as an enormous amount of must have information on everything you need to know to survive and enjoy the city of Dubai.

ISBN 976-8182-60-1 **Retail Price** Dhs.65 €18

Geneva Explorer

Following the hugely popular style of the **Explorer** city guides, the **Geneva Explorer** too, has raised the bar for quality guidebooks in the region. A resident team of writers, photographers and lovers of life have sold their souls to exhaustive research, bringing you a guidebook packed with insider recommendations, practical information and the most accurate coverage around. Written by residents thoroughly familiar with the inside track, this is THE essential must-have for anyone wanting to explore this multicultural haven. **(Due out 4th quarter 2004)**

ISBN 976-8182-44-x **Retail Price** Dhs.65 €18

Oman Explorer

As the list of fascinating insights grew beyond the city limits of Muscat, the **Oman Explorer** was born. Now covering the whole of this largely unspoilt country, this guidebook has become an in-depth catalogue of the region's life, leisure and entertainment. Based on the legendary formula of the **Dubai Explorer**, every aspect of existence in Oman is covered, with no stone left unturned. This is essential reading for anyone exploring this gorgeous country – be it residents, visitors or business trippers. **(Due out 4th quarter 2004)**

ISBN 976-8182-07-5 **Retail Price** Dhs.65 €18

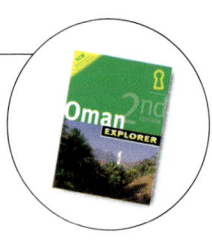

Explorer Activity Guides

Why not visit stunning marine life and mysterious wrecks, or stand poised on the edge of a natural wadi or pool in the mountains? Get a tan and a life with our activity guidebooks.

Family Explorer (Dubai & Abu Dhabi)

The one and only handbook for families in Dubai and Abu Dhabi has finally arrived. Jam packed with hundreds of innovative ideas, you can now enjoy a multitude of both indoor and outdoor activity options with your little ones, or follow the guidance and tips provided on practical topics such as education and medical care. Written by experienced parents residing in the Emirates, the **Family Explorer** is, without a doubt, the essential resource for families and kids aged up to 14 years. **(Due out 3rd quarter 2004)**

ISBN 976-8182-34-2   **Retail Price** Dhs.65 €18

Off-Road Explorer (UAE)

You haven't truly been to the Emirates until you've experienced its delights off the beaten track. Dear to the hearts of the indigenous and the insane, this pastime involves hours of zooming 4x4s up sand dunes and hours of digging them out again! The **Off-Road Explorer (UAE)** is a brilliant array of outback route maps designed for the adventurous and the anxious alike. Satellite images superimposed with step-by-step route directions, safety information and stunning photography, make this a perfect addition to your four wheeler.

ISBN 976-8182-37-7   **Retail Price** Dhs.95 €29

Underwater Explorer (UAE)

Opening the doors to liquid heaven in the UAE, this handy book details the top 58 dive sites that avid divers would not want to miss. Informative illustrations, shipwreck data & stunning marine life photographs combined with suggested dive plans cater to divers of all abilities. Whether you're a passionate diver or just pottering, you will not want to be without this crucial resource.

ISBN 976-8182-36-9   **Retail Price** Dhs.65 €18

Off-Road Explorer (Oman)

Coming Soon!

FAMILY EXPLORER

Explorer Photography Books

Where words fail, a picture speaks volumes. Look at the world though new eyes as the lens captures places you never knew existed. These award winning books are valuable additions to bookshelves everywhere.

Dubai: Tomorrow's City Today

Stunning photographs shed light on the beauty and functionality of contemporary Dubai, a city that is a model of diversity, development and progress. Explore its historical highlights, municipal successes, innovative plans and civic triumphs, as you wonder at the grandeur in store for the future.

ISBN 976-8182-35-0 **Retail Price** Dhs.165 €45

Images of Abu Dhabi & the UAE

This visual showcase shares the aesthetic and lush wonders of the emirate of Abu Dhabi as spectacular images disclose the marvels of the capital and the diversity of astounding locations throughout the seven emirates.

ISBN 976-8182-28-8 **Retail Price** Dhs.165 €45

Images of Dubai & the UAE

Images of Dubai shares the secrets of this remarkable land and introduces newcomers to the wonders of Dubai and the United Arab Emirates. Journey along golden beaches under a pastel sunset, or deep into the mesmerising sands of the desert. View the architectural details of one of the most visually thrilling urban environments in the world, and dive undersea to encounter the reef creatures that live there. This book is for all those who love this country as well as those who think they might like to.

ISBN 976-8182-28-8 **Retail Price** Dhs.165 €45

Sharjah's Architectural Splendour

Take a guided tour of some of the highlights of Sharjah's architecture. Through the lens, this book captures small, aesthetic details and grand public compounds, the mosques and souks of this remarkable city. Striking photographs are linked together with text that is both analytical and informative. Whether you are a long term resident or a brief visitor, this volume of images will undoubtedly surprise and delight.

ISBN 976-8182-29-6 **Retail Price** Dhs.165 €45

Other Products

Apart from our wondrous array of city guides, activity guides and photography books, we offer other titles so innovative, they cannot be categorised. From the Hand-Held Explorer (our revolutionary digital guidebook) to the Street Map Explorer (your guide to getting around), these popular products have been bought, used, loved and lived.

Hand-Held Explorer (Dubai)

The **Dubai Explorer** goes digital. Interactive, informative and innovative, this easy to install software for your PDA offers you all the info from your favourite guidebook at your fingertips. Browse through restaurant reviews at the push of a button, scroll through and peruse a multitude of activities, and dive into a mountain of must know data at a glance. Your PDA will be undernourished without it!

ISBN 976-8182-40-7   **Retail Price** Dhs.65 €18

Street Map Explorer (Dubai)

The most accurate and up to date map on Dubai has arrived! The **Street Map Explorer (Dubai)** is a concise and comprehensive compendium of street names, cross referenced with an A to Z index of businesses and tourist attractions. In this fast developing city, this expansive and handy guidebook will soon become your favourite travel mate and a standard tool for navigating this ever-growing metropolis.

ISBN 976-8182-10-5   **Retail Price** Dhs.45 €18

Dubai Tourist Map

This much awaited second edition of the **Dubai Tourist Map**, compiled and published by Dubai Muncipality, offers visitors and residents the best chance of getting from A to B. Key places of interest are highlighted and brief descriptions of the main tourist attractions are enhanced by colour photographs. An index of the community street and building numbering system ensures that the city can be easily navigated. This map is a must for anyone in Dubai.

ISBN 976-8182-16-4   **Retail Price** Dhs.35 €14.95

Zappy Explorer (Dubai)

Aptly dubbed the 'ultimate culture shock antidote', this guide is **Explorer's** solution to the complexities and perplexities of Dubai's administrative maze. A clear, straightforward set of procedures assists residents through the basics of life in this city, from opening a bank account and connecting your phone to buying a car and marrying your true love. Including detailed information on ministry and government department requirements, what to bring lists, reference maps and much more, the **Zappy Explorer** is your best chance of getting things done next to bribery or force!

ISBN 976-8182-25-3   **Retail Price** Dhs.65 €18

Home Sweet Home

Overview	3
Moving to the UAE	**3**
Culture Shock & Children	4
Facts & Figures	**6**
Population	6
Business & Social Hours	6
Safety/Security	8
Local Media	8
Money	9
Climate	9
Photography	9
Culture & Lifestyle	**9**
Culture	9
Language	10
Food	10
Dress	10
Places of Worship/Religion	11
Support Groups & Social/Cultural Groups	11

Entering the UAE	**11**
Visas	11
Health Requirements	12
Travel Insurance	12
Getting Around	**12**
Buses	12
Taxis	12
Cars	12
Road Safety	14
Driving	14
Holidays & Annual Events	**15**
Holidays	15
Annual Events	15
Housing	**15**
Property Rental	15
Property Purchase	16
Relocation	16
Insurance	17

Baby Proofing the Home	17
Pets	17
Domestic Services	**18**
Babysitting	18
Domestic Help/Maids/Housecleaners	20
Laundry	20
Gardening	20
Plumbing/Maintenance/Home Improvements	21
Locks & Keys	21
Electricity	21
Telecommunications	21
Television	21
Rubbish Disposal	21
Recycling	21
Insects/Rodents	22
Dangerous Bugs	22
Annual Events	**22**

Medical

Introduction	**27**
Health Card	27
Private Medical Insurance	27
Emergencies	28
Pharmacies/Chemists	28
Medical Care	**28**
Medical Institutions	28
General Practitioners	29

Paediatricians	29
Dentists/Orthodontists	30
Opticians	30
Dermatologists	32
Chriopodists	32
Maternity	**32**
Antenatal & Birth	32
Mental Health	**35**

General Safety & First Aid	**36**
First Aid	36
Stings & Bites	36
Burns	36
Common Concerns	37
Alternative Medicine	**37**

Education

Education	**41**
Toddler Groups	43
Nurseries & Pre-Schools	44

Schools	50
Tertiary Education	55

Special Needs	**56**

Shopping

Shopping	**61**
Places to Shop	**61**
Shopping Malls	61
What & Where to Buy	**66**
Baby Equipment	66

Baby Equipment Hire	68
Baby & Kidswear	68
Books & Stationery	70
Food	70
Hairdressers – Kids	71
Home Furnishings & Accessories	71
Home Safety	72

Interior Design	72
Maternity Clothes	73
Musical Instruments	73
Pets	73
Portrait Photographer/Artist	74
Sporting Goods	74
Toys & Crafts	76

Activities

Sports & Activities	83	Martial Arts	102	**Beach, Health & Sports**	
Amusement Centres	83	Mini Golf	103	**Clubs**	**119**
Amusement Parks	86	Moto-Cross	104	Beach Clubs	119
Basketball	86	Mountain Biking	104	Health & Sports Clubs	121
Boat & Dhow Charters	86	Netball	104		
Creek & Coastal Cruises	87	Paintballing	106	**Beaches & Parks**	**122**
Bowling	88	Plane Tours	106	Beaches	122
Camel Racing	88	Play Centres	106	Beach Parks	123
Camping	90	Rollerblading	107	Parks	124
Canoeing	91	Rugby	107		
Climbing	92	Running	107	**Expand Your Horizons**	**126**
Crazy Golf	92	Sailing	108	Art Classes	126
Cricket	92	Sand Boarding/Skiing	109	Clubs & Associations	127
Diving	93	Snorkelling	109	Dance Classes	127
Dune Buggy Riding	94	Squash	110	Drama Groups	128
Fishing	95	Swimming	112	Language Schools	130
Football	95	Tennis	113	Libraries	131
Golf	96	Trekking	114	Music Lessons	132
Gymnastics	98	Triathlon	114	Summer Camps	133
Hockey	99	Wadi & Dune Bashing	114		
Horse Riding	99	Walks	115	**Museums, Heritage &**	
Ice Hockey	100	Water Parks	116	**Culture**	**135**
Ice Skating	100	Water Skiing	116	Museums – City	135
Jet Skiing	101	Water Sports	118	Museums – Out of City	136
Karting	101	Windsurfing	118	Zoos	139
Kite Flying	101	Yoga	118	Tour Operators	140
Kite Surfing	101				
				Weekend Breaks	**140**

Birthday Parties

Birthday Parties	**151**	Ice Skating	158	Sporty Parties	162
		Karting	158	Water Parks	163
Indoor Venues	**151**	Museums	159		
Amusement Centres	151	Play Centres	159	**Parties at Home**	**163**
Arty Parties	151	Sporty Parties	161	Birthday Cakes	165
Bowling	152			Organisers & Entertainers	167
Cinema	153	**Outdoor Venues**	**161**	Party Accessories	167
Clubs, Hotels &		Beaches	161		
Restaurant Venues	153	Paintballing	161	**Theme Parties**	**170**
Fast Food	156	Parks	162	**Out Of Town Parties**	**170**

Going Out

Going Out	**177**	**Restaurants**	**184**	**Cafés & Coffee Shops**	**193**
Icons - Quick Reference	178	Abu Dhabi	184	**Foodcourts**	**196**
Friday Brunch	178	Dubai	188		

Maps   200

Index   240

Are you relocating to Dubai or Abu Dhabi ?

You are probably wondering how you are going to find the time and energy to plan your move ?

You don't have to.

At In Touch Relocations, we know the in's and out's of settling newcomers into Dubai or Abu Dhabi. We can assist with your home-find, utilities hook up, drivers licence, school enrolment, shopping mall guide etc. The list is extensive and guaranteed to save your family from the stress, frustrations and hassles such a move generates.

At In Touch Relocations we can tailor-make a relocation package that will suit your needs. So as you take up your exciting new position, you can focus on these challenges knowing your family is being well taken care of.

Using In Touch Relocations is a proven cost effective solution to a hassle free move.

- City orientation • Settling in • Home find assistance • Education services
- Departure service • Document attestation • Help desk support

Give your family a positive feeling about being in the United Arab Emirates and working for your company – contact In Touch Relocations, your dedicated relocation experts

Call for a free consultation
Tel +971 4 332 88 07
Fax +971 4 332 83 93

In Touch
RELOCATIONS

intouch@emirates.net.ae - www.intouchdubai.com

Home Sweet Home
EXPLORER

Home Sweet Home

Overview	3	*Entering the UAE*	11	*Domestic Services*	18
		Visas	11	Babysitting	18
Moving to the UAE	3	Health Requirements	12	Domestic Help/Maids/	
Culture Shock & Children	4	Travel Insurance	12	Housecleaners	20
				Laundry	20
Facts & Figures	6	*Getting Around*	12	Gardening	20
Population	6	Buses	12	Plumbing/Maintenance/	
Business & Social Hours	6	Taxis	12	Home Improvements	21
Safety/Security	8	Cars	12	Locks & Keys	21
Local Media	8	Road Safety	14	Electricity	21
Money	9	Driving	14	Telecommunications	21
Climate	9			Television	21
Photography	9	*Holidays & Annual Events*	15	Rubbish Disposal	21
		Holidays	15	Recycling	21
Culture & Lifestyle	9	Annual Events	15	Insects/Rodents	22
Culture	9			Dangerous Bugs	22
Language	10	*Housing*	15		
Food	10	Property Rental	15	*Annual Events*	22
Dress	10	Property Purchase	16		
Places of Worship/Religion	11	Relocation	16		
Support Groups &		Insurance	17		
Social/Cultural Groups	11	Baby Proofing the Home	17		
		Pets	17		

MUST HAVE

As you drive round the UAE you will notice an alarming number of young children standing up between the front seats or evening riding, unsecured, in the front of the car. Despite the audacity of these drivers this irresponsible behaviour is in fact illegal and is especially dangerous when the driving here leaves a lot to be desired. Children should always wear a seatbelt or be secured in a car seat, a number of which can be found in Mothercare. See [p.15].

MUST DO

The UAE has a zero tolerance policy to drink driving and the penalties are more than a slap on the wrist. If you have an accident, even a minor prang, and the police discover you have been drinking then you can expect to do jail time. If you cause injury to another person as a result of that accident then the sentence will reflect the extent of the damages. Also police have begun doing spot checks so you could be stopped even if you haven't been involved in an accident. Taxis are plentiful and cheap so use them, even if you've just had the one. See [p.12]

MUST KNOW

In the last year or so property rental prices, especially villas in the mid range price bracket, have substantially increased. While a year ago you could easily find a three bedroom villa with shared pool in Mirdif for Dhs.60,000 (popular with families) annually you are now looking at Dhs.70,000+. However, pundits believe that as the buyers' market takes off, more properties for rent will be available, forcing rents to go down. Also, offering to pay your annual rent in one cheque, if you can afford it, rather than the usual two or three, can get you a sizeable discount. See [p.15]

FAMILY EXPLORER

Overview

Well ma and pa, it's off to the UAE. By this time, whether you're preparing to depart or are just arriving, you're probably reeling with anticipation, nerves, excitement and maybe even a little fear. However, topmost on your mind would most likely be a million questions about everything from housing and medical care to what you're going to do on a Saturday... err... Thursday afternoon (it's ok, you'll get used to it). Well, take heart. You're far from the first family to relocate here and Explorer has tapped into the experience of some of the most adventurous veteran expat parents to put together this handy guide that answers the majority of your questions.

No matter where you're coming from, you're in for a period of adjustment and there's no way of getting around that. However, once you've unstuck yourself from some of the inevitable red tape, set up home, figured out where the shops are, and recovered from the jet lag, you'll find that for the most part, the Emirates is extremely family oriented with a regular offering of events developed specifically for children or families. Additionally, a number of facilities, especially in Abu Dhabi and Dubai, offer safe and sometimes even educational play opportunities. Match that with the natural attractions of beach, mountain and desert, and you begin to understand why parents are so happy with this environment.

Dubai Creek

Outside of facilities and events, you will find that the culture too is quite family oriented, and families stay out with children even late at night. Because of this, most facilities are geared to accommodate children, and the staff are usually tolerant and helpful. You will also find that people are very forward about speaking to (and sometimes even touching) your little ones, which may take a while to get used to. While you will of course, want to keep an eye on your children, you will soon get used to the environment and begin to feel that your children are safe here.

So, where do you begin? Right here of course. With this completely revised and revamped edition of the *Family Explorer*, you will find guidelines to an abundance of activities available in the Emirates. From Brownies to bowling and camping to cricket, the range includes a full description of available parks, cinemas, museums, clubs and any other entertainment option you can think of. However, as you well know, keeping a family going is about much more than just activities at the weekends. So, we have also included a section on Medical Care [p.26], which explains not only how to get your health card and insurance sorted out, but also gives helpful advice on hospitals, paediatricians, having a baby, specialists, and even some basic first aid. Also, we have taken a careful look at education in the Emirates and provided you with a complete guide to the different types of schools, what you and your children can expect from them, as well as any other information you will need to know about nurseries, kindergartens and tertiary education. Also, a very useful Shopping section [p.60] tells you where to find all the necessities, such as toys! Finally, when it's all done and you want to leave the cooking to someone else, flip to Eating Out [p.177] for a comprehensive guide to the best family friendly restaurants in Abu Dhabi and Dubai.

Moving to the UAE

If you're preparing to move to the UAE, there are a few things to bear in mind as you're getting yourself and your family ready to go. First and foremost, be up for the change. Experienced expats know that the transition from your home country to another can be an exciting yet possibly stressful time, especially for children who are accustomed to routine. If it is your first experience abroad, you will soon discover this. You should also be aware that culture shock is a very real phenomenon and most people go through it in one form or another. It can be helpful to familiarise yourself with the signs and stages of culture shock, so you can minimise or work through some of the issues that come up in the process of adapting.

As you prepare for your move, it is advisable to learn all that you can about the UAE and the specific Emirate that you are relocating to. Then, depending on the age of your children, talk to them positively about what the move will entail, what kind of changes they're going to experience, and mention some of the exciting things they will come across once they arrive (camels and the beach are the two most popular options). Downloading photos from the Internet or purchasing books with photos of people and places might also prove helpful (*Images of Dubai & the UAE* by Explorer Publishing offers an excellent pictorial coverage).

Keep in consideration any special dietary/medical needs you or your children may have. The UAE is a modern country with a solid infrastructure and state of the art healthcare. Nevertheless, if a member of your family requires special treatment or medication, it would be worth your while to contact one of the hospitals and/or paediatricians in your prospective emirate and confirm that those needs can be met. Most likely, you won't have a problem, but you'll feel more comfortable knowing for sure.

Bring along photos of close friends and family members for your new home (or even pets who couldn't make the trip). This is especially helpful for younger children and will make re-familiarisation easier when grandparents, aunts, uncles, cousins or old friends come to visit, or when you're home on vacation.

Remember to bring copies of immunisation records and medical histories for your child, as they will be necessary for school.

Finally, try to ensure that all those you would like regular contact with (ie, grandparents) have access to email and the Internet, and know how to use it. International phone calls can become expensive and with the time differences, keeping in touch can be difficult. With email, however, you can maintain regular contact. Sending pictures or posting them to a Website is a great way to share your experiences with loved ones back home.

Culture Shock & Children

Moving from one place to another inevitably involves a period of serious transition. Culture shock is technically not a state of shock but a series of stages that an individual goes through when adjusting to new surroundings, whether a different country, a new city or even a new school or job. Generally, these stages begin with some form of euphoria or excitement, where you or your children are thrilled by the new surroundings and everything is refreshing and new. When these differences become negative and day to day operations are frustrating due to unfamiliarity, depression or adjustment difficulties set in. Finally, if all goes well, some type of adaptation stage is reached where the adjustment is made and life goes on. For each individual, this can take different lengths of time and manifests itself in several ways. To make things more difficult, you may be going through the same stages at the same time. It is important that you recognise this process of acculturation in yourself and your children.

Home Sweet Home

ايرنيست لوسطاء التأمين ش.ذ.م.م
Earnest Insurance Brokers L.L.C.

HOME SWEET HOME !

HOW SECURE IS YOURS?

We can *insure* your home and personal belongings
giving you full protection 24 hours a day.

For all your INSURANCE needs:
Contact Frank O'Sullivan or Sridhar on 04 338 5400 or
Mobile 050 5599726 / 050 5599782

The following pointers may help:
- Find familiar shops and places. You may not want to eat pizza or shop at Toys R' Us, but your kids will initially find comfort in these familiar surroundings.
- Try to put your children in contact with other expat kids who have made the adjustment. Group activities that interest your child, such as sports or art classes, will give them something to look forward to and an opportunity to meet other children with similar interests.
- Accentuate the positive and understand what your child is going through. This is not the time for harsh words or making your child feel guilty about missing home, so don't brush off or dismiss his/her frustrations. On the contrary, encourage children to express their irritations, fears or concerns, so they feel that someone's listening to them.
- Try your best to establish a familiar routine. It may provide an oasis of stability in a suddenly confusing world.
- Relax around your house. There is a temptation to be on the go all the time when you first arrive, but a weekend of settling in can be beneficial to your family.

Remember that the entire family is experiencing the same, but reacting in different ways. Since you have a huge influence on your children, be careful with negative comments or reactions and work hard on making your own adjustments so that you are able to help the rest of your family.

So what can you expect once you get here? Your first few days in the Emirates will be dominated by two overwhelming observations. Firstly, everything is new, modern and BIG! Whether it's the skyline of Sheikh Zayed Road in Dubai, the Corniche in Abu Dhabi or one of the massive shopping complexes found throughout the country, you will be impressed. Considering how little was here 15 - 20 years ago, the sheer scale and sophistication of architecture will leave you stunned. Secondly, diversity is the norm and everyday, you will come across people from a variety of cultures. For many people this is a good thing and one of the great attractions of living here, but even for the most open minded of individuals, dealing with so many different types of people can take some getting used to.

If you arrive in the summer months (especially August or September), you will notice one thing above all else. It's hot! No, not just hot... words like scorching, baking, sweltering and oppressive spring to mind. You'll find yourself spending a lot of time indoors, even though it's bright and sunny outside. Take heart. The weather will cool down by October or November, and by February, you'll be gloating in front of your friends about how you spent your weekend at the beach, while they were shovelling snow back home. It's definitely worth the wait.

Facts & Figures

Population

The population of the UAE stands at around 3.5 million, with 65 - 70% of the people living in Abu Dhabi or Dubai. Expats living and working in the Emirates significantly outnumber the local Emirati population. The majority of these expats are labourers from countries such as India and Pakistan. This means that men greatly outnumber women (2.4 men to every woman in Dubai) as low income labourers are not permitted to bring their families with them. Many other nationalities are also well represented throughout the Emirates in different fields and professions, which makes for a rich diversity. Unfortunately, it also means that outside of those working with the government or possibly in education, expats seldom fraternise with locals. There are of course, exceptions to this rule. Locals, in general, are quite friendly and inviting.

> **Living in the UAE**
>
> There are many attractions of living in the UAE including a better standard of life, higher than the average salary at home (and tax free) and a cheaper cost of living. The UAE is also a safe place to live in comparison to many other countries and prides itself on being nearly 'crime free'. Also the warm climate and freedom to explore the desert and mountains inspires in many people a sense of adventure that they might not have at home and gives them memories that last a lifetime.

Business & Social Hours

Social hours are Mediterranean in style – normally people get up early, often have an afternoon siesta, then eat and socialise until late in the evening.

Traditionally, there's no concept of the weekend, although Friday has always been the holy day. This means that in the modern UAE, the weekend has established itself on different days for different

The Specialists

أخصائيو

Property   **Relocation**   **Interiors**

We offer a unique one - stop service covering all aspects of Real Estate, Relocation and Interior Decoration.

The Specialists has been established since 1996 and is an integral part of Dubai's local business and expatriate community. Our team brings together an unrivalled knowledge and understanding of one of the worlds fastest growing desirable locations. Our services include Real Estate Sales and Rentals, Practical and Cultural Orientation Programmes and Soft Furnishing and Home Decoration. Our full compliment of services are driven by the ongoing satisfaction of a happy customer. We can respond quickly and provide competitive pricing ensuring a welcoming experience for all companies, employees and families that are moving to Dubai or within the Emirates.

www.dubaiuae.com   +971 4 3312662   info@dubaiuae.com

people. Government offices and some private companies are closed on Thursday and Friday. Other companies take a half day on Thursday and all day Friday, and still others take Friday and Saturday as their weekend. Understandably, these differences cause difficulties since families do not necessarily share weekends.

Schools generally follow the Thursday/Friday weekend option and hours vary, with a start time of 07:00 or 08:00 and a finish time of between 12:00 and 16:00. Schools finish earlier on Wednesdays and extracurricular activities are after school hours.

Government offices are open 07:30 - 13:30. Private sector office hours vary between split shift days (generally between 08:00 and 13:00, reopening at either 15:00 or 16:00 and closing at 18:00 or 19:00) or straight shifts (usually 09:00 - 18:00 with an hour for lunch).

Ramadan

Business and social hours change dramatically during Ramadan, including school hours, so be prepared to do a bit of routine juggling for the month. You will also notice that the cities/streets become a great deal quieter during this time, apart from during the evenings. Non-Muslims must respect the laws of the holy month and refrain from eating, drinking and smoking in public places during daylight hours.

Shop opening times are usually based on split shift hours, although many outlets in the big shopping malls remain open all day. Closing times are usually 22:00 or 24:00. On Fridays, many places are open all day, apart from prayer time (11:30 - 13:30), while larger shops in the shopping malls only open in the afternoon at 16:00 or 17:00. During the holy month of Ramadan, timings may change, even for the larger shopping centres.

Safety/Security

Crime, especially against children, is seemingly non existent in the Emirates. As mentioned by expat parents, one of the pluses of living here is the overwhelming sense of safety wherever you go. This obviously doesn't mean that you'll want your youngsters to roam unattended, but you'll find yourself quite comfortable in the park or in crowded situations. You will also be happy to find that the police are genuinely friendly and helpful, especially where children are concerned.

One worry you may have as a parent is the traffic situation. Driving, for the most part, is fast and undisciplined, and the sheer lunacy of some drivers is a popular topic of conversation among resident expats. Although the laws clearly state that children must be in the back of the vehicle in a secured car seat, these are all too often ignored, even by parents who should know better.

Are you sure this is safe?

Local Media

Locally published English language newspapers, such as Gulf News, Khaleej Times and The Gulf Today are readily available here, and feature international and local coverage. The Guardian, International Herald Tribune, USA Today and other international newspapers are also widely available, although they're usually a day or two out of date.

Recently, the UAE market has seen an explosion of local English language magazines (most are Dubai focused). Many are aimed at a specific target audience or are entertainment based. Additionally, most international magazines (including parenting based titles) are sold in markets and news stands. The majority of magazines are European, but quite a few North American titles or editions can also be found.

Some local magazines: Ahlan, Aquarius, Connector, Emirates Woman, Gulf Business, Parent Plus, Viva, What's On and Time Out.

For resident information, Explorer books are ideal, providing you with the most comprehensive coverage of the Emirates. Beginning with the *Abu Dhabi Explorer* and the *Dubai Explorer*, you'll find important information on cities, what to do and where to go, along with detailed maps. For the more adventurous, the *Underwater Explorer*, features scuba dive sites around the UAE, and the *Off-Road Explorer* offers adventurous routes with easy to follow instructions and directions. The *Zappy Explorer* covers mundane matters, such as getting a driving licence, applying for a work permit or paying the bills.

Satellite and cable television is quite popular, showing films, sports and news, as well as local stations. There are a number of English language radio stations that often appear indistinguishable from one another and mostly play bubble gum pop and commercial hit numbers from the Top Ten charts. Unfortunately, the radio market has yet to cater to differing or alternative tastes.

Money

The UAE Dirham (Dhs. or AED) is the local currency. Divided into 100 'fils', the dirham is available in notes of 5, 10, 20, 50, 100, 200, 500 and 1000. Additionally, coins of Dhs.1, 50 fils and 25 fils are available. The dirham is fixed to the US dollar at a mid rate of US $1 ~ Dhs.3.6725. The exchange rates of all major currencies are published daily in the local newspapers and exchange houses are widely available offering good service and rates.

Cash is very much the preferred method of payment throughout the Emirates. However, credit cards are becoming increasingly accepted, especially in shopping centres and larger restaurants. In the smaller eateries, souks and outside of larger cities, you will certainly want to have cash available. Getting change too, can be an issue outside of the larger venues, so try to hold on to your smaller bills.

Climate

While summers are exceedingly hot (highs can reach 48° C/118° F), temperatures during the rest of the year vary from bearable to lovely, ranging from the mid teens to high twenties in the winter months. Match that with virtually guaranteed blue skies (rainfall is around 13 cm per year) and you'll find that your family will want to spend a lot of time outside. A trip to the wilderness or the beach for some great weather is definitely one of the highlights of living in the Emirates, but if you're not accustomed to year round sunshine, you should be aware of some safety concerns. Sun exposure is a very real threat, even during the winter months or on overcast days. Parents should be especially careful with children and ensure that proper sunscreen (widely available) is worn, as well as protective clothing, such as a hat, sunglasses and possibly long sleeves. Additional care should be taken to ensure adequate hydration for everyone. If you're going out, it's always a good idea to carry a couple of litres of water per person in the car.

Photography

Standard 35 mm film and the means to develop it are readily available in the Emirates. Developing is generally offered at a reasonable price and is usually of standard one hour quality. If you are a professional photographer or require a film that is hard to find, you will have to go to more specialised shops, such as Grand Stores for Fuji (04 352 3641) or UCF (United Colour Films) for Kodak (04 336 9399). If you're in the market for a new camera, consider making the jump to digital photography so it is much easier to send photos home. Either way, you'll want to have a good camera to record your adventures.

Sandman smiles for the camera!

Culture & Lifestyle

Culture

To simplify matters, there are two broad cultures in the Emirates – the local Emirati culture and the expat culture. What's more, the lifestyle of Emiratis in larger cities, such as Abu Dhabi and Dubai, will greatly contrast the lifestyle of those Emiratis in more rural settings. With so many ethnic groups represented, expat culture too, will certainly manifest itself in different ways to different people. Between these two cultures, although there are certain separations, both the 'locals' and the 'expats' interact in public, frequently, smoothly and readily.

The result of this mixture, whether it is in Dubai, Al Ain or Abu Dhabi, is a vibrant and dynamic community that offers opportunities to attend cultural events ranging from camel races to rock concerts. Residents and visitors to the Emirates can choose from every varying option. Those wanting to experience the traditional ways of life don't have to look very far to find cultural centres, museums, festivals and other special events dedicated to highlighting and prolonging the cultural heritage of the Emirates. Conversely, an extended stay will also offer opportunities to take in the latest Hollywood films, an occasional touring orchestra, or visit one of many clubs, bars and exquisite restaurants. As the Emirati culture is very family oriented and many expat workers are here with their families, you will find many opportunities for family entertainment. The trick is to keep your eyes and ears open for upcoming events (often events aren't well publicised) and also to keep your mind open to the many possibilities this rich mix of cultures affords to children and adults alike.

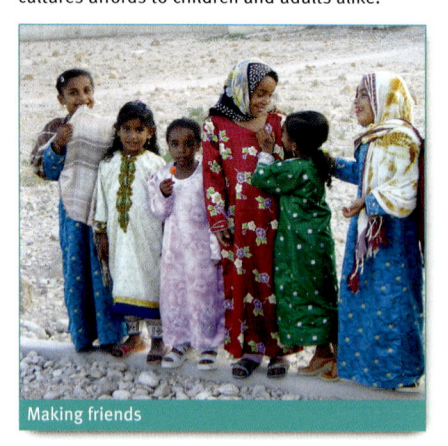

Making friends

Language

Arabic is, of course, the official language of the Emirates and widely spoken, but English is very much the lingua franca throughout the Emirates. Newspapers, radio, television and street signs are all in English, and business, too, is generally conducted in English. In other words, shop assistants, waiters and pretty much anyone else you come across and need to communicate with will probably speak English, especially in Abu Dhabi and Dubai. There are also many schools where English is the medium of instruction. Should you still want to learn Arabic, classes are available.

Food

A wide range of western food products, especially from the UK and Europe, are available in grocery stores throughout the Emirates, so you needn't worry about getting your kids accustomed to Arabic meals. Grocery stores and markets offer a full range of baby products, from formulas and cereal to baby food (with some stores stocking organic products). Additionally, with so many cultures and nationalities represented, you will come across products from all over the world, offering you the ideal opportunity to be adventurous.

Some of the brands and products available here are: Pampers, Huggies, Nanny's, Gerber, Aptalmi, Nestle, gluten free milk, rusks, Johnson & Johnson, Bebe Comfort and soya milk.

Eating out (or ordering in) is a favourite pastime in the Emirates and there are hundreds of restaurants offering almost every type of cuisine imaginable. As local culture is very family oriented, you'll find that most restaurants (even some of the outlets in the five star hotels) welcome children and often offer seating in family areas. Restaurants and even food stands (that usually seve shawarma sandwiches made from mutton or chicken, falafel sandwiches and the like) are kept to a high standard of hygiene and are regularly inspected, so safety generally isn't an issue. However, you may want to exercise parental judgement from time to time.

Another point to note is that most families take advantage of the bottled water delivery services, which are extremely convenient, delivering 20 litre bottles and collecting the empties. Tap water throughout the Emirates is safe for drinking and cooking, but doesn't always taste that great. Restaurants usually serve bottled water.

Dress

The majority of the national population in the Emirates wears traditional Arab attire – the 'dishdash(a)', which is a long (usually white) full length shirt-dress with a headdress called the 'gutra' for men and the 'abaya' and 'sheyla', the long black robe and headscarf, for women. Many women also wear gloves and a veil covering their face.

While the Emirates is, in many ways, a very traditional Muslim country, there is no dress code which states that women must cover themselves in public, meaning that you can basically wear whatever you want. However, it is sensible to be respectful of the local customs and beliefs, and to strive for modesty or at least decency when in public. Beach attire is acceptable (on the beach, of course) and you won't feel uncomfortable in a bathing costume or a bikini, especially at the larger beach hotels. Dubai is the most liberal of the emirates, with Abu Dhabi and Al Ain becoming more conservative respectively. Additionally, during the holy month of Ramadan, it is only respectful for women to be especially mindful of dress and opt for the more conservative outfits in their wardrobe.

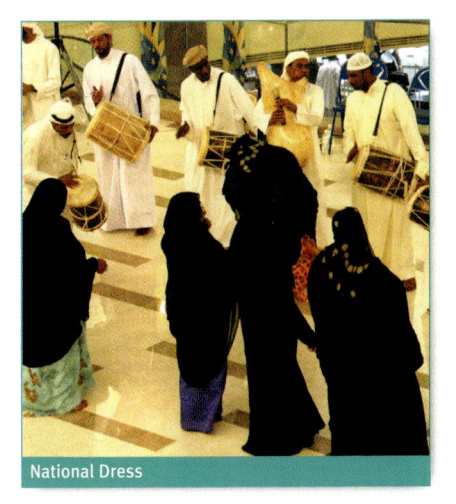

Winters in Dubai are naturally quite mild, so summer clothing is suitable throughout the year, although you and your children will want to have a few sweatshirts, jumpers or lightweight jackets to choose from. Oddly enough, you will still need these when visiting restaurants or the cinema, as the air conditioning is liberally employed. Additionally, sun exposure is a very real issue, so hats, sunglasses and sunscreen should be among the items to pack.

Places of Worship/Religion

Islam is the official religion of the UAE, but other religions are respected and people are free to congregate and worship. Al Ain, Abu Dhabi and Dubai all have Christian churches offering services throughout the week and active church communities. Several denominations are represented. There is also a Hindu temple in Dubai. Above is a list of Christian churches in the Emirates.

Churches

Abu Dhabi

Arabic Evangelical Church	02 443 4350
Evangelical Community Church	02 445 5434
St Andrew's Episcopal Church	02 446 1631
St George's Orthodox Church	02 446 4564
St Joseph's Roman Catholic Church	02 446 1929

Al Ain

St Mary's Church (Catholic)	03 721 4417

Dubai

Emirates Baptist Church	04 349 1596
Holy Trinity Church (Anglican)	04 337 0247
Jesus Christ Latter Day Saints	04 395 5447
St Mary's Church (Catholic)	04 337 0087
The Evangelical Community Church	04 884 6623
The Mor Ignatius (Orthodox)	04 884 4382
United Christian Church of Dubai	04 344 2509

Support Groups & Social/Cultural Groups

Living overseas is a great adventure packed with new encounters and once in a lifetime experiences, but it can also be difficult at times. You're away from your extended family, you or your spouse (or both of you) may be working a great deal, and sometimes you just feel plain homesick. The latter can be especially true for stay at home mums. But be strong – whatever you're going through, there's usually someone else in a similar situation. Fortunately, a sizeable network of support and cultural groups are available to help you along or to simply offer some comfort. So remember, their help is only a phone call away. For a list of support groups, refer to Medical Care [p.26].

Entering the UAE

Visas

Visa requirements for the UAE vary greatly between nationalities. Regulations should always be checked before travelling since details can change with little or no warning. Except for GCC Nationals, all visitors require a visa. However, citizens of the countries listed on p.12 are granted a free visit visa on arrival. Children with their own passports also require visas.

Tourists from Eastern Europe, China and South Africa may obtain a 30 day, non renewable tourist visa sponsored by a local hotel or tour operator before entry into the UAE.

National Dress

No Visa Required

Citizens of Andorra, Australia, Austria, Belgium, Brunei, Canada, Cyprus, Denmark, Finland, France, Germany, Greece, Holland, Hong Kong (with the right of abode in the United Kingdom), Iceland, Ireland, Italy, Japan, Liechtenstein, Luxembourg, Malaysia, Malta, Monaco, New Zealand, Norway, Portugal, San Marino, Singapore, South Korea, Spain, Sweden, Switzerland, United Kingdom, United States of America and Vatican City receive an automatic, free visit visa on arrival in Dubai. This visa is valid for 60 days, but can be renewed for a further 30 days on payment of a fee.

Health Requirements

No health certificates are required for entry to the Emirates, except for those visitors who have been in cholera or yellow fever infected areas in the previous 14 days. However, it's always wise to check health requirements before departure for restrictions may vary depending on the situation at the time.

Malarial mosquitoes are rarely a problem in the cities, as they mostly exist in damp surroundings, such as the wadis and mountain pools. Short term visitors who plan to visit the countryside may be advised to take tablets for malaria. Check requirements before leaving your home country.

Hospitals and paediatric clinics throughout the Emirates offer any necessary immunisations, including annual boosters for children. However, you may wish to arrange for them before arriving, especially if you're only visiting. Polio, tetanus and hepatitis (A and B) are recommended. If your children are of school age, the school will require your child's immunisation records and medical history.

Travel Insurance

All visitors to the Emirates should have travel insurance – just in case. Choose a reputable insurer with a plan that suits your needs and that covers any activities you may plan to do whilst here. Make sure this insurance also covers 'blood money' in case you are involved in an accident involving a death and you are found guilty. For families settling in the Emirates, please see Health Insurance [p.17].

Getting Around

In the Emirates, getting from point A to point B is usually a relatively simple affair due to the excellent motorways and a variety of travel options. Following are the various options you can choose from to get to where you're going. As with anything, having kids can complicate matters, but you should still be able to find an acceptable mode of transport for getting around town.

Buses

Abu Dhabi, Al Ain and Dubai offer a bus service which is generally used by lower income workers. They are probably not the best option for parents and children. If you would like to give the bus a go, contact the Dubai Municipality (800 4848). For Abu Dhabi, call 02 443 1500.

Taxis

Taxis are readily available throughout the Emirates. Most have meters, and travellers, especially women, should try to use these licensed vehicles. If you do find yourself in a non metered taxi, be sure to agree on a price before the journey. Additionally, when travelling alone in one, women would probably prefer to ride in the back seat. Some taxis do not have back seat belts, however you can request for one that does when ordering the taxi. Parents should be aware that taxis do not provide car seats for infants or small children, but the driver will certainly wait while you install yours in his car. Do not hesitate to tell the driver to reduce the speed if his driving is making you uncomfortable.

A point to remember is that taxi drivers aren't always an authority on how to get around the city, so you may find yourself giving directions. If you're new in the city, it's worth having directions or at least the phone number of wherever you're going.

Cars

Buying a Car

Most individuals and families staying in the Emirates for an extended period will opt to buy their own car. Public transport is not the best of options in the Emirates, and while taxis are cheap

Bumps & Babes, Beauty & Fashion, Health, Interiors, Investment, Property, On-line Book-Club, Recipes, Slimming, & Travel.
Plus UAE Local Pages, Qatar Local Pages and more franchises to come....

ExpatWoman.com
your magazine on-line

Its free, its friendly & its written for you

A resource for expatriate women of all nationalities, living anywhere.

- a monthly magazine on-line;
- a growing archive of readers' stories;
- a very active chat board;
- local news, views, competitions and offers; and
- a busy social calendar of events from fashion shows to privilege shopping mornings, breakfasts to high tea to dinners…

www.ExpatRegister.com
For all expats, past and present, all nationalities, living anywhere.

It's easy and quick to register,

and it's *FREE!*

Keep track of old friends and don't lose your new ones.

Sign Up Today and Spread the Word....!

and plentiful, they don't offer the same level of freedom as having your own wheels. As you spend more time here, you'll find yourself wanting to get out and explore. There are several reasons why most families go for a 4 wheel drive, if they can afford one. Primarily, these cars offer more options for the weekend, such as off-roading, camping and exploring the wilderness. Additionally, a larger vehicle affords a little more respect on the roads, meaning that you are more visible and less likely to be cut up.

There are various avenues to try when looking for a vehicle to buy. Car dealers are plentiful and the local newspapers feature a daily classified section of cars and 4 WDs for sale.

In addition, noticeboards in the larger grocery stores usually list several cars for sale. It is highly recommended that anyone buying a car via this method should have it thoroughly checked by a mechanic – looks can be deceiving and the previous owner could have been less than kind to the car, leaving you with a load of headaches.

Once you decide to buy a car, refer to the *Zappy Explorer* for a step by step guide to arranging the insurance and registration of your car.

Road Safety

Roads and highways throughout the Emirates are quite well developed and maintained. Although this means getting from place to place is easy, it also means that traffic can move very swiftly and accidents, unfortunately, are a regular occurrence. Most are slight fender benders with no injuries, but the occasional serious ones do occur. Motorists should be cautious at all times and especially vigilant of other drivers. Parents should also make sure that children are secured in approved car seats. Even though the law states that it is illegal, you will often see children riding in the arms of parents in the front seat.

Driving

Driving in the Emirates does not involve the mass congestion and sheer lunacy of some countries around the world, but it can still be a bit of a white knuckle experience. While most drivers are at least courteous, it seems there is an ever increasing number of bad drivers behind the wheel who are insistent on always pushing their vehicles to its maximum speed, weaving recklessly through traffic or just plain not paying attention. For that reason, a healthy dose of defensive driving on your part is a good idea.

Car Seats

It really can't be emphasised enough how important it is to keep children restrained in an approved car seat. Accidents are far too common and even a slight bump can be serious for a child riding unbuckled or in the arms of an adult. Besides, you already have your hands full watching out for other drivers, pedestrians, cyclists and crossing camels, to have to worry about Junior and what he's doing to your lovely leather upholstery with that chocolate bar.

Roundabouts

If you're in an outside lane on a roundabout, you should be prepared to take the next exit, or have the person to your left do so. Oddly, the inside lanes have right of way, so it's not uncommon for someone to take a right from the middle lane. Using your indicator at all times is advisable.

Non Verbal Communication

When you do get cut up or when a Landcruiser comes barrelling up to your rear bumper with its lights flashing, DO NOT under any circumstances make an obscene gesture with your fingers or any other part of your body. Ticking off the wrong person – anyone, really – can get you in more

In the Driver's Seat

trouble than you want. If you're really mad, make a note of the license plate number, count to ten, then call the Traffic Police's toll free hotline (800 4353) and report the offender.

Speed Limits

Speed limits are usually 60 - 80 km/hr in town and 100 - 120 km/hr on highways. Radar cameras (both fixed and temporary) record violations, so there's really no talking your way out of a ticket. If you think you've been 'flashed' (ie, the camera tracked and recorded your speed), you can confirm and pay online at www.dubaipolice.gov.ae. Alternatively, you can just wait until you renew your vehicle registration, at which point you may have the national debt of a small country in speeding fines!

Driving & Alcohol

The police enforce a strict zero tolerance policy across the Emirates. If you're in an accident (even one where you're not at fault) and you are found to have been drinking and driving, your insurance is automatically void. No excuses. So don't do it. Be smart and responsible, and get a taxi. They're cheap and you really don't have to worry about your car getting broken into if you leave it somewhere overnight.

Holidays & Annual Events

Holidays

Public and private sector holidays revolve around Muslim traditions with a few national celebrations included. Don't expect to have holidays such as Christmas, although if your children are at school, they will probably be on a semester break. Generally, Muslim holidays aren't announced until a few days before the actual start of a holiday (confirmation in accordance with the lunar calendar). This can make travel plans difficult. Many families who have the luxury, save their travel time for school holidays or during the summer when the weather is just short of unbearable.

Annual Events

With a few notable exceptions, most of the annual events taking place in the Emirates are family friendly. Some, such as the Dubai Shopping Festival or Dubai Summer Surprises, are specifically geared towards family entertainment while others, such as Great British Day or the annual Rugby 7s tournament, offer a good time for everyone. In general, any daytime event will be more family oriented, while after dark festivities are a good time to employ a babysitter. Having said that, the local culture promotes doing things as a family, so don't be surprised if you see young children up very late.

Housing

Property Rental

The majority of Dubai residents rent their home for the duration of their stay. Rents over the past few years have consistently risen and, in general, are very high. However, although prices at the lower end of the market have seen a decrease, accommodation at the higher end (over Dhs.45,000 for apartments and Dhs.100,000 for villas per annum) should drop eventually due to supply exceeding demand and freehold property ownership now becoming an option for all. Prices at the lower/middle end are expected to remain firm due to a heavy demand. Rents are always quoted for the year, unless otherwise stated.

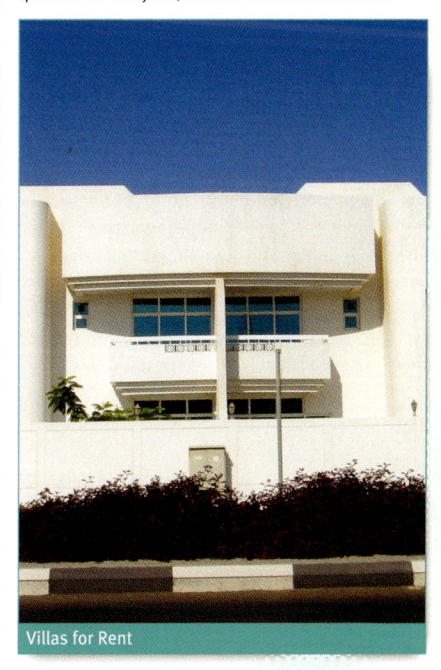

Villas for Rent

Most families have some sort of rental agreement or housing allowance provided along with their employment contract. This is generally sufficient to cover housing costs, but will not cover utilities, such as water or electricity. Housing ranges from apartments in older buildings or modern high rises to detached villas. Villas are probably more suitable for families as they are generally more spacious and usually have a garden. Many villas are part of a compound, which may include a swimming pool and other facilities.

Property Purchase

While in the past, only GCC Nationals could own residential property, options for expatriate land ownership are on the increase in Dubai. The summer of 2002 brought the long awaited news of freehold property ownership for people of all nationalities. The option of property purchase is yet another government scheme to encourage foreign investment in the Emirates.

With opportunities for long term visas and mortgages, buyers have been flocking to the various upmarket developments, snapping up properties in record time. The Dubai Palm Island sold all of its 2,000 villas and townhouses (costing Dhs.1.7 million - 4.6 million) in just over two weeks.

Currently, non GCC Nationals are only permitted to own land in certain developments: Emaar Properties' Dubai Marina, Emirates Hills, The Greens, The Meadows, The Lakes and Arabian Ranches; Dubai Palm Developers' Dubai Palm Islands (Jumeirah and Jebel Ali) and Jumeirah Islands, and Estithmaar's Jumeirah Beach Residence. Furthermore, new projects are sprouting up at breakneck speeds.

For further information on property ownership, contact Dubai Palm Developers (04 390 3333), Emaar Properties (04 800 4990) or Estithmaar (04 399 1114).

Non GGC ownership is very much in its infancy stage; this area is likely to change radically.

Relocation

Whether you're just moving to the Emirates or ending your stay, you will want to work out how to transfer your personal belongings. Outside of what can be carried on the plane as luggage, you have the choice of sending possessions by sea or air. Airfreight is more expensive, but also more efficient and might be the best choice for smaller amounts. Sea freight, although much slower, is far less expensive and surprisingly easy. The important thing to remember is to go with a professional shipping or relocation company.

If you choose to move larger quantities, you will need to contact a removal company (there are several operating in the Emirates that are part of a larger international network). Most will offer free consultations and guide you through the shipping process.

It is worth noting that furniture stores such as IKEA, THE One and Home Centre have a flourishing trade in the Emirates and hence, you can often find quite good deals. So, if you're thinking that your old bed or chest of drawers needs replacing, you may want to think about leaving them behind. Quality children's furniture such as beds, cribs, changing tables and related gear is widely available at prices that are comparable to Europe or North America, and meet requisite safety standards. What's more, a handful of specialty shops sell expensive designer furniture for babies, for those with more refined tastes.

Moving Tips

- Book moving dates well in advance
- Don't forget insurance; purchase additional for irreplaceable items
- Make an inventory of the items (keep your own copy!)
- Ensure everything is packed extremely well and in a way that can be checked by customs and repacked with the least possible damage; check and sign the packing list
- Keep a camera and film handy to take pictures at each stage of the move (valuable in case of a dispute)
- Include a few favourite toys, books, blankets etc, in your luggage, or send them ahead as it can take a while for freight to arrive

When your belongings arrive in Dubai, you may need to be present while Customs authorities open the boxes to ensure nothing illegal or inappropriate has been brought into the country. Assisting in this process can be exhausting; the search may take place outdoors over a few hours with your belongings strewn on the floor. After this, depending on your agreement with the removal company, either their Dubai representative will help you transport the boxes to your new home, or you would have to make the arrangements locally.

Insurance

Health Insurance

Health cover is recommended for expats in the Emirates. Residents are entitled to relatively low cost treatment at government hospitals and clinics, however, these low prices do not include x-rays and other such necessary treatment. Your employer may or may not arrange health insurance, so look for it as part of your contract. Whatever your circumstances, the cover offered needs to be analysed carefully to ensure that it is adequate for your family's needs. Getting cover can be a lengthy procedure, so you can get travel insurance for the interim. For a list of insurance companies, refer to Medical Care [p.26]. See [p.28] for more details.

Household Insurance

No matter which part of the world you live in and however safe the place appears, it is always wise to insure the contents of your home. There are many internationally recognised insurance companies operating in the Emirates. Check the Yellow Pages or Hawk Business Pages for details.

The general information that insurance companies need when forming your policy is your home address in the UAE, a list of household contents and valuation, and copies of invoices for items worth over Dhs.2,500. Cover usually extends to theft, storm damage, fire etc, and for an additional fee, you can insure personal items outside the home (such as jewellery, cameras and so on).

Main Agents	
Abu Dhabi	
Alliance Insurance	02 632 6067
Norwich Union	02 677 4444
Dubai	
Alliance Insurance	04 605 1111
National General Insurance	04 222 2772
Northern Assurance	04 331 8400
Norwich Union	04 324 3434

Baby Proofing the Home

If you're moving with children, you will already know the basics of child proofing a home. Other than the universal tips, there are very few necessary precautions specific to UAE homes. Most places here have tiled floors, which can be slippery for little ones in stockinged feet and make for hard falls. Many villas also have stairs which need to be secured. Here are some extra tips to make your home as disaster proof as possible. The equipment mentioned can be found at toy stores, such as Toys 'R' Us and other baby supply shops. Ace Hardware also stocks a variety of home safety equipment. See the Shopping Section [p.60] for more information.

- Most doors within the house have key locks, so be sure to remove the keys from all the locks and store them in a safe place. Remember to label them for later use

- Install gates at the top and bottom of stairs and secure balconies. You might also want to put perspex on any wrought iron railings (common in staircases)

- Double sided carpet tape will stop carpets and rugs from sliding on tiled floors

- Many immersion heaters are set to ridiculously high temperatures and can cause serious burns to small children and even unsuspecting adults. If your water is too hot (higher than 120 degrees), have your building maintenance adjust it or call a plumber. You may also want to consider an anti scald device, best installed by a plumber

Do remember that children are naturally inquisitive and will probably be a lot better at finding loopholes in your safety system than you. It's important that you keep an eye on them, but accept that you're doing your best – lying awake at night worrying about what you've forgotten won't help at all.

Pets

Most of us grow so fond of our pets that we would no more think of leaving them behind than we would any other member of the family. What's more, a pet that travels with a family can act as an important stabilising influence on young children trying to adjust to new surroundings. If you have a pet and are considering bringing it, rest assured there are lots of pet owners in the Emirates and many migrated here with their pets.

Pet stores selling supplies, special foods and animals are common in the UAE, especially in Abu Dhabi and Dubai, and most markets stock cat and dog food. Veterinary services are plentiful and professional, with prices similar or less expensive than what you're probably used to paying. Kennels and catteries are available for when you're away.

Before you decide to transport your pet, thoroughly reconsider your new housing arrangements. Most landlords will not forbid pets, but a family living in an apartment is crowded enough already without a big dog taking up additional space.

Note that many cultures within the Emirates (including Arabic) do not welcome dogs; most people are afraid of dogs and will avoid them or become very frightened, agitated or downright angry if the animal gets too close. Because of this, a short lead and a lot of respect are necessities when you are in public. Dogs are generally forbidden on public beaches, although this law is not strictly enforced on every beach.

The Bodyguard

In recent years, people walking their pets has become a more common sight in the UAE. This is great on the one hand because more people are learning the joys of owning a pet. On the other hand, the increase has meant a rise in the numbers of stray and abandoned pets. If you're planning on bringing a pet, make sure it's one that you will keep and take with you when you leave. The same applies if you are thinking of adopting – just remember that adorable puppies become dogs and cute kittens become furniture scratching cats. If you're in the market for a pet, consider contacting one of the local veterinary practices. They can put you in touch with an organisation or individual who will match you with a lovely stray that will love you all the more for giving it a good home.

Bringing Your Pet into the UAE

The only country from where you cannot bring a pet into the UAE is India (except for dogs). Importing a pet from some Asian countries requires a 21 day quarantine. You must first obtain an import permit from the Ministry of Agriculture & Fisheries (04 295 8161). The permit normally takes between 1-2 days to process. It is mandatory to microchip all pets arriving into the UAE from any country.

Dubai Kennels & Cattery (04 285 1646) can help you obtain an import permit, Customs clearance, collection and delivery from the airport, quarantine (if necessary) and/or boarding of your pet if required. Quarantine applies to any pet under the age of 4 months, regardless of the origin. Some of the local kennels/catteries can be used for the quarantine period. If you choose not to use their services, either your local vet or your airline should be able to advise you on any necessary requirements.

Taking Your Pet Back Home

The regulations for 'exporting' your pet depend on the laws of the country to which you're moving. Your local vet, kennels or the airline that you are travelling with can inform you of the specific regulations relevant to your destination, such as quarantine rules etc.

Cats & Dogs

Your pet must be vaccinated regularly and wear a Municipality ID disc (supplied on vaccination) on its collar at all times. The Municipality controls Dubai's huge stray population by trapping and putting down animals. If your pet is trapped without an ID disc, it will be treated as a stray. It is advisable to sterilise all pets and keep them on your premises. Once sterilised, they are less inclined to wander and also less exposed to the dangers of traffic and disease.

Domestic Services

Babysitting

Families who opt for domestic help, such as a maid (live in or otherwise), will generally arrange babysitting with that individual. Others may be able to ask a neighbour's housemaid to babysit. Alternatively, babysitting services are often advertised in the classifieds of the Gulf News or Khaleej Times. Either way, the same amount of care should be taken as in your home country. Gymboree in Abu Dhabi (02 665 8882) and Dubai (04 345 4422) provide a service during the day where you can leave your child in their professional care.

There are very few reported incidents of child abuse or other inappropriate behaviour towards children from housemaids or babysitters in the Emirates. In general, they probably prefer an evening spent with your young ones to other activities (work related). At the same time, many

DUBAI KENNELS & CATTERY
Established 1983

> Shopping then breakfast then **shopping** then lunch then **shopping** then a really yummy dinner... then a tummy-rub and our midnight chews... and then tomorrow we start all over again!

> Do you have a special arrangement with the handlers?

worldwide pet relocation, boarding, grooming, dog training, collection & delivery

...dogs, cats, birds, rabbits, tortoises, hamsters...

+971 4 285 1646 / info@dkc.ae / www.dkc.ae

are young and lack experience with small children, so you may want them to spend time with your family while you are there for supervision and training. This also gives children a chance to become familiar with this new person. Be quite clear about dietary rules and other areas that you may take for granted. And, of course, be sure to leave your contact information (mobile number and the number of where you are going) along with the number of a nearby friend who would be willing to help in case of an emergency.

Be sure to agree on a price when you make the arrangements. Most sitters charge between Dhs.10 - 25 per hour, but remember that these women work hard, some doing several jobs at once, so be fair. You should also confirm with live in housemaids that they are willing to babysit on their evenings off – don't simply take that service for granted. Unless you have an existing agreement with them to take responsibility one or two nights a week, evening babysitting should be considered as overtime.

Domestic Help/Maids/Housecleaners

Although you may never have considered hiring a domestic helper before, many people in the Emirates do, as the service is comparatively cheap and easy to arrange. For the busy or the lazy, it means the house is spotless and shirts are always pressed, and for mum and dad, it means an extra helper and an easy to find babysitter.

To employ the services of a full time live in domestic helper, you must have a minimum monthly salary of Dhs.6,000. The helper cannot be related to you or of the same nationality. As the employer, you must sponsor the person and deal with all residency papers, including medical tests etc. Single people and families where the wife isn't working may face difficulties sponsoring a helper. It is normally best to find someone through an agency dedicated to hiring domestic helpers.

The residence visa for a maid costs Dhs.5,000 (Dhs.4,800 for the government fee, Dhs.100 for the residence visa and Dhs.100 for the labour card). Residency is only valid for one year. You can obtain a residence visa card through the normal channels after which, some embassies (for example, the Philippines) require to see the labour contract of your newly appointed maid. This is to ensure that all paperwork is in order and that the maid is receiving fair treatment. There will normally be a minimum wage stipulated by the embassies. It is illegal to share a maid with another household.

An alternative and cheaper option is to arrange part time home help; a number of agencies offer domestic help on an hourly basis. The standard rate is Dhs.20 - 25 per hour, with a minimum of two hours per visit. The number of hours required will obviously depend on the size of your accommodation and the level of mess. The service includes general cleaning, washing, ironing and sometimes babysitting.

Domestic Help Agencies	
Abu Dhabi	
Delight Cleaners	02 678 9216
Solutions	02 443 0445
Dubai	
Helpers	04 395 6166
Home Help	04 355 5100
Maids to Order	04 393 0608
Molly Maid	04 398 8877
Ready Maids	04 272 7483

Laundry

Laundry services are abundant and inexpensive. They offer washing, dry cleaning, ironing and folding, and will usually collect and deliver as well. While any dry cleaner or laundry service will happily handle your baby or children's clothes, we have yet to find a nappy service in the Emirates.

Gardening

Most villa compounds have an on site gardener, whose services are either part of the rental agreement or require a separate fee. If not, you will need to arrange your own gardener (of course you could always do the work yourself…). Find one by asking around your neighbourhood.

Cost of gardeners depends on the size of your garden and how frequently you want them to tend to it. If you call them six days a week, you would be paying anywhere between Dhs.200 - 450 a month (according to the covered area).

You may want to look into getting a well. If you're paying your own water bills, you could actually save yourself quite a sum in the summer months by installing one. Ask a neighbour who already has one regarding the quality of water in your area – sometimes it can be too salty. To have a well installed, you need to check with a nursery/garden shop (not all of them provide this service). They will bore a hole and feed in a pipe to which they add a motor and connect a hose. You will also need a power socket somewhere in the garden to eventually run it. Make sure they go deep enough, or you may discover that you need their services once again to bore deeper, which will of course, cost you more. Boring costs anywhere between Dhs.400 - 650 and the motor, Dhs.250 - 650.

Plumbing/Maintenance/ Home Improvements

Most apartment buildings or villa compounds should come with plumbing and general maintenance services. If not, your best bet is either to contact your landlord for help or to consult the Yellow Pages. Remember that, in the Emirates, word of mouth is the most reliable advertisement, so it's a good idea to ask friends and neighbours for suggestions.

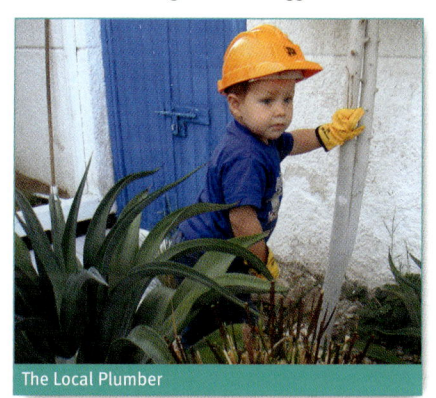

The Local Plumber

Locks & Keys

Usually, your landlord or building supervisor will be willing to make duplicate keys, fix locks or open accidentally locked doors. If they're not, duplicate keys can be made in hardware stores or various shops around town. Unlike many places, the cost of calling a locksmith won't exceed that of just going ahead and buying a new house!

Electricity

There's plenty of it! The electricity supply in the Emirates is 220/240 volts and 50 cycles. Sockets are the same as the three point British system. The electrical service is generally good without frequent interruptions or power fluctuations, but it may be worth buying uninterrupted power supplies or surge protectors for sensitive equipment.

Telecommunications

The UAE features ultra modern telecommunications capabilities. Long distance, Internet, cellular and wireless services are all available and handled by the government owned Etisalat. Although Etisalat is currently a monopoly organisation, a plan to privatise this sector is being finalised. For more information, refer to the *Zappy Explorer* for step by step instructions on how to get connected.

Television

Local television is mostly broadcast in Arabic, and when it isn't, it is usually not of the highest quality. Fortunately, there are several satellite television providers broadcasting western news, entertainment and sports programmes as well as children's channels. In addition, video and DVD rentals are available throughout the Emirates, giving couch potatoes another option.

Rubbish Disposal

Getting rid of your rubbish is extremely convenient in the Emirates. Many apartment buildings have a rubbish chute on every floor for you to just drop your refuse in. If it's too big, simply leave it next to the chute and someone will take it away… eventually. If it's particularly ugly or smelly, do everyone a favour and take it down yourself, or notify your building management that you need it removed. If you're in a villa, you'll need to take your garbage to the nearest bin, which is emptied regularly. There's no regular 'rubbish day', so you won't have to worry about putting the bins out or anything along those lines. And again, if you have something big to get rid of, say that old couch or some spare tyres, they'll take those away too, just as long as they're next to the bin.

Recycling

Recycling hasn't caught on widely here, so there's no kerbside or automatic collection. However, it is available for those who are willing to make the effort. Most Spinneys supermarkets have a recycling centre where you can leave aluminium cans, plastic bottles and newspapers. Additionally, you will see men on bicycles looking around bins for pieces of cardboard, which they then take to be recycled.

Insects/Rodents

Insects, especially in the home, are not much of a problem. You may run across the occasional cockroach, spider, gecko, cricket or ant in the house, but there are very few dangerous creepy crawlies around, and those that exist are not very abundant. Unfortunately, rats and mice are more prolific, especially in heavily populated areas. There have been no reported cases of rabies in the Emirates since 1994. The camel spider, a common arachnid found in the Emirates, is not dangerous despite its ferocious appearance. However, the Australian redback should be taken more seriously (refer to Dangerous Bugs on [p.22]).

Pesticides

Pesticides and sprays are available through gardening centres or hardware stores. Remember that most pesticides are very strong chemicals, which are dangerous to have around the house. You may be better off using a special trap or just waiting for the problem to take care of itself. Other alternatives include blocking suspected entry points (with screens, caulk or sealant), repairing leaky faucets, storing food in sealed containers or the refrigerator, and keeping rubbish in a bin with a tight lid.

Before going down the chemical warfare route, consider whether you really have a problem or are you panicking over a couple of creepy crawlies? Is your swarm a seasonal occurrence, such as bugs coming into your house due to heavy rains? Are they dangerous? Are there any other measures you can take, such as replacing screens or sweeping up regularly? The point is that most bug problems, especially in the Emirates, are slight and tend to be of the non biting variety, meaning that they pose a lesser threat than using dangerous pesticides.

Dangerous Bugs

There are a few poisonous or dangerous insects worth mentioning. Almost every species of spider in the world carries poisonous venom – the ones we have to worry about are the ones whose venom and delivery system (fangs) are strong enough to do us damage. In the Emirates, the female Australian redback spider is one such dangerous customer. It doesn't appear in great numbers but can be found just about anywhere, even in private gardens and dark, quiet garden sheds and garages. It can be recognised by the red spot on the back of its round black body. Fortunately, bites are rare and when they do occur, are almost never fatal for adults. Children and the elderly, or those with extreme allergies are more susceptible. If you or someone in your family has a suspected bite by a redback or other poisonous spider, you will need anti-venom. Unfortunately, the bite is not always felt or immediately detected, but within 10 - 60 minutes, symptoms appear which may include anxiety, severe muscle cramping in the back and abdomen, headaches, nausea, vomiting and profuse sweating. If someone has been bitten, do the following:

- Keep the victim as calm as possible
- If you can find the bite, wash it thoroughly and apply an antiseptic, such as iodine
- Apply a wet compress or ice to reduce the pain and slow the spread of venom
- Get to a hospital emergency room, especially if the victim is a child or an older person. Even if the bite isn't that dangerous or the victim isn't showing symptoms, it's best to avoid complications

Given the desert climate, scorpions are also common but you won't find them that often in your house or garden. In the mountains and deserts, the small yellowish scorpion is the one to avoid. It is more harmful to humans than the larger black one. Scorpion bites are rarely fatal but again, children, elderly people and those with allergies to the bite will certainly warrant special attention. In the event of a bite:

- Keep the victim as calm as possible
- Apply a wet compress or ice to reduce the pain and slow the spread of venom
- If the following symptoms appear, get the victim to a hospital immediately: profuse sweating, difficulty swallowing, blurred vision, loss of bowel control, jerky muscular reflexes and respiratory distress

The best way to avoid such bites is to remember not to stick unguarded hands into dark places and under rocks or sticks. When on camping trips, check shoes before putting them on. Also, if you see a spider, scorpion or other potentially dangerous creature (although fascinating to watch), STAY AWAY FROM IT! For more information on bites and stings, refer to Medical Care [p.26].

Annual Events

Abu Dhabi and Dubai play host to several popular annual events, many of which make a great day out for families – you'll find a list of the more established yearly happenings below. In addition, if you tap into the local 'word of mouth' grapevine, you'll get to hear about numerous other events organised by societies, clubs or schools in your area throughout the year.

Al Ain Flower Festival
This colourful event takes place each spring, and showcases landscaping genius and a vibrant range of flowers and shrubs in the park near Jahili Fort. The annual festival parade, which seems to attract virtually all the residents of Al Ain, features throngs of children dressed up in multi coloured flower costumes. The exact dates for the 2005 Al Ain Flower Festival will be available nearer the time – keep in touch with the Al Ain Municipality (03 763 5111).

Dog Show, The (www.nadalshebaclub.com)
Families flock to this annual event in February, where you're guaranteed to bump into wet-nosed, waggy-tailed dogs of all shapes, sizes and colours, from pretty poodles to slobbery labradors! Proud owners can enter their pampered pooches into one of the competitive classes, which are usually judged by overseas experts. If it's excitement you're after, then you'll enjoy the thrills and spills of the Dog Agility Course and displays by the Dubai Police. Bouncy castles, kids' activities and stalls all add to the show atmosphere.

Dubai Raft Race (www.dimc-uae.com)
The harbour comes alive over Raft Race weekend, when teams turn out on coloured rafts to battle against each other on the water. It's a great spectator event, and there are also many land based activities to keep the family busy in between race watching. International bands provide musical entertainment, there are plenty of stage activities and beach games, and enough refreshment tents to ensure you don't go thirsty! A word of warning though – this event gets crowded, so keep a careful eye on younger children.

Dubai Shopping Festival (www.mydsf.com)
Dubai is a renowned shoppers' paradise all year round, but once a year in January, the city dusts off its fairy lights and pulls out all the stops for a whole month of carnival fun and shopping mania. (Abu Dhabi also hosts a shopping festival every year in early March). Daily attractions include live music, stage shows, funfairs and magnificent fireworks displays, not to mention the chance to strike it big with one of the legendary prize draws. Detailed listings of activities can be found in daily newspapers or on local television channels.

Dubai Summer Surprises (www.mydsf.com)
With the promise of 'Big Fun for Little Ones!', Dubai Summer Surprises (DSS) provides a range of indoor entertainment for families during the sweltering summer months. Held from mid June to the beginning of September, each week represents a different theme or surprise, such as heritage, knowledge, arts, food etc. Entertainers and cartoon characters can be found bringing smiles to little faces all around the city, and the shopping malls and parks all have long lists of daily activities.

Dubai Tennis Open (www.dubaiworldcup.com)
Held in the middle of February at the Dubai Tennis Stadium, this is a well supported event. It is established on the international tennis circuit and offers the chance for the sporty kids to see top seeds, both male and female, in an intimate setting, battling it out for game, set and match.

Great British Day (www.britbiz-uae.com)
Organised by the British Business Group, this celebration of all things British takes place annually on a Friday in February. Held in Dubai, it is attended by thousands of people every year, all hankering for traditional goodies like fish and chips, and traditional cream teas. For entertainment, there is a Punch and Judy show, plus a variety of games, tombolas, bouncy castles, paint-balling, face painting and live music, all rounded off at the end of the day by an impressive fireworks display. The proceeds go to charity.

Terry Fox Run (www.terryfoxrun.org)
This popular fund raising charity event is held once a year on a Friday morning, usually during February/March. The race covers ten kilometres, and is held in both Abu Dhabi and Dubai. Anyone may enter (each competitor should be sponsored) and take part in any way – from serious runners, walkers or cyclists to those being pushed in a pram or on roller blades. Even pets can participate!

Check the daily newspapers two months prior to February/March for contact details of the race organisers, or nearer to the event, listen out for items on the radio. All proceeds go to cancer research.

www.foresightrp.com

RP robs people of their sight, with your help it could be cured

Katy Newitt is severely visually impaired due to *Retinitis Pigmentosa*. RP is a hereditary disease that causes people throughout the world to lose their sight and eventually go blind. Imagine flowers and trees, friend's faces, children's smiles, fading away.

Once an incurable disease, new advances mean that there is now hope. With your help to fund more research there could be a cure for RP within 5 years. Bring light back into the lives of people with RP.

FORESIGHT

For more details on how you can help this cause
Tel: Katy Newitt 050 5659044, E-mail: info@foresightrp.com

Medical
EXPLORER

Medical

Introduction	27	Dentists/Orthodontists	30	**General Safety & First Aid**	**36**
Health Card	27	Opticians	30	First Aid	36
Private Medical Insurance	27	Dermatologists	32	Stings & Bites	36
Emergencies	28	Chriopodists	32	Burns	36
Pharmacies/Chemists	28			Common Concerns	37
		Maternity	**32**		
Medical Care	**28**	Antenatal & Birth	32	**Alternative Medicine**	**37**
Medical Institutions	28				
General Practitioners	29	**Mental Health**	**35**		
Paediatricians	29				

MUST KNOW

While government healthcare is available many people opt for private care financed by medical insurance, either independently subscribed or provided as part of an employment package. However if you are intending to have a baby medical insurance from your employer may not cover childbirth and most private insurers have a waiting period of at least ten months before pre-natal care can be claimed. See [p.28] for a list of insurers

MUST DO

Within two weeks of giving birth in the UAE your child must be registered at the Ministry of Health and have a valid residence visa within four months. If this is not done and the required documentation processed the baby will not be able to leave the country. But don't panic some of the work is done for you with the hospital preparing the Arabic certificate once you have provided them with copies of both parents' passports and a marriage certificate, along with a Dhs.50 fee.

Aerial view of Abu Dhabi

Introduction

The quality of medical care in the Emirates is generally regarded as quite high and visitors should have little trouble receiving appropriate treatment, whether from the government or from privately run hospitals and clinics. There has been an enormous investment in healthcare and the UAE Ministry of Health keeps in close touch with medical research all over the world.

Although visitors face no specific health risks, the climate can be oppressive during the summer months. Even if you have arrived here from a warm climate, do not underestimate the heat and humidity of summer in the Gulf. With standard summer temperatures of over 100°F and high humidity it is sensible for all members of the family to take extra care. Cover up, use high protection sun cream, stay inside in the middle of the day and drink lots of water (when you're feeling thirsty, your body is already dehydrated). In addition, children of all ages may suffer from colds and allergies more frequently while adapting to their new environment – constant air conditioning certainly seems to spread the germs faster.

With a health card (see below) and a minimal fee, UAE Nationals and expatriate residents are allowed health care at the government run hospitals and clinics. There are also various private hospitals and clinics offering a wide range of facilities and procedures.

Remember! Your health is important. Choosing the right physician leads to a healthier lifestyle as well as peace of mind. Check out what is available NOW instead of waiting until you have a crisis on your hands.

Health Card

It is mandatory for all expat residents to have a health card to reside (and work) in the UAE. This card enables you to use government hospitals and clinics for free, or to receive treatments and prescriptions at very reduced rates. The card is available for a fee, and for children, is valid for the duration of their residency. Adults have to renew theirs annually.

If you do not have a health card, government hospitals will treat you in the emergency. However, you will either need to produce one after 24 hours or make arrangements to go elsewhere.

The basic annual cost of a health card is Dhs.100 for 0 - 10 year olds and Dhs.200 for 10 - 18 year olds. In addition, each visit to a government facility is charged – approximately Dhs.20 (including medicine) for a paediatrician and Dhs.50 for a specialist. Urgent cases are free. Adult health cards cost Dhs.300, plus Dhs.200 for the initial medical examination, which includes a blood test for AIDS and Hepatitis. Children under 18 do not need this examination.

To apply for a health card, a Ministry of Health application form must be submitted (typed in Arabic) to the acting public health hospital or clinic of the emirate, along with the following: one passport photocopy with visa stamp or visa application form, covering letter from sponsor, two passport size photographs and the necessary amount in dirhams. It can be quite hectic and time consuming, so try to go as early in the morning as possible.

Private Hospitals and Clinic Approved Cards: Some private medical insurance schemes are recognised by the Ministry of Health and cancel the need to obtain a UAE health card. However, the card must be notarised by the Ministry of Health at a cost of Dhs.200. Check with the private hospitals whether they run such a scheme.

Private Medical Insurance

Health insurance is recommended for private medical care as treatment can become very expensive. Schemes are usually linked to American or European medical insurance, and the

Al Noor Hospital, Abu Dhabi

type of cover can vary considerably, from a basic Emirates plan to a Middle East/Asia plan or a worldwide plan (usually excluding America). Dentistry is not generally covered, except in special cases or with more expensive medical insurance.

Medical Insurance Companies

Abu Dhabi

Alliance Insurance	02 633 6747
Nasco Karaoglan Group	02 671 3000
Oman Insurance	02 626 8008

Dubai

Alliance Insurance	04 605 1111
BUPA International	04 331 8688
Dubai National Insurance Co.	04 269 1300
Nasco Karaoglan Group	04 352 3133
Oman Insurance	800 4746

Many families arrange health insurance before leaving their home countries, or have it included as part of their employment package. Nevertheless, expats who need local medical insurance have a number of options. For further information, contact some of the companies listed above. The A to Z Business Pages and Yellow Pages (available from Etisalat) are also good sources of information.

Emergencies

During a true emergency, any government hospital will accept you without a referral for treatment, although they may transfer you to a hospital better equipped to deal with your problem. However, if you cannot produce a health card after 24 hours, you will need to make arrangements to go elsewhere. The alternative would be to apply for one (and this could take time).

Emergency Numbers

Location	Ambulance	Police	Fire	Coast Guard
Abu Dhabi	998	999	997	02 673 1900
Al Ain	998	999	997	–
Dubai	999	999	997	04 345 0520

Keep a handy record of useful numbers (your doctor, local hospitals, clinics and a dentist) and other emergency services (fire and police) by your telephone, in your wallet and in the car.

Pharmacies/Chemists

There are numerous pharmacies in the UAE, the majority of which stock the same items at similar prices. The larger pharmacies may also carry a range of baby care products, sunscreens, cosmetics, vitamins etc. You can try practising your bargaining skills; if requested, they may give a discount.

Opening hours: Timings vary, but in general are 9:00 - 13:30 & 16:30 - 22:00, Saturday - Thursday, and 16:30 - 22:00 on Fridays. Some pharmacies, especially ones in malls, remain open throughout the day. Few open on a Friday. Names and numbers of 24 hour 'duty' pharmacies are listed in the daily newspapers.

Medical Care

Medical Institutions

There are many government hospitals, private hospitals, clinics and health practitioners available in the Emirates (refer to the table). When choosing medical services, go by word of mouth. Asking your consulate or embassy for a list will be helpful. The decision of which facility to use may well depend on the urgency of the complaint and your location.

Government hospitals offer 24 hour emergency treatment for everyone. Health card holders can also benefit from various treatments at a reasonable price at government clinics. But be prepared to wait, since the clinics are often very busy. Take some story books, colouring books or a favourite toy for your child – it will make the waiting time easier and less stressful. Arabic and English (of varying standards!) are the common languages. People are generally helpful and friendly, even though at times their approach lacks the tender touch of private healthcare.

A & E

In Abu Dhabi, the Central Hospital handles most accident cases and general treatments; the Mafraq is the capital's main government hospital. The Sheikh Khalifa Medical Centre, which otherwise only treats Nationals, has an accident and emergency section which is open to all and will especially, never turn you away if a child is involved.

In Dubai, the Rashid Hospital is the main hospital for trauma and traffic accidents. In Al Ain, you have Al Jimi and Tawam hospitals.

Note: This is an Explorer guidebook for children. Hence, we have listed the more child orientated centres. However, all hospitals offer health care for all ages.

Hospitals

Abu Dhabi

Al Noor Hospital Emergency	02 626 5265
Golden Sands Medical Hospital	02 642 7171
Mafraq Hospital Emergency	02 582 3100
National Hospital Emergency	02 671 1000
New Medical Centre Hospital Emergency	02 633 2255
Sheikh Khalifa Medical Centre Emergency	02 612 2000
The Corniche Hospital (Maternity Only) Emergency	02 672 4900

Al Ain

Al Ain Hospital (Al Jimi) Emergency	03 763 5888
Emirates International Hospital	03 763 7777
Oasis Hospital Emergency	03 722 1251
Specialised Medical Care Centre Emergency	03 766 2291
Tawam Hospital Emergency	03 767 7444

Dubai

Al Amal Hospital	04 344 4010
Al Baraha Hospital Emergency	04 271 0000
Al Maktoum Hospital Emergency	04 222 1211
Al Wasl Hospital Emergency	04 324 1111
American Hospital Emergency	04 336 7777
Belhoul European Hospital Centre	04 345 4000
Dubai Hospital Emergency	04 271 4444
International Private Hospital Emergency	04 221 2484
Iranian Hospital Emergency	04 344 0250
Rashid Hospital Emergency	04 337 4000
Welcare Hospital Emergency	04 282 7788

American Hospital

General Practitioners

Whereas in places such as the UK, your first port of call for most medical conditions would be the family GP, families here tend to see a range of doctors. The children go to a paediatrician and the women go to a gynaecologist or often, a female GP, while the husbands have a male GP. Clinics here are very well equipped (several with x-ray equipment) and specialists are at hand. Skin, ENT, urinary and even heart specialists can be found within the local community. The American and Welcare Hospitals are also well set up to deal with most problems that arise.

To find a GP, just pick a clinic that is preferably near your residence or workplace. Call and ask to see a male or female GP, according to your preference. (Actually, the way it usually works is that 'mum' carefully selects a paediatrician and the rest of the family obediently signs up with doctors in the same clinic.) Although you can find a GP in any hospital or clinic, listed in the table below are some names that are quite well known.

General Practitioners

Abu Dhabi

Centre Medical Franco – Emirien Emergency	02 626 5722
Dr McCulloch	02 633 3900
Gulf Diagnostic Centre	02 655 8090

Al Ain

Al Dhahery Clinic	03 765 6882
Emirates Medical Centre	03 764 4744
Family Medical Clinic	03 766 9902
Hafeet Medical Centre	03 764 1565
Hamdan Medical Centre	03 765 4797
Mahboob Clinic	03 765 4631
New Al Ain Medical Clinic	03 764 1448
Sulaiman Clinic	03 764 1009

Dubai

American Hospital	04 309 6877
Dr Akel's Medical Centre	04 344 9150
Dubai Physiotherapy Clinic	04 349 6333
General Medical Centre	04 349 5959
Manchester Clinic	04 344 0300

Paediatricians

There are some excellent paediatricians operating in the Emirates and although a few are mentioned in this Explorer guidebook, that should not in any way detract from the others. The doctors mentioned here however, come highly recommended and are well established and active in the community.

Do not regard this as an exclusive list. Choose a clinic in a convenient location and a doctor you trust and feel comfortable with. ENT bugs are very common here and pre-school children, in particular, will be frequent visitors at the doctor's. By the time they reach school level, they seem to build up resilience. If you hail from Northern Europe, you will notice that here, antibiotics are prescribed often and are available freely – some pharmacies don't even ask for a prescription, although they should. The pharmacies are well stocked and can probably help you with most minor ailments, saving you the trouble of going to a doctor. This comes in especially handy if you don't have medical insurance. They're a good first port of call for minor problems like coughs and colds.

Paediatricians

Abu Dhabi

Dr Latifa Shah	Gulf Diagnostic Centre	02 665 8090

Dubai

Dr Anil Gupta	American Hospital	04 309 6887
Dr Ejaz Waseem	Manchester Clinic	04 344 0300
Dr Ian Jefferson	American Hospital	04 309 6887
Dr Keith Nicholl	Dubai Physio Clinic	04 349 6333
Dr Rita Kovesdi	Dubai London Clinic	04 344 6663

Dentists/Orthodontists

You will find a range of well known and established dentists that are competent professionals. Look for one that is convenient for you, near to work or home. Bear in mind though, that treatments, even check ups, are not cheap. You will notice that cosmetic dentistry is very popular and not just among the teens. In today's image conscious world the UAE is no exception in striving for perfection and pearly white teeth can be bought. The total bill for achieving dental perfection could also set you back Dhs.20,000. For normal dental care, check ups are recommended every six months and you'll probably see the hygienist too. If you're unsure about the six fillings and removal of a wisdom tooth you've been told that you need, get a second opinion. You can also expect completely pain free treatment here, which makes you wonder why it isn't the norm elsewhere.

> **Monthly Medical**
>
> The monthly Connector and Aquarius publications are a good source of information on matters of health and medical practitioners. www.expatmum.com also features a medical section with a facility that allows you to email any queries to Manchester Clinic.

Dentists/Orthodontists

Abu Dhabi

Advanced Dental Clinic	02 681 2921
American Dental Clinic	02 677 1310
Austrian Dental Clinic	02 621 1489
Barbara Dental Clinic	02 626 9898
British Dental Clinic	02 677 3308
Dr Elisabeth Dental Clinic	02 626 7822
Faxius Dental Clinic	02 672 3445
Gulf Diagnostic Centre	02 665 8090
International Dental Clinic	02 633 3444
Maher Dental Clinic	02 666 3588
Swedish Dental Clinic	02 681 1122

Al Ain

Al Bahri Dental Clinic	03 764 3273
Al Hijjar Dental Clinic	03 765 8155
Canadian Dental Clinic	03 766 6696
City Dental & Medical Centre	03 764 2252
Gulf Dental Clinic	03 765 4373
Modern Dental Clinic	03 766 4764
New Al Ain Dental Clinic	03 766 2059
Tabrizi Dental Clinic	03 766 2133
Thabit Medical Centre	03 765 4454

Dubai

American Dental Clinic	04 344 0668
British Dental Clinic	04 342 1318
Dr Akel's Medical Centre	04 344 9150
Dr David Fairclough's Dental Clinic	04 344 2687
Dr Michael's Dental Clinic	04 349 5900
Drs Nicholas & Asp	04 345 4443
Dubai London Clinic	04 344 6663
Finn Dental Clinic	04 297 4003
German Dental Clinic	04 332 4499
Jebel Ali Medical Centre	04 881 4000
Jumeirah Beach Dental Centre	04 349 9433
Manchester Clinic	04 344 0300
Scandcare Dental Clinic	04 345 9431
Seven Dental Centre	04 395 2177
Swedish Dental Clinic	04 223 1297
Talass Orthodontic & Dental Centre	04 349 2220

Physios, Osteopaths & Chiropractors

Whether it's executives with their sedentary lifestyles, or physique conscious forty somethings pumping it out in the gym, people here keep the physios busy. There are some very skilled practitioners here, and word of mouth is the best way to find one.

Drs Nicolas & Asp
SPECIALISED DENTAL CARE FOR ALL THE FAMILY

When you suggest taking your child to the Dentist does this happen?

Well don't worry anymore. At Drs. Nicolas & Asp we are used to bringing a smile to Children's faces. We look after all our Children & Young Adults needs in a caring, relaxed & understanding manner

KID'S CORNER

Play area for our younger children
Kid's Library
Colouring competitions Every month
'Small Mouths' Education programme

KID'S SERVICES

Fluoridation and Sealants
Cool Braces in Cool Colours.
Customised Mouthguards for Contact Sports

So come to the place where we keep your child smiling.

Clinic Hours are Saturday-Thursday,
8:00am-8:00pm.
Tel: 345 44 43 for an appointment.
24 Hour Emergency Service Pager No. 919 41 341.

DRS. NICOLAS & ASP
DENTAL CENTRE

مركز دكتور نيقولا
و آسب لطب الاسنان

CARING IS OUR CONCERN

Jumeirah Beach Road
Opposite Dubai Marine Beach Club

Al Jasar

Physios, Osteopaths and Chiropractors

Abu Dhabi

Abu Dhabi Health and Fitness Club	02 443 6333
Chiropractic Speciality Clinic	02 634 5162
Gulf Diagnostic Centre	02 665 8090

Dubai

Canadian Chiropractic Centre	04 342 0900
Chiropractor	04 344 4316
Dubai Physiotherapy Clinic	04 349 6333
General Medical Centre, The	04 349 5959
Gulf American Clinic	04 349 8556
Orthosports Medical Centre	04 345 0601
Osteopathic Health Centre	04 344 9792

Dermatologists

A life flooded with sunshine is beautiful, but you should also be aware of the risks involved, such as moles: watch out for changes in them. Look for a darkening in colour, roughness and/or bleeding. It's always better to get them checked once in a while, just to be reassured that there are no problems. Removal of moles can be done simply and painlessly at clinics. You can also have a variety of other skin disorders treated there, right through to cosmetic surgery, and you have a wide choice in both clinics and hospitals for any of these treatments.

Dermatologists

Abu Dhabi

Dermatologist & Cosmetic Centre	02 445 7100

Dubai

Manchester Clinic	04 344 0300
Medlink Clinic	04 344 7711

Chriopodists

In a land where sunshine and swimming are the norm unfortunately so is the spread of fungal infections, especially amoung children who tend to share the same paddlig pools. Persistant verrucas can be a bit of a problem, especially once your child has begun school (many of which have swimming pools) or nursery where soft play areas require bare feet. Therefore it is important for the whole family to pay special attention to foot cleanliness as socks aren't there to protect you now that the sun's permanentely out!

Chriopodists

Abu Dhabi

Chiropractic Specialist Centre	02 634 5162

Dubai

Canadian Chiropractic Centre	04 344 0412
Chiropody Centre Dubai	04 349 9055
Dubai Physio Clinic	04 349 6333
Dubai Podiatry Centre	04 343 5390

Maternity

Antenatal & Birth

Abu Dhabi, Al Ain and Dubai have their own government maternity hospitals. Both the Al Wasl Hospital in Dubai and the Corniche Hospital in Abu Dhabi have excellent modern facilities and specialise in obstetrics, gynaecology and paediatrics. Currently under active development are the departments of neurology, oncology and orthopaedics for children, and the wards are quite friendly and cheerful. Health cards are required and for your stay you will also need your marriage certificate; a very important document in this country.

Most Western expats in the Emirates opt to have their babies in one of the private hospitals. A deciding factor for going government or private is if you have medical insurance that covers maternity, or a nest egg for the special occasion. You may decide to go private but for all multiple births, and

Public (Government) Hospital

DUBAI LONDON CLINIC

SPECIALIST SERVICES AVAILABLE

- Obstetrics
- Gynaecology
- Antenatal Care
- Well Baby Clinic
- Paediatrics
- Diabetes
- Dental
- Internal Medicine
- Gastroenterology
- Family Practice
- Diagnostic Imaging
- Pathology Laboratory
- Periodontal

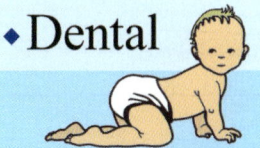

Here At The Dubai London Clinic We Provide A Warm, Friendly and Family Atmosphere With Not Only Professional But Caring Staff

P.O Box 12119, Dubai, U.A.E., Tel: (9714) 3446663 Fax: (9714) 3446191
E-Mail: dlc@emirates.net.ae

MEDICAL	8AM-1PM & 4-7PM SATURDAY – WEDNESDAY
	8AM – 1PM ON THURSDAY
DENTAL	8AM - 7PM SATURDAY - WEDNESDAY
	8AM - 1PM ON THURSDAY

if there are any complications, you will be referred to the government hospital in your emirate.

Private hospitals offer packages that cover full antenatal care, hospitalisation and delivery. The basic birth package will cost around Dhs.10,000. You can also arrange for your own gynaecologist to deliver your baby. For that, just take a package less the delivery charges and use that money to pay your doctor directly. The staff at these hospitals is more than capable of looking after you, but sometimes a woman prefers to have her own doctor attend.

You may decide to go to one of the government hospitals and not bother with the private ones. Many expatriate women do. The standard of care is still high and the cost is lower, although there have been recent increases. English is not the first language in government hospitals but everyone speaks it. Another deciding factor is that, in the unlikely event of anything going wrong, neonatal facilities are far better in the government hospitals. Pain relief is available and your husband can be present at the birth but may not be allowed in the labour room. You will have to share a room with three other ladies (which may give you an insight into diverse cultural customs!) If you want your child's delivery to be a truely 'Arabic' experience, this is the place to be. However, they generally will not tell you the sex of the baby prior to birth.

To register with a government hospital, show up at one, armed with your medical card and marriage certificate, within the first three months of pregnancy. They prefer not to register after the first 12 weeks of pregnancy, but in the case of an emergency, they will not turn you away. Some would argue that, even if you're planning to have your baby elsewhere, it is still useful to register with the government hospital to have your details on file just in case. The monthly check ups cost Dhs.50 and the staff are very nice, but the comfort is still nowhere close to that of wandering around in your private clinic. In the past, the organisation was such that, when you would arrive promptly for your ten o'clock appointment, you would find 50 women waiting before you. However, we are given to understand that the level of efficiency has improved quite considerably. It would still be wise to make an appointment for later in the morning as they become far more efficient as lunchtime approaches. Also, don't forget to take a book to while the wait.

Shopping

In Dubai, you can get specialised help for fitting maternity bras from Bernadette Banks (04 331 3648). For hiring a breast pump, call Sonia Winter (04 344 3978). The Jenny Rose Boutique (04 349 0902) in both the Beach Centre and Burjuman offers an extensive and exclusive range of maternity wear for the fashionable mother to be. For more information on where to buy items for your new baby, refer to the Shopping section [p.60].

Few Facts

- Contraception is freely available in the UAE
- For a vasectomy, you need to contact a urologist
- It is illegal to terminate a pregnancy in the UAE
- It is also against the law to have a child outside of marriage

Natural Childbirth

A question that has been voiced on more than one occasion is: What options are available in the Emirates for delivering in a more natural method and environment? Well, the option of home birth is completely ruled out. It is actually illegal to give birth at home (deliberately, that is... accidents of course, can happen.) To seek help on this matter in a professional environment, contact either Sonia Winter (04 344 3978 or 050 453 4980) or Jane Daly (04 344 7314 or 050 655 3084). They will be happy to advise you regarding your options.

Overall, Dubai is a great place to have a baby. Find yourself a gynaecologist who you're comfortable with (there's absolutely nothing wrong with seeing a couple in the early stages), and you're really spoilt for choice. Below are a few that come highly recommended.

Obstetricians & Gynaecologists

Abu Dhabi	
Al Noor Hospital	02 626 5265
Corniche Hospital	02 672 4900
Gulf Diagnostic Centre	02 665 8090
New Medical Centre	02 633 2255
Al Ain	
Al Ain Hospital (Al Jimi)	03 763 5888
Emirates International Hospital	03 763 7777
Oasis Hospital	03 722 1251
Specialised Medical Care Centre	03 766 2291
Tawam Hospital	03 767 7444
Dubai	
American Hospital	04 309 6879
General Medical Centre	04 349 5959
Medlink Clinic	04 344 7711
Welcare Hospital	04 282 7788

Registering a Birth

Every expatriate child born in the UAE must be registered at the Ministry of Health within two weeks and have a residence visa within four months of birth. Without the correct documentation, the baby will not be able to leave the country.

The hospital where the delivery took place will prepare the birth certificate in Arabic upon receipt of hospital records, photocopies of both parents' passports, a marriage certificate and a fee of Dhs.50. Take the birth certificate for translation into English to the Ministry of Health Department of Preventive Medicine (there's one in every emirate). They will endorse and attest it for a fee of Dhs.10.

Once this is done, ensure the child is registered at your embassy or consulate (you may also want to arrange for a passport for your baby), then apply for a residence visa through the normal UAE channels.

Before giving birth in the UAE, it is worth checking the regulations of your country of origin for citizens born overseas.

Immunisation

Currently, for entry into the UAE, no health certificates or particular immunisations are required, unless visitors have been in a cholera or yellow fever infected area in the previous 14 days. Nevertheless, ensure that your family's vaccinations are up to date, especially for polio, tetanus and hepatitis A and B. The Health Authority in the UAE will recommend any additional vaccinations if and when required. Most medical centres and clinics offer immunisation programmes.

Malaria, once a major problem in the country, has now been virtually eradicated. Still, care should be taken when in wet areas, such as wadis and mountain pools, especially when camping. Covering up to prevent bites, and using sprays and anti mosquito coils is recommended.

All schools require the child's up to date immunisation record and medical history. It is compulsory for every school to have a registered nurse and a vaccination programme that starts from the age of five. The vaccines or immunisations recommended by Dubai Health Authority for children from 0 - 15 years of age are as follows:

Recommended Immunisation Schedule

Age	BCG (Tuberculosis)
At birth	1st dose HBV (Hepatitis B)
At birth	2nd dose HBV
1 month	1st dose Pertussis (Whooping Cough)
2 months	1st dose DPT (Diphtheria, Pertussis, Tetanus), Injected Polio & Hemophilis Influenza (HIB)
2 months	2nd dose DPT & Injected Polio and HIB
4 months	3rd dose DPT , Oral Polio , HIB and 3rd dose HBV
6 months	Measles
9 months	MMR (Measles, Mumps, Rubella)
15 months	DPT & Oral Polio Booster and HIB
1½ years	Hepatitis A, Meningitis
2 years	Hepatitis A, 2nd dose
2½ years	DPT & Oral Polio Booster, MMR Booster
4 - 6 years	DT (Diphtheria, Tetanus) & Oral Polio Booster
10 years	Tetanus Booster every 10 years

Mental Health

Psychiatrists, psychologists and stress management specialists are widely present in the Emirates. They hail from a variety of medical backgrounds, and you can choose the approach that most appeals to you. To get in touch with one, either ask your GP for a referral or look in Connector (monthly magazine). Overleaf are some of the areas they cover.

Counselling/Psychology/Psychiatry

Abu Dhabi	
Al Noor Hospital	02 626 5265
New Medical Centre (Psychiatry Only)	02 633 2255
Gulf Diagnostic Centre	02 665 8090
Al Ain	
Al Ain Hospital (Al Jimi)	03 763 5888
Specialised Medical Care Centre	03 766 2291
Tawam Hospital	03 767 7444
Dubai	
Al Rashad Psychiatry Clinic	04 398 9740
Comprehensive Medical Centre	04 331 4777
Dubai Community Health Centre	04 344 6700
Dr Akel's Medical Centre	04 349 4880
Dr Roght McCarthy Psychology Clinic	04 394 6122
Welcare Hospital	04 282 7788

- Psychiatry
- Psychological Therapies & Assessments
- Marriage & Family Counselling
- Speech Therapy
- Special Needs Educational Help in English & Arabic
- Courses & Workshops for Teachers
- Courses & Workshops for Parenting
- Workshops for Children and Teens
- Workshops for Self Development

General Safety & First Aid

All children in cars should be in the appropriate childseat restraints for their age and weight. Pay close attention to the manufacturer's instructions and observe the recommendations with regard to fitting. It is extremely dangerous for a child to sit in a front seat where an airbag has been fitted; the bag designed to cushion the impact for an adult can prove fatal to a child. In the UAE, it is in fact illegal for children under the age of 10 to sit in the front seat. If you have visitors with young children, you can hire equipment from Rent-A-Crib or Abu Dhabi Mums (refer to the Shopping section [p.60]).

First Aid

It is advisable to keep two kits; one permanently in the house and another ready to take with you on day or weekend trips out of the city. Do not forget to add any special medication that you or your family may need, and include a list of emergency phone numbers – just in case.

Immediately replace any item that you use, so that the kit is complete and ready at all times. Check the expiry date of medicines occasionally to make sure that everything is up to date.

First aid kits can be bought at a number of places such as pharmacies, Carrefour and Ace hardware.

Stings & Bites

Marine Stings

If swimming in the sea, it would be advisable to have with you in your bag, one of the three items below:

- A large bottle of vinegar (for jellyfish stings) – pour vinegar over the injury for a few minutes, then wash off
- Sodium bicarbonate (baking soda) – apply a paste of equal parts of sodium bicarbonate and water to the area which has been stung
- Powdered meat tenderiser or talcum powder – papin, present in the tenderiser, inactivates venom. Dust the powder on the infected area.

Spines should be removed by a professional medical person. If there's a reaction such as severe inflammation or fever, go to a hostpital

Insect Stings

When stung, remove the sting carefully and apply a cold compress. Cut an onion in half and apply the cut face to the infected area. If there's a strong reaction to the sting, use antihistamine tablets (check allowed dosage first according to age). If stung near the throat or windpipe, go directly to a hospital.

Snake Bites

In case of a bite:

- Lie the casualty down and keep them calm and still
- Try to keep the affected part below the level of the heart
- Wash the wound thoroughly in warm soapy water
- Arrange medical help

If possible (and without encouraging another bite), kill the snake and take it to the hospital for identification.

Burns

Sunburn

If sunburnt:

- Put the casualty in the shade
- Gently sponge the skin with cool water
- Apply calamine lotion, after sun lotion or yoghurt (for mild burns)
- Give sips of water

If in any doubt, obtain medical help as quickly as possible.

Minor Burns

If burns are minor and the skin is not broken, gently rub it with a slice of raw potato.

Major Burns

For severe burns, it is best to go to the nearest hospital or phone an ambulance.

Common Concerns

Meningitis

In the UAE, children have to be vaccinated for meningitis at two years of age. All parents worry about this swift and potentially fatal disease. A combination of some of the following symptoms could lead to meningitis: a high fever, stiff neck, headache or neck pain, vomiting, sensitivity to light, a rash, or small red or purple black spots resembling bruises, usually found on the armpits, groin, ankles and areas where pressure is applied. Call your doctor or hospital if you are at all concerned.

Ear Problems

One of the benefits of living in the Emirates is the outdoor lifestyle; daily use of an easily accessible swimming pool (in a villa, apartment block or compound) may be wonderful, but can cause problems such as recurrent ear infections. For this, grommets are recommended. They also help when on a plane (which is inevitable whilst living here). A grommet is a tiny cylinder tube put through a hole punched in the eardrum. They take over the job of ventilating the middle ear cavity from the blocked eustachean tubes (these are the ones that block off when the plane is landing/taking off). It is a short procedure (about 15 minutes) done under general anaesthesia.

In fact, the worst part of the procedure for both mother and child, is applying the general anaesthetic, which can be a little distressing, but it's over in a matter of seconds and, for most children, there are no ill effects. Many mothers report that they 'cannot believe the change' in their child after the procedure. Grommets are often applied to very young children (pre-talking) who may have been labouring a constant dull earache for some time, but unable to tell anyone about it.

Alternative Medicine

As with everywhere else in the world, more and more people are turning to alternative therapy. In the Emirates you can find acupuncture, aromatherapy, holistic therapy, homeopathy, hypnotherapy, I ching, food allergists, reflexology, reiki, yoga and zone therapy. If it works, don't knock it. For more therapies, refer to the small ads and Green Pages at the back of Connector, or try the notice board on www.Expatwoman.com.

Cosmetic Surgery

Although you will never meet anyone who has ever had any cosmetic surgery (or admits to it), the number of clinics is constantly on the rise. The services offered include everything from liposuction to breast enhancement/reduction and varicose vein treatment to Botox. Ask around for recommendations and consult some surgeons first before committing yourself to any major surgery and expense.

Well Woman & Well Man

Women are pretty good at going for the annual breast examinations and pap-tests. All the clinics offer facilities. Mammograms are recommended for all women over 40 (to at least take a baseline scan for future comparisons). You hear so many stories of breast cancer being detected too late; why take the risk?

Men are prone to heart disease, testicular and prostrate cancer. Many are under corporate health schemes but if your husband is not, book him in for an annual check up.

Support Groups

Abu Dhabi	
American Women's Association (pager)	91 155 823
AA Recovery helpline	02 443 6325
Abu Dhabi Ladies	02 6673024
Abu Dhabi Mums	02 448 2562
Eating Disorder Support Group	02 665 8090
Parentcraft	02 655 8090

Dubai	
CARE (Cancer Awareness for Residents of the Emirates)	04 324 1111
Al Anon Family Groups (AA)	04 343 0446
Adoption Support Group	04 349 4496
Attention Deficit Hyperactive Disorder	04 394 6643
AA Recovery Helpline	04 394 9198
Birth Days	04 344 3978
Breastfeeding Telephone Support	050 453 4670
Fertility Support Group	050 646 5148
Mums & Toddlers Group	050 667 5220
Overeaters Anonymous	050 668 4640
SANDS (Stillbirth & Neonatal Death Society)	04 344 0534
Twins, Triplets or More	050 654 0079

children's oasis
nursery is proud to announce the opening of

- Warm, caring & friendly atmosphere.
- Dedicated & professional staff.
- British Curriculum.
- 3 months to 4 1/2 years, Nursery & Day care.
- Bright, spacious classrooms & garden.
- An adventure filled journey of discovery & learning.
- A division of Children's Oasis Nurseries.

kidz inc.
nursery
at the Dubai Marina

Education
EXPLORER

Education

Education	41	School & Nursery Table	48	**Special Needs**	56
Toddler Groups	43	Schools	50		
Nurseries & Pre-Schools	44	Tertiary Education	55		

MUST DO

Although the skyline of the UAE is constantly burgeoning and new schools are on the horizon, at present there still remains a shortage of places so it is well worth putting your child on a waiting list even before they reach school age. This also applies for nursery schools, especially the more popular ones, so it may be worth visiting them when your pregnant. Many waiting lists don't require a fee until you actually register your child. See [p.48] for the 'At a glance' table.

MUST KNOW

The Montessori method of education encourages learning through play and discovery, rather than through formal teaching methods. In theory, it helps young children develop their natural instincts and abilities in an individualised environment. Of the nursery schools in Dubai, some follow the Montessori methods very strictly, while others merely incorporate certain Montessori principles into their existing curriculums. Check with the school for more details.

MUST HAVE

When you register your child at a school or nursery there are a few essential documents that the school requires. These include a passport copy with valid residence visa, original transfer certificates from your child's previous school, vaccination certificates and a birth certificate. Check with each school what they require in advance in case you need to send home for certain things. See [p.42].

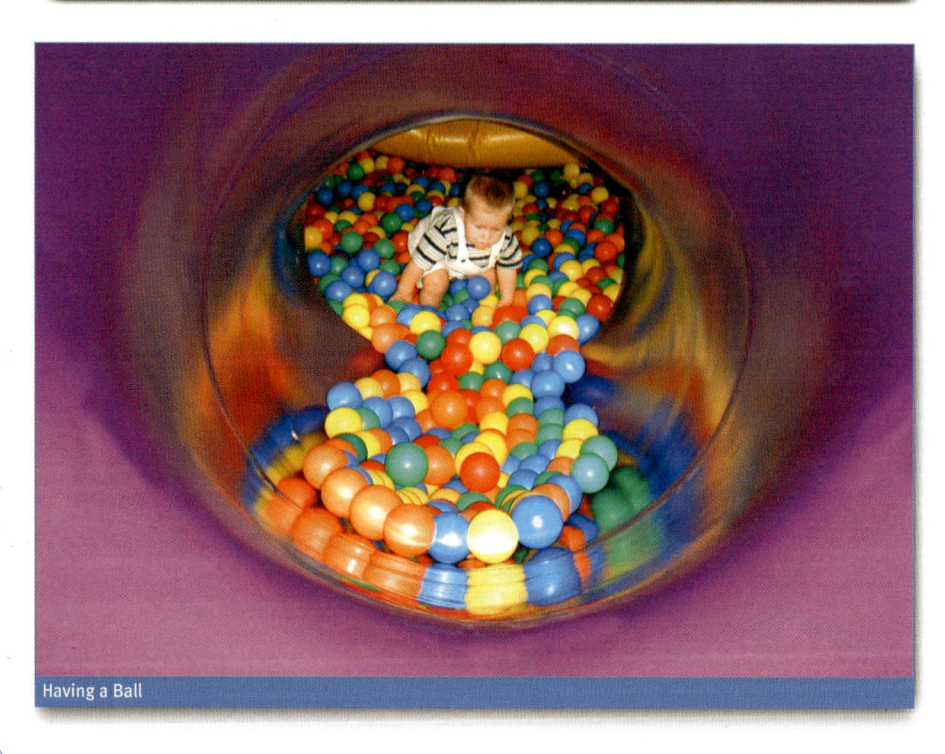

Having a Ball

Education

Due to the UAE's diverse expatriate culture, the education system here is extremely varied. You'll find many schools offering the same curriculum as those in your home country, or at least a very close equivalent. If possible, you should try to investigate schools on your preliminary visits to the UAE, whilst finalising jobs and accommodation, since registration should be done in advance - new schools are opening all the time, but the shortage of places at good schools is a common expat complaint! There is no free or government subsidised education for expats here, but many companies do offer their employees assistance with paying school fees.

All schools are fully registered and approved by the Ministry of Education and the Municipality. The establishments listed in this guide are just some of the options available in Abu Dhabi and Dubai, and mainly those offering the British or American curriculums. The 'At a Glance' table at the end of this section is a quick reference guide to facts such as fees, age range, area, contact details, etc. for selected schools. Remember that word of mouth is often the strongest recommendation, so friends and colleagues may have loads of valuable advice.

Multinational Environment

Most schools in the UAE encourage a multinational atmosphere of tolerance and understanding. Your child will be able to make friends with other children from different nationalities and discover new cultures, beliefs, dress codes, etc.

School Starting Age

Generally, children start school at the age of four. Most schools follow a system of 'four years old before the first of September of the school year in question', unless otherwise stated. If your child has a birthday after that, he or she will usually have to wait until the following year to start 'big school'.

School Curriculum

As mentioned earlier, most schools listed here offer the British or American curriculums. Children from elsewhere, like South Africa, Australia or Europe, may have to consider changing curriculums when they start school here. Check with your home country's Ministry of Education or with their Embassy in the UAE about the compatibility of the UK/US curriculums with those back home.

School Year

The school year for most establishments is divided into three terms:

Term 1 (Winter Term) – September to December

Term 2 (Spring Term) – January to March

Term 3 (Summer Term) – April to June

School Week

The school week for most educational facilities runs from Saturday to Wednesday. This was established by a new Federal ruling in 1999 and, depending on your company, may be different to your working week (refer to Social & Business Hours in *Home Sweet Home [p.2]*).

School Hours

School timings vary, with a start time of between 07:00 - 08:00 and a finish time of between 12:00 - 16:00. Nearly all schools finish earlier on Wednesdays. Sports and other extracurricular activities take place after school hours.

Acceptance

Acceptance of a pupil is at the discretion of the school. It usually depends on the number of places available in each group and on the priority of receipt of the original application, and is also subject to any current Ministry restrictions. Priority is often given the siblings of current or ex-pupils. Places are usually limited, particularly at the top schools, so get your kids' names on the waiting lists early!

To gain a more accurate picture of a student's academic skills and to screen for any learning difficulties, some schools evaluate candidates before they are admitted. In order to secure a place, most schools ask for a non-refundable admission fee.

> **Did you know?**
> The academic year of the Southern hemisphere is very different to the academic year of the Northern hemisphere, so students may have to repeat six months or jump six months. The numbers of the grading are also not always the same – you could be repeating Grade 4, but in fact jumping a year. Check with the school.

Teachers

Almost without exception, internationally qualified, certified and experienced teachers make up the staff of UAE schools. Teachers have regular in-service training in order to keep up to date with current methodology and practice. If you are concerned about the level of qualifications that teachers have, check with the individual schools - you should find that most have strict requirements for hiring new staff, and that standards are high.

Class Sizes

For primary and secondary schools, the average class size is usually between 18 to 25 students. Classrooms are fully air-conditioned.

Application Requirements

In accordance with the current UAE Ministry of Education requirements, the following documentation is necessary for every new child enrolling in a school. Compliance is usually mandatory for admission approval by the UAE Ministry of Education. The school will supply an application form, which should be completed and returned to the school along with:

- School registration fee
- Photocopy of pupil's passport with UAE entry stamp or residence visa stamp
- Photocopy of birth certificate
- Passport size photographs of pupil (always take more than you think you'll need!)
- Copy of the child's immunisation record and medical history
- Original copy of the most recent school report

For applicants within the UAE, a transfer certificate from the previous school (usually you will need the original request from the old school to the new school and Dhs.15. This will be processed by the new school who will pay the Dhs.15 to the Ministry).

Applicants outside the UAE must provide a transfer letter from their child's previous school stating which year/grade they are in. The original transfer certificate of students from schools in any country other than the United Arab Emirates, the USA or Western Europe must be attested by the Ministry of Education, Ministry of Foreign Affairs and the UAE Embassy in that country. The original document and two copies of the transfer certificate must contain the following information: date of enrolment; year group placement; date the child left the school; school stamp and signature. The year group is of vital importance, as it will dictate in which year the child will be placed in their new school.

School Fees

School fees tend to be on the high side here, and this should be an important consideration when you are negotiating a package with your company. Many companies do provide education allowances for employees' children. Please note that all fees listed in the table are approximate and can change (usually increasing) at any time.

School Fees – The Small Print

Usually a full term's notice in writing is required when withdrawing a pupil from school

Fees are payable in advance

Some deposits can be deducted from the first terms fee

Include an amount ranging from Dhs.100 - 300 per year for your child's medical examination

Some schools give discounts on tuition fees for a second child/children

There can be separate miscellaneous charges for books, extracurricular activities and examination fees etc.

School bus shuttles usually run to major communities with door to door drop off, but these can cost up to Dhs.1500 per term

School Meals

School meals are not provided and children have to take a lunch box. Drinking water is available in all schools. Some secondary schools have limited facilities for purchasing food and drink at the school.

School Uniform

Wearing a uniform is usually obligatory in Arabic and Asian schools and those offering schooling under the British national curriculum. American, French and German schools don't usually require a uniform, except sometimes for sports. Uniforms can sometimes be bought directly from the school, but usually from school outfitters. A standard uniform package including sweater, sports and swimwear, but excluding socks and shoes, will cost between Dhs.300 and Dhs.400 depending on the age of the child. At least two sets are required. All clothing should be clearly labelled with your child's name.

Healthcare

Schools have well equipped medical dispensaries under the control of a full time nurse who works in liaison with a visiting school doctor. In addition to monitoring immunisation programmes, the nurse is available at any time during school hours to administer first aid and to carry out routine medical examinations. Immunisations are given at regular intervals throughout the school year by the school medical staff and it is important that records of immunisations given outside the school are made available. The UAE immunisation programme is based on recommendations for the region from the World Health Organisation and it may differ from the one in your country of origin. If hospital treatment is required, the nurse will telephone the parents and liaise with them over necessary action. It's advisable for parents to get health cards issued for their children by the Department of Health & Medical Services. Refer to the section on **Medical Care** [p.26].

Arabic

Following Ministry of Education guidelines, Arabic is taught from pre school, so that children have the opportunity to learn the language of the country in which they reside. The course is set out by the Ministry of Education and places emphasis on speaking and listening and the context of each session is relevant to the age of the child. For those whose native language is Arabic, there are extra sessions in small groups. Sessions focus on developing knowledge and understanding of the Arabic language and Islam.

Toddler Groups

Having a baby or raising a toddler in a strange city is sometimes exciting and sometimes daunting. Invariably you've left behind your support network of grandparents, aunties and uncles, who would normally share their experiences with you and also babysit from time to time! Toddler groups are a superb way to get your tot socialising, and you'll meet loads of other mums who are in the same boat as you - you'll be swapping ideas and comparing notes in no time!

Abu Dhabi

Abu Dhabi Mums

Location → Various locations · Abu Dhabi | 02 673 2968
Hours → Various
Web/email → mcgraths@emirates.net.ae | Map Ref → UAE-A3

This group has over 200 members and welcomes ladies who are either mums to be, or already mums of children up to school age. They meet at various indoor and outdoor locations throughout the week.

They have a baby equipment scheme, whereby you can hire various items on a weekly basis, and have also negotiated discounts with several local shops and services. They also arrange a monthly mums' night out - time off for good behaviour!

St Andrews Playgroup

Location → St Andrews Church · Al Mushrif | 02 681 4913
Hours → Various
Web/email → na | Map Ref → 3-C3

This group for new born to pre school children is run by mums and is a great place to meet other mums and have a chat while keeping a close eye on the kids. It's held in the St Andrews Church hall which is equipped with toys suitable for newborns and toddlers. The group is non profit, but a small fee is levied to cover coffee/tea, biscuits and the hiring of the hall.

Dubai

Dubai Adventure Mums

Location → Various | 050 656 5837
Hours → Various
Web/email → www.dubaiadventuremums.com | Map Ref → na

DAM is a community of women who combine the opportunity of meeting new friends with the pursuit of excitement. They currently have members aged 17 - 70, made up of 34 different nationalities. Their monthly challenges have included activities such as quad biking, sand boarding, sailing, go karting and indoor rock climbing! New members are encouraged to come along to meetings, which take place on the first Sunday of every month. Call Debbie Magee for more information, on the above number or via email at info@dubaiadventuremums.com.

Mums and Tots Group

Location → Nr Ramada Hotel Bur Dubai | 050 656 5837
Hours → 09:30 - 11:30
Web/email → anncassidy100@hotmail.coom | Map Ref → 12-C1

This well established, informal mums' group has been going for the past 14 years. All mums (and dads!) are welcome, and the focus is on meeting like minded people and making friends. The meetings take place in a huge hall that is crammed with toys to keep the kids busy while mums chat over coffee. This group is highly recommended, especially if you're new to Dubai or new to motherhood. Contact Ann on the above number for more info and directions.

Costs: Dhs.15 per meeting, which includes tea/coffee, biscuits and snacks for the kids.

Mirdif Mums

Location → Various locations · Mirdif | 050 654 8953
Hours → Various
Web/email → mirdifmums@yahoo.com | Map Ref → 15-E4

This friendly support group is mainly for all the mums in the growing Mirdif area and its surrounds. They organise a busy timetable of activities, including coffee mornings at members' houses, meetings at various play centres around Dubai, and get togethers at parks and beaches. For a detailed timetable, check the website. The group is run by Bonnie Scott-Laws, who can be contacted on the above number or by email at the above address.

Mother to Mother

Location → Dubai Country Club · Al Awir Rd | 050 452 7674
Hours → Wednesdays 09:30 - 11:30
Web/email → na | Map Ref → 13-A1

This is a non-profit support group for mums of children up to three years. They meet once a week at Dubai Country Club. For more information, contact Ilsie at the above number or on 04 348 3754.

Look Who's Teething!

Mothers and Miracles

Location → Le Meridien Mina Seyahi | 04 390 5102
Hours → Various
Web/email → www.mothersandmiracles.co.za | Map Ref → 15-D1

Mothers and Miracles offers a structured, interactive learning programme, designed to stimulate children between three months and three years, in the areas of intellect, emotions, creativity, physical movement, social interaction and music. The programme, developed by a leading early childhood educationalist, encourages the active participation of the parent in each session, guiding and encouraging the child through each activity.

Contact: Karen Pereira on the above number or on 050 450 1993, or via email on mothersmiracles@sahmnet.ae.

Nurseries & Pre-Schools

There are many wonderful nursery schools in the UAE, so when you're ready for the big milestone of packing your little one of for their first day at 'school', you'll have no problem finding a nursery that suits you. In general, most nursery schools operate on a mornings only basis, although there are quite a few that offer late timings more suitable for working parents.

Choosing a Nursery

When choosing a nursery there are several important considerations;

Location: A nursery that is close to your home or office has obvious advantages, especially if you have other children already at school and you need to keep your school run simple!

Teacher: Ask to meet the teacher beforehand and trust your parental instincts - after all, your child will be spending quite a few hours with him or her.

Facilities: Visit several schools to see what's on offer - check for classroom size, outside play areas, any glaring safety hazards, cleanliness, etc.

Atmosphere: Try to visit during a normal day when other children are there - do they seem happy, contented and well supervised? Standards here are high, but check whether a school is suitable for your child specifically - is it too rigid, too wild, too noisy or not active enough? This will depend largely on what your child is used to at home.

Flexibility: This is particularly important for working parents - many nurseries offer late classes and early drop off times.

Fees: Nursery school fees tend to vary significantly and depend on the age of your child, how many days he or she goes to school, drop off and pick up times, optional transport and catering requirements, etc. In addition to the term fees, you will also be asked to pay a medical fee, a registration fee and possibly a deposit. Visit several schools and judge what is the best option for your child in relation to your budget. Try not to put too much stock into the cost - the most expensive nurseries are not necessarily the best!

And don't forget, the most popular nurseries in Dubai are always over-subscribed, with waiting lists of up to a year, so if you have a preferred option, get your tot's name down early!

Abu Dhabi

First Steps Kindergarten & Primary School

Location → Al Karama St. · Abu Dhabi | **02 445 4920**
Hours → 08:00 - 13:00
Web/email → www.firststeps.ae   Map Ref → UAE-A3

With the luxury of a well equipped outdoor play area with paddling pool, an indoor gymnasium and an art room, First Steps focuses on developing social skills. The use of the British curriculum prepares the child for a smooth transition into the education system.

Age range: 14 months - four years
Late hours: na

Giggles English Nursery

Location → Tourist Club Area | **02 677 8934**
Hours → 07:30 - 14:00
Web/email → navasha@hotmail.com   Map Ref → UAE-A3

Established in 1987, Giggles welcomes all nationalities through its doors. A first aider is provided on site and, like many other nurseries, the British curriculum is in place. A transport bus is available for an extra fee.

Age range: 18 months - four years
Late hours: na

Humpty Dumpty Nursery

Location → Khalidia Palace Htl · Al Ras Al Akhdar | **02 666 3277**
Hours → 07:30 - 14:00
Web/email → lisamarieblackburn@hotmail.com   Map Ref → 5-C3

Providing full time and part time care for babies, toddlers and children up to the age of four years.

Groups are supervised by well qualified staff, all of whom have completed comprehensive Medic First Aid courses, specifically for the care of babies and children.

Age range: 12 months - five years
Late hours: na

Sesame Street Private Nursery

Location → Shk Rashid B Saeed Al Makt St | **02 641 2766**
Hours → 08:00 - 13:00
Web/email → ala123@emirates.net.ae   Map Ref → na

The development of early phonetic, conversational and pre writing skills is balanced with manipulative and role playing skills, sand and water activities and early co-ordination skills in the gym. Class sizes are restricted to provide quality, education on an individual level. They also have school bus services.

Age range: two - three and a half years
Late hours: Can extend to 13:45

Stepping Stones Nursery

Location → 13th Street · Khalidiya | **02 681 5583**
Hours → 07:30 - 12:15
Web/email → na   Map Ref → na

The children learn by playing games, class themes, craft activities, cooking and 'pretend play'. The covered outdoor play area has wooden play equipment, cars and bikes and there's also an indoor gym. They offer an American/British curriculum.

Age range: 18 months - four years
Late hours: Can extend to 13:15

Dubai

Children's Oasis Nursery

Location → Umm Suqeim | **04 348 8981**
Hours → 08:00 - 12:30
Web/email → www.childrensoasisnursery.com   Map Ref → 12-B1

Popular for its family atmosphere, there are now three locations for this nursery. They encourage family visits and stress the importance of communication with parents and teachers. Split into four different age groups, the home routine is closely followed for infants, and daily activities are planned for the toddlers.

Age range: three months - four years
Late hours: Can extend to 17:00
Other branches: The Lakes (04 390 5010); Dubai Marina (04 390 5100)

Emirates British Nursery

Location → Umm Suqeim
Hours → 08:00 - 13:30
Web/email → www.ebninfo.ae
04 348 9996
Map Ref → 12-A2

Fun is the order of the day at this nursery, which recognises playtime as an important factor in a child's early development. Both locations are spacious and well planned, with multilingual staff and an in house nurse. A summer school (a lifesaver for working mums!) is available during July and August.

Age range: 11 months - four years
Late hours: Can extend to 15:00
Other branches: Mirdif (04 288 9222)

Gulf Montessori Nursery

Location → Nr Choithrams · Al Garhoud
Hours → 08:00 - 13:00
Web/email → www.gulfmontessori.com
04 282 7046
Map Ref → 15-D1

Providing plenty of opportunities for play, creativity and social interaction in a nurturing and activity-based environment. Tuition is by fully qualified Montessori staff, lessons are in Arabic, English and French. Annual fees include breakfast and lunch. The nursery also runs a summer school.

Age range: two - five years
Late hours: na

Jumeirah International Nursery

Location → Jumeira 2
Hours → 08:00 - 12:30
Web/email → www.jinspire.com
04 394 5567
Map Ref → 12-D2

One of the oldest nurseries in Dubai, Jumeirah International Nursery stresses the importance of early childhood development. Educational activities follow the standards set by UK OFSTED (Office for Standards in Education) and individual care and attention is given in a safe and balanced environment.

Age range: eight months - four years
Late hours: Can extend to 16:00

Jumeirah International Nursery School

Location → Nr Post Office   Al Wasl Rd
Hours → 08:00 - 12:30
Web/email → www.jinschools.com
04 349 9065
Map Ref → 12-E1

Claiming to be the best equipped and largest pre school facility in the region, they promise to offer your child an atmosphere that is warm, safe and secure, whilst presenting them with carefully chosen age appropriate learning experiences. Teachers and caregivers are both experienced and well trained.

Age range: 18 months - four and a half years
Late hours: Can extend to 13:30

Kids' Cottage

Location → Beach Rd · Umm Suqeim
Hours → 08:00 - 12:30
Web/email → www.kids-cottage.com
04 394 2145
Map Ref → 12-C1

This cheerful nursery offers an activities based curriculum for children over the age of 12 months. The premises features well equipped classrooms, a physcial development hall, a learning centre and an outdoor play area, and parents can check up on their kids at any time via a webcam (access is password protected).

Age range: 12 months - four years
Late hours: Can extend to 13:30

Kids' Island Nursery

Location → Umm Suqeim
Hours → 08:00 - 12:30
Web/email → www.kidsislandnursery.com
04 394 2578
Map Ref → 12-E1

Kids' Island aims to create a relaxed and caring atmosphere, in which children follow the British curriculum. The nursery is open all year round, thanks to their summer school, and there is also a weekly 'mums and tots' group. They have four large, outdoor shaded play areas as well as an Activity Room and Playroom.

Age range: 12 months - four years
Late hours: Can extend to 13:30

e-Kids

Kids' Village

Location ➜ Umm Suqeim	04 348 5991
Hours ➜ 08:00 - 12:00	
Web/email ➜ na	Map Ref ➜ 12-B2

This Montessori school has an outside play area, partly shaded for the hotter months and play times are scheduled into the kids' daily Montessori activities. The pet turtle, Huchi Puchi, is a great hit with the kids!

Age range: 14 months - five years
Late hours: Can extend to 16:00

Ladybird Nursery

Location ➜ Nr Post Office · Jumeira	04 344 1011
Hours ➜ 08:00 - 12:30	
Web/email ➜ na	Map Ref ➜ 12-E1

Ladybird strikes an interesting balance between a traditional nursery and Montessori, by providing the usual bright and cheerful environment, toys, dressing up clothes and soft play, whilst spending some time each day encouraging the children to explore the Montessori materials.

Age range: 18 months - four years
Late hours: Can extend to 13:30

Little Land Montessori

Location ➜ Beach Rd · Umm Suqeim	04 394 4471
Hours ➜ 08:00 - 12:30	
Web/email ➜ www.littleland-montessori.com	Map Ref ➜ 12-B1

Joint owned by a neonatal specialist and a qualified Montessori teacher, this professional team has created a relaxing environment for little ones. The six classrooms, split according to age group, all have child friendly names like 'Winnie the Pooh' and 'Twinkle Toes'. Little Land will also assist parents with the trials and tribulations of potty training!

Age range: 15 months - four years
Late hours: Can extend to 14:00

Palms Nursery School

Location ➜ Nr Safa Park · Al Wasl Rd	04 344 7017
Hours ➜ 08:00 - 12:30	
Web/email ➜ www.palmsnursery.com	Map Ref ➜ 12-D1

There are seven classrooms and play areas plus a soft play classroom designed especially for children of nursery age. The aim is to offer a curriculum that will help the children acquire the skills and values that enable them to develop socially, physically and emotionally.

Age range: 22 months - four years
Late hours: Can extend to 13:30

Safa Kindergarten Nursery School

Location ➜ Off Al Wasl Rd · Al Safa	04 342 9575
Hours ➜ 08:00 - 12:30	
Web/email ➜ www.safanurseries.com	Map Ref ➜ 15-D1

Both branches of this nursery operate in the same way, according to the Montessori teaching method. Activities include educational play, singing, playhouse activities and water play. The choice of Arabic or French as a second language is introduced to children above the age of three. A variety of field trips are arranged throughout the year, and there is an annual sports day, fancy dress day and various concerts.

Age range: 12 months - four years
Late hours: Can extend to 14:00
Other branches: Safa II (04 344 3878)

Small Steps Nursery School

Location ➜ Mirdif	04 288 3347
Hours ➜ 08:00 - 12:00	
Web/email ➜ smallstepsnursery@hotmail.com	Map Ref ➜ 15-E4

This is a nursery run by British staff in the heart of the Mirdif community. With a covered outside play area, and opportunities for water play and soft play, they offer your child a fun environment in which to play and learn.

Age range: 12 months - four years (pre school)
Late hours: Available up to 13:30

Small World Nursery

Location ➜ Nr Dubai Zoo · Beach Rd, Jumeira	04 345 7774
Hours ➜ 08:00 - 12:30	
Web/email ➜ www.smallworldnurserydubai.com	Map Ref ➜ 13-B1

Small World offers a balanced educational structure, combining academic learning with physical education. The well equipped facilities include a library, sandy play area, a role playing room and outside play areas.

Age range: 18 months - four years
Late hours: Can extend to 13:30
Other branches: Small World II (04 349 9770)

Schools at a glance...

School	Age	Area	Phone
Abu Dhabi			
Abu Dhabi Grammar School (Canada)	3.5 - 16+	Khaleej Al Arabi St	02 666 2900
American Community School of Abu Dhabi	4 - 16+	Khalidiya	02 681 5115
American International School	3 - 16+	29th Street, Airport Road	02 444 4333
Cambridge High School	3 -18	New Mussafah	02 552 1621
International Community School	3 - 17	23rd St, off Muroor Rd	02 448 9900
International School of Choueifat	3 - 18	Airport Rd, opp Abu Dhabi Islamic Bank	02 446 1444
The British School Al Khubairat	3 - 18	Airport Rd	02 446 2280
Dubai			
Al Mawakeb School	3 - 17	Al Garhoud & Al Barsha	04 347 8288
American School of Dubai	4 - 18	53B St, Al Wasl	04 344 0824
British National Curriculum School, The	3 - 14	Beach Road, Jumeira	04 344 1614
Cambridge High School, The	3 - 18	Al Garhoud	04 282 4646
Dubai American Academy	4 - 17	Interchange 4, Al Barsha	04 347 9222
Dubai College	11 - 18	Al Sufouh Rd, nr Knowledge Village	04 399 9111
Dubai English Speaking School	4 - 11	Oud Mehta Road, Bur Dubai	04 337 1457
Emirates International School	4 - 18	Jct 4, nr Dubai College, Shk Zayed Rd	04 348 9804
English College, Dubai	11 - 18	Off Shk Zayed H'way, Umm Suqeim	04 394 3465
Horizon School	3 - 11	Nr Park n' Shop, Jumeira	04 394 7879
International School of Choueifat	3 - 18	Btn Jct no.4 & no 5 Umm Suqeim	04 399 9444
Jebel Ali Primary School	4 - 11	Jebel Ali Village	04 884 6485
Jumeirah College	9 - 17	Behind Park N Shop, Al Wasl Road	04 395 4950
Jumeirah English Speaking School	3 - 11	Near Safa Park	04 394 5515
Jumeirah Primary School	3 - 9	Al Wasl Road, Jumeira	04 394 3500
Lycee Georges Pompidou	3 - 11	Oud Mehta Road, Bur Dubai	04 337 4161
Oxford School, The	3 - 18	Nr Galadari Driving Institute, Al Qusais	04 254 3666
Regent School	3 - 11	Jumeira 1, Nr Iranian Hospital	04 344 2409
St. Mary's Catholic School	5.5 - 18	Opp Indian High School, Bur Dubai	04 337 0252

Nurseries at a glance...

Nurseries	Age	Area	Phone
Abu Dhabi			
First Steps	14 months - 4 yrs	Al Karama Street	02 446 0960
Giggles English Nursery	18 months - 3.5 yrs	Airport Rd/Tourist Club Area	02 677 8934
Humpty Dumpty	12 months - 5 yrs	11th Street, Al Bateen Area	02 666 3277
Sesame Street Private Nursery	2 years - 3.5 yrs	Sheikh Maktoum Bin Rashid St	02 641 2766
Stepping Stones	18 months - 4.5 yrs	13th Street, Khalidiya	02 681 5583
Dubai			
Children's Oasis Nursery	3 months - 4 yrs	Umm Suqeim; Dubai Marina; Lakes	04 348 8981
Emirates British Nursery	11 months - 4 yrs	1 in Mirdif; 1 in Umm Suqeim	04 348 9996
Jumeirah International Nursery	8 months - 4 yrs	Jumeira 2	04 394 5567
Jumeirah International Nursery School	18 months - 4 yrs	Nr Post Office, Al Wasl Rd	04 349 9065
Kids' Cottage	12 months - 4 yrs	Beach Road, Umm Suqeim	04 394 2145
Kids' Island Nursery	14 months - 4 yrs	Umm Suqeim	04 394 2578
Kids Village	14 months - 5 yrs	Jumeira, Umm Suqeim	04 348 5991
Ladybird Nursery	18 months - 4 yrs	Nr Post Office, Jumeira	04 344 1011
Little Land Montessori	15 months - 4yrs	Beach Rd, Umm Suqeim	04 394 4471
Palm's Nursery School	22 months - 4 yrs	Nr Safa Park, Al Wasl Rd	04 394 7017
Safa Kindergarten Nursery School	12 months - 4 yrs	Off Al Wasl Rd, Route 15	04 344 3878
Small Steps Nursery	12 months - 4 yrs	Mirdif	04 288 3347
Small World Nursery	18 months - 4.5 yrs	Beach Rd, Nr Zoo	04 345 7774
SuperKids Nursery	11 months - 5 yrs	Mirdif	04 288 1949
Tender Love and Care	4 months - 4 yrs	Dubai Media City Boutique Offices	04 367 1636
Tiny Home Montessori	22 months - 5.5 yrs	Beh Dubai Zoo, Jumeira 1	04 349 3201
Yellow brick road	4 months - 5 yrs	Garhoud	04 282 8290

*All nurseries that have late pick up timings are shown in brackets

Schools at a glance...

Timings	Bus	Uniform	Curriculum	Students per Class
08:00 - 15:00	Yes	Yes	Canadian (Nova Scotia)	20
08:00 - 15:00	No	No	American	16
08:00 - 15:00	Yes	Yes	American	17
08:00 - 13:50	Yes	Yes	British	25 - 28
07:40 - 14:30 (KG 08:00 - 12:30)	Yes	Yes	International	On request
07:50 - 15:00 (primary) 16:00 (secondary)	Yes	Yes	British & American	On request
07:30 - 14:30	Yes	Yes	British	On request
08.00 - 15.00	Yes	Yes	American	20 - 28
08:00 - 15:00	No	Yes	American	18 - 24
08:00 - 13:20	Yes	Yes	British	20 - 25
08:00 - 13:45	Yes	Yes	British	25 - 30
07:45 - 14:45	No	Yes	American	24
07:50 - 15:25	Yes	Yes	British	20 (max)
07:45 - 14:15	No	Yes	British	25
08:00 - 15:00	Yes	Yes	International	On request
07:45 - 15:00	Yes	Yes	British	20 - 25
07:35-13:10	Yes	Yes	British	20
07:50 - 15:00 (primary) 16:00 (secondary)	Yes	Yes	British & American	On request
07:45 - 13:30	Yes	Yes	British	24
07:45 - 15:30	Yes	Yes	British	22
07:45 - 13:45	Yes	Yes	British	20
07:40 - 14:15	Yes	Yes	British	18 - 24
08:00 - 13:15	Yes	No	French	28
08:00 - 13:40	Yes	Yes	British	25
8:00 - 13:30	Yes	Yes	British	15
7:45 - 13:15	No	Yes	British	30

Nurseries at a glance...

Timings	Bus	Uniform	Curriculum	Students per Class
08:00 - 13:00	Yes	Yes	British	12
07:30 - 14:00	Yes	Yes	British	10 - 15
07:30 - 14:00	No	No	British	On request
08:00 - 13:00 (13:45)	Yes	Yes	American	20
07:30 - 12:15 (13:15)	No	No	British and American	On request
08:00 - 17:00	No	No	British	15
08:00 - 15:00	Yes	No	British	18
08:00 - 16:00	Yes	No	British	12 - 18
08:00 - 14:30	Yes	No	British	18
08:00 - 13:30	No	No	British	8 - 15
08:00 - 14:00	No	No	British	12 - 15
08:00 - 12:30 (13:30)	No	No	Montessori	10 - 12
08:00 - 12:30 (14:00)	No		Montessori	12 - 18
08:00 - 12:00 (16:00)	Yes	No	Montessori	15 - 20
08:00 - 12:30 (13:30)	No	No	British	12
08:00 - 12:30 (14:00)	Yes	Yes	International	
08:00 - 12:00 (13:30)	Yes	No	British	10
08:00 - 12:30 (13:30)	Yes	Yes	British	15 - 16
08:00 - 13:30 (16:00)	Yes	No	Montessori	15 - 20
08:00 - 12:30 (17:00)	No	No	International	See review
08:00 - 12:00	No	No	Montessori	15 - 20
07:30 - 15:00 (19:00)	No	No	British	20

Education

FAMILY EXPLORER

Super Kids Nursery	
Location ➔ Mirdif	04 288 1949
Hours ➔ 08:00 - 13:00	
Web/email ➔ www.superkidsnursery.com	Map Ref ➔ na

Super Kids is a small yet popular nursery serving the ever growing Mirdif community. The focus is on providing a warm, cosy 'home away from home' environment. Facilities include a large, shaded outside play area, an activity gym and a music room. Hot lunch and transport are optional extras.

Age range: 11 months - five years
Late hours: Can extend to 16:00

Tender Love and Care	
Location ➔ Dubai Media City	04 349 3201
Hours ➔ 08:00 - 12:30	
Web/email ➔ www.tenderloveandcare.com	Map Ref ➔ 11-D1

Activities here are planned week to week, and parents are notified of the monthly theme plans. Facilities include a gymnasium and garden, and snacks are provided twice during the day. Infants have their own sleeping room with cots. The child to adult ratio is as follows: infants 4:1, toddlers 6:1, pre school 8:1. The nursery also has a 'daily drop in' service (two to four years only), for a minimum of three hours.

Age range: 11 months - five years
Late hours: Can extend to 16:00
Drop in service: 09:00 - 17:00. Dhs.100 for three hours (including one snack). Dhs.25 for each additional hour.

Tiny Home Montessori	
Location ➔ Nr Dubai Zoo - Jumeira	04 349 3201
Hours ➔ 08:00 - 12:00	
Web/email ➔ na	Map Ref ➔ 13-B2

This nursery opened in 1989 and strictly follows the Montessori curriculum. All staff are qualified with the international Montessori school of teaching. Classrooms are designed according to the Montessori method and there is a play area on site. Monthly themes and field trips are organised throughout the year.

Age range: 22 months - five and a half years
Late hours: na

Yellow Brick Road Nursery	
Location ➔ Opp Irish Village - Al Garhoud	04 282 8290
Hours ➔ 07:30 - 15:30	
Web/email ➔ www.yellowbrickroad.ws	Map Ref ➔ 15-D1

This purpose built nursery, accommodates 180 children in 9 classes and a baby room. Children are taught the British curriculum. Outdoor facilities are particularly appealing and include a paddling pool. Breakfast and lunch are prepared for the children, on the premises.

Age range: Four months - five years
Late hours: Can extend to 19:00

Schools

If there's one golden rule you should follow when it comes to planning your child's education, it is that you MUST get your child's name on the waiting lists of your preferred schools as early as possible. Many an expat will be happy to tell you, at great length, about the difficulty they had finding a school place for their own children. So even though your child may still be in nappies, and you feel a bit silly going round to the 'big' schools, you should at least visit a few to see what's on offer and join the queue! The good news is that with all the new developments and big projects currently under construction in the UAE, there is bound to be a whole crop of new schools popping up over the next few years.

> **Boarding Abroad**
>
> Jo Bowen, 04 3488 085 and Fiona Wells, 04 348 4683 keep a list of children at boarding schools and will be able to help you with advice, as well as information relating to discounted flights for listed children (university/college students equally qualify).

The list of schools which follows includes primary and secondary schools in Abu Dhabi and Dubai. In Abu Dhabi, most schools tend to cater for children of all ages, from the time they start primary school until the day they graduate from high school. In Dubai however, there are several schools which are specifically for the primary school grades.

Most of the schools listed below follow either the British, American, or International curriculums. If you can't find a school offering the exact curriculum of your home country, in most cases the UK and US systems are universally accepted. (Check with your Embassy here to make sure).

Yellow Brick Road Nursery

hand in hand step by step

Give your child the very best...

The **Yellow Brick Road Nursery philosophy** is unique and special to ensure all the children's individual needs are cared for in a loving, safe, secure & homely environment.

❋ **Our multicultural and multilingual Nursery staff** is a wonderfully dedicated team of professional women who justly reflect Dubai's unique cultural diversity. Their combined knowledgeable experience in early-years teaching methods is of great value for the children's early-learning development.

❋ **The Nursery learning programmes** are planned following the British Foundation Curriculum with an integration of the specialised Montessori and Steiner learning methods.

❋ **The Nursery activities** are based on a daily life that is gentle and unhurried; a beautiful inspiring environment for young children to create, initiate and imagine freely.

...the only choice for your child.

"The most beautiful & unique pre-school learning years your children could ever experience, a dream come true for parents & children"

Nursery Hours: 7.30 am to 7.30 pm.
Saturdays to Thursdays.
Nursery Ages: Four months to Four years.

Contact Us:
Tel: 04 2828290, Fax: 04 2828214
Email: yellowbr@emirates.net.ae
Website: yellowbrickroad.ws
Al Garhoud Residential Complex,
Opposite Irish Village.

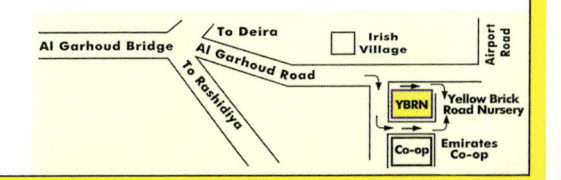

Al Garhoud Bridge — To Deira — Al Garhoud Road — To Rashidiya — Irish Village — Airport Road — YBRN Yellow Brick Road Nursery — Co-op — Emirates Co-op

The location of the school will obviously be an important factor in your selection, and not just so that the drop off and pick up route is simple. If all your children's school friends live near the school, but you live on the other side of town, you may find yourself living behind the wheel of your car while you taxi them about!

Fees vary considerably for each school, and are subject to change at short notice, so discuss this with each school at the time of your visit. And don't forget the hidden costs, such as transport, medical fees, school trips, books, uniforms, etc.

Abu Dhabi

Abu Dhabi Grammar School

Location → Khaleej Al Arabi St	02 666 2900
Hours → 08:00 - 15:00	
Web/email → www.agsgrmmr.sch.ae	Map Ref → 3-E4

This school, founded in 1994, follows the Nova Scotia curriculum of Canada. It has nearly 500 students, split into pre school, elementary level, junior high and senior high. School facilities include a library, swimming pool, gymnasium, art studio, music room, science labs and two computer rooms.

Age range: Three - 18 years
Curriculum: Nova Scotia (Canada)

American Community School of Abu Dhabi

Location → Khalidiya	02 681 5115
Hours → 08:00 - 15:00	
Web/email → www.acs.sch.ae	Map Ref → 9-E1

ACS was established in 1972 by the American Embassy. All teaching staff are American, and

Buses – you wait for one then five come!

priority for places is given to children of American citizens (although other English speaking students can attend, space permitting). Apart from the high quality education offered here, the school also boasts facilities such as a swimming pool, gym, media centre, sports and recess fields, a fitness centre and computer facilities.

Age range: Four - 17 years
Curriculum: American

American International School

Location → 29th St · Airport Rd	02 444 4333
Hours → 08:00 - 14:40	
Web/email → www.aisa.sch.ae	Map Ref → 5-E1

AISA offers a complete American high school diploma program and a parallel international program. English is the language of instruction in all classes with the exception of Arabic, as a foreign language, in Islamic Studies, and French.

Age range: three - 17 years
Curriculum: American

British School Al Khubairat, The

Location → Airport Rd	02 446 2280
Hours → 08:00 - 13:00	
Web/email → www.britishschool.sch.ae	Map Ref → 3-C3

The school's overriding aim is to provide education for English speaking children in accordance with the best teaching practices, in order to enable them to qualify for subsequent education in the UK within their own age groups, without disadvantages.

Age range: Three - 18 years
Curriculum: British

Cambridge High School

Location → New Mussafah	02 446 1444
Hours → 08:00 - 13:50	
Web/email → www.tchs-auh.sch.ae	Map Ref → 13-B1

This school provides education based on the British curriculum for children from kindergarten to year 13. The recreational facilities include a playground for the kindergarten section, a swimming pool, tennis and volleyball courts, science and computer labs, music and art studios, a library and a canteen. The school currently has around 700 pupils from over 45 different countries, and a diverse range of professional staff.

Age range: Three - 18 years
Curriculum: British

International Community School

Location → 23rd Street · off Muroor Rd
Hours → 07:40 - 14:30
Web/email → www.ics.co.ae
02 448 9900
Map Ref → 3-B1

ICS offers a mixed curriculum (UK/US) for students from KG1 to grade seven, while grades eight upwards study the British Curriculum (GCSE). Although English is the language of instruction, the school also has strong Arabic and French programs. In order to encourage a balanced education, music, art and physical activity are all incorporated into the curriculum.

Age range: Three - 17 years
Curriculum: British

International School of Choueifat

Location → Airport Rd
Hours → See timings below
Web/email → www.sabis.net
02 446 1444
Map Ref → 3-C3

The school system is a unique method of education that allows students to learn more in a shorter time and with less effort. New students take placement tests to check whether they have attained the minimum expected standards in English and mathematics.

Age range: Three - 18 years
Curriculum: British and American
Timings: 08:00 - 17:00 Thu 08:00 - 13:00 Fri closed

Dubai

Al Mawakeb School

Location → Nr Volvo Showroom · Garhoud
Hours → 08:00 - 15:00
Web/email → www.almawakeb.sch.ae
04 285 1415
Map Ref → 15-D1

Al Mawakeb boasts a student body of over 3000 pupils on its two campuses, representing over 40 nationalities. Although English is the language of instruction, there are strong programmes in Arabic and French. The school provides kindergarten, elementary, intermediate and secondary levels of teaching. Facilities on each campus include a guidance counselling centre, a school clinic, a library, arts workshops, and science and computer labs.

Age range: Three - 17 years
Curriculum: American
Other Branches: Al Barsha (04 347 8288)

American School of Dubai

Location → St 53B · Al Wasl
Hours → 08:00 - 15:00
Web/email → www.asdubai.org
04 344 0824
Map Ref → 13-A2

Dubai Academy offers children an enriched American curriculum. It provides a college preparatory programme in the English language to students from around the world. Supplementary classes include physical education, karate, art, piano, organised sport and after hours native language instruction.

Age range: Four - 18 years
Curriculum: American

Cambridge High School, The

Location → Garhoud
Hours → 08:00 - 13:45
Web/email → www.tchs-dxb.sch.ae
04 282 4646
Map Ref → 15-D1

Please refer to the review of Cambridge High School Abu Dhabi (p.52) for more information.

Age range: Three - 18 years
Curriculum: British

Dubai American Academy

Location → Al Barsha · Interchange 4
Hours → 07:45 - 14:45
Web/email → www.dubaiacademy.org
04 347 9222
Map Ref → 12-A3

Dubai American Academy provides high quality education, following the American Curriculum. The school currently has over a thousand students representing more than 60 countries. In terms of facilities, there is a cafeteria, computer and science labs, a gymnasium, library, swimming pool, athletics track and an auditorium.

Age range: Four - 17 years
Curriculum: American

Dubai College

Location → Nr Knowledge Village · Al Sufouh Rd
Hours → 07:50 - 15:25
Web/email → www.dubaicollege.org
04 399 9111
Map Ref → 11-D1

Students at Dubai College are encouraged to develop their intellectual, physical, creative and social skills, and therefore the school boasts a diverse range of facilities. Sporting activities include athletics, rugby, soccer, netball, tennis and swimming; and non sporting activities such as music, public speaking and drama are also available. There are currently just over 700 pupils at the school.

Age range: 11 - 17 years
Curriculum: English National Curriculum

Dubai English Speaking School

Location → Oud Metha Rd · Bur Dubai 04 337 1457
Hours → 07:45 - 14:15
Web/email → www.dessdxb.com Map Ref → 13-E4

DESS first opened in a single room of a villa in 1963, and has since grown into a highly respected school wih top class facilities and around 700 pupils. The curriculum is based on the British National Curriculum and prepares students for secondary education either here or in the UK. Facilities and activities include computers, music, swimming, dance, a library and various sports.

Age range: four - 11 years
Curriculum: British

Emirates International School

Location → Jct 4, Shk Zayed Rd 04 348 9804
Hours → 08:00 - 15:00
Web/email → www.eischool.com Map Ref → 12-A2

EIS aims to foster independent thinking with a balanced approach to education and an international curriculum. Facilities include fully equipped classrooms, computer and science labs, a library, a theatre and a canteen. Extra curricular activities include drama, music, swimming and basketball.

Age range: four - 18 years
Curriculum: International Curriculum

English College Dubai

Location → Umm Suqeim 04 394 3465
Hours → 07:45 - 15:00
Web/email → www.englishcollege.ac.ae Map Ref → 12-D2

English College Dubai has a varied extra curricular programme offering activities such as chess, rugby, tennis, trampolining, choir, netball, football (boys and girls), athletics, table tennis, golf and even rock climbing! Students are encouraged to unlock their own potential and explore their unique talents. The multicultural environment at the school promotes tolerance and understanding.

Age range: 11 - 18 years
Curriculum: British

Horizon School

Location → Nr Safa Park · Jumeira 04 342 2891
Hours → 07:35 - 13:10
Web/email → www.horizonschooldubai.com Map Ref → 12-D2

Horizon opened in 1992 with just 15 pupils, and today it has expanded to a large complex complete with top class facilities and over 300 children. Students receive English Curriculum education, and can choose from afternoon activities such as football, netball, rounders, karate, swimming, dancing, cookery and drama. The school has recently moved to a new location, although a sister school will remain in the original buildings (near Park 'n Shop, off Al Wasl Rd). Children from both Horizon primary schools will have automatic entry to Horizon College, which is set to open in September 2005.

Age range: 11 - 18 years
Curriculum: British
Other branches: Safa Horizon School (04 394 7879)

International School of Choueifat

Location → btn Jct no 4 & no 5 · Umm Suqeim 04 399 9444
Hours → See timings below
Web/email → www.sabis.net Map Ref → 12-C1

This school is part of the worldwide SABIS school network. Refer to the Abu Dhabi International School of Choueifat review [p.53] for further information.

Age range: Three - 18 years
Curriculum: British and American Curriculums
Timings: 07:50 - 15:00 (primary); 07:50 - 16:00 (secondary)

Jebel Ali Primary School

Location → Jebel Ali Village 04 884 6485
Hours → 07:45 - 13:30
Web/email → www.jebelalischool.com Map Ref → 10-E3

This friendly primary school first opened its doors in 1977 and is now one of the oldest schools in Dubai. Today it educates close to 500 pupils in 22 classes, following the British Curriculum. It occupies two sites, one for the Infant Department and one for the Juniors. Both have access to swimming pools and grassed areas. After school activities include soccer, cricket, netball, golf, gymnastics, squash, drama, cooking, music and computers.

Age range: Four - 11 years
Curriculum: British Curriculum

Jumeirah College

Location → Behind Park N Shop · Al Wasl Rd
Hours → 07:45 - 15:30
Web/email → www.jc-dxb.sch.ae
04 395 4950
Map Ref → 12-C2

This school follows the British Curriculum. Although the children attending this school represent 40 different nationalities, the majority of students are British and all teaching is done in the English language. The school offers all the regular sporting and cultural extra curricular activities, as well as some more unconventional pursuits such as trampolining, ballet, waterskiing, horse riding, rock climbing, and karate.

Age range: Nine - 17 years
Curriculum: British

Jumeirah English Speaking School

Location → Nr Safa Park · Al Wasl Rd
Hours → 07:45 - 13:45
Web/email → www.jessdubai.org
04 394 5515
Map Ref → 12-D2

The school caters for English speaking children aged three to 11 years, and there are four classes in each year group from Foundation I to Year 6. Preference will be given to British passport holders, those holding debentures, and those with siblings higher up the school.

Age range: Three - 11 years
Curriculum: British

Jumeirah Primary School

Location → Al Wasl Rd · Jumeira
Hours → 07:40 - 14:15
Web/email → www.jpsdubai.com
04 394 3500
Map Ref → 12-D2

JPS is one of the most well known primary schools in Dubai, and provides a high quality British Curriculum education. The school boasts high standards both academically and with discipline, and has a balanced range of afternoon activities. The campus facilities are impressive - there is a well stocked library, an active art department, a specialist music department, up to date computer facilities, a large gymnasium, a 25 metre swimming pool, tennis courts, playing fields (both grass and astroturf), and a separate play area for the Foundation stage.

Age range: Three - nine years
Curriculum: British

Oxford School, The

Location → Nr Galadari Driving Inst.· Al Qusais
Hours → 08:00 - 13:40
Web/email → www.oxford.sch.ae
04 254 3666
Map Ref → UAE-C2

This British National Curriculum School uses a wide range of materials from the UK to prepare students for higher education. The school campus consists of a nursery/kindergarten unit, computer centre, science labs, a library, a large multi purpose hall and fully equipped classrooms. Sports facilities include an indoor swimming pool and extensive outdoor sports fields, with activities such as swimming, football, basketball, cricket and table tennis on offer.

Age range: Three - 18 years
Curriculum: British

Regent School

Location → Nr Iranian Hospital · Al Wasl Rd
Hours → 08:00 - 13:30
Web/email → www.regentschooldxb.com
04 344 2409
Map Ref → 12-D1

The academic development of students at Regent School is carefully balanced with a range of extra curricular activities such as sports, drama and arts. Regent School is moving to new premises in The Greens from September 2005.

Age range: Three - 11 years
Curriculum: British

St. Mary's Catholic School

Location → Opp Indian High School · Bur Dubai
Hours → 07:45 - 13:15
Web/email → www.stmarysdubai.com
04 254 3666
Map Ref → 14-A4

Founded in 1968, St. Mary's retains the discipline of convent education, combined with the tolerance and diversity of an internationally representative student body. Pupils of all religions are welcome at the school. In addition to various sports activities, other extra curricular activities include drama, music, debating, cookery and chess.

Age range: Five and a half - 18 years
Curriculum: British

Tertiary Education

In the past, many expat school leavers returned to their home countries to pursue quality tertiary education. This was understandably a tough time for many families, not just because of the distances, but also because of the expense. An added complication is that male children over the age of 18 are considered as adults, and unless they are either enrolled in higher education or working, they could face having to leave the country as they are no longer allowed to fall under the sponsorship of their parents.

However, the UAE has made dramatic progress in the area of tertiary education over the past few years. There are several internationally renowned institutions which have opened local branches, offering accredited diplomas and degrees. A more recent development has been the completion of Knowledge Village, a connected community of educational institutions aimed at developing the region's talent. It contains a number of foreign branches of particular universities or colleges, which provide internationally recognised academic programs. So, although many expat school leavers still choose to study at the top universities in their home countries, it is at least reassuring to know that there are a few more local options than there were before.

The following institutions offer a range of internationally recognised degrees and diplomas to all students, regardless of gender, nationality, race or religion.

Abu Dhabi

Abu Dhabi University (02 558 8999)
www.adu.ac.ae

Dubai

American University of Dubai (04 399 9000)
www.aud.edu

British University in Dubai
www.buid.ac.ae

Cleopatra & Steiner Beauty Training Centre (04 324 0250)
www.cleopatrasteiner.com

Emirates Aviation College (04 282 4000)
www.emiratesaviationcollege.com

Knowledge Village (04 390 1111)
www.kv.ae

University of Southern Queensland in Dubai (04 390 1161)
www.usqindubai.com

University of Wollongong (04 395 4422)
www.uowdubai.ac.ae

Special Needs

If your child has severe physical or learning difficulties, there are several organisations you can contact in order to find out what activities or facilities are available according to their special needs.

Several of the mainstream schools will try to accommodate children suffering from dyslexia, ADD and other relatively manageable issues. (You may be able to get more information about dyslexia specifically from the Dyslexia Support Group, a voluntary organisation run by mums, which offers advice and support to families. Contact Anita Singhal on 04 344 0738 or Carolyne Palmer on 04 344 6657 for more information). It will depend on the individual needs of each child and you will have to talk to each of the schools, to find the best place for him/her. Some of the schools have small, dedicated units (JPS for dyslexia, Horizon for special needs) and some take a more integrated approach, possibly with the help of an individual tutor (at your expense) if that is what is needed.

Whatever the special needs of your child are, you should be able to find some kind of support network here in the UAE. And if not, you could even start your own support group.

Abu Dhabi

Al Noor Speech, Hearing & Development Centre	
Location → Abu Dhabi	02 449 3844
Hours → na	
Web/email → uae_alnoor@hotmail.com	Map Ref → na

This charity organisation takes in students who cannot afford to go to other centres in Abu Dhabi. Students are accepted with all types of disabilities and are of all ages. The centre provides formal and informal education and also vocational training.

Future Centre	
Location → Villa 17, 26th St · Al Nahyan St	02 666 9625
Hours → 08:00 - 14:00	
Web/email → www.future-centre.com	Map Ref → 3-D4

Open to all nationalities between the ages of three and 20. Classes exist for students with ADD/ Behavioural Disorders, Down Syndrome, Cerebral Palsy and Traumatic Brain Injury. There is also a small Autism unit.

Dubai

Al Noor Centre

Location → Nr Safa Park · Umm Suqeim | 04 394 6088
Hours → 08:00 - 13:00
Web/email → www.alnooruae.org | Map Ref → 12-C2

Al Noor Centre first opened its doors in 1981 with just 8 pupils. Today it caters to over 200 children with special needs, from childhood up to adulthood. Annual music and sports events are held annually in which the pupils take part.

British Therapy Service

Location → Opp Al Hanna Centre · Mankhool | 04 398 2246
Hours → 09:00 - 18:00
Web/email → www.britishtherapy.com | Map Ref → 13-C2

With one clinic in Sharjah, and another in Dubai, the British Therapy Service offers occupational therapy for children, focusing on children with leaning difficulties in mainstream schools, such as dyslexia and dyspraxia. They also offer adult rehabilitation.

Dubai Community Health Centre

Location → Nr Jumeirah Beach Park · Jumeira | 04 395 3939
Hours → 09:00 - 19:30
Web/email → dchc73810@hotmail.com | Map Ref → 12-D1

The Centre provides psychiatric, psychological and special needs services for adults and children. Services include psychiatry, psychological therapies and assessments, marriage & family counselling and speech therapy. Workshops are conducted for teachers, parents, children and self-development.

Dubai Special Needs Center

Location → Nr Gulf News Bld · Shk Zayed Rd | 04 344 0966
Hours → 08:30 - 13:30
Web/email → dcsneeds@emirates.net.ae | Map Ref → 12-E1

The centre is dedicated to enriching the education of children with learning disabilities. The many facilities include therapy departments, 2 libraries, a music room, an arts and crafts room, a gymnasium and swimming pool. Classes are taught in Arabic and English.

Gulf Montessori Centre

Location → Bank St, Bur Dubai | 04 335 2073
Hours → See timings below
Web/email → www.gulf-montessori.com | Map Ref → 14-A2

Although not just for special needs teaching, the Gulf Montessori Centre helps organise workshops for people who work with children, with special needs. Common disabilities in the classroom like dyslexia, autism, attention disorders or Down Syndrome are also covered.

Timings: 09:00 - 12:00 15:30 - 18:30 Thu 08:30 - 13:00

Manzil Centre for Challenged Individuals

Location → Sharjah | 04 393 1985
Hours → Various
Web/email → www.manzil.ae | Map Ref → na

This new centre (opening in November 2004) will provide a professional, caring environment for individuals with special needs, and will aim to develop their potential to function in society.

Rashid Paediatric Therapy Centre

Location → Bank St, Bur Dubai | 04 335 2073
Hours → See timings below
Web/email → www.gulf-montessori.com | Map Ref → 14-A2

This non profit, non government humanitarian organisation caters to children with special needs. It provides the basic activities of a normal school, but has special activities and therapies that have been developed specifically for challenged children. It is a private charity which relies solely on donations to meet its operational costs.

Timings: 09:00 - 12:00 15:30 - 18:30 Thu 08:30 - 13:00

Riding for the Disabled Association of Dubai

Location → Desert Palms Polo Club | 04 323 8003
Hours → Various
Web/email → rdaddubai@hotmail.com | Map Ref → UAE D2

This charity organisation provides horse riding lessons to children and young adults with special needs. Children with many different challenges, such as Down Syndrome, Autism and Cerebral Palsy, have enjoyed the physical benefits of horse riding, as the movement of the horse's body aids muscle relaxation. Contact Pat Bellairs on the above email address for further information.

INSIDERS' CITY GUIDE

9th EDITION

Dubai Explorer

BUY ME YOU GENIUS!

Published with Passion

Buy it, read it, love it, live it!

We all know how quickly this city changes, it seems you blink and a new building appears on the skyline. So to keep you up to date with all things shiny and new, in the 9th edition of Dubai Explorer we've made it our business to satisfy your pleasure.

Only available at the best bookstores with the right attitude, as well as hotels, supermarkets, hardware stores or directly from Explorer Publishing.

Passionately Publishing...

EXPLORER

Phone (971 4) 335 3520 • Fax (971 4) 335 3529 • Email Info@Explorer-Publishing.com

Insiders' City Guides • Photography Books • Activity Guidebooks • Commissioned Publications • Distribution

www.Explorer-Publishing.com

Shopping
EXPLORER

Shopping

Shopping	61	Baby Equipment Hire	68	Interior Design	72
		Baby & Kidswear	68	Maternity Clothes	73
Places to Shop	**61**	Books & Stationery	70	Musical Instruments	73
Shopping Malls	61	Food	70	Pets	73
		Hairdressers – Kids	71	Portrait Photographer	
What & Where to Buy	**66**	Home Furnishings &		/Artist	74
Baby Equipment	66	Accessories	71	Sporting Goods	74
		Home Safety	72	Toys & Crafts	76

MUST SEE
While the UAE is well geared up to cater for children of all ages and from designer threads to bargin basics shopping for your kids is by no means a chore. You will find internationally renowned names such as Mothercare & Toys 'R' Us in both Abu Dhabi and Dubai. Also the lesser known chain, The Babyshop is also located in both emirates and sells a wide range of clothing, baby equipment and toys, and the till receipt will be a pleasant surprise too. See [p.66]

MUST HAVE
With year round sunshine protecting your little ones from the harmful UV rays is a top priority. As well as keeping your kids in the shade as much as possible and avoiding going out in the hot midday sun it is also important to use a good sunscreen. High factor sun creams such as the paediatric recommended Coppertone Water Babies 45 SPF can be found in sports shops, some baby stores and most chemists in the various shopping malls. See [p.75]

Mercato Shopping Mall

Shopping

Whatever you need for your children you're more than likely to find it in Dubai, which has justifiably become known as the shopping capital of the Middle East. While Abu Dhabi's shopping choice is more limited – expat residents used to regularly head for Dubai on shopping trips for many items – today there is greater variety available than ever before. You may choose to check out Dubai for more important purchases, to see a better range of furniture shops for example. There is even Sharjah for some furniture bargains.

This section takes a brief look at the main shopping malls and other retail outlets devoted to children. There are also many other specialist shops and it's worth taking the time to explore the variety that exists in terms of range, brand, price and quality. In contrast to the other chapters, the Abu Dhabi and Dubai shopping information is collated.

Like working hours, shop opening hours vary considerably. Outlets in the shopping malls are generally open 10:00 - 22:00, while individual stores close for the lunchtime break, usually between 13:00 - 16:30. During the holy month of Ramadan, shops often open and close later in the day.

See also: Aquarius and Connector monthly magazines carry a shopping directory, or check the Yellow Pages. Additionally, the UAE Local Pages section of www.expatwoman.com gives some general information on shopping in the Emirates.

Places to Shop

Shopping Malls

Shopping malls are one of the attractions of shopping in the Emirates. They house a variety of outlets all under one roof, selling everything from children's clothes and toys to brand name fashions and groceries. The malls are generally modern, spacious and fully air conditioned – offering a great escape from the heat.

A good time for a major shopping spree is during the Dubai Shopping Festival and Dubai Summer Surprises when the majority of stores have sales, special deals and draws or raffles. However sales do spring up all year round so watch the daily newspapers for adverts and details. Raffles are also very popular but it may seem rather tedious completing all those raffle ticket stubs when you do your weekly shop. You may think that it's not worth the time, but you never know when your luck will come in. You could find yourself winning a shiny new car - it does happen!

> **Bits 'n' Bobs**
>
> Keep the bedroom tidy! OK, so it maybe a losing battle, but Ace Hardware sells various sizes of colourful plastic boxes with lids, which neatly stack on top of each other. These are ideal for storing pieces of Lego and such like. THE One has a slightly pricier, more upmarket range of storage options and of course, there's also IKEA.

The key to finding a real bargain is to know the 'right price' before you enter the shop. So, if you are planning some significant purchase – be it a computer, a carpet or a piece of jewellery - research the pre-sale price in several shops in the weeks leading up to the festival.

Many of the malls provide entertainment aimed specifically at kids, from amusement centres or arcade games to special play areas for younger children. These are generally very popular and conveniently allow parents to relax or shop in peace, although they can become expensive. Additionally, a few malls have cinemas as part of the complex. Most also have a foodcourt, with a variety of outlets that are good for a quick meal or a snack, including of course the ubiquitous hamburger joints!

In Dubai, during the Shopping Festival and Summer Surprises, the larger malls hold special family events, such as dancing or magic shows. These performances are always popular and involve acts from all around the world.

Abu Dhabi

Abu Dhabi Mall

Location → Nr Beach Rotana Hotel · Al Meena | 02 645 4858
Hours → 10:00 - 22:00   Fri 15:30 - 22:00
Web/email → www.abudhabi-mall.com   Map Ref → 4-C2

This mall has opened up a completely new world of shopping in Abu Dhabi and features a host of famous stores and brands. Should you require information, there are customer service representatives on hand to assist. The desk is located on level 1 in the Palm Court.

Fotouh Al Khair Centre

Location → Shk Rashid B Saeed Al Makt St **02 621 1133**
Hours → 10:00 - 22:00
Web/email → fotouhkc@emirates.net.ae   **Map Ref** → 4-E3

Known locally as the Marks & Spencer building, several of the world's favourite brands are jammed into this spacious mall – Wallis, Monsoon, Mango, Nine West and many more.

Fotouh Al Khair Centre

Marina Mall

Location → Breakwater · Abu Dhabi **02 681 8300**
Hours → 10:00 - 22:00   Fri 14:00 - 22:00
Web/email → www.marinamall.ae   **Map Ref** → 5-D4

Located on the Breakwater, well away from the hustle and bustle of the city, the spacious Marina Mall provides a breath of fresh sea air. Underneath the impressive tented roof, 160 local and international retail outlets keep visitors entertained day and night. Worth visiting for home furnishings are Pier Import and the ever-popular IKEA, while the basement is dominated by Carrefour hypermarket. Foton World and the nine screen cinema ensure that this mall also scores highly for entertainment.

Dubai

Al Bustan Centre

Location → Nr Al Mulla Plaza · Al Twar **04 263 0000**
Hours → 10:00 - 23:00   Fri 16:00 - 23:00
Web/email → www.al-bustan.com   **Map Ref** → 15-E1

Part of a large residential complex, the Al Bustan Centre offers over 100 varied retail outlets, including Sandra and Monalisa for kids' clothes, plus jewellery, greeting cards and swimwear shops. The stores are all on ground level, alongside a multi-cuisine foodcourt with seating for 500, a cinema and a popular children's amusement centre called Fantasy Kingdom.

Al Futtaim Centre

Location → Muraqqabat Street · Deira **04 222 5859**
Hours → 10:00 - 22:00
Web/email → info@alfuttaimsons.com   **Map Ref** → 14-C3

Located in the heart of Deira, the Al Futtaim Centre offers a good range of children's wear in Marks & Spencer; and toys, clothes and nursery accessories in the well known Toys 'R' Us. For those of you who remember, the large play area at the rear of M&S is no longer there – it made way for a more extensive clothing range. However, the café survived the refurbishment and has a good menu. The store also sells a limited range of M&S food.

Within Toys 'R' Us there is a supervised play area. If you have a mobile phone with you, it's a pleasant option for you and the children to go your separate ways while you have a look around. There is some covered parking at the rear, and open parking beyond that.

Al Ghurair City

Location → Al Rigga Rd · Deira **04 222 5222**
Hours → 10:00 - 22:00   Fri 14:00 - 22:00
Web/email → www.alghuraircity.com   **Map Ref** → 14-B3

Nearer than you think, the Al Ghurair Centre is a big mall with many interesting shops – especially for ladies. For children's wear, there's Mothercare, BHS, Benetton and several specialised outlets. You will find kids party clothes and gift ideas at Funland, while Fun Corner provides the entertainment. There's also a good foodcourt that suits a variety of tastes. You can borrow a pushchair or wheelchair from customer services on the ground floor, where they also offer free gift wrapping. Another advantage is that this mall is rarely overcrowded.

It makes a pleasant and convenient morning of shopping to visit the Al Ghurair Centre and then go on to M&S and Toys 'R' Us at the Al Futtaim Centre. They are no more than five minutes apart.

Beach Centre, The

Location → Nr Dubai Zoo · Jumeira
Hours → 09:30 - 13:00 16:30 - 21:30
Web/email → na
04 344 9045
Map Ref → 13-A1

Downstairs in The Beach Centre you will find Baby Casa, for beautiful baby cribs and cots, and the White Star shops, one for books and the other for teachers' aids; a treasure trove of educational toys and crafts. Upstairs there's Jenny Rose for stylish maternity wear and Studio Al Aroosa for beautiful portrait photography. There is also the Sheikh Mohammed Centre for Cultural Understanding – with extremely friendly and helpful staff, it's worth a look and will give visitors a different and interesting perspective on Dubai.

For children there's Network Games; a mini amusement arcade and a bank of computers loaded with various shoot 'em up, fast car games… the sort of thing kids love and parents hate! At Kuts 4 Kids let your tots watch cartoons on the mini TVs while they have their hair cut and there's also a party shop for all party accessories, where a clown or magician can also be booked.

BurJuman Centre

Location → Trade Centre Rd · Bur Dubai
Hours → 10:00 - 22:00 Fri 16:00 - 22:00
Web/email → www.burjuman.com
04 352 0222
Map Ref → 14-A3

One of the largest malls in Dubai, this airy shopping centre has plenty of fashionable shops for all ages, offering a range of prices and styles.

There's a large foodcourt, plus three entertainment centres: Toby's Jungle Adventure and Fun City (04 359 3336; under 9's) and Fun World (04 352 2922; 5 year olds to adults). Baby strollers are available from the information desk on level 1 and baby changing facilities are located on levels 1 and 2. Plenty of underground parking.

Deira City Centre

Location → Opp Dubai Creek Golf Club · Deira
Hours → 10:00 - 22:00 Fri 14:00 - 22:00
Web/email → www.deiracitycentre.com
04 295 1010
Map Ref → 15-D1

This very popular mall offers a comprehensive range of shops to suit all requirements and budgets. For children's needs, the outlets are endless – Carrefour (food, toys, clothing, shoes), Mothercare, Early Learning Centre, IKEA, Woolworths (the South African chain, not the UK/US Woolworths), Next, Debenhams… plus shops selling sportswear, shoes, books, cards and wrapping, theme shops, a children's hairdresser, designer wear… and much more.

BurJuman Centre

FAMILY EXPLORER

At one end of the mall is Magic Planet, a large amusement centre with an extensive foodcourt. At the other end, IKEA has a supervised play area and a video room for older children that's available for IKEA shoppers. Upstairs from IKEA, a section of the mall is dedicated to restaurants and fast food outlets, with a cinema at the far end. Here you will also find Virgin Megastore, a dedicated Hello Kitty store, Magrudy's and more.

Deira City Centre is usually busy and gets particularly crowded at weekends and in the evenings, when the extensive covered parking can get gridlocked.

Jumeirah Centre

Location → Nr Jumeira Mosque · Jumeira | 04 349 9702
Hours → 09:00 - 13:00 16:00 - 22:00 Fri 16:00 - 21:00
Web/email → www.dubaishoppingmalls.com | Map Ref → 13-B1

Previously known as Markaz Al Jumeirah, this mall includes well stocked toyshops to keep youngsters occupied while adults visit the boutiques, Body Shop, antique and furniture shops. There's also a DVD/video store, florist, optician, pharmacist, photo developers, travel agency and more. Specific shops for children are Mothercare and the Tree House (toys). There's also a swimwear shop on the first floor selling UV sun protection suits. Food outlets include Baskin Robbins and cafès on both floors.

Jumeirah Plaza

Location → Nr Jumeira Mosque · Jumeira | 04 349 7111
Hours → 09:30 - 13:00 16:30 - 21:30 Fri 16:30 - 21:30
Web/email → www.dubaishoppingmalls.com | Map Ref → 13-B1

Often referred to as the 'pink plaza', this mall is the one next to the blue one (Markaz Al Jumeirah) on Jumeira Beach Road, just along from Jumeira Mosque. It's a delight to browse around (as appose to trek as you find yourself doing in the larger malls) with lots of gift shops selling interesting items. The Plaza also has a children's hairdresser, bookshop, a good beachwear shop and on the first floor, an arts, crafts and hobby shop, greeting card and birthday party supplier, sports store, accessory shops and you can also find some beautiful and unusual imported furniture.

Another treasure is tucked away in a corner downstairs – a second-hand bookstore. This sells a good range of children's classics at very reasonable prices and when you've finished with them you can return them for half of what you paid. The Dome coffee shop offers an excellent range of cakes and pastries, as well as lunches and a good menu of kid's meals for a teatime treat. Adjacent to the coffee shop, Fun Corner has glass walls so you can sit and have a coffee, flick through one of the magazines available for diners, while watching your child playing. It's a small Fun Corner but perfect for pre-schoolers, and it is fully supervised. Parking is available underground or on the street.

Lamcy Plaza

Location → Nr EPPCO HQ · Oud Metha | 04 335 9999
Hours → 10:00 - 22:00 Fri 10:00 - 22:30
Web/email → lamcydxb@emirates.net.ae | Map Ref → 13-E4

Built around the theme of the famous Tower of London in the UK, Lamcy Plaza has a range of open-plan shops selling clothes, toys and shoes. Books Plus on the third floor (fourth level) is one of the largest bookshops in the Middle East. The play area, LouLou Al Dugong's, on the ground floor, is extensive and offers fun for children up to the age of about eight. Even the lobby of the mall is a hub of activity, frequently hosting various family shows and promotional events. There is a huge food court to the right of the lobby. The centre provides regular entertainment for children, especially during events like Dubai Shopping Festival or Dubai Summer Surprises. It is very busy at the weekends, particularly Fridays.

Magrudy's Shopping Mall

Location → Beach Rd · Jumeira | 04 344 4192
Hours → 09:00 - 13:30 16:00 - 20:00
Web/email → www.magrudy.com | Map Ref → 13-B1

Something of an institution, Magrudy's three main shops are built around an open-air courtyard. On offer are a greeting card, toy, swimwear, uniform, gift and knitting shop with a separate bookshop and shoe shop. Other outlets include a popular ladies couturier, jewellers, and a pharmacist. Upstairs is a private medical centre. Gerard's cafè, set in the middle of the mall, is a popular meeting point for a chat and a break from shopping. In the cooler months especially, it's lovely to sit outside and enjoy a mid-morning cappuccino.

Mazaya Centre

Location → Bt Interchange 1 & 2 · Shk. Zayed Rd | 04 343 8333
Hours → 10:00 - 13:30 16:30 - 22:00
Web/email → www.mazayacentre.com | Map Ref → 12-E2

This mall is rather hidden away, but is located in a lovely spacious building. There is a good range of shoe shops, ladies' fashions, lingerie, three or four children's clothing outlets and a small Spinneys. Homes R Us and Pier Import are both great home furnishing stores and Fast Track Computer Games and Giant Kingdom Kiddi Rides provide the entertainment for children.

Mercato

Location → Jumeira Beach Road · Jumeira | 04 344 4161
Hours → 10:00 - 22:00 Fri 14:00 - 22:00
Web/email → www.mercatoshoppingmall.com | Map Ref → 12-E1

Mercato is one of the newer malls in Dubai and a very pleasant place to shop. With the high, glass ceiling the designers have created an atmosphere of shopping al fresco – but always at the perfect temperature of course. Shops include Adams, Virgin Megastore and an array of ladies' fashion outlets, plus Spinneys, so you can do the grocery shopping amid stylish surroundings. There are also a number of cafes to stop for a well deserved coffee or light lunch. Older children can even be left at the cinema while you enjoy the shops.

Oasis Centre

Location → Oasis Centre · Al Quoz | 04 339 5459
Hours → 10:00 - 22:00 Fri 16:00 - 22:00
Web/email → www.landmarkgroupco.com | Map Ref → 12-C2

You can easily spot the Oasis Centre from the Sheikh Zayed Road. It incorporates a number of retail outlets, a foodcourt and a Fun City family entertainment centre in an oasis-themed landscape.

This mall is a favourite with families so expect to dodge more than a few excited children. Outlets include Home Centre, Baby Shop, Shoe Mart, Splash and Ladybird. Lifestyle sells a hotchpotch of goods; it's great for filling party bags and stockings, and also good for gifts, particularly for little girls (if you ever need anything pink and covered in feathers, this should be your starting point). Petland is also a popular stop for children to browse, but be careful what you leave with! Constant supervision in Fun City allows parents to shop while their children are looked after. The foodcourt is home to a number of fast food outlets, and on the other side of the mall is an Italian restaurant/cafè. The centre has covered parking for 600 cars.

Souk Madinat Jumeirah

Location → Madinat Jumeirah · Umm Suqeim | 04 366 8888
Hours → 10:00 - 23:00
Web/email → www.jumeirahinternational.com | Map Ref → 12-A1

Taking a stroll through the Souk Madinat is like experiencing a shopping spree before the modern day's ubiquitous mall was born. Which is exactly what makes shopping here so refreshing. While recognised names in fashion, electronics and jewellery appear they are intersperced with charming bazzar style shuttered shops selling authentic marketplace wares such as spices, handicrafts and Arabian gifts. While the UAE's climate makes high street shopping impossible the Souk Madinat allows you to wander up and down alleyways devoid of the synthetic facade that you cannot escape in the many shopping malls. Kids are also catered for with fashion boutiques and the Early Learning Centre.

Spinneys Centre

Location → Spinneys Centre · Umm Suqeim | 04 394 1657
Hours → 08:00 - 23:00
Web/email → www.spinneys.com | Map Ref → 12-C2

This compact yet comprehensive, bright and airy centre offers carefully selected retailers who provide for everyday and more specialist shopping requirements. A large Spinneys supermarket dominates the centre. Other outlets include a shoe repairer, optician, pharmacy, dry cleaner, film developer, DVD and music shop, confectioner, bookshop, card and gift shop, (Petals - ideal for presents and special items around the home) and, next door, an MMI liquor store. For kids, Mothercare and the Uniform Shop provide clothes and accessories, while the Fun Corner play centre is recommended for entertainment. There's also a coffee shop and a fast food outlet, plus plenty of outside parking.

Town Centre

Location → Jumeira Beach Road · Jumeira | 04 344 0111
Hours → 10:00 - 22:00 Fri 17:00 - 22:00
Web/email → www.towncentrejumeirah.com | Map Ref → 12-E1

There are many good reasons to look around Town Centre, not least DKNY (men's and ladies' fashions), Belleamie (for ladies lingerie and swimwear) and Nine West (shoes). You will also find Hobbyland, Party Zone and the Music Room upstairs. Recently opened on Fuddruckers old site is Cafè Ceramique – definitely worth a visit. The concept is that you enjoy a coffee, then you and/or your children choose a piece of earthenware and paint it, returning a week later to collect it after glazing. They have pieces especially for children.

Wafi Mall

Location ➜ Umm Hurair (2) · Dubai
Hours ➜ 10:00 - 22:00   Fri 16:30 - 22:00
Web/email ➜ www.waficity.com
04 324 4555
Map Ref ➜ 15-C1

This attractive mall is easily recognised by the three glass pyramids atop a large complex on the road near Al Garhoud Bridge, Bur Dubai side. The atrium of the mall often houses speciality displays and entertainment (usually at Ramadan, Eid and Christmas), which are extremely popular with children up to about eight years.

The mall is characterised by its designer shops for both adults and children. Jashanmal (department store) offers children's clothes, shoes and accessories. Other outlets for children (clothes, furniture and toys) are Oshkosh B'gosh, Color 4 Kids and Early Learning Centre. Entertainment is provided by Encounter Zone, which has two sections to appeal to younger and older children, and popular food outlets include Subway and Pizza Corner.

What & Where to Buy

Baby Equipment

Other options ➜ Baby Equipment Hire [p.68]

The choice of stores selling nursery equipment is somewhat limited. Mothercare and the Baby Shop (in both Abu Dhabi and Dubai) each have an extensive range of clothes, accessories, toys and nursery paraphernalia. In addition there are a few smaller boutiques located in the various malls which sell cots and bedding accessories such as Descamps (Bur Juman, Dubai, 04 3555563). Toys 'R' Us (located both in Abu Dhabi and Dubai, for more details see p. 78), although famed for its huge display of toys, also has a good range of cots, changing tables, carseats and pushchairs.

Baby Shop

The Baby Shop stocks everything for the newborn, including feeding equipment, bedding, bathing accessories, cots, prams, strollers and toys. The selection is extensive. There is also a wide range of reasonably priced clothes and shoes for children up to the age of nine years, as well as a good choice of books, toys and stationery.

Abu Dhabi
Airport Road – 02 634 7012
09.30 – 13.00 16.30 – 22.00 Sat – Thurs 16.30 – 22.00 Fri
Tourist Club Area – 02 644 7739
09.30 –22.00 Sat – Thurs 16.30 – 22.00 Fri

Dubai
Zabeel Road, Karama – 04 335 0212
09.30 – 13.00 16.30 – 22.00 Sat – Thurs 16.30 – 22.00 Fri
Web/email ➜ www.landmarkgroupco.com
Near Ramada Continental Hotel, Deira – 04 266 1519
10.00 – 22.00 Sat – Thurs 14.00 – 22.00 Fri
Oasis Shopping Centre – 04 338 0965

Mothercare

Good quality, no-nonsense nursery equipment, including carseats, mattresses, and bedding are on sale at Mothercare, plus essentials for the newborn to three year olds. Outlets also sell maternity wear and clothes for boys and girls up to the age of eight.

Abu Dhabi
Abu Dhabi Mall – 02 645 4894
Khaladiya, 32nd Street – 02 681 2966
Najda Street – 02 621 9700

Dubai
Al Ghurair Centre – 04 223 8176
Bur Juman Centre – 04 352 8916
Deira City Centre – 04 295 2543
Lamcy Plaza – 04 334 0742
Jumeirah Centre – 04 349 4019
Spinneys Centre Umm Suqeim – 04 394 0228

Dubai

Babycasa

Location ➜ Beach Centre, The · Jumeira
Hours ➜ 09:30 - 13:00 17:00 - 22:00 Fri closed
Web/email ➜ beachctr@hotmail.com
04 344 4119
Map Ref ➜ 13-A1

Full of beautiful things, this shop is dedicated to cots, cribs and changing stations.

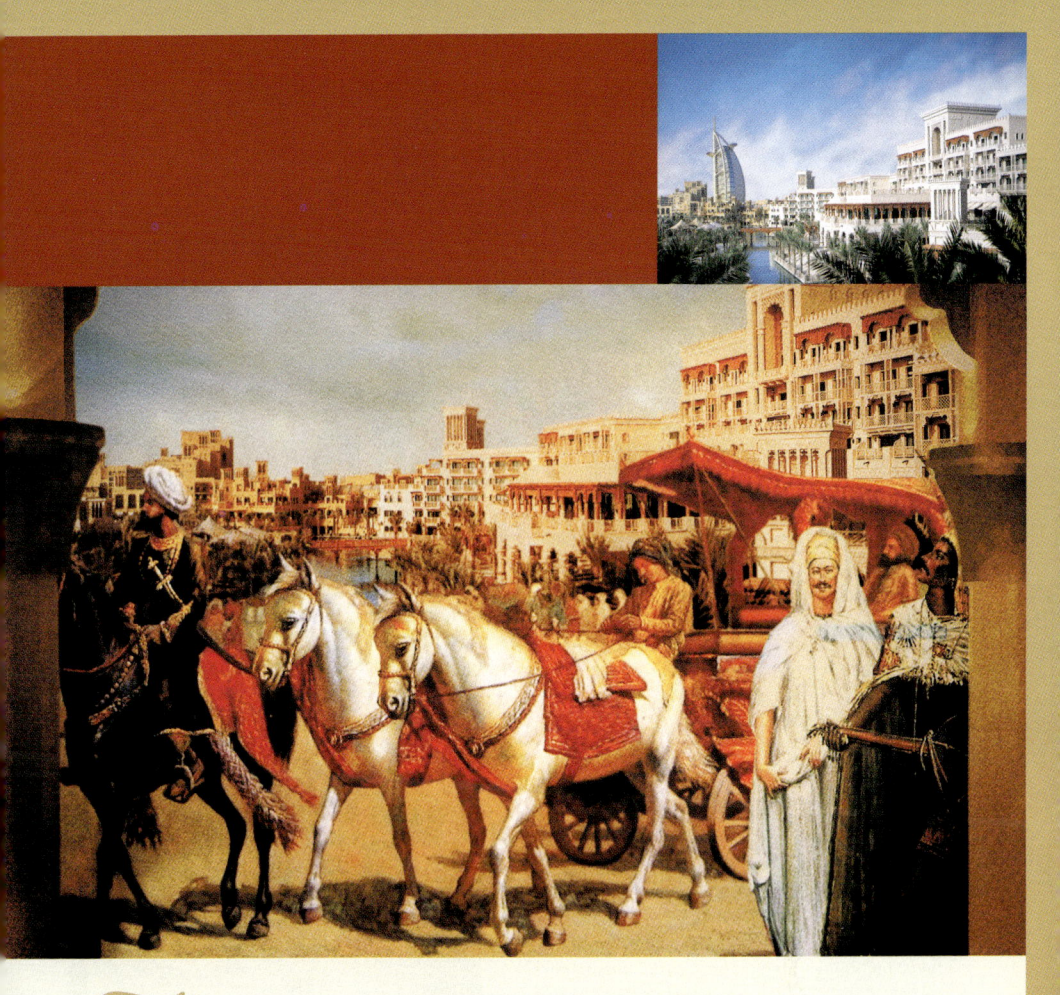

The Tale Of The New Arabian Legend.

It is said there is a place so lavish and so majestic that legends are born and you can experience tomorrow's history today. They call it Madinat Jumeirah - a stunning Arabian beach resort in Dubai. A monumental destination where the natural beauty of the region is captured in a re-creation of ancient Arabia. One kilometre of beautiful private beach borders two magnificent grand boutique hotels, Mina A´Salam and Al Qasr including 29 stand-alone Dar Al Masyaf traditional courtyard summer houses, the pinnacle of luxury and sun drenched spaciousness. At the vibrant heart of the resort, Souk Madinat Jumeirah, a shopping and dining experience unique in the world and a sanctuary of serene care and relaxation, the region's first Six Senses Spa.

Experience authentic Arabia visit www.madinatjumeirah.com

Madinat Jumeirah®
THE ARABIAN RESORT · DUBAI

Come Live The Legend.

JUMEIRAH INTERNATIONAL®

Mummy & Me	
Location → Al Maktoum St · Deira	04 228 2029
Hours → 09:00 - 13:00 17:00 - 21:00 Fri 17:00-21:00	
Web/email → na	Map Ref → 14-B3

Mummy & Me stocks quality nursery clothes and shoes for newborns and children up to 16 years. Nursery equipment includes cots, pushchairs, changing tables, feeding and bedding accessories, plus a good selection of gifts for babies.

Baby Equipment Hire

Abu Dhabi Mums	
Location → Various locations · Abu Dhabi	050 492 9738
Hours → Timings on request	
Web/email → www.abudhabimums.ae	Map Ref → UAE-A3

This voluntary social group keeps a stock of baby equipment for hire, all of which has been donated by families leaving Abu Dhabi. It's a non-profit arrangement; you simply pay a Dhs.50 deposit on taking the items and a small fee for a week's hire.

Rent a Crib, Dubai	
Location → See website · Dubai	050 588 7917
Hours → Timings on request	
Web/email → cribrent@37.com	Map Ref → na

This hire service is ideal for visitors with babies or small children, or for any short-term needs. A range of equipment is available, from furniture to toys including highchairs, cots, pushchairs, rocking horses, slides, sterilizers, breast pumps, baby monitors and more. Prices are reasonable, starting at Dhs.30 per week, and delivery is free.

Baby & Kidswear

Dedicated stores such as Mothercare and the Baby Shop can be found in both Abu Dhabi and Dubai (see reviews on p.66) and have an extensive range of clothes, and accessories from birth to age eight and nine respectively. There are also a number of specialised baby and kids fashion and footwear stores so you can kit your kids out in the latest trends!

Abu Dhabi

Nowadays there's a great choice of children's wear in Abu Dhabi and you no longer need to trek to Dubai. For shoes there are a couple of the major chains, plus speciality shops such as Clarks (Sheraton Residence Building, Khalidiya area, 02 665 4814) and Hush Puppies (Fotouh Al Khair Centre, 02 621 5068).

Dubai

Many of the major international department stores selling children's clothes, shoes and accessories can be found in Dubai, including British Home Stores (04 227 6969), JC Penny (04 295 3988), Next (04 295 2280), Woolworths (the South African chain, 04 295 5900) and Marks & Spencer (04 222 2000). Debenhams (04 2940011) also has a huge section (on the third level) dedicated to baby and kidswear and you can even get designer names such as Jasper Conran if you want the best dressed baby in town! Also worth a peek is Westwood (04 294 9292) where you will find a fantastic selection of clothes in a range of prices as well as the excellent shoe brand Pablosky. Prices for clothes in the department stores are usually higher than in their country of origin so you may want to explore a few of the boutiques dotted around the various malls. Deira City Centre has numerous funky baby and kidswear outlets that offer clothes at affordable prices including Reset (04 295 0855), Ovo (04 295 0885) and Okaidi (04 295 9923), or if you don't mind spending a bit more there's Baby Gap in Studio R (04 2950261), Elle (04 295 1551) and Monsoon (04 295 0725).

Matching Outfits

Adams 0 - 10

This store sells a good selection of clothes and accessories, including shoes, swimwear, hats, sunglasses, bags and nightclothes for children aged 0 - 10 years.

Abu Dhabi
Abu Dhabi Mall – 02 644 0608
Dubai
Bur Juman Centre – 04 355 2205
Deira City Centre – 04 294 5576
Lamcy Plaza – 04 337 6002
Mercato – 04 349 2272

Benetton

Generally classified as casual wear, Benetton is ideal for unisex fashions and a range of clothing for trendy 0 - 12 year olds.

Abu Dhabi
Abu Dhabi Mega Mall
Dubai
Al Ghurair Centre – 04 221 1593
BurJuman – 04 351 1331
Deira City Centre – 04 295 2450
Jumeira Centre, Al Markhaz Jumeira – 04 349 3613
Lamcy Plaza – 04 334 7353

Prémaman

Fashionable clothes for 0 - 18 months can be found at Prémaman, plus mobiles (of the hanging not ringing variety!), presents for newborns and maternity wear. Stores also cater for toddlers and 2 - 8 year olds, and some stock accessories.

Abu Dhabi
Abu Dhabi Mall – 02 645 8600
Dubai
BurJuman Centre – 04 351 5353

Shoe Mart

Shoe Mart offers a range of shoes, including Clarks and Salamander, to suit all occasions and sizes from infants up. Back to school shoes and socks are available, and other accessories include bags and stationery items. You will find a good range that's competitively priced.

Abu Dhabi
Madinat Zayed area – 02 634 6461
Sat – Thurs 09.30 – 13.30 16.30 – 23.00 Fri 16.30 – 23.00
TCA – 02 644 9543
Sat – Thurs 10.00 – 23.00   Fri 14.30 – 23.00
Dubai
Near Ramada Hotel, Bur Dubai – 04 351 9560
Sat – Thurs 9.30 – 13.30 & 16.30-22.00 Fri 16.30 – 22.00
Near Abu Hail Centre, Deira – 04 262 2125
Sat – Thu 10.00 – 22.00 Fri 16:30 – 22:00
Lamcy Plaza – 04 337 9811
Oasis Center – 04 338 0440

Dubai

Jamil Fashions

Location → Hor Al Anz, nr Al Mulla Plaza | 04 262 6808
Hours → 09:30 - 13:30 16:30 - 22:30
Web/email → na | Map Ref → 14-E4

Jamil Fashions sells a large selection of reasonably priced clothes and shoes for any age; babies to adults. The stock changes frequently and sometimes includes well known brand names. Outlets also sell school bags and have a separate toy department.

Magrudy's Shoe Shop

Location → Magrudy Shopping Mall · Jumeira | 04 344 4192
Hours → 09:00 - 20:00 Fri 16:30 - 20:30
Web/email → magrudyadm@emirates.net.ae | Map Ref → 13-B1

Magrudy's is excellent for back to school requirements, offering a good range of shoes (in different width fittings) and socks according to school specifications. The shop supplies Clarks and Startrite shoes and they will measure your child's feet to ensure they get the right size. To avoid the September scramble, try doing your school shoe shopping in August!

Shoe City

Location → Deira City Centre · Deira | 04 295 0437
Hours → 10:00 - 22:30 14:00 - 22:00
Web/email → shoecity@emirates.net.ae | Map Ref → 15-D1

School, leisure, sports, casual or smart, Shoe City offers a good selection of shoes and sandals for all ages. Hush Puppies and Disney collections are also available, plus an automatic foot measuring machine.

Secondhand Clothes

Dubai Charity Association

Location → Al Rigga Rd · Al Rigga Rd, Deira | 04 268 2000
Hours → 08:00 - 13:00 17:00 - 19:30
Web/email → dca@emirates.net.ae | Map Ref → 14-B3

All profits from this charity shop go to the Dubai Centre of Special Needs. The shop sponsors 18 children and contributes towards the purchase of special equipment. It's run on a volunteer basis, so help is always welcome, as are donations. You can leave your clothes here for sale and when/if sold, the price is split 50/50 between you and the charity. If items haven't sold after two months, the prices are halved.

Books & Stationery

Other options → Libraries [p.131]

A reasonable selection of English language books is sold in the Emirates, covering a broad range of subjects, from children's books to the latest bestseller or coffee-table books about the UAE. You will also find that a variety of foreign magazines and daily newspapers are flown in regularly. Most of the larger hotels have small bookshops offering a limited choice.

You are unlikely to find as extensive a range of books and bookshops as in your home country, although the number of outlets is increasing. The cost of books varies, but you will find that foreign newspapers and magazines are always more expensive than at home.

In addition to the following list, the supermarkets carry a reasonable selection of books and magazines.

Books Gallery

Books Gallery offers a good range of books for adults and children, plus the store sells some soft toys and gifts.

Abu Dhabi
Abu Dhabi Mall – 02 6443869
Dubai
The Village, Jumeira – 04 344 5770

Dubai

Magrudy's Book Shop

Location → Magrudy's Shopping Mall · Jumeira | 04 344 4193
Hours → 09:00 - 20:00 16:00 - 20:00 Fri 16:30 - 20:30
Web/email → www.magrudy.com   Map Ref → 13-B1

Magrudy's has an enormous range of children's books and English textbooks for different ages. If they haven't got what you want immediately, their online order and delivery service operates at very competitive rates. Children have a comfortable reading corner so they can read and leave parents to browse in peace. In addition to books, Magrudy's sells cards, wrapping paper and school accessories as well as a good selection of toys suitable for 0 - 12 year olds, including arts, crafts and hobbies. It's a great shop for presents and there's also a Lego table where children can play while parents browse.

From Harry Potter to Hello Kitty!

Food

You will find an excellent range of stores and supermarkets selling all types of food to cater for the country's multi-national inhabitants!

Prices vary drastically. Both manufactured goods and produce are imported from all over the world, and some items are double what they would cost in their country of origin. However, fresh goods such as fruit and vegetables can be amazingly cheap, especially if bought from the fruit and vegetable markets. A typical basket of goods would be comparably priced, if not cheaper than the UK, but probably not as competitive as in the USA, Australia or South Africa.

In residential areas there are plenty of 'corner' shops, good for milk, bread and a few essentials. Some are open 24 hours a day and most will deliver groceries if you ask.

However, while most items are available, there are some speciality foods that you can't buy. In particular, packaged baby food is limited in brand and selection, although the major supermarkets, such as Choithrams, Carrefour, Park 'n' Shop, Spinneys and Abela Superstore (Abu Dhabi) do stock jars and powdered milk. Recently Heinz baby food tins have found their way to the shelves. Abela also has a good range of expat-attractive products including European cheese, plus you can order special meats, etc for Christmas.

Hairdressers – Kids

You can take them to your own salon of course but, in both Abu Dhabi and Dubai, you can find hairdressers dedicated solely to kids, helping to make the trip for a haircut less intimidating than it can be in adult salons! Expect to pay between Dhs.20 - 35 per visit. There is no need to book, you can just turn up. Extras offered may include video entertainment in appropriately decorated surroundings, as well as face painting for Dhs.10 - 15, or hair braiding and henna tattoos. Most salons also sell a range of hair products and accessories.

Abu Dhabi
Toy Town, Abu Dhabi Mall – 02 645 5567
Kids Land Saloon, Marina Mall – 02 681 6316
Dubai
Just 4 kids beside Clock Tower – 04 295 8646
Union coop, Jumeira – 04 394 5997
Opposite Karama Centre, Karama – 04 396 4502
Kutz 4 kids – 04 344 8355
Rashidya — 04 285 3211
Beach Centre, Jumeira – 04 344 8355
Snoopy Salon – 04 349 8989
Jumeirah Plaza

Home Furnishings & Accessories

For good quality furniture and household items at reasonable prices, the most popular furniture outlets in Dubai are IKEA, THE One and a whole range of importers of Asian furniture and artefacts.

At one time, most people headed for Sharjah to Lucky's, Khan's and Pinkies (06 534 1714) for the treasure troves of Indian teak and wrought ironware, although these bargain finds are not really suitable for children's rooms. However, the gap in the market was spotted and in recent years many Asian furniture shops, covering a number of regional specialities, have opened in Dubai. For Indonesian indoor and outdoor furniture, try The Warehouse (04 344 0244). Aquarius (04 349 7251), which is also in the Jumeirah Centre, always has an interesting range of reasonably priced wooden furniture. Pagoda House (04 339 5909) was opened by a lady who developed her tastes while living in Singapore. Then there's Cottage Furniture (04 339 5909), Carpe Diem (04 344 4734), Apollo (04 339 1358), Home Centre (04 339 5111), Marina Gulf Trading (04 295 9570) and Showcase Antiques (04 348 8797). With many people in Dubai living in bigger houses than they would back home, there is a great temptation to fill the available space so homewares accessory stores have become popular. THE One has a great range of 'room fillers' as well as some fun furnishings for childrens' rooms. Also if you're after the obligatory bean bag for your kids room then try KAS (04 344 1179) which has every style from fluffy pink to oriental.

In Abu Dhabi too, the range has much improved in recent years. The major stores are listed below, but you could also visit Gemaco (Airport Road, 02 633 9100), Shadows (Najda Street, 02 631 4404) and Home Centre (02 626 2621).

Colour 4 Kids

Colourful, enduring, practical and interesting furniture for kids' bedrooms can be found at Colour 4 Kids. With everything from beds and bunks to desks, chairs, cupboards, bookshelves and tents, all colour coordinated, mix and match, to fit into any room; you'll be hard pushed to make a decision!

Abu Dhabi
Abu Dhabi Mall – 02 645 6117
Dubai
Wafi Shopping Mall – 04 324 0477
Zabeel Road, Karama – 04 335 4166

IKEA

Complete bedroom sets and bedding (100% cotton) for babies upwards can be found in the kids' section at IKEA. Matching curtains can be made to order. The store also sells safety equipment for around the home for toddlers, including corner protectors, cupboard stoppers and non-slip mats, plus soft or wooden toys, lamps, kids tents, feeding accessories, high chairs and utensils.

Home Sweet Home

The restaurant is very popular with children, offering a good menu at reasonable prices. A play area and separate video room provide free, supervised entertainment for children while parents shop in the store.

See also: Eating Out [p.195]

Abu Dhabi
Marina Mall – 02 681 2228

Dubai
Deira City Centre – 04 295 0434

THE One

In addition to the brightly coloured range of bedroom furniture (which includes a selection of beds and bunk-beds, chests of drawers and desks), THE One sells play rugs, beanbags, children's lamps, books, backpacks, photo frames and all manner of soft toys for kids. It's one of the best places in town to find a plush toy camel for a baby back home!

Abu Dhabi
Khaladiya – 02 681 6500
Sat – Thurs 09.00 – 22.00 Fri 14.00 – 22.00

Dubai
Beach Road – 04 342 2499   Map Ref → 13-B1
Sat – Thurs 09:00 - 22:00 Fri 14:00 - 22:00
Web/Email → www.theoneme.com

Wafi City – 04 324 1224
Sat – Thurs 10:00 – 22.00 Fri 16.30 - 22.00

Sahara Centre – 06 531 2223
Sat – Thurs 10.00 – 22.00 Fri 14.00 – 22.00

Home Safety

IKEA stocks baby-proofing items for the home, but ask a member of staff to guide you, otherwise you could be searching for hours! The Baby Shop sometimes stocks a few corner cushions and cupboard locks but the range is somewhat sporadic, and the same applies to Debenhams which have had baby proofing kits on display in the past, although not on a regular basis.

ACE Hardware

Ace Hardware stocks a range of baby proofing accessories such as cupboard, toilet seat and drawer locks as well as wall plug covers. They also have a good range of furnishings for kids' bedrooms including colourful stick on borders. Their range of paints is fantastic, if you're up for a bit of creative redecorating.

Abu Dhabi
Airport Road – 02 449 0441
Sat - Fri 10.00 – 22.00

Dubai
Sheikh Zayed Road – 04 355 0698
Sat - Fri 09.00 – 21.00

BurJuman Centre – 04 355 0698

Interior Design

If you are itching to flex your artistic muscles or are simply fed up with plain white walls, the first point of call should be a maintenance company, since they may agree to decorate your rooms at a very reasonable rate (on the basis that you provide the paint). For a selection of paints, visit Ace Hardware [p.72] or your local Jotun paint shop. However, if you're feeling truly creative, the larger Spinneys stores stock Crown paint stencils with options for themed bedrooms such as princess or football.

However, it is wise to check with your landlord before you start painting and remember, your contract may stipulate that the walls must be their original colour when you leave.

Dubai

MacKenzie Associates

Location → On Request · Dubai   **050 453 4232**
Hours → Timings on request
Web/email → mackenziea1@yahoo.com   Map Ref → na

If you're looking for something a little more special, contact Fiona to discuss your requirements and completely transform your room or rooms. Talented artists can produce murals with fairytale castles, landscapes, jungle scenes and even painted ceilings resplendent with angels or flying elephants! Versatile styles, specialist paint finishes and reasonable prices are the order here, as is a willingness to travel anywhere in the Emirates.

Creative Art Centre

Location → Nr Choithrams · Jumeira   **04 344 4394**
Hours → 08:00 - 18:00
Web/email → artcentr@emirates.net.ae   Map Ref → 12-E1

Based in two villas, the Creative Arts Centre is a great place for a browse. They offer art in many forms and are one of the few places in Dubai that sells both original and poster art for children's bedrooms.

Maternity Clothes

Maternity wear is easily available in stores, such as Mothercare, Marks and Spencer's, Debenhams and Next. However, speciality stores are few and far between, although several have cropped up in Dubai in the recent years, such as Jenny Rose (04 349 0902), Great Expectations (04 345 3155) and Formes (04 324 4856). Dorothy Perkins in Lamcy Plaza (04 335 9999) has also introduced a good, although small, maternity section and Westwood in Deira City Centre (04 295 5900) has an affordable and fashionable range. Abu Dhabi still has some catching up to do in the maternity wear department. So, you will have to either settle for the more established retail chain outlets or opt for elasticated waists and extra large sizes!

Musical Instruments

Other options → Music Lessons [p.132]

Abu Dhabi

Whether you are already an accomplished musician, or have recently decided to explore your musical talents, you may find the selection of musical instrument stores in Abu Dhabi a little disappointing. AKM Music Centre (02 621 9929) has a decent range (including pianos) – they also sell sheet music. If you can't find what you're looking for, it may be worth a trip to Dubai where you'll find get a wider choice.

Dubai

There are a number of shops in Dubai that sell musical instruments. It's advisable to shop around to check the different models and prices available at any given time – check the Yellow Pages for a good list of suppliers (see Music Instruments – Dealers), or ask your child's music teacher for recommendations. Remember to check the availability of accessories for certain instruments before you purchase, since this could be a problem in the future.

Second-hand pianos go like hot cakes and supermarket ads and the classifieds are the usual source of information. Piano tuners can be found through music shops or recommendations by music teachers.

Popular shops in Dubai include: Thomsun Music, Deira (04 266 8181), suppliers of Yamaha instruments; Melody House Musical Instruments, opp. Hamarain Centre (04 227 5336); Zak Electronics & Musical Instruments, Karama (04 336 8857) and Deira (04 269 5774).

Pets

The voluntary organisations K9 Friends (04 347 4611) and Feline Friends (Abu Dhabi 02 665 5297; Dubai 050 451 0058) are always grateful for permanent or temporary homes for unwanted cats and dogs. The websites www.k9friends.com and www.felinefriendsuae.com both have regularly updated sections listing cats and dogs available for adoption, with photos and details of their character. Although K9 Friends is based in Dubai, it's still worth giving them a call from Abu Dhabi. Feline Friends operates out of Abu Dhabi and Dubai. Check out the regular feature for both organisations in the Saturday edition of the Gulf News.

Although there are animal souks in the area and they are considerably cheaper than petshops, they are not for the faint-hearted and it is advisable to stick to the reputable petshops. The CITES protected list is disregarded in these souks, and the animals are often diseased and kept in very cramped and overcrowded cages. Depending on your sensitivity a trip to the animal souk in Meena, Abu Dhabi or the plant and pet souk in Satwa, Dubai may be worthwhile, as pet food and bedding are often cheaper here than at the pet shops.

If you have your own pet, particularly a cat or dog, make sure that you get a municipality ID tag (they require immunisation certificates and charge just Dhs. 10) to attach to the collar with a contact name and phone number in case it wanders off. Check the Yellow Pages, Hawk Business Pages or Connector for details of vets in your area.

There are a few petshops about, in Abu Dhabi there's Pet Land (02 667 2223) and Wonder Sea Fish (02 667 3957) and in Dubai, Pet Zone (04 321 1424) and Petland (04 338 4040).

Man's Best Friend

Portrait Photographer/Artist

Abu Dhabi

Steve & Mary Smith Photography

Location ➜ On Request · Abu Dhabi | 050 641 5462
Hours ➜ Timings on request
Web/email ➜ stevesmithphotos@hotmail.com   Map Ref ➜ na

Based in the UAE for over 20 years, Steve and Mary Smith take family portraits, school groups, corporate and other photography anywhere in the UAE.

Dubai

Le Studio Mystique

Location ➜ Mazaya Centre · Trade Centre 1&2 | 04 343 9234
Hours ➜ 10:00 - 22:00 Fri 16:30 - 22:00
Web/email ➜ lsm@emirates.net.ae   Map Ref ➜ 12-E2

This studio covers all family photography from portraits to modelling, parties to weddings, plus they have a range of cute costumes available for children's portraits. All the photography is digital, so customers are able to view pictures on screen before ordering copies. A further branch has opened in Mercato shopping mall.

Paul Thuysbaert Photography

Location ➜ Villa 56A · St 27D, 214 · Al Garhoud | 04 286 8802
Hours ➜ Timings on request
Web/email ➜ www.ptphotography.com   Map Ref ➜ 15-D1

If you want the standard snapshot of little Johnny in his school uniform, then this is not for you. However, if you have always wanted a unique and timeless black and white (or colour, if you prefer) photograph of the most important people in your life, then contact Paul Thuysbaert.

Sandra Metaxa

Location ➜ On Request · Dubai | 04 348 4650
Hours ➜ Timings on request
Web/email ➜ spy013@emirates.net.ae   Map Ref ➜ na

Sandra takes charming children's photographs, particularly in local dress, in her studio in Jumeira. Her rates are reasonable and she soon puts children at ease. She's also available for weddings and family/home photographs.

Studio Al Aroosa

Location ➜ Beach Centre, The · Jumeira | 04 344 1663
Hours ➜ 09:30 - 13:00 16:30 - 21:00 Fri closed
Web/email ➜ studioalaroosa@hotmail.com   Map Ref ➜ 13-A1

You only need to look at the various examples hanging in the studio window to see the beautiful work done at Studio Al Aroosa.

Sporting Goods

If you wish to shop around for specific sports clothing or equipment, most of the shopping malls in Dubai have a number of sports stores that are worth a visit. In Abu Dhabi, try the Abu Dhabi and Marina Malls. Prices don't fluctuate much between stores but depend on the brand name.

Alternatively, it may be worth asking your child's coach for advice; for example, if looking for a tennis racket. They will probably stock a line themselves and have the right size for your child.

The golf clubs have their own pro shops where sets of clubs can be purchased and cut down to size if necessary (see Beach, Health & Sports Clubs, Outdoor Activities). Other golf shops selling a reasonable range of equipment are mentioned below.

For horse riding equipment, take advice from the riding clubs. The key requirement, however, is a good fitting hat. Sizes and fit vary from make to make and you need to be careful to buy a good fitting, quality hat, with a kite mark, to ensure your child's safety. Two good stockists are listed here. There are other tack shops at the camel souk, but you should know what you're looking for – you can easily save over Dhs.100 buying a cheap hat for example, but at the cost of safety. If you are unsure as to how your child will take to the sport, the riding schools will loan you a hat for the first few weeks. You will find jodhpurs and boots at all the stockists, at a

> **Ball Skills**
>
> *All the major sports stores stock footballs – mostly size 5s. Or you can buy them for a fraction of the price in the souks, but they won't be the same quality. According to Michael Owen, children should hone their dribbling skills using a solid size 2 ball, which is what the Brazilians use. Remember not to really kick it though – you'll hurt your foot! An air-inflated size 4 ball is best for children to play with – if you can find one; they're good ideas for birthday presents from family back home.*

range of prices. If you know sizes, you may find it cheaper to ask visiting family members to bring them from home. Initially, a pair of comfortable trousers and shoes with a heel can be used. Trainers are not suitable.

Bicycles can be purchased from the larger toy shops (Toys 'R' Us have a good and affordable range, see p.78) and specialist bike shops. If you are in Dubai, head to Satwa for a bicycling bargain! They may not look so swish (and you might want to check them over yourself before they are used), but they are considerably cheaper than elsewhere. Servicing costs next to nothing.

Heat Waves

Heat Waves stocks a good range of beachwear and accessories for every age, size and activity. Speedo costumes can be ordered according to school colours. 'Floaties' (swimming costumes with a built-in float) are available for newborns to five year olds, as well as costumes with nappies for babies. They always stock a colourful range of UV sunsuits and, with coordinating bags, shoes, hats and wraps, both you and your tot can be stylishly dressed for the beach!

Abu Dhabi
Foutouch Al Khair – 02 621 3775
Sat – Thurs 10.00 – 14.00 Fri 17.00 – 22.00

Dubai
Jumeira Plaza – 04 344 9489   (women and children's wear)
Jumeira Plaza – 04 344 7441   (men and boys' wear)
Town Centre Mall – 04 342 0445
Le Meridien Dubai · Al Garhoud – 04 399 3161
10:00 – 22:00
Web/Email → heatwave@emirates.net.ae

Sun & Sand Sports

Sun & Sand Sports caters for all the family, selling a selection of clothing (eight years plus for kids), shoes and equipment, including junior rackets, beach and water sports gear.

Abu Dhabi
Hamdan Street – 02 674 6299
Sat – Thurs 10.00 – 13.00 16.00 – 22.00 Fri 16.00 – 22.00
Marina Mall – 02 681 8330

Dubai
Deira City Centre – 04 295 5551
BurJuman Centre – 04 351 5276
Al Ghurair Centre – 04 222 7107
Sports Market, opposite Jumeirah Centre – 04 3443799
Sat – Thu 10:00 – 22:00 Fri 18:00 – 22:00
Jumeirah Centre – 04 349 5820

Dubai

Al Hamur Marine

Location → Beach Rd, Jumeira | 04 344 4468
Hours → 16:30 – 20:30
Web/email → na | Map Ref → 13-B1

A good selection of snorkelling gear for children can be bought at Al Hamur Marine. In addition, they sell UV suits, lifejackets, fishing tackle, body boards, noodles, helmets for skateboarding, sandcastle building sets, goggles … etc.

Emirates Sports Stores

Location → Jumeirah Plaza · Jumeira | 04 344 7456
Hours → 09:00 – 21:30   Fri 17:00 – 21:30
Web/email → www.dubaishoppingmalls.com | Map Ref → 13-B1

Emirates Sports Stores sells a comprehensive range of shoes, junior rackets and accessories for all sports, including water sports.

Emirta Horse Requirements

Location → Al Kawakeb Bld · Shk Zayed Rd | 04 343 7475
Hours → 10:00 – 14:00 16:30 – 20:30
Web/email → emirta@emirates.net.ae | Map Ref → 13-A3

Emirta stocks a huge of riding equipment, including clothing, hats and boots suitable for children aged four years and above. Bridles, saddles and grooming accessories can also be purchased here. Remember to ask for a riding school discount.

Golf House

This Dubai based chain of stores offers a good selection of clubs, bags, clothing and accessories. Sets are sold according to age and size, from 3 - 12 years. Good for gift ideas for dads and grandads too!

BurJuman Centre – 04 351 9012
Lamcy Plaza – 04 334 5945
Deira City Centre – 04 295 0501
Jebel Ali Hotel – 04 883 6636

Horse World Trading

Location → Camel Souk · Nad Al Sheba | 04 339 3183
Hours → 08:00 – 13:00 16:00 - 20:00 Fri closed
Web/email → hworld@emirates.net.ae | Map Ref → UAE-C2

This is a small shop, but it stocks a very good range of quality riding equipment – all well known brands. It's run by two Englishwomen, Catrina and

Annabelle, who are both qualified riding instructors with many years experience. What they don't have, they can usually source within a few weeks, so it's always worth asking.

Picnico General Trading (Dubai)

Location → Jumeirah Beach Road · Beach Rd | 04 394 1653
Hours → 09:00 - 21:00   Fri 16:30 - 21:00
Web/email → picnico@emirates.net.ae | Map Ref → 12-D1

This shop is dedicated to camping and outdoor equipment. It offers a varied selection of goods, including backpacks and small tents specifically for children. It's located by a petrol station, halfway along the Beach Road on the right as you're heading towards Dubai from Umm Suqeim.

Scuba Dubai Shop

Location → Trade Centre Apartments | 04 331 7433
Hours → 09:00 - 13:00   16:00 - 20:30   Thur 09:00-19:00
Web/email → na | Map Ref → 13-B3

Located next to the dive centre, this is one of the best-stocked shops in Dubai, offering honest and unbiased advice on all aspects of diving in the region. They also stock children's snorkelling and diving equipment, including wetsuits suitable for children over 12 years.

Wheels Trading

Location → Sahara Tower, Shk Zayed Rd · Dubai | 04 331 7119
Hours → 09:00 - 13:00   16:00 - 21:30   Fri am closed
Web/email → na | Map Ref → 13-B3

Wheels Trading sells a comprehensive range of sturdy, colourful bikes for children aged three years and up. In addition to road bikes and special bicycles designed for handicapped people, they sell mountain bikes suitable for those over seven years. They also offer proficient service and repair facilities, plus all sorts of accessories including helmets.

Wolfi's Bike Shop

Location → Between Jct 2 & 3 · Shk Zayed Rd | 04 339 4453
Hours → 09:00 - 19:00   Fri closed
Web/email → www.wolfisbikeshop.de | Map Ref → 12-C2

Staff at Wolfi's have bags of experience that they are happy to share; they will go out of their way to help biking enthusiasts find just the right widget for their sprocket, searching the net and ordering from abroad if necessary. Stocking bikes to suit the smallest beginners through to serious adult riders, they also have a wide range of accessories and safety equipment, including Sigg aluminium water bottles from Switzerland, which are both leak proof and taste free.

Toys & Crafts

Traditional toys and games of this region reflect the influence of the sea, particularly in those played with by boys, such as boat racing, building small ships and playing with seashells. The materials for building were gathered from the seashore and included items like leaves and date palms, bones from dead birds, skeletons such as star fish and pieces of coloured glass. Other popular games were 'tag' and horse racing with small palm tree 'horses'. Girl's games were generally played in and around the home and incorporated singing and poetry. One of the more energetic games was similar to hopscotch.

Games, Sets and Match!

Times have changed, however, and toys are now dominated by plastic and electronic gadgetry. In the UAE, you can find pretty much everything you can get back home, plus a lot more! For more significant purchases, like Little Tykes houses or ride in cars, there's a thriving second hand market operating via supermarket noticeboards.

The major toyshops are detailed here, but it's also worth taking the time to check what is available in the souks. You won't find the quality that you will find elsewhere, but prices are much cheaper. For bits and pieces, at Eid and Christmas for example, children will be delighted with the Dhs.5 police motorcyclist or the singing, belly dancing dolly for Dhs.15! Apart from children, these shops are great for silly presents for friends and family back home.

Arts & Crafts

For creative kids who like to dabble in arts and crafts, tools of the trade can be found at any of the following stores. If you're looking for anything in particular, try contacting each individual store before embarking on a wild goose chase. Stores are sprawled throughout the city and you can find yourself shop hopping if you don't plan ahead. Also see Arty Parties in the Birthday Parties section [p.151].

Abu Dhabi

Craft Corner

Location → Lulu Refreshments Bld · Airport Rd | 02 622 2563
Hours → See below
Web/email → CCAbuDhabi@aol.com | Map Ref → 4-E3

Craft Corner has an extensive range of quality arts and crafts supplies including face paints, drawing books, ceramic paints, stencils and silk paints. They also offer craft classes, for more information, see Art Classes in the Activities section [p.126].

Timings: Sat - Tue 09:30 - 13:30 17:00 - 19:00, Wed - Thu 09:30 - 13:30 Fri closed

Dubai

Art Shop

Location → 1st Floor, Jumeirah Plaza · Jumeira | 04 349 0627
Hours → 09:30 - 14:00 16:00 - 21:30 Fri am closed
Web/email → na | Map Ref → 13-B1

Located at Dubai International Arts Centre, this little shop has a wide range of art supplies. Plus you may just be tempted to sign up for one of the courses as you're passing through.

The Art Shop stocks a range of hobby crafts and art supplies for children and adults – from learn to draw books and paints for clay and silk, to stencils, origami paper, Styrofoam balls and raffia. They also have air drying clay (moulds to any shape, no firing necessary) and Fimo clay for modelling jewellery, magnets, and so on, with many different colours of clay.

Elves & Fairies

Location → Jumeirah Centre · Jumeira | 04 344 9485
Hours → 09:30 - 13:30 15:30 - 20:30
Web/email → jmeadows@emirates.net.ae | Map Ref → 13-B1

In addition to the usual arts and crafts items, Elves & Fairies sells Snazaroo face paints, party sets, accessories and books. The shop also stocks cross stitch kits for kids, the Osborne collection of books on arts, crafts and hobbies, stamps for making gift cards (good as presents), plus customised rubber stamps for names, and so on. The truly creative can buy wall stamps with children's designs, which are great fun to use on walls, furniture and fabric. The shop also offers rubber stamping tuition.

Emirates Trading Establishment

Location → Nr Al Nasr Cinema · Al Karama | 04 337 5050
Hours → 08:00 - 21:00 Fri closed
Web/email → etenmoo1@emirates.net.ae | Map Ref → 13-E4

This stationery shop stocks a good range of materials for the more serious artist, from oils or watercolours to silk paints, plus 'how to' books for budding artists. They also sell a great choice of craft kits aimed at children over eight years old. There is another branch in the Arts Centre in Jumeira.

Men at Work

Toys & Games

Carrefour

Carrefour sells a good and reasonably priced selection of popular toys, games, sports and fishing gear, backpacks and much more! There are plenty of items that make great gifts, plus inexpensive clothing and accessories for all ages.

Abu Dhabi
Airport Rd – 02 448 4300

Dubai
Al Shindagha – 04 393 5737
Deira City Centre – 04 295 1600

Early Learning Centre

These stores stock a colourful and interesting range of quality toys and accessories that are both fun and educational. Items are displayed by age range – very helpful if you are not sure what to buy and what is suitable for what age. Gift wrapping available.

Abu Dhabi
Abu Dhabi Mall – 02 645 4766
Marina Mall – 02 681 8868
Fotouh Al Khair Centre – 02 621 5863

Abu Dhabi
BurJuman – 04 359 7709
Deira City Centre – 04 295 1548
Wafi City – 04 324 2730
Spinneys Centre, Umm Suqeim – 04 394 1204

Toys 'R' Us

The biggest toyshop in the UAE (Deira) sells everything from pencils and cards to bicycles or climbing frames. The latest and greatest games, videos, puzzles, models, books, stationery and toys of all shapes and sizes can be bought here for ages 0 and up. Toys 'R' Us offers an extensive range of baby and nursery equipment with a selection of brands and prices.

Abu Dhabi
Mina Zayed – 02 673 2332
10.00 – 22.00   16.00 – 22.00

Dubai
Salah Al Din Road – 04 224 0000   Map Ref → 13-E4
10.00 – 22.00 every day
Web/Email → info@alfuttaimsons.com

Dubai

Hobby Centre

Location → Airport Rd · Deira   04 295 5512
Hours → 09:00 - 13:30 16:30 - 21:00 Fri closed
Web/email → www.hobbycentre-uae.com Map Ref → 14-C4

This shop is for serious flyers, drivers, sailors and racers aged ten years and over! The Hobby Centre is a major supplier of remote control cars, aeroplanes and boats – they offer free demonstrations and also a free after sales lesson service.

Wasco White Star

Location → Beach Centre, The · Jumeira   04 342 2179
Hours → 10:00 - 23:00   Fri 15:00 - 23:00
Web/email → wasco@suco.co.ae   Map Ref → 13-A1

This small, unusual shop stocks a range of teachers' aids and is a real treasure chest for educational and craft-related toys, as well as unusual gift ideas.

Camel Race

fun for everyone...

Bronte X-back
Dhs 110

Umina V-back
Dhs 70

Nobbys Racer
Dhs 40
Dhs 45

Coogee Sportsback
Dhs 80

Umina X-back
Dhs 70

Junior Pro Goggles
Dhs 45

Available at select Beyond the Beach & Al Boom Marine Stores

Goggles are available in all stores. Junior swimwear is available at Spinneys Centre Umm Suqeim, Al Bahar (Jumeirah Beach Rd.)
Call Retail Head Office, for details 04 2895578

ZOGGS

AL BOOM MARINE

BEYOND THE BEACH

Time to Head for the Hills

While the UAE may be fast becoming the Middle East's most modern metropolis there still remains a vast desert and mountainous expanse waiting to be explored. While you might be able to take yourself out of the city you can't always take the city out of you, so getting lost in the UAE's 'outback' could be a problem. Or not...when equipped with this off-road route guide that has easy to follow instructions, satellite imagery, distances, land marks, points of interest and driving tips for difficult terrain.

- Satellite Maps & GPS Co-ordinates
- Driving & First Aid
- Wildlife Guide
- Outdoor Activities
- Archaeology & Heritage

Passionately Publishing...

EXPLORER

Phone (971 4) 335 3520 • Fax (971 4) 335 3529 • Email Info@Explorer-Publishing.com

Insiders' City Guides • Photography Books • Activity Guidebooks • Commissioned Publications • Distribution

www.Explorer-Publishing.com

Activities
EXPLORER

Activities

Sports & Activities	83	Moto-Cross	104	Health Clubs & Sports	
Amusement Centres	83	Mountain Biking	104	Clubs	121
Amusement Parks	86	Netball	104		
Basketball	86	Paintballing	106	**Beaches & Parks**	**122**
Boat & Dhow Charters	86	Plane Tours	106	Beaches	122
Creek & Coastal Cruises	87	Play Centres	106	Beach Parks	123
Bowling	88	Rollerblading	107	Parks	124
Camel Racing	88	Rugby	107		
Camping	90	Running	107	**Expand Your Horizons**	**126**
Canoeing	91	Sailing	108	Art Classes	126
Climbing	92	Sand Boarding/Skiing	109	Clubs & Associations	127
Crazy Golf	92	Snorkelling	109	Dance Classes	127
Cricket	92	Squash	110	Drama Groups	128
Diving	93	Swimming	112	Language Schools	130
Dune Buggy Riding	94	Tennis	113	Libraries	131
Fishing	95	Trekking	114	Music Lessons	132
Football	95	Triathlon	114	Summer Camps	
Golf	96	Wadi & Dune Bashing	114	& Activities	133
Gymnastics	98	Walks	115		
Hockey	99	Water Parks	116	**Museums, Heritage &**	
Horse Riding	99	Water Skiing	116	**Culture**	**135**
Ice Hockey	100	Water Sports	118	Museums – City	135
Ice Skating	100	Windsurfing	118	Museums – Out of City	136
Jet Skiing	101	Yoga	118	Zoos	139
Karting	101			Tour Operators	140
Kite Flying	101	**Beach, Health & Sports**			
Kite Surfing	101	**Clubs**	**119**	**Weekend Breaks**	**140**
Martial Arts	102	Beach Clubs	119		
Mini Golf	103				

MUST SEE

Big Red sand dune at the side of the Dubai – Hatta road is an impressive sight and a great photo opportunity. There are also a couple of independent quad bike companies at the foot of the sand dune who hire out basic quad bikes as well as few of the 250cc big boys. However, while the rental prices may be relatively cheap less experienced drivers, especially kids, would be better opting for tour operators such as Desert Rangers who provide basic training and constant supervision. See [p.140]

MUST KNOW

While camping is a great family getaway, and the weather here lends itself to at least six months of perfect temperatures for a couple of nights under the stars, recent law enforcement has dampened the activity somewhat. While setting up camp in whatever picturesque spot you found was once possible beach and camping regulations have created limitations on both camping and cooking on the beach. However, a camping permit can be obtained from the Municipality. See [p.90]

MUST DO

Rugby is a much loved sport here, especially with Dubai on the international Rugby 7s circuit, with the annual tournament in December drawing crowds, including many families, from all around the UAE as well as the rest of the Gulf states and the world. With avid followers the sport has become popular with kids and the Dubai Exiles Club offer a junior training programme for budding players. See [p.107]

Sports & Activities

Other options → Going Out [p.176]

Dubai is overflowing with a fab array of activities, both indoor and out, for the kids, or the big kid in you. Whether they (or you!) fancy daring the Jumeirah Sceirah at state of the art water park, Wild Wadi, or catching the latest Disney Pixar creation at one of the many multi-screen cinemas there is more than enough on offer for all ages and weather conditions. During the pleasant winter months, before the heat and humidity rise, water sports and beach pursuits will keep the whole family busy from sunrise to sunset. As for the stickier summer months you can still escape cabin fever with a range of air conditioned activities from amusement arcades to play centres.

If your flock are forever giving you the run around then the wide variety of sports activities available could be just the thing to tire them out, instead of them tiring you out! Whether they are a budding Tiger Woods or Venus Williams there is virtually every sport under the sun (or in the sports hall) on offer. Even the more educational activities are fun, with interactive museums and cool cultural sites.

Alternatively, if you and the family want to escape the hubbub of the city, be it camping under the stars or lapping up the luxury of a five star hotel then check out the weekend break suggestions at the end of this section.

Amusement Centres

Other options → Amusement Parks [p.86]

Admission is generally free to all the amusement centres and you pay as you go until your pockets are empty! The age range tends to be for 3 years and above.

Abu Dhabi

Action Zone

Location → Tourist Club · Tourist Club Area | 02 676 8669
Hours → 10:00 - 24:00
Web/email → adclub@emirates.net.ae | Map Ref → 4-B3

Ideal for kids over 5 years of age, Action Zone provides unlimited fun on all the electronic games machines, rides and the soft play area.

Prices: An initial Dhs. 3 per card; Dhs.3 - Dhs.15 per ride

Foton World

Location → Marina Mall · Breakwater | 02 681 5526
Hours → 10:00 - 23:00
Web/email → na | Map Ref → 5-A2

This high tech amusement outlet has a large range of electronic games, carousels and other funfair rides – a good option for keeping the kids busy while the parents shop.

Prices: Dhs.35 (unlimited access to all rides)

Foton World

Fun World

Location → Opp Cultural Foundation · Al Hosn | 02 632 2255
Hours → 10:00 - 13:30 16:30 - 23:00 Thu 10:00 - 23:00
Web/email → na | Map Ref → 5-A3

Fun World has rides and attractions offering a pleasurable experience for children and adults alike. Try out the bumper cars, mini flight, soft play area, video machines, or Dooby's Backyard area which consists of a playground area, fun art area, sand art area and computer section.

Prices: Dhs.2.50 per token; Dhs.20 (for a 'ride all you can' wristband); Dhs.50 (20 tokens plus 5 free tokens); Dhs.100 (40 tokens plus 10 free tokens)

Toy Town

Location → Abu Dhabi Mall · Al Meena | 02 645 5567
Hours → 09:30 - 23:00   Fri 15:00 - 22:00
Web/email → toytown@emirates.net.ae | Map Ref → 4-C2

Beware of the gigantic spiders, snakes and gorillas lurking among the amusement rides! This jungle themed amusement centre includes a water slide, bumper cars and a roller coaster.

Prices: Dhs.2 - 10 per game/ride

Dubai

City 2000

Location → Hamarain Centre · Deira
04 266 7855
Hours → 10:00 - 23:00   Fri 16:30 - 23:00
Web/email → city2000@emirates.net.ae   Map Ref → 14-C4

City 2000 offers video games and rides in an air conditioned environment. From racing on a track or bombing in a fighter plane, there is a great range of simulator style amusements. For little ones there are funny videos and the latest rides.

Prices: Dhs.2 per game/ride; Dhs.3 for simulator games

Encounter Zone

Location → Wafi Mall · Umm Hurair (2)
04 324 7747
Hours → 10:00 - 22:00   Fri 13:30 - 22:00
Web/email → ezone@emirates.net.ae   Map Ref → 15-C1

Divided into two sections, Encounter Zone offers a range of action packed fun for all ages from electronic games to arts and crafts activities. Galactica is for teenagers and adults, and Lunarland is for kids aged 1 - 8 years.

Prices: Dhs.5 - 15 per activity (Lunarland); Dhs.10 - 22.50 per activity (Galactica); Dhs.2 - 8 per video game; Dhs.50 all day pass excluding video games (Sat - Wed); Dhs.20 morning pass excluding video games and arts and crafts activities (Sat - Thurs 10:00 - 14:00)

Fantasy Kingdom

Location → Al Bustan Centre · Al Qusais
04 263 2774
Hours → 10:00 - 23:00   Fri 14:00 - 23:00
Web/email → www.al-bustan.com   Map Ref → 15-E1

Themed as a medieval castle, Fantasy Kingdom offers adventure, fun and excitement. The centre is located in the comfort of a 24,000 square feet indoor play area, which is divided into sections for different age groups.

Prices: Dhs.2 per token with no entrance fee (tokens become cheaper the more you buy).

Fun World

Location → BurJuman Centre · Bur Dubai
04 352 2922
Hours → 10:00 - 22:00   Fri 14:00 - 22:00
Web/email → www.burjuman.com   Map Ref → 14-A3

BurJuman offers something for all ages with Toby's and Fun City for the very young, and Fun World for the next stage on. Some of the machines and rides are aimed at the young, but there's a focus on entertainment for teens.

Magic Planet

Location → City Centre · Deira
04 295 4333
Hours → 10:00 - 24:00   Fri 12:00 - 24:00
Web/email → www.deiracitycentre.com   Map Ref → 15-D1

Ride the carousel or Ferris wheel, swing through Clarence camel's adventure zone, or test your skills on the bumper cars and latest video games. For a more leisurely route, watch the world pass from the City Express train or safari car.

Prices: Pay as you play, using Dhs.2 cards (they become cheaper the more you buy); Dhs.50 Planet All Day Special (unlimited access)

Sharjah

Adventureland

Location → Sahara Centre · Sharjah
06 531 6363
Hours → 10:00 - 22:30
Web/email → www.adventureland-sharjah.com   Map Ref → UAE-C2

Adventureland is spacious with a balanced mix of rides and attractions. It covers 70,000 square feet of fun space indoors and caters to all ages, from fun rides for toddlers young kids to teenage videogames and adult thrill rides, truly living up to its name as the ultimate family entertainment destination.

Prices: The rides vary from Dhs.3 - 7. Membership is Dhs.50 and allows Dhs.30 worth of rides, discounts in the mall and a host of other benefits

Foton World

Location → Top Floor, Al Taawum Mall · Sharjah
06 577 4455
Hours → 10:00 - 22:00   Friday 14:00 - 22:00
Web/email → na   Map Ref → UAE-C2

Foton World is a fantasy destination for the whole family to explore. Based on the globe, it combines fun, entertainment and education, as well as the opportunity to savour cuisine from around the world. With its hanging vines, towering trees and greenery, Africa has much to offer the younger guests with slides, flumes and rope bridges. In dramatic contrast, Antarctica is a sculptured wonderland of icebergs, melting snow and crevasses, with penguins, polar bears and other arctic animals bringing this crystal world to life. Ride the thrilling Ice Coaster and speed into the hidden icicle cave, or go underwater in the Ocean. Foton World also operates the amusement centre in Manar Mall, Ras Al Khaimah.

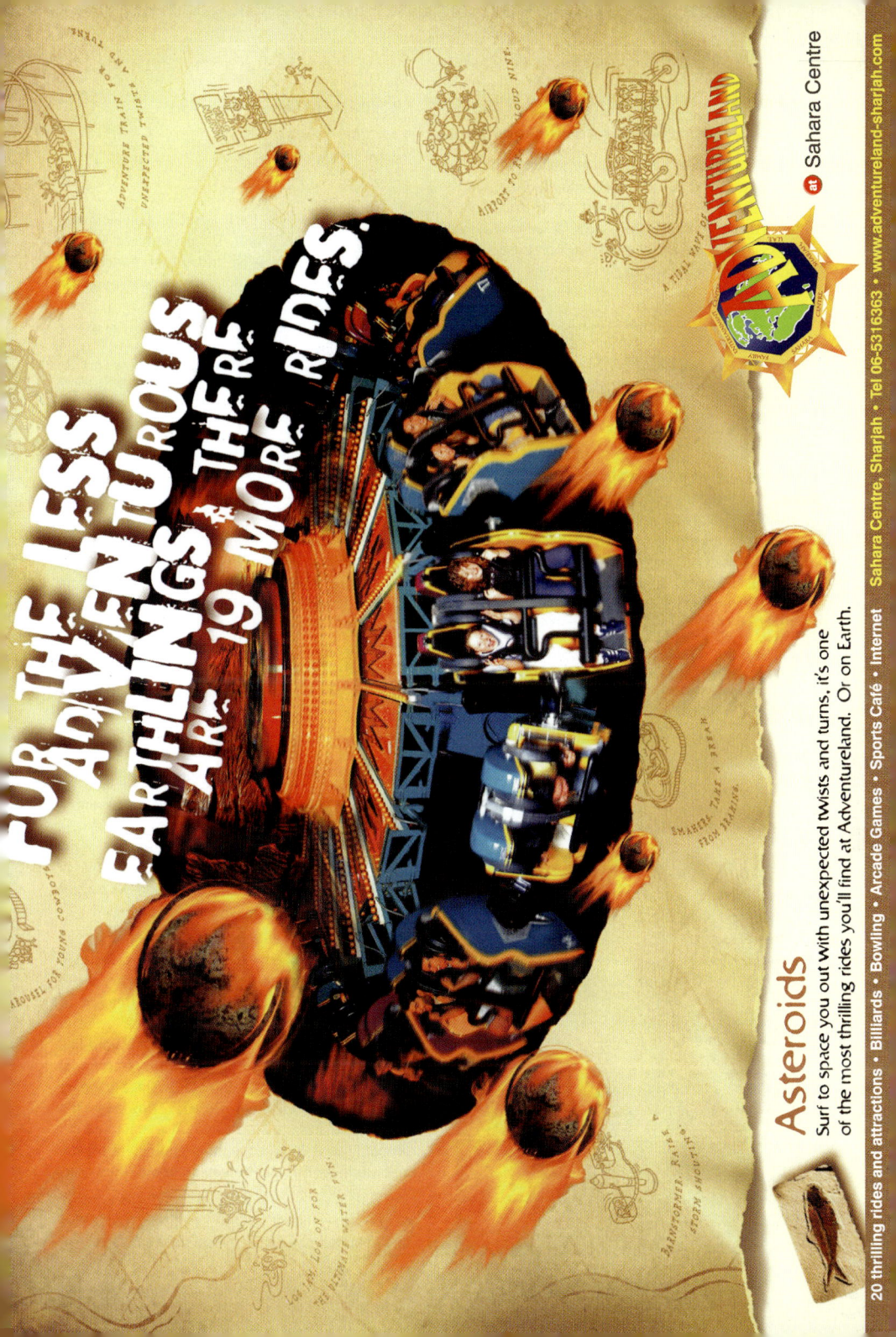

FUN FOR THE LESS ADVENTUROUS EARTHLINGS THERE ARE 19 MORE RIDES.

Asteroids
Surf to space you out with unexpected twists and turns, it's one of the most thrilling rides you'll find at Adventureland. Or on Earth.

ADVENTURELAND at Sahara Centre

20 thrilling rides and attractions • Billiards • Bowling • Arcade Games • Sports Café • Internet   Sahara Centre, Sharjah • Tel 06-5316363 • www.adventureland-sharjah.com

Amusement Parks

Other options → Amusement Centres [p.83]

All the amusement parks charge an admission fee with pay as you go rides once you are in. Children have the space to run around freely under adult supervision. Although there are no large Amusement Parks in Abu Dhabi, it is worth the short trip across to Al Ain to have a fun day out with the kids.

Al Ain

Hili Fun City & Ice Rink

Location → Mohammed Bin Khalifa St · Hili | 03 784 5542
Hours → See timings below
Web/email → www.hilton.com | Map Ref → 7-D1

It's the largest amusement park in the Gulf and covers a total area of 86 hectares. Thrilling rides including runaway trains and alien encounters will excite all age groups. Admission is free for children under the age of 3.

Prices: Weekdays Dhs.10 (8 ride coupons), Thu & Fri Dhs.15 (12 ride coupons)

Timings: Winter: 16:00 - 22:00 Sun - Wed & 09:00 - 22:00 Thu, Fri and public holidays. Tue & Wed are women and children only. Closed Sat. Summer: 17:00 - 23:00 Sun - Wed & 9:00 - 23:00 Thurs, Fri and public holidays

Dubai

Fruit & Garden Luna Park

Location → Al Nasr Leisureland · Oud Metha | 04 337 1234
Hours → 09:00 - 22:30
Web/email → www.alnasrleisureland.ae | Map Ref → 13-E4

This park has rides for everyone aged 4 and above. Rides include go-karts, bumper cars, a roller coaster and many more.

Prices: Dhs.10 per adult; Dhs.5 per child (under five years of age)

Play Time

WonderLand Theme & Water Park

Location → nr Creekside Park · Umm Hurair (2) | 04 324 1222
Hours → See below. Sundays closed.
Web/email → www.wonderlanduae.com | Map Ref → 15-C1

A theme and water park attraction divided into three areas - Main Street, Theme Park and Fujifilm SplashLand, each with individual specialised entertainment. Throughout the park there are a variety of food outlets.

Prices: Dhs.75 per adult; Dhs.65 per child; Dhs.20 under 4 years of age

Timings: Timings vary according to season. Call for details on specified days for ladies, families, schools and special offers

See also: Splashland — Water Parks (Activities, p.116).

Basketball

Basketball hasn't really taken off in the UAE but courts can be rented at the Aviation Club and Dubai Country Club, plus there is a public court at Safa Park (04 349 2111) in Dubai. LG InSportz (04 347 5833) offers a basketball coaching programme for 6 - 9 year olds. Abu Dhabi Health & Fitness (02 443 6333) also offers coaching for all levels. However, currently there doesn't seem to be much team activity, so it looks like lone net practice for the time being.

Boat & Dhow Charters

Other options → Creek & Coastal Cruises [p.87]

Large independent groups can try chartering a dhow from the fishermen at Dibba to travel up the coast of the Mussandam. Be prepared to haggle hard — knowing a bit of Arabic may smooth things along. Expect to pay around Dhs.2,500 per day for a dhow large enough to take 20 - 25 people.

You'll need to take your own food and water, etc, as nothing is supplied except ice lockers that are suitable for storing supplies. Conditions are pretty basic. However, you will have limited freedom to plan your own route (camping is only allowed in certain areas) and to see the beautiful fjord-like scenery of the Mussandam from a traditional wooden dhow. Visas aren't required since in theory you won't be entering Oman. However, it's possible to arrange stops along the coast and it's probably best to take camping equipment for the night, although you can sleep on board.

The waters are crystal clear, although the weather can seriously reduce visibility for divers, and turtles and dolphins can be seen from the boat. It's ideal for diving, but hire everything before reaching Dibba (try the Sandy Beach Diving Centre — see Diving [p.93]). Alternatively, spend the days swimming, snorkelling and lazing, and for an extra Dhs.800 hire a speedboat for the day.

Abu Dhabi

Blue Dolphin Speed Boat Charters

Location → Htl Inter-Continental · Bainuna St | 02 666 9392
Hours → Timings on request
Web/email → www.interconti.com | Map Ref → 5-D3

Blue Dolphin has 31 foot Barracuda speedboats, equipped with two 140 hp engines available for charter. The boats can be hired for four hours or alternatively on an hourly basis.

Prices: Dhs.800 for four hours; Dhs.250 per hour (minimum two hours)

Dubai

Al Boom Tourist Village

Location → Umm Hurair (2) | 04 324 3000
Hours → 20:00 - 22:30
Web/email → www.alboom.co.ae | Map Ref → 15-C1

Al Boom Tourist Village has seven dhows, ranging in capacity from 20 - 280 passengers. Along with each private charter, they offer a range of menus, such as sea paradise, international delicacies, local delights, Far Eastern feast and Indian cuisine.

Prices: Ranging from Dhs.500 per hour for Al Taweel (single deck, 20 passenger capacity), to Dhs.3,000 for Kashti (double deck, 150 passenger capacity).

Creek Cruises

Location → Nr DCCI · Deira | 04 393 9860
Hours → 20:30 - 22:30
Web/email → www.creekcruises.com | Map Ref → 14-B3

There are two dhows available for charter, for any kind of occasion, and these are suitable for groups of between 20 and 200 people. Facilities include an air conditioned deck, an Arabic style majlis, a professional sound system and dance floor.

Contact: For further information, contact the above number or 050 624 3793
Prices: Dhs.1,500 per hour (minimum two hours). Catering can be provided from Dhs.80 per person upwards.
Location: Far end of Quays 1 and 2

Khasab Travel & Tours

Location → Warba Centre · Deira | 04 266 9950
Hours → Timings on request
Web/email → www.khasab-tours.com | Map Ref → 14-C3

Visit the Mussandam Peninsula on a dhow, with the chance of seeing dolphins, going swimming and snorkelling, or just enjoying the scenery of the area. Flights can also be arranged to the Mussandam and weekend breaks or longer holidays in Khasab.

Costs: Adults Dhs.150 for a half-day, four hour cruise with refreshments; Dhs.250 full-day, including lunch. At some times of the year children under 12 are free and there are special rates for groups. Although the Mussandam is part of Oman, no visas are required for this trip

Creek & Coastal Cruises

A boat trip is an exciting and unique way to spend an afternoon, and can be quite reasonably priced, depending on the type of craft you choose. Kids will love it and learning about the workings of a boat and the sea in general can be a valid educational experience. Even just sailing past the hive of activity along the creek provides great entertainment. As with any water based activity, constant adult supervision is recommended.

Age Range: 4+

Dubai

Pleasure boats are available for hire from the waterfront by the Heritage & Diving Village, Al Shindagha. A boat ride can be combined with a tour around the Village and Sheikh Saeed Al Maktoum's House, making a fascinating outing for residents and visitors of all ages. Trips in SeaScope, a semi submersible craft, also depart from here. Further details can be obtained from Sam Tours (04 393 8901). For the more adventurous (children over the toddler stage), an abra or water taxi will take you across the Creek from the Textile Souk to the Al Seef Road part of Bur Dubai for just 50 fils per passenger. For Dhs.35 - 50 you can hire the boat and driver for a half hour tour along the Creek - an enjoyable and different way to pass the time, particularly if you have visitors. Don't forget to agree the price before you board. Strict parental supervision is advisable.

See also: Heritage & Diving Village (Museums & Heritage)

Dubai

Creekside Leisure

Location → Opp Dubai Municipality HQ · Deira | 04 336 8406
Hours → Timings on request
Web/email → www.tour-dubai.com Map Ref → 14-B3

Creekside Leisure operates daily guided tours of Dubai in a traditional Dhow. This one hour trip includes a brief history of the city, places of interest, souks, forts and palaces, and offers the chance to see Dubai from a new perspective. Hot and cold refreshments are available on board. School trips and private parties (up to 50 children) can be arranged, and they have recently introduced a two hour dinner cruise, the 'Floating Majlis', featuring a belly dancer, hubbly bubbly, an Arabic meal and soft drinks.

Guided Tours: Timings - 11:30, 15:30 and 17:30; Cost – Dhs.35 per adult, Dhs.20 per child, children under five are free

Groups: Dhs.20 per child, including one free soft drink

Floating Majlis: Timings – 20:30 – 22:30 nightly; Cost – Dhs. 175 per adult, Dhs.85 per child

Danat Dubai Cruises

Location → Nr British Embassy · Bur Dubai | 04 351 1117
Hours → 08:00 - 18:30
Web/email → www.danatdubaicruises.com Map Ref → 5-B2

Luxury coastline cruises and creek tours are provided on Danat Dubai (Pearl of Dubai), a 110ft air conditioned catamaran. A daily 75 minute Scenic Sunset Cruise, including a complementary cocktail and soft drinks, costs Dhs.65 per adult, with children aged 5 - 12 years Dhs.40 and under 5's free. Other specialities include a daily Dining Delight two hour cruise with buffet dinner and belly dancer, for Dhs 175/adult and Dhs 115/child. Danat Dubai also accepts group charters for special functions and coastal cruises into and out of the popular marinas along the coast from Jazira to Ajman. For timings, contact the above number.

Bowling

Growing in popularity, bowling is great fun and good entertainment. Children aged 6 and up are generally allowed to participate, provided they are strong enough to hold and throw the lightest ball, which weighs around 6 lbs. Most bowling alleys in Abu Dhabi and Dubai offer party packages. Refer to the Birthday Party section [p.150] for further information on individual outlets.

Abu Dhabi

Abu Dhabi Tourist Club

Location → Nr Le Meridien Htl · Tourist Club Area | 02 672 3400
Hours → 08:00 - 24:00
Web/email → adclub@emirates.net.ae Map Ref → 4-B3

This 12 lane centre has a simple layout with no frills, although soft drinks and snacks are available. Ideal for escaping the heat in the summer months.

Prices: Dhs.7 for one game; Dhs.3 for shoe rental. Take your own socks, or buy them for Dhs.4.

Camel Racing

A morning at the camel racetrack may not be as glamorous as an afternoon at Ascot, but it is definitely something a little different and certainly memorable. This extraordinary sport features a unique blend of competition and camaraderie as owners, jockeys and camels mingle before the race. For visitors, this is an opportunity to see a truly traditional local sport up close. Races take place during the winter months, usually early on Thursday and Friday mornings at the tracks in Dubai, Ras Al Khaimah, Umm Al Quwain, Al Ain and Abu Dhabi. Additional races are often held on National Day and other public holidays. Admission is free, but you may have to sacrifice your usual weekend lie-in, since the races start very early and are usually all finished by 8:30! After the race you can browse around the camel market shops, which sell a range of camel accessories, but of particular interest are the 100% cotton blankets at bargain prices. The Digdagga racetrack in Ras Al Khaimah is situated on a plain between the dunes and the mountains about 10km south of the town. If you're the outdoors type you can make a really memorable weekend of it - simply set up camp in the big red dunes overlooking the racetrack, wake up early to catch the races and then head back for a freshly cooked campfire breakfast. In Abu Dhabi and Al Ain, races are usually held at the Sowaihan racetrack (about 130km from Abu Dhabi along the road to Al Ain) and at the Al Ain racetrack (about 25km from the centre of Al Ain, along the road to Abu Dhabi).

For more information, call the Emirates Heritage Club (02 4456456)

TOUR DUBAI
Creekside Leisure

FLOATING MAJLIS

Daily Dinner Cruises
Private Dhow Charters

Tel: 336 8406

TOUR DUBAI
Creekside Leisure

DAILY GUIDED CREEK TOURS

Departs 4 times a day at 11.30 - 1.30 - 3.30 and 5.30 pm.
Near Intercon Hotel.

Tel : 336 8407

TOUR DUBAI
Creekside Leisure

TOURS & SAFARIS

Exclusive private tours
Corporate group events

Tel: 336 8409

Camping

Other options ➜ Wadi & Dune Bashing [p.114]

The UAE is a great place for camping, probably because it is so informal, with no real campsites but just a wealth of peaceful spots to set up camp. However it is worth noting that camping laws have become a bit more constrictive and you may need a permit to camp on the beach (without one the fine is Dhs. 3000). Contact the Public Parks and Recreation Section (336 7633) for clarification. Although weatherwise it is best to camp from October to May, with a bit of planning camping in mountain and oasis sites is tolerable in the hot summer months. In general, very little rain and warm temperatures mean that you can camp with much less equipment and preparation than in other countries. It can be enjoyable for families with children of any age, although a certain amount of care is needed to avoid the occasional insect, primarily mosquitoes. The best defence, if you are camping near water during the cooler months, is to cover up as much as possible and to use plenty of mosquito repellent.

For younger, first time campers it can help at bedtime to have a familiar toy and a torch inside the tent. Baby's bottles can be prepared at home, stored in the cool box and warmed up in hot water at the campsite. For the hire of camping cots for babies, see Rent-a-crib in the Shopping section of the book [p.68]. However, do bear in mind that young children can become sick and deteriorate rapidly, so don't camp too far from available medical facilities.

First Time Camper

Many families start off with a trip to Jebel Ali beach; not too far from civilisation with the added bonus of a bracing early morning swim. There are many other locations worth a camping visit including around the Hajar Mountains (in the north near Ras Al Khaimah or east and south near Hatta or Al Ain) and the huge sand dunes of Liwa. For more information on good camping locations refer to the Off-Road Explorer (UAE).

Checklist

Whether you go for one night or a week, the basic equipment required is the same and should include:

- Camping stove, firelighter, wood or barbecue and charcoal
- Water (drinking, washing and vehicle)
- Torches and spare batteries (head torches are great, since they allow your hands to remain free)
- Binoculars, compass, GPS, lighter, multi-purpose penknife
- First aid kit and mosquito repellent (see First Aid list - Medical Care)
- Basic tool kit, tow-rope, shovel, spare tyre
- Cool box, food and drink
- Small accessible cooler for supply of drinks and snacks en route
- Rubbish bags, toilet rolls, tissues and wet wipes
- Tent, foam mattress, sleeping bag. Substitute a mosquito net for a tent in summer
- Pans, plastic plates, mugs, cutlery, kettle, wooden spoon. Cheap and practical items can be bought in the household souks
- Fold down table for eating
- Chairs or mat to sit on
- Animal and bird reference books to answer all those questions!
- Beach ball, bat and ball, bucket and spade, surf board and some indispensable toys
- Camera, spare films and batteries
- Jumpers or equivalent for cooler winter evenings

For longer trips and ones through difficult terrain:

- Always travel with more than one vehicle
- Pack the load equally in the vehicle, with heavy items on the bottom. Tie down if necessary
- Heavy-duty plastic boxes (available from Ace Hardware, along with other camping essentials) are ideal for packing similar items together

- Ice is a must for the cool box. Food should be tightly packed and stored in watertight containers. Emarat and EPPCO shops, open 24 hours, sell ice, made from drinking water, by the bag at a cost of Dhs.3 each. Around the Emirates, ice factories sell ice by the block or crushed for Dhs.5 per block. One block is sufficient for two cool boxes. The ice is made from tap water
- Campsites should always be left spotless and free of litter. For long weekends, desert, mountain and camping trips can be combined with a final night's stay in a hotel or motel, providing that little bit of luxury at the end of an outdoor adventure

Canoeing

Other options → Tour Operators [p.140]

For teenagers interested in wildlife, a canoe trip through the mangroves at Khor Kalba Nature Reserve on the East Coast is a stimulating and enjoyable way of passing leisure time. Take a bird book with you and try to spot the White Collared Kingfisher, which only breeds here and is in danger of extinction. The Khor (creek) is easy to find, just follow the coast road past Fujairah and the town of Kalba and you eventually reach a single lane bridge at the start of the mangroves. There are many places to camp, but remember to take all rubbish away with you. The reserve is a unique and protected area, so treat it with respect – take only photographs and leave only footprints.

Other mangrove areas where it's possible to canoe are around the coastal lagoons of Umm Al Quwain, on the Ras al Khaimah creek between the new and old towns, and north of RAK before Rams. For further information, refer to the *Off-Road Explorer's* Hatta to Kalba route. If you would rather go a professionally organised trip, see the entry for Desert Rangers [p.91].

Abu Dhabi

Al Jazira Hotel and Resort

Location → Ghantoot Area | 02 562 9100
Hours → Timings on request
Web/email → na | Map Ref → na

A number of one and two man canoes are available, which are ideal for beginners, as long as they're big enough to hold the paddles. The resort provides life jackets, paddles and basic instruction. Dhs.30 for 30 minutes or Dhs.60 for an hour.

Prices: Dhs.50 for 10 minutes; Dhs.400 for six coaching lessons

Palm Beach Leisure Club

Location → Al Diar Gulf Htl · Al Maqtaa | 02 441 4777
Hours → 9:00 until sunset
Web/email → www.aldiarhotels.com | Map Ref → 1-D3

A small number of open canoes are available for hire for paddling around the calm waters off the club's beach. Suitable for children and adults alike. Canoes are available from 09:00 to sunset.

Prices: Dhs.20 for 30 minutes; Dhs.40 for 60 minutes. A day entry charge is applicable to all except club members, their guests or residents of the hotel

Dubai

Desert Rangers

Location → Dubai Garden Centre · Shk Zayed Rd | 04 340 2408
Hours → 08:30 - 14:30
Web/email → www.desertrangers.com | Map Ref → 12-A2

Initial instruction is followed by brief hands-on manoeuvres to develop skill and confidence and then an instructor guides you around the mangrove lagoon at Khor Khalba Nature Reserve. Only a basic level of fitness and strength is needed. Children under 10 must be accompanied by an adult.

Costs: Dhs.300 per person with a 50% discount for under 12's

Jebel Ali Sailing Club

Location → Al Sufouh | 04 399 5444
Hours → 09:00 - 20:00   Thu & Fri 09:00 - 22:00
Web/email → www.jebelalisailingclub.com | Map Ref → 2-C1

For children aged eight years and older, four week kayaking courses of four weeks duration are held periodically through the year. All kids' classes are run on Thursday mornings.

Fujairah

Beach Hut, The

Location → Sandy Beach Motel · Al Aqqa | 09 244 5050
Hours → 08:00 - 17:30
Web/email → www.sandybm.com | Map Ref → UAE-E2

Rent a kayak or take a paddleboat around the popular Snoopy Island. It is recommended that kids below 12 be accompanied by an adult, especially if they don't know how to swim. Life jackets are provided.

Prices: Hire single kayaks for Dhs.30 per hour; double kayaks Dhs 50 per hour

Ras Al Khaimah

Al Hamra Fort Hotel

Location → Opp RAK Ceramics | 07 244 6666
Hours → 09:00 - 17:00
Web/email → www.alhamrafort.com   Map Ref → UAE-D1

Single and double kayaks and paddle boats are available for hire to hotel guests only, at Dhs.40 for half an hour, Dhs.50 for one hour. Wake and kneeboarding, banana boat rides, tube rides and surf bikes are also available.

Climbing

The eroded and shattered terrain of the Hajar Mountains provides some excellent climbing routes, particularly in the Ras Al Khaimah, Dibba and Hatta areas. In addition there are some really good crags around Al Ain/Buraimi and the area near the Oman border including the infamous 'Wonderwall'. To date, more than 200 routes have been climbed and named. Although the majority of routes are in the higher grades, there are many easier ones on which new or younger climbers can sharpen their skills. Techniques and safety procedures can be learned on an indoor climbing wall in Dubai before young climbers tackle the great outdoors.

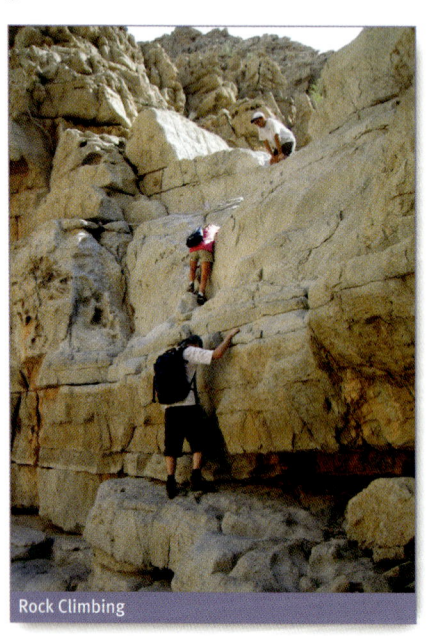

Rock Climbing

Dubai

Pharaohs Club

Location → Pyramids · Umm Hurair (2) | 04 324 0000
Hours → 07:00 - 22:00   Fri 07:00 - 21:30
Web/email → www.pyramidsdubai.com   Map Ref → 15-C1

The only indoor climbing wall in Dubai. It comprises a varied set of walls for climbing routes and bouldering, with crash mats for safety during low level climbs and ropes in place on all routes. All courses are run by experienced instructors. For the 'Children's Club', children older than seven are instructed in the basic techniques of rock climbing. Gift vouchers can be purchased from the club for any number of lessons. These make a good 'alternative' birthday presents for young climbers, or for any adventurous child who has yet to try it.

Prices: Dhs.40 per class (one hour)

Crazy Golf

Abu Dhabi

Al Diar Gulf Hotel & Resort

Location → Al Diar Gulf Htl · Al Maqtaa | 02 441 4777
Hours → 09:00 - 22:00
Web/email → www.aldiarhotels.com   Map Ref → 1-D3

A 9 hole obstacle course is available at the Gulf Hotel for all budding Nick Faldos! Cost is Dhs.5 for 30 minutes of play.

Dubai

Hyatt Golf Park

Location → Hyatt Regency · Deira | 04 209 6741
Hours → 15:30 - 23:00
Web/email → www.dubai.hyatt.com   Map Ref → 5-B1

For details refer to the Hyatt Golf Park review – Mini Golf [p.103].

Cricket

Other options → Annual Events [p.22]

With the large numbers of enthusiastic fans from all over the cricket playing world like India, Pakistan, Sri Lanka, England, Australia and the UK, it's no surprise that cricket is a very popular sport in the UAE. Car parks, rough land and grassy parks all sprout stumps at weekends and evenings, as a mix of ages comes out to play. Cricket Coaching is widely available, and in schools where it is not featured in the sports curriculum, it is often offered as an after school activity.

Major international matches are held regularly in the Emirates, mainly at the grounds in Sharjah, where it's possible to see some of the world's best teams, cheer your own side on and maybe even collect an autograph or two!

To set up your own informal pitch in your garden or the park, inexpensive cricket sets can be found in Satwa or Karama.

Abu Dhabi

Abu Dhabi Cricket Council

Location → Salam Street · Abu Dhabi
Hours → 08:00 - 13:30 19:00 - 22:00
Web/email → www.uaecricket.com
02 558 8331
Map Ref → 4-C2

Founded to promote and run cricket affairs in the emirate, the council organises various inter company matches, seven a side games and annual competitions throughout the year. There are currently 45 local clubs registered, with over a thousand players of all nationalities.

Dubai

Darjeeling Cricket Club

Location → Nr Dubai Country Club · Al Awir Rd
Hours → See timings below
Web/email → coxoil@emirates.net.ae
04 333 1746
Map Ref → na

Matches of 25 overs start at 09:00 and 13:30 every Friday, while net practice takes place under floodlights on Tuesdays. In early March, there's a six a side Gulf tournament and the rest of the year sees matches against visiting test sides.

Membership: Dhs.650 per playing member; Dhs.250 per social member. A non member match fee of Dhs.20 is levied

LG InSportz

Location → Jct 3, Shk Zayed Rd · Shk Zayed Rd
Hours → 09:30 - 21:30
Web/email → www.insportzclub.com
04 347 5833
Map Ref → 12-B2

Qualified coaches guide children in all areas of the game, helping them to hone their skills and sharpen their techniques.

Prices: Dhs.20 per child (12 years and under); Court booking per hour Dhs.100

Diving

Once children over eight can snorkel comfortably, they are generally ready for the next step - diving! PADI has recently introduced the Bubblemaker experience for those aged 8 - 12. This involves a small amount of theory and the chance of blowing some bubbles in the safety of a pool. The 'discover scuba' dive for 12 years and older offers pool training, some theory and video work, with a chance to dive in the sea with an instructor. This is also a good introduction for first time adult divers to get a taste of the sport. The 'junior open water' course, also for 12 years and up, is an internationally recognised certificate course. At the age of 15 this can be upgraded to full 'open water diver'. A parent's consent and signature is necessary before a child participates in any of the courses.

There are many organisations offering diving trips and training. The main centres that cater for children are mentioned below. Popular dive sites can be found on both coasts, but in general you'll find wreck diving in the Arabian Gulf and the more natural sites on the East Coast.

Abu Dhabi

Abu Dhabi Sub Aqua Club

Location → Al Meena Zayed · Abu Dhabi
Hours → Timings on request
Web/email → www.the-club.com
02 673 1111
Map Ref → 4-A3

The club has around 100 members, including about 20 who are instructor standard, and is an official overseas branch of the British Sub Aqua Club (BSAC), so safety standards are high. A range of training courses are regularly held for all standards of diver.

Membership: To join the Sub Aqua Club, membership of The Club is required first

Al Jazira Diving Centre

Location → Al Diar Jazira Club · Ghantoot Area
Hours → 09:00 - 18:00
Web/email → na
02 562 9100
Map Ref → UAE-B3

This centre offers a variety of programmes from discovery to advanced courses. People completing the open water course get a licence allowing them to scuba dive anywhere in the world. They also offer a bubble maker course for kids aged 8 - 12 years. For more information, contact Irmgard Mackenbrock, Recreation Manager (050 476 3436).

Golden Boats

Location → Nr Central Bank Bld · Al Bateen | 02 666 9119
Hours → Timings on request
Web/email → golbomat@emirates.net.ae   Map Ref → 5-D3

Golden Boats offers a variety of water sports, including fishing, skiing and wind surfing, as well as diving trips for certified divers and scuba courses with a qualified instructor for beginners. Courses are available for adults and children aged between 8 - 12 years.

Location: Activities are available at four centres: Le Meridien Abu Dhabi, Khalidia Palace Hotel, Raha Beach Centre and Marine Sports Club Centre

Prices and Timings: Thurs 20:00 – 01:00, Arabic theme night party for Dhs.150. Fri 10:00 – 17:30, Family Day, Dhs.100 (adults) & Dhs.50 (kids between 6 - 12 years)

Dubai

Al Boom Diving

Location → Nr Iranian Hospital · Al Wasl Rd | 04 342 2993
Hours → 10:00 - 20:00
Web/email → www.alboommarine.com   Map Ref → 13-B2

Courses for all ages are offered here and are complemented by regular snorkelling and diving trips to various locations in the UAE and Oman. The Aqua Centre shop offers a range of equipment for rent and sale for small people and adults alike.

Courses: Bubblemaker course for 6 – 10, Dhs.250 for a lesson. Under 10's then progress to the Seal Team course, which includes 5 pools dives, for Dhs.1,000. The Open Junior Water course is for children age 10+ and consists of 5 theory sessions, 5 pool dives and 4 ocean dives, for Dhs.1,700

Pavilion Dive Centre

Location → Jumeirah Beach Htl · Umm Suqeim | 04 406 8827
Hours → 09:00 - 18:00
Web/email → www.jumeirahinternational.com   Map Ref → 12-A1

This PADI Gold Palm resort dive centre boasts its own marina, training pool, classrooms and beach frontage and offers the full range of PADI diving courses, from beginner to instructor.

Prices: Children aged 8 - 11 can get a basic introduction via the bubblemaker course; a series of half hour lessons at Dhs.150 each. 8 - 10 year olds can go for their first PADI certified course, 4 one and a half hour sessions, at a cost of Dhs.900. The next stage is the Discover Scuba dive course; 2 days, starting with an introduction in the pool and moving out to open water – Dhs.350

Scuba Dubai

Location → Trade Centre Apartments | 04 331 7433
Hours → 09:00 - 13:00 16:00 - 20:30 Thu 09:00 - 19:00
Web/email → www.scubadubai.com   Map Ref → 13-B3

PADI, BSAC and technical diving courses are taught here. Bubblemaker, for 6 – 8 year olds; 45 – 60 minute sessions, Dhs.60 a session. The Junior Open Water program is a certified PADI course; Dhs.1,700 for five one hour theory sessions, two pool dives and two half-day open water dives.

Contact: For more information phone Croydon on 050 551 8254

Scubatec

Location → Sana Bld · Al Karama | 04 334 8988
Hours → 09:00 - 13:30 16:00 - 20:30
Web/email → scubatec@emirates.net.ae   Map Ref → 13-D3

This five star IDC centre, licensed by PADI and TDI, offers instruction in Arabic, English, German or Urdu. They offer the Bubblemaker course for 8 - 10 year olds and the Open Water Junior course, priced at Dhs.1,500 for 5 theory sessions, 5 pool dives and 4 sea dives.

Khor Fakkan

7 Seas Divers

Location → Nr Khorfakkan Souk · Khorfakkan | 09 238 7400
Hours → 08:00 - 20:00
Web/email → www.7seasdivers.com   Map Ref → UAE-E2

This PADI five star IDC dive centre offers daily day and night trips to a variety of sites. Training is given from beginner to instructor level. 8 – 12 year olds can do the Bubblemaker course, and over 12s can join in the 'discover scuba' dive.

Dune Buggy Riding

This exhilarating sport of dune driving in small lightweight buggies is available in the Emirates for teenagers (15 years+). There are independent companies operating along the Dubai – Hatta road at the Big Red sand dune, and although rental from these companies is relatively cheap, less experienced drivers may find that tour operators are the safer option (see Desert Rangers [p.91]), as they provide basic training and constant supervision.

On yer quad bike

Fishing

Children love to fish and the shores on both coastlines of the UAE provide good beach and surf fishing. Fishing has become increasingly popular in recent years, and the UAE Government has introduced regulations to protect the fish stocks off the coast of the UAE. You will need to apply for a recreational fishing licence from the Municipality and fill out an application form. For more details contact the Municipality hotline (800 4567). This licence is free of charge and is well worth applying for because if you are caught fishing by the police without a licence you will be fined. As well as the beaches and lagoons, Jumeira beach front in Dubai is a good place – try the end of the promenade. The creek front in Creekside Park, Dubai is also a popular spot, as is the Breakwater in Abu Dhabi.

The more adventurous, with cash to spare, may consider deep sea fishing. Drinks are usually provided but check before you set off. The fishing season runs from September/October through to April, although it is still possible to catch sailfish and queenfish in the hot summer months. Fish commonly caught in the waters off the UAE include king mackerel, barracuda, tuna, trevally, bonito, kingfish, cobia and dorado or jacks. As you tend to go out for whole or half days, it may not be a suitable activity for younger children. Below is a table listing a few options for fishing trips - check with the individual company for any child age restrictions.

Fishing	
Abu Dhabi	
Al Dhafra	02 673 2266
Al Jazira Hotel & Resort	02 562 9100
Blue Dolphin Company LLC	02 666 9392
Le Meridien Abu Dhabi	02 644 6666
Palm Resort	02 677 3333
Dubai	
Bounty Charters	04 348 3042
Club Joumana	04 804 8058
Dubai Creek Golf & Yacht Club	04 295 6000
Fun Sports	04 399 5976
Le Meridien Mina Seyahi Beach Resort	04 399 3333
Yacht Solution	04 348 6838
Khor Fakkan	
Oceanic Hotel	09 238 5111

Football

Other options ➔ Sporting Goods [p.74]

Football is played, watched and loved all around the world and the UAE is no exception. It is also a great sport for kids to make friends and keep active.

Football coaching is widely available, particularly in Dubai, with many clubs and groups offering weekly lessons and regular mini tournaments. Abu Dhabi also has several football clubs in operation. And don't forget there are the parks and beaches, although check park rules first as some don't allow ball games. Various organised tournaments are great, giving children the chance to compete regularly in friendly events and helping to hone their skills.

Buy it like Beckham

Satwa in Dubai is a great place to find copy football strips for most of the major European and international teams. And you can iron your child's name on the back of the shirt with letters bought from the same shops at Dhs.1 each. Top, shorts, socks and a cap will set you back around Dhs.50 - 60. For the very keen, who may spot the difference, send home for the real thing or look up your favourite team's web site for mail order options.

Abu Dhabi

Abu Dhabi Nomads Club

Location → Various locations · Abu Dhabi | 02 672 4900
Hours → Timings on request
Web/email → shieldsy18@hotmail.com | Map Ref → 1-D3

The club trains and plays at Al Jazira Sports Club on Monday evenings. Although membership is currently at full capacity, they are always looking for new players of a good standard.

Contact: Alan Groves, Chairman (02 698 9246); David Shields, Secretary (050 446 8735).

E-sports Football Academy

Location → Various locations | 050 698 0048
Hours → Call for timings
Web/email → www.e-sportsdubai.com | Map Ref → na

E-sports offers football, tennis and swimming coaching, and runs the Advanced Centre of Excellence, at the Dubai Exiles club, as well as the Junior Football League, run in Abu Dhabi. View their website for full details of all their activities.

Dubai

Active Sports

Location → Various locations | 04 288 2773
Hours → Call for timings
Web/email → valkclm@emirates.net.ae | Map Ref → na

Active Sports offers Thursday morning football coaching in Safa Park, and other venues through the week for ages 4 – 12.

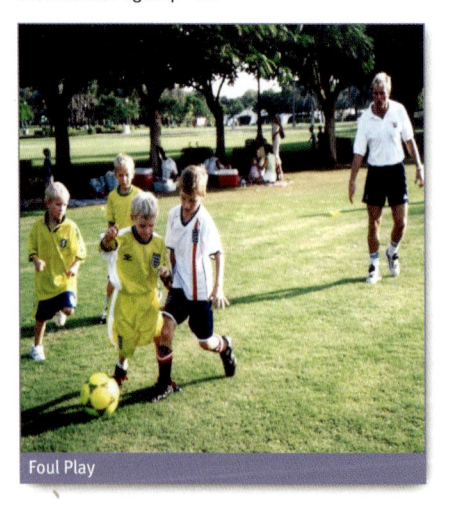

Foul Play

Dubai Country Club

Location → Nr Bu Kidra Interchange · Al Awir Rd | 04 333 1155
Hours → 08:00 - 22:00
Web/email → www.dubaicountryclub.com | Map Ref → 6-A2

The club runs coaching sessions for children, by age group, on Thursday mornings. five to ten year olds play from 9:00 to 13:00, and children over ten play from 15:30 to 18:00. Contact the club for details of their periodic tournaments, which usually coincide with school holidays.

LG InSportz

Location → Jct 3, Shk Zayed Rd · Shk Zayed Rd | 04 347 5833
Hours → 09:30 - 21:30
Web/email → www.insportzclub.com | Map Ref → 12-B2

Along with a variety of other sports, Insportz offers a complete football coaching programme for 6 – 11 year olds. They are based in Safa Park and also host indoor sessions at their air-conditioned facilities.

UAE English Soccer School of Excellence FZ-LLC

Location → Various locations · Dubai | 050 476 4877
Hours → Various
Web/email → masty57@hotmail.com | Map Ref → na

The training alternates between the five a side grass pitches and two polyurethane pitches. The academy trains children from 3 ½ - 13 years. There are a couple of 30 minute beginners' sessions and thereafter the programmed one-hour training sessions run daily, split by age groups.

Golf

Other options → Annual Events [p.22]

The UAE is widely known as the Gulf's premier golfing destination, with excellent year-round facilities and many important tournaments being held here. Dubai has a number of first class international courses which stand in stark contrast to the desert surroundings. However, there are also a number of brown (sand) courses which make for a novel game, and some that have both grass and sand (and not just in the bunkers!). On the international scene, Dubai is host to the Annual Desert Classic, which is part of the European PGA (Professional Golf Association) Tour. In Abu Dhabi, Al Ghazal Golf Club hosted the first World Sand Golf Championship in March 2004. This annual event will be held again in March 2005. There are also monthly local tournaments and annual competitions, which are open to all, such as the Emirates Mixed Amateur Open, the Emirates Ladies' Amateur Open (handicap of 21 or less), the Emirates Men's Amateur Open (handicap of 5 or less) and the Abu Dhabi Duty Free Medal.

Golf Pro

Abu Dhabi

Abu Dhabi Golf & Equestrian Club

Location → Al Tahnoon Street · Al Mushrif | 02 445 9600
Hours → 06:00 - 23:00
Web/email → www.adec-web.com   Map Ref → 3-D3

The Academy runs six week courses for juniors aged 5 - 16, dealing with all aspects of the game. There are also special junior open days to make sure the children are kept in the right group for their age and ability level.

Registration: Dhs.150 including a. T-shirt, cap and towel. Dhs.300 for six weeks' coaching, which includes a digi card (10 buckets of balls)

Abu Dhabi Golf Club by Sheraton

Location → Umm Al Nar St | 02 558 8990
Hours → 06:00 - 24:00
Web/email → www.adgolfsheraton.com   Map Ref → 1-A1

Facilities include two 18 hole par 72 grass courses, a driving range, putting and pitching greens and a golf academy. Junior Roll Up, every Thursday 15:00 to 16:00, allows juniors (nine years and under) to turn up for a one-hour coaching session, no booking required. Junior membership is available (under 16 years).

Junior membership: Dhs.1000 (annual); Dhs.600 (6 months); Dhs.350 (3 months)

Junior Roll Up: Dhs.10 (members); Dhs.15 (non-members)

Al Ghazal Golf Club

Location → Nr Abu Dhabi Int Airport · Abu Dhabi | 02 575 8040
Hours → 08:00 - 20:00
Web/email → golfclub@emirates.net.ae   Map Ref → na

Home to the World Sand Golf Championship, this 18 hole sand course and 9 hole grass course is situated 2 minutes away from the capital's airport. Facilities include a golf academy, driving range and licensed clubhouse. Junior membership is available (under 18 years) and no joining fee is required.

Junior membership: Dhs.660 per annum

Rotana Junior Golf League

Location → Golf & Equestrian Club · Al Mushrif | 02 445 9600
Hours → 06:00 - 22:30
Web/email → na   Map Ref → 3-D3

Kids can learn as members of the golf league from September to April. Tournaments are held on Thursday mornings and pre-coaching sessions are offered on Wednesdays at 16:00 for Dhs.20.

Prices: Membership – Dhs.100; Tournament Fees – Dhs.30 (3 hole) and Dhs.40 (9 hole)

Dubai

Dubai Country Club

Location → Nr Bu Kidra Interchange · Al Awir Rd | 04 333 1155
Hours → 08:00 - 22:00
Web/email → www.dubaicountryclub.com   Map Ref → 6-A2

An 18 hole sand course. Carry your own piece of fairway for driving up to the 'browns'. Browns are the sand course equivalent of greens and are regularly brushed to give them a true roll. The club also has a floodlit driving range. Individual lessons can be booked.

Dubai Creek Golf & Yacht Club

Location → Al Garhoud | 04 295 6000
Hours → 06:30 - 19:00
Web/email → www.dubaigolf.com   Map Ref → 15-D1

The newly renovated Creek course is set to open in January 2005, and will be a par 71 measuring around 6800 yards. The Academy provides professional instruction for all ages and abilities. Facilities include a hi-tech video swing analysis room and a 9 hole par 3 course. The Golf Academy runs an exstensive junior coaching programmes.

Prices: For details on junior coaching sessions contact the club

Emirates Golf Club

Location → Emirates Hills · Jct 5, Shk Zayed Rd	04 380 2222
Hours → 06:00 - 23:00	
Web/email → www.dubaigolf.com	Map Ref → 11-C2

World class practice and teaching facilities are combined with expert instruction to provide the perfect learning environment for all ages and levels of play. Golfing tots, aged 4 - 6 years, can learn the basics on the kindergarten course.

Prices: Ages 7 – 10 years, Dhs.850 for members and Dhs.900 for non-members. Ages 11 - 14 years, Dhs.950 for members and Dhs.1,050 for non member

Montgomerie Golf Club

Location → Emirates Hills	04 390 5600
Hours → 05:30 - 20:00	
Web/email → www.themontgomerie.com	Map Ref → 11-C2

The 18 hole par 72 course has the world's largest green. Practice facilities include a golf academy, driving range, short game and putting practice areas, a skill honing 9 hole par 3 course, plus a swing studio with state of the art swing analysis software.

Prices: Dhs.350 for the junior coaching programme for children ages 7+

Nad Al Sheba Club

Location → Nad Al Sheba	04 336 3666
Hours → 07:00 - 01:00	
Web/email → www.nadalshebaclub.com	Map Ref → na

This 18 hole floodlit links style course has professional coaches running the junior programme, offering group and individual lessons for all levels of ability from September throughout the school year. A ten week course is offered each term, suitable for children aged 6 - 16.

Prices: Dhs.795 for the ten week course, including a golf club which is made specifically for your child's height

UAE Golf Association

Location → Creek Golf Club · Al Garhoud	04 295 6440
Hours → 09:00 - 17:00	
Web/email → www.ugagolf.com	Map Ref → 15-D1

This non-profit organisation is the governing body for amateur golf in the UAE. Its aims are to make golf more affordable and accessible in the UAE, with a programme to support junior players and the development of the national team.

Prices: Affiliate membership starts at Dhs.200 per year. UGA membership runs from 1 Jan to 31 Dec

Jebel Ali

Club Joumana

Location → Jebel Ali Htl · Jebel Ali	04 804 8058
Hours → 06:00 - 21:00	
Web/email → www.jebelali-international.com	Map Ref → 10-A1

This 9 hole par 36 course is spikeless and includes a well-stocked pro-shop, floodlit driving range, instruction from PGA professionals, putting green and short game facilities. Junior coaching clinics are arranged for groups of 8 – 15 children, age 6+.

Prices: One to one sessions are priced at Dhs.130 for half an hour, Dhs.250 for a full hour. Visitors are welcome on a 'pay as you play' basis

Contact: For more information contact the above or Brad direct on 050 450 1536

Gymnastics

Most schools offer children the chance to enjoy gymnastics, either within school PE lessons or as an extracurricular activity in the afternoons or at weekends. Age Range 18m+.

Dubai

Dugym

Location → Various locations	050 553 6283
Hours → Call for timings	
Web/email → na	Map Ref → na

Suzanne Wallace and her team run gymnastics classes for children aged 18 months to 18 years. Dugym classes are held at the Dubai Country Club, the Ballet Centre and at several schools. Lessons are Dhs.30 per hour.

Recreational Gymnastics Club

Location → JESS · Al Wasl Rd	04 348 6590
Hours → 09:00 - 12:00 Thu 14:30 - 16:30	
Web/email → tonyruth@hotmail.com	Map Ref → 12-D2

Classes are held on Thursdays during term time. The children are divided into groups according to age and ability. Children between four and twelve years can register, no previous gymnastics experience is necessary. The cost is Dhs.30 per hour.

Reebok Fitkids	
Location → Various locations	050 768 1211
Hours → See below	
Web/email → na	Map Ref → na

Kerrie Campbell runs gymnastics classes on Thursdays, for 4 - 7 year olds at the Ballet Centre, 09:00 - 09:45, and for 8 -11 year olds at JESS, 17:30 - 18:15. Six week courses cost Dhs.150.

Hockey

Other options → Ice Hockey [p.100]

This popular British game isn't played in the local schools, but enthusiasts can join a club to take part in this enjoyable and challenging social sport.

Abu Dhabi

Abu Dhabi Hockey Club	
Location → Various locations	02 674 4410
Hours → Timings on request	
Web/email → na	Map Ref → na

The club takes part in various tournaments held each year in Abu Dhabi, Dubai and Sharjah. The club is usually able to field men's, women's and mixed teams, depending on what tournament is being played. They also run a mini hockey league. For further details contact Manish on the above number or on 050 621 0534.

Dubai

Darjeeling Hockey Club	
Location → Darjeeling Cricket Club · Al Awir Rd	04 333 1746
Hours → 20:00 - 22:00	
Web/email → darjeelinghockey@hotmail.com	Map Ref → na

Members range from ex professionals to complete beginners (coaching is available), all are welcome. Team players are both men and women. Generally over 18s play, but a keen and talented teenager would be welcome to go along.

Prices: Annual membership of the hockey section is Dhs.650 per playing member; Dhs.250 per social member.

Horse Riding

Other options → Annual Events [p.22]

Horse riding is a popular activity in the Emirates for adults and children. See the shopping section for advice on tack and where to buy it (see Sporting Goods [p.74]). Pony rides are an easier introduction to riding for little ones, and also a pleasant way for them to come into contact with animals they can pet.

Giddy-Up

Abu Dhabi

Abu Dhabi Equestrian Club	
Location → Nr Immigration Office · Al Mushrif	02 445 5500
Hours → Timings on request	
Web/email → na	Map Ref → 3-D3

The riding club offers comprehensive instruction from beginner to jumping, endurance desert riding and stable management courses. All levels of riders are welcome – the starting age is 5 years and up. Riding gear is compulsory.

Prices: Dhs.50 for one hour

Dubai

Emirates Riding Centre	
Location → Nr Camel Race Track · Nad Al Sheba	04 336 1394
Hours → See timings below	
Web/email → emrc@emirates.net.ae	Map Ref → na

The centre has 147 horses and facilities include an international sized floodlit arena, riding school and dressage arenas as well as a lunging ring. Training in show jumping, dressage and musical dressage is offered. Trail rides and hacks are also available.

Lesson timings: Summer 06:30 - 08:30 and 17:00 - 19:00. Winter 07:00 - 10:00 and 16:00 - 18:00. Rides for little ones are available every afternoon from 16:30, at a cost of Dhs.15 for ten minutes (cost includes hat)

Jebel Ali Equestrian Club

Location → Jebel Ali Village · Jebel Ali | 04 884 5485
Hours → 08:00 - 11:30 16:00 - 19:00 Fri closed
Web/email → na | Map Ref → 10-E3

A range of services are offered to children and adults. Beginners can learn to ride here and for the more experienced, hacking, dressage and jumping are offered. Group lessons, packages and private lessons are available, and the registration fee per rider is Dhs.120, or Dhs.300 per family.

Jebel Ali

Club Joumana

Location → Jebel Ali Htl · Jebel Ali | 04 804 8058
Hours → 06:00 - 21:00
Web/email → www.jebelali-international.com | Map Ref → 10-A1

The riding centre has five horses, an outdoor arena and keeps livery on request. Individual half hour lessons and one hour desert rides are available. The riding instructor is available for lessons from Tuesday to Sunday, between October and June each year.

Ice Hockey

Ice hockey has grown as a popular team sport for youngsters in the UAE. It's a great way to burn off some energy, as it is quite physically demanding, although you might have to face the odd sprained or broken bone!

Abu Dhabi

Abu Dhabi Falcons Ice Hockey

Location → Abu Dhabi Ice Rink · Old Airport Rd | 02 446 1788
Hours → See website
Web/email → www.abufalcons.com | Map Ref → 2-B1

Dedicated to the development of youth ice hockey in a fun and safe environment, the club has a youth league with three teams that participate in local tournaments. Hockey camps are held annually for boys and girls, with professional coaches flown in from Canada.

Contacts: Club President, Vincent Saubestre on the above number

Dubai

Dubai Junior Ice Hockey

Location → Al Nasr Leisureland · Oud Metha | 04 348 2702
Hours → 17:00 - 19:30 Sat & Sun
Web/email → chadwick@emirates.net.ae | Map Ref → 13-E4

Started five years ago and now boasting a membership of 94 children between the ages of 6 and 17, the club runs practice sessions from September to April. Highlights include mini hockey camps where participants receive training from professional Canadian coaches.

Prices: Currently Dhs.450 (subject to change)

Dubai Sandstorms Junior Ice Hockey Club

Location → Al Nasr Club | 04 344 1885
Hours → 17:30 - 21:00
Web/email → na | Map Ref → 13-E4

This club was established to provide boys and girls (6 - 18 years) with the opportunity to learn ice hockey. The emphasis is on participation, teamwork and sportsmanship. No previous experience is necessary since participants are placed in teams based on their age, size and level of skill. The season runs from mid September to mid May, with practices held twice a week. Throughout the season, matches are played against Dubai, Abu Dhabi, Al Ain and Oman teams, with an international tournament scheduled for March each year. The registration fee of Dhs.600 includes an ice hockey jersey, and covers all practices and games during the season.

Age Range: 6+

Ice Skating

Other options → Ice Hockey [p.100]

Ice skating may seem an odd choice in the middle of the desert but it's great fun, not to mention a useful skill base for other cool sports like roller-blading and skiing. The younger they start, the nearer they are to the ground, making the inevitable falls easier to take!

The ice skating rinks in both Abu Dhabi and Dubai are excellent venues at any time of the year and an obvious option in the hotter months. Don't forget to take sweaters, as the rinks are cold. It's also a good idea to take your own socks, rather than having to buy them specially. Refer to the Birthday Parties section for details on individual ice rinks [p.150].

Jet Skiing

Other options → Beach Clubs [p.119]

The sight of jet skis at the first lagoon between Dubai and Sharjah, near Al Mamzar Beach Park, or near Al Garhoud Bridge, on the opposite side of the bridge to Dubai Creek Golf & Yacht Club is common. Most are available for hire at approximately Dhs.100 for half an hour. Many hotels also have jet skis for hire.

Note that a 1998 law limits jet skiers to within a 500 metre boundary from the shore, with the threat of legal action for exceeding this limit. With all the aquatic traffic, you may find the waters of Dubai Creek a little murky, and other locations offer a cleaner environment, as well as stricter controls and better safety records.

Abu Dhabi

Al Jazira Hotel and Resort	
Location → Ghantoot Area	02 562 9100
Hours → Timings on request	
Web/email → na	Map Ref → na

Safety is a top priority here - you are connected to the jet ski by a safety chord, which stops the engine once it's disconnected. This, and wearing a life jacket, helps prevent accidents. Prices start at Dhs.50 for 15 minutes (speeds of up to 40kmph are possible).

Dubai

Fun Sports	
Location → Various locations, see below	04 399 5976
Hours → 09:00 - 17:00	
Web/email → www.funsport-dubai.com	Map Ref → na

Fun Sports is one of the leading water sports companies in Dubai. Their huge range of activities includes fishing, sailing, windsurfing, wakeboarding, jetskiing, knee boarding, banana rides, kayaking, power boat rides, parasailing and sunset cruising.

Karting

Other options → Dune Buggy Riding [p.94]

Karting tends to be a favourite with most kids. It isn't really restricted by age, although a child must be able to reach the pedals to take part.

Abu Dhabi

Leisure Games Centre	
Location → Nr Tourist Club · Tourist Club Area	02 679 3330
Hours → See timings below	
Web/email → saeed-lgc@hotmail.com	Map Ref → 4-B3

The track has several features, including an electronic circuit timer, two hairpin bends, a U-turn and straights. Training is provided each week, targeting different age groups, from 7 - 50 year olds. The karts are fitted with two stroke engines (200cc, 250cc and 390cc).

Prices: Dhs.30 for 10 minutes on the track. If you find yourself hooked on the sport, you can buy your own kart for Dhs.9,000

Timings: Weekdays 09:00 - 12:00 & 17:00 - 24:00; Wed, Thu & Fri 09:00 - 12:00 & 16:00 - 01:00

Dubai

Formula One Dubai	
Location → Dubai Exiles Rugby Club · Dubai	04 338 8828
Hours → 15:00 - 22:00	
Web/email → f1dubai@emirates.net.ae	Map Ref → 15-C1

F1 Dubai offers a range of racing opportunities for kids and adults. The outdoor short circuit is approximately 400 metres in length and the long circuit, 750 metres. They also cater for children's parties, full supervision is provided.

Age: 8+ (Adults 12+)

Prices: Dhs.40 per child (10 min) ; Dhs.50 per adult (10 min)

Kite Flying

With so much open space here and few obstacles (such as trees) to restrict flight kite flying has become popular. Just watch out for people when the wind is strong and never fly a kite near an overhead electric pylon. Most good toy shops sell kites. The Hobby Centre in Dubai is particularly good, refer to Toys & Games in the Shopping section [p.78].

Kite Surfing

Other options → Windsurfing [p.118]

In this relatively new sport which verges on the extreme, you harness the power of the wind to achieve high speeds and jump high over waves. Faster than windsurfing, it is a dangerous sport for many an over-confident, under-wary or just plain unlucky participant so it is better to start with a few lessons. You can connect with other kite surfers, and find out more about the sport, by visiting the website of the official UAE kite surfing association (http://groups.msn.com/uaekitesurf/welcome.msnw). There are two or three dedicated beaches you should head for. Avoid areas where there are swimmers or other water sports.

Martial Arts

A number of martial arts disciplines are available in Dubai and Abu Dhabi, teaching all ages from the very young through to adults. For shy children it gives them a well deserved confidence boost and for boisterous kids it is a good arena for learning discipline and self-control.

Mortal Combat

Abu Dhabi

Baroudy's Sports Club

Location → Golden Tower · Corniche | 02 626 8122
Hours → 09:00 - 21:00
Web/email → tbaroudy@hotmail.com   Map Ref → na

This club teaches taekwondo, which embraces the traditional beliefs of honour, integrity, loyalty and compassion. Not only is it a form of self-defence, but also it improves physical fitness, mental discipline, self-control, concentration, timing and emotional calmness. The club also runs a children's summer camp.

Contact: Tony Baroudy on the above number or 050 621 4399

Emirates Sports Centre

Location → Tourist Club Area | 02 676 6757
Hours → 09:00 - 13:00 16:00 - 21:30
Web/email → na   Map Ref → 4-C3

Lessons in karate and kung fu are available, conducted by experienced instructors. There are separate classes for ladies, children and girls. They will also arrange grading sessions with certificates issued from their international headquarters in Malaysia to successful candidates. Contact Mr Hamid on the above number for more information.

Prices: Starting from Dhs.100 per week (2 lessons); Dhs.250 (6 lessons)

Golden Dragon Kung Fu Institute

Location → Airport Rd | 02 632 5109
Hours → 08:00 - 13:00 16:00 - 22:00 Fri 17:00 - 21:00
Web/email → luhuiming@hotmail.com   Map Ref → 4-C3

The focus is on basic Shaolin arts including Shaolin fist, stick, knife, sword and spear play and southern fists. Ladies and children have an experienced female coach who teaches Tai Chi, Shaolin, self-defence and varieties of kung fu.

Oriental Karate & Kobudo Club

Location → Tourist Club Area | 02 677 1611
Hours → Timings on request
Web/email → www.orientalkarate.com   Map Ref → 4-B3

The chief instructor at this club is Sensei Ali Mohammed who's a 5th dan in karate and a 4th dan in kobudo martial arts. He offers separate sessions for adults and children, for all levels of ability and age. Lessons are held at various places around Abu Dhabi, and transport is available for children upon request.

Locations: Madinat Zayed (02 634 5080); Airport Road (02 445 7375); Khalifa Street (02 622 4182)

Prices: Dhs.100 per month (2 classes per week)

Dubai

Ballet Centre, The

Location → Behind Jumeira Plaza · Jumeira | 04 344 9776
Hours → 09:00 - 12:30 15:00 - 18:30
Web/email → na   Map Ref → 13-B2

Abdurahiman (7th Dan black belt) teaches taekwondo for beginner, intermediate and advanced levels. This form of martial arts teaches children mental calmness, courage, strength, humility, integrity, perseverance and self-control. Classes are of one hour duration.

Dubai Aikido Club

Location → Dubai Karate Centre · Al Wasl Rd
Hours → See timings below
Web/email → www.aikido-uae.net
04 344 4156
Map Ref → 13-A2

Dubai Aikido Club was established in 1995 and is affiliated to the Aikikai Aikido world headquarters, Japan and to the Aikido Association International, USA. For further information contact John Rutnam, Chief Instructor.

Timings: Classes are held on Sunday and Tuesday 17:30 - 18:30 for children and families and 19:30 - 21:30 for the general public

Dubai Karate Centre

Location → Nr Emirates Bank · Al Wasl Rd
Hours → See timings below
Web/email → na
04 344 7797
Map Ref → 13-A2

A team of black belt, JKA qualified instructors teach a style of karate called shotokan, as well as aikido and judo. They offer tuition from beginner to black belt for anyone aged six years and above.

Timings: Courses are held on Saturday, Monday and Wednesday evenings between 17:00 - 19:00, depending on experience, and the fees include three sessions a week

Prices: Dhs.100 initial registration fee, then Dhs.200 monthly membership fee. Uniforms cost Dhs.100 from the club

Golden Falcon Karate Centre

Location → Behind Sony Jumbo · Al Karama
Hours → 08:30 - 12:00 16:30 - 22:30
Web/email → www.goldenfalconkarate.com
04 336 0243
Map Ref → 13-D4

Affiliated to the Karate Budokan International and the UAE Judo, Taekwondo and Karate Federation, classes in judo, taekwondo and fitness are held according to demand. Call instructors Suresh and Sathian for further details.

Jumeirah Beach Club

Location → Nr Jumeira Beach Park · Jumeira
Hours → Sat & Wed 08:00
Web/email → www.jumeirahbeachclub.com
04 344 5333
Map Ref → 12-E1

The children's monthly activity programme includes karate and taekwondo instruction for the over fives. Classes last for one hour and are held on various afternoons at a cost of Dhs.25 per lesson. Open to non-members.

Mini Golf

Other options → Golf [p.96]

Mini golf has all the appeal of formal golf, but without the seriousness! It is a great activity for families.

Dubai

Aviation Club, The

Location → Nr Tennis Stadium · Al Garhoud
Hours → 06:00 - 23:00
Web/email → www.aviationclubonline.com
04 282 4122
Map Ref → 15-D1

The 9 hole, par 27 pitch and putt course is open to members only. A series of Junior Golf Tournaments are scheduled throughout the year with events for the under 8s, under 12s and under 16s, which are open to all.

Hyatt Golf Park

Location → Hyatt Regency · Deira
Hours → 15:30 - 23:00
Web/email → www.dubai.hyatt.com
04 209 6741
Map Ref → 5-B1

Hyatt Golf Park has a nine hole pitch and putt grass golf course and also an 18 hole crazy golf course. Clubs are provided and golf balls can be purchased for Dhs.8 each. The park is floodlit in the evenings.

Prices: pitch and putt: one round Dhs.15, two rounds Dhs.25; crazy golf: Dhs.10 per person (ball and club included)

Hatta

Hatta Fort Hotel

Location → 110Km from Dubai ·
Hours → Timings on request
Web/email → www.jebelali-international.com
04 852 3211
Map Ref → UAE-D3

This popular out-of-town hotel offers a choice of mini golf or a nine hole cross country fun golf course. Each hole is par 3, ranging from 68 to 173 yards. Golf instruction and lessons are available.

Prices: Day visitors on Fridays and public holidays purchase a voucher at the entrance (Dhs.40 for adults, Dhs.20 for children), which is redeemable against hotel facilities, including lunch

Moto-Cross

Other options → Karting [p.101]

From four years and above, young daredevils can race in the Pee Wee division, while the main junior class is for those aged eight and above. Chances are high that Dad – and the odd Mum - will be interested and take the little ones along!

Abu Dhabi

Abu Dhabi MX Club

Location → Various locations | 02 634 5527
Hours → Timings on request
Web/email → na | Map Ref → na

MX race classes are organised in Umm Al Quwain and Dubai for all skill levels, and both boys and girls are welcome to join. Enthusiastic beginners can initially borrow a bike, helmet, etc, although availability may be limited depending on the day.

Contact: Klaus Schwingenschloegl on 050 612 4614
Prices: Annual Fee – Dhs.350 family; Dhs.250 individual

Dubai

Dubai Youth Moto-Cross Club

Location → Various locations | 04 333 0659
Hours → Timings on request
Web/email → www.dubaimotocross.ae | Map Ref → na

This active club operates two tracks; a junior and cadet track for riders aged up to ten years, and a senior track for 80cc and 125cc riders. Riders are graded by age and ability, with beginners as young as five competing.

Contact: For more information contact Shaun Whitley (050 553 7812) or visit the above website

Mountain Biking

Although parts of the Emirates offer challenging terrain for keen mountain bikers, there are some areas where younger cyclists can go biking, especially in the wadis and mud flats north of Abu Dhabi and Dubai. Popular flat areas run along the coastline from Ajman to north of Umm al Quwain and you can see many tracks as you drive along the road to Ras Al Khaimah. Stay on the well established routes and take time to enjoy the beautiful bird life that can be seen here. Always make sure that you know where you are going, stick to the tracks, take plenty of water and protect yourself from the sun. It's also advisable for the whole family to wear proper cycling helmets.

Dubai

Biking Frontiers

Location → Various locations | 050 450 9401
Hours → Timings on request
Web/email → www.bikingfrontiers.com | Map Ref → na

All competent mountain bikers are welcome. Your own bike, helmet and proper gear are essential. The group also enjoys camping, hiking and barbecues.

Contact: Paul or Pete via the above Website

Desert Rangers

Location → Dubai Garden Centre · Shk Zayed Rd | 04 340 2408
Hours → 08:30 - 14:30
Web/email → www.desertrangers.com | Map Ref → 12-A2

Whether you're a fanatical biker craving challenging terrain, or a complete beginner preferring a gentler introduction to the delights of off road biking, Desert Rangers will determine a suitable route depending on your requirements and group size.

Cost: Dhs.300 per person, inclusive of bike, helmet, guide, pick up and drop off and soft drinks

Mountain Biking

Netball

This popular sport is enjoyed by many young girls at school level, and there is also a thriving social league in the Emirates. It's a good team sport that can be enjoyed right through to adulthood.

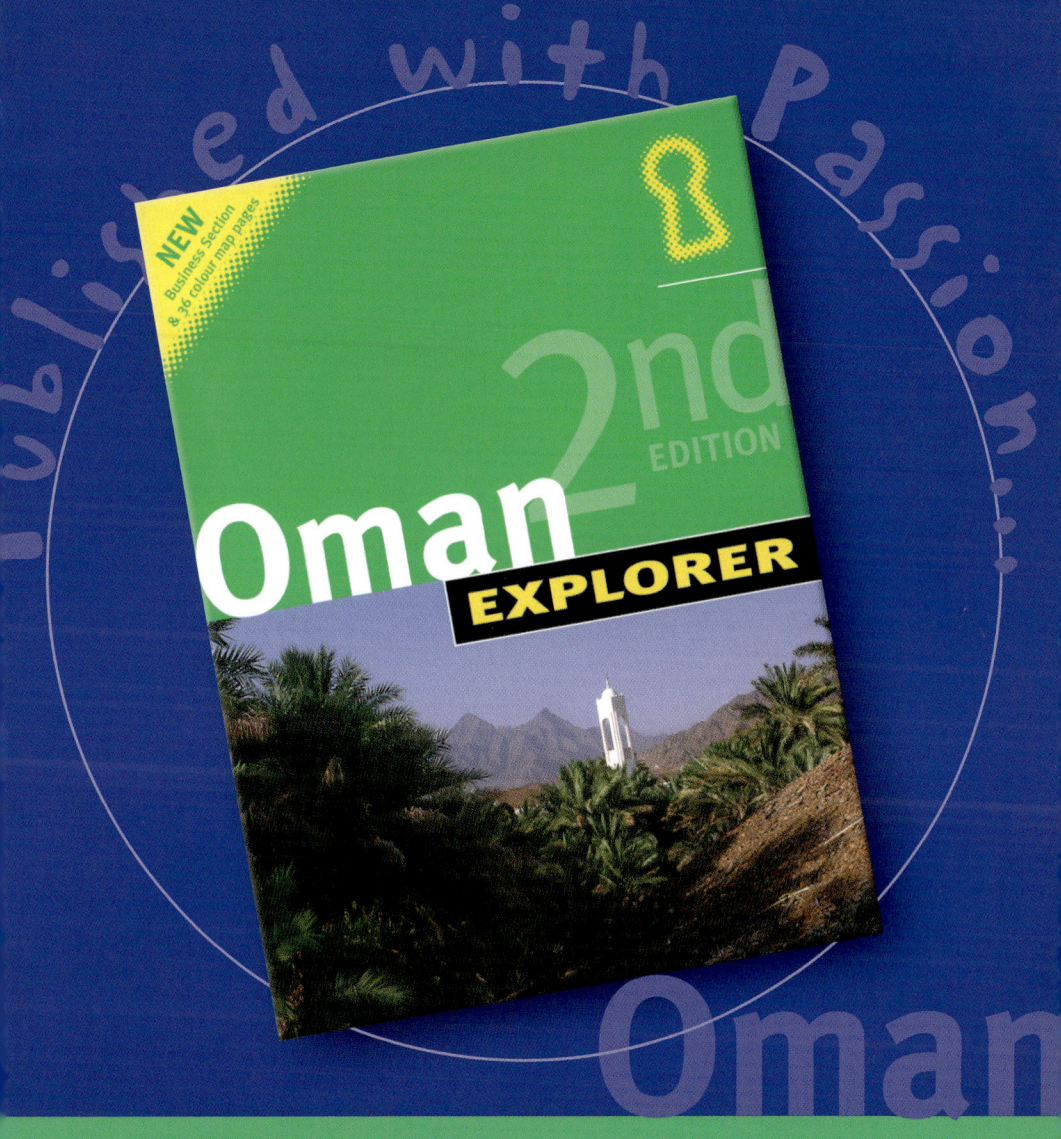

Life's a journey... take a guide

Ain't no mountain high enough (even the Hajar) or river wide enough (even the Wadi Bani Khalid) to keep us from bringing this book to you. From Arabian charm to the call of the wilderness, get ready to explore. It's Oman, it's breathtaking and it's time you bought this book.

Only available at the best bookstores with the right attitude, as well as hotels, supermarkets, hardware stores or directly from Explorer Publishing.

Passionately Publishing...

Phone (971 4) 335 3520 • Fax (971 4) 335 3529 • Email Info@Explorer-Publishing.com
Insiders' City Guides • Photography Books • Activity Guidebooks • Commissioned Publications • Distribution

EXPLORER
www.Explorer-Publishing.com

Abu Dhabi

Abu Dhabi Down Netball League

Location → Various locations | 050 536 3821
Hours → Call for timings
Web/email → na   Map Ref → UAE-A3

There is a junior team (girls aged 13 and above) that plays in the league, they practice on Saturday evenings and play matches on Tuesday evenings. For further information please contact Natalie.

Dubai

Dubai Netball League

Location → Dubai Exiles Club · Al Awir Rd | 050 450 6715
Hours → Wed 18:30 - 22:30
Web/email → na   Map Ref → 6-A2

There are over 15 teams divided into three divisions. Players range from teenagers to grandmothers, and beginners to experts. Games are played from September to May on Wednesday nights. Team training is on a Sunday or Monday night. Contact Sandra, afternoons only.

Paintballing

This combat activity is currently only available in Dubai. For children and adults alike, it's a thrilling way to release stress. This team game involves trying to shoot your opponents, and thus eliminate them, with air guns that fire pellets of water-soluble dye. Protective clothing is provided. Battle tactics are vital! Ideal for ages 10+.

Dubai

Pursuit Games

Location → WonderLand · Umm Hurair (2) | 04 324 1222
Hours → Timiings on request
Web/email → wonderld@emirates.net.ae   Map Ref → 15-C1

You need a minimum of six players (maximum 40). For further information, contact Kaz on 050 651 4583. An adult must accompany children between 10 - 12 years.

Prices: Dhs.70 for a typical two hour game with 100 paintballs, gun and gas. An extra 100 paintballs costs Dhs.50

Plane Tours

Live the high life and see the Emirates from the skies with a flight along the coast, stopping for breakfast in another Emirate. You can buy a gift voucher for a flight - an unusual birthday gift for that friend who already has everything!

Fujairah

Fujairah Aviation Centre

Location → Fujairah Int Airport · Fujairah | 09 222 4747
Hours → Timings on request
Web/email → www.fujairah-aviation.ae   Map Ref → UAE-E2

Flights last from 30 minutes (at Dhs.100 per person) to four hours which will enable you to see almost the entire UAE. A longer tour for 1 - 3 people costs Dhs.480 per hour. The following are some suggested itineraries, although the pilots can prepare other routes especially for you.

Scenic Flight 1: Fujairah – Dibba – Masafi – Fujairah

Scenic Flight 2: Fujairah – Hatta – Al Dhaid – Masafi – Fujairah

Scenic Flight 3: Fujairah – Al Ain – Abu Dhabi – Dubai – Sharjah – Ajman – Umm Al Quwain – Ras Al Khaimah – Dibba – Fujairah

> **Pre Flight Checks**
>
> A trip to the toilet before boarding is advisable for younger flyers. Young ones should drink during take off and landing to ensure that their little ears don't get blocked. Always have drinks in your hand luggage, and a back up supply of sweeties should be relied upon to make them swallow!

Play Centres

Other options → **Play Centres - Birthday Parties [p.159]**

All the main shopping malls have play centres or areas offering a variety of entertainment for children, and are a popular hangout for mums and tots during weekday mornings, and for young school children in the afternoons and at weekends. You generally pay for an hour or two's play, and while some centres also offer pay as you go machines once inside, toddlers are generally happy to just play in the soft play/ball pit areas. Some centres also provide organised morning activities, like Sand Art, at around Dhs.10, which is always a big hit with little ones. At many of the centres, supervision is good enough for you to leave children over four years of age to amuse themselves, whilst you go shopping or relax. You leave your mobile number and the staff contact you if your child needs you. For details on individual play centres refer to the Birthday Party section [p.159].

Rollerblading

Other options ➔ Beaches [p.122]

This exciting sport is great fun and good exercise – many parks provide excellent locations for roller blading. Both the Corniche and Breakwater in Abu Dhabi have long paved areas and the spectacular view is an added bonus! In Dubai, try Creek Park and Safa Park for smooth, wide pathways with few people and enough slopes and turns to make it interesting, or along the promenade at Jumeira beach front, where you have the additional benefit of the superb scenery. Age range 7+

Rugby

Other options ➔ Annual Events [p.22]

With Dubai on the Rugby 7s circuit the UAE has a special fondness for this gentleman's 'bit of rough' sport. It is also popular with school boys of all nationalities, both to play and watch. Many schools offer rugby either as part of the curriculum or as an after-school activity.

It's MY Ball!

Abu Dhabi

Abu Dhabi Rugby Football Club

Location ➔ Madinat Zayed · Abu Dhabi	050 662 3069
Hours ➔ Timings on request	
Web/email ➔ na	Map Ref ➔ 4-A3

The mini section currently has over 200 kids turning up to the weekly training sessions. Games are played at the Military Stadium, with after match activities taking place at the Crowne Plaza Hotel. Players and non-players of all skill levels are welcome.

Contacts: Club Captain, Aubrey Roberts (050 662 3069); Ladies Coach, Clare Shryane (050 626 1661); Riaan Smuts (050 536 3718), for minis and youth

Dubai

Dubai Exiles Rugby Club

Location ➔ Nr Dubai Country Club · Al Awir Rd	04 333 1198
Hours ➔ 08:00 - 22:00 Timings on request	
Web/email ➔ www.dubaiexiles.com	Map Ref ➔ 6-A2

Training sessions are scheduled throughout the week with the 1st and 2nd XVs meeting on Sundays and Wednesdays and veterans on Tuesdays and Saturdays. There's also training for children (the minis, age range 7 - 16) on Mondays and Wednesdays. Sessions begin in September and run until mid April.

Running

For over half the year, the weather couldn't be better for running in the Emirates, and you'll find dedicated runners clocking up the miles all over the UAE. In the hottest months, the evenings, and the early mornings especially, are the best times to be out.

If you or your child are seriously interested in the sport, then there are a number of clubs and informal groups that meet regularly to run together, with some runs being competitive or training runs, for the variety of events organised throughout the year. Regular short distance races are held, as well as a variety of biathlons, triathlons, duathlons and hashes, which provide a reasonably full and varied schedule.

Two of the more popular races are the 'Round the Creek' relay race and the epic Wadi Bih Run. For the latter, teams of five run the 70 km from Ras Al Khaimah on the west coast to Dibba on the east, over mountains topping out at over 1,000 metres. Runners take turns to run different stages with a support vehicle and this event, held annually, attracts up to 300 participants. The Dubai Marathon, held in January, is growing in popularity. The Marathon is run in conjunction with a 10km road race and a 3km charity race. The Terry Fox Run, held annually in aid of cancer research, is particularly popular with families and all are welcome, from serious runners to mums with prams and tots on trikes!

Contacts: Wadi Bih race, John Gregory (050 647 7120) or arabex. Terry Fox Run: www.terryfox.com. Dubai Marathon: www.dubaimarathon.org

Abu Dhabi

Abu Dhabi Striders	
Location → Various locations	050 441 4886
Hours → 18:00 Wed	
Web/email → na	Map Ref → na

Members are from all walks of life and standards of fitness. At each training session a choice of 3, 5, 8, 10 and 15 km courses are marked out. Predict your time for your chosen distance; walk/run against the clock; and the runner closest to their prediction wins a prize.

Contacts: Ash (050 692 8601) or Steve Reay on the above number

Dubai

Dubai Road Runners	
Location → Safa Park · Al Wasl	04 394 1996
Hours → Sat 18:30	
Web/email → www.dubai-road-runners.com	Map Ref → 3-D2

The objective is to run either a 3.5 km or 7 km track around the park. A Dhs.5 entrance fee is charged, and most people try to run this standard course against the clock. The club also organises competitions and social events.

Contact: Graham Rafferty (050 624 3213)

Sailing

Other options → Annual Events [p.22]

In winter, the temperatures are perfect for sailing and water sports in general, while in the summer you can escape some of the scorching heat that prohibits other land-based sports. Sailing is a popular pastime in Dubai, with many people being members of one of the sailing clubs on Jumeira Beach or Al Mina Al Siyahi. Membership of the clubs generally allows you to use the leisure facilities, the club's beach, to join in the activities, rent sailing and water sports equipment, and moor or store your boat (always an extra cost!).

Children can start messing about in their parents' boats from a very young age, building up their confidence in the water. They tend to learn to swim early here, but even the most confident swimmers should still wear life jackets. An interested child could probably start lessons from the age of six. There's quite a healthy racing scene for a variety of classes of boat and competitors are welcome to take part from any age, depending on their competency.

If you prefer not to take the reigns, many companies will take you out on a cruise, either for a couple of hours or for a full day, for pleasure or for fishing.

Abu Dhabi

Abu Dhabi Catamaran Association	
Location → Hiltonia Beach Resort · Corniche	02 443 5339
Hours → Timings on request	
Web/email → na	Map Ref → 4-D3

The association offers advice to prospective owners, access to spare parts, tools, and lots of friendly 'know how' to all levels of sailor. In addition, there's a social club with many racing get-togethers and outings. Membership fees are reasonable and new members are always welcome.

Contact: Commodore Kingsley Ashford-Brown on the above number

Abu Dhabi Sailing Club	
Location → The Club · Al Meena	02 673 1111
Hours → Mon & Thu	
Web/email → www.the-club.com	Map Ref → 4-A3

The Club supports three fleets, and boats are syndicated to members who qualify as helms. They are then responsible for its maintenance and seaworthiness. Organised races are held on most Monday and Thursday afternoons, while Fridays are generally for cruising.

Membership: Abu Dhabi Sailing Club is now a sub-section of The Club. ADSC members must also be members of The Club. Annual fee for membership of the sub-section is Dhs.950

Dubai

Dubai Offshore Sailing Club	
Location → Beach Rd, Jumeira	04 394 1669
Hours → 09:00 - 17:00	
Web/email → www.dosc.org	Map Ref → 12-C1

Children's sailing day is every Thursday with water based games and activities in the morning and sailing in the afternoon. Young sailors (5+ years)

are taught to rig and handle optimists, toppers and lasers. Holiday camps combine sailing with one or two nights camping.

Fun Sports

Location → Various locations, see below | 04 399 5976
Hours → 09:00 - 17:00
Web/email → www.funsport-dubai.com | Map Ref → na

Offering multi-hull sailing, with professional sailing instructors available to teach beginners and improvers. For bookings contact Suzette on the above number or 050 453 4828.

Locations: The company operates at the following beach clubs: Hilton Dubai Jumeirah, Metropolitan Resort & Beach Club, Oasis Beach Hotel, Ritz-Carlton Beach Club and Le Meridien Mina Seyahi

Jebel Ali Sailing Club

Location → Al Sufouh | 04 399 5444
Hours → 09:00 - 20:00   Thu & Fri 09:00 - 22:00
Web/email → www.jebelalisailingclub.com | Map Ref → 2-C1

Courses of four weeks duration include sailing, windsurfing, power boating and kayaking. The cadet club (8 -15 year olds) provides water and land based activities, and is generally held on Thursday mornings, but also has climbing, hiking and overnight camping.

Timings: With prior booking school groups can learn to sail on Sunday, Monday and Tuesday mornings. Tuesdays between 09:00 - 12:00 are for ladies only

Contact: Sharon Allison or Colin Slowey

Sand Boarding/Skiing

Other options → Tour Operators [p.140]

It might not be as glamorous as snow but sand skiing can still be great fun. It's a quick sport to learn and it doesn't hurt when you fall. One of the favourite areas is the huge dune affectionately known as 'Big Red', which is half way to Hatta, on the left by the main road.

Boards are usually standard snowboards but, as the sand is quite hard on them, they often can't then be used for snowboarding. Some sports stores sell 'sand boards', which are cheaper and more basic. As an alternative for children, a plastic sledge or something similar is enough to give a lot of fun.

All the major tour companies take tours to sand board the highest dunes and offer basic instruction on how to stay up, how to surf and how to fall properly! This can be available either as part of another tour or as a dedicated sand boarding tour. A half-day sand boarding tour costs Dhs.175 - 200. See Desert Rangers [p.91] for details.

Snorkelling

Other options → Diving [p.93]

With children learning to swim from as young as three, snorkelling can be a fun, as well as educational, activity for kids of all ages (depending upon their swimming ability). On the East Coast, the well known Snoopy Island, opposite the Sandy Beach Motel, and Sharque Island in the Bay of Khorfakkan, offer great snorkelling opportunities at shallow depths. Young swimmers are guaranteed to see pretty corals, sea cucumbers, colourful fish and sea urchins. At low tide you can walk to Snoopy Island, alternatively you need to swim. Sharque Island is only accessible by boat.

> **Snorkelling Safety**
>
> In shallow waters, be careful where you put your feet so as not to damage the coral and watch out for sea urchins.
>
> Also to avoid sunburn on unsuspecting shoulders, children should wear a UV suit or t-shirt, not forgetting suncream all over. T-shirts also help to avoid jellyfish stings. Wear plastic shoes or sandals in the shallows when exploring the islands. The rocks can be sharp on tender feet!

Young children tend to feel more confident about snorkelling from the shore, where they can get to a place where they can put their feet down, than from the side of a boat. This is something to bear in mind if you are booking a holiday; look out for a house reef that is easily accessible.

Abu Dhabi

Blue Dolphin Company LLC

Location → Htl Inter-Continental · Bainuna St | 02 666 9392
Hours → 08:00 - 13:00   16:00 - 19:00
Web/email → www.interconti.com | Map Ref → 5-D3

Snorkelling equipment can be hired per person or alternatively, the company can arrange group trips to snorkelling areas, such as off Ras Al Ghurb Island.

Prices: Equipment rental Dhs.50 per day

Dubai

Al Boom Diving

Location → Nr Iranian Hospital · Al Wasl Rd | 04 342 2993
Hours → 10:00 - 20:00
Web/email → www.alboommarine.com   Map Ref → 13-B2

Al Boom Diving offers opportunities for snorkelling on the East Coast. Equipment is available for sale, alternatively hire a full set for the day for Dhs.50, or you can hire items individually for Dhs.20 (fins, mask and snorkel). They also offer kayaking.

Scuba Dubai

Location → Trade Centre Apartments | 04 331 7433
Hours → 09:00 - 13:00 16:00 - 20:30 Thu 09:00 - 19:00
Web/email → www.scubadubai.com   Map Ref → 13-B3

For those wishing to arrange their own snorkelling trips, equipment can be rented on a 24 hour basis, collecting one day and returning the next. Rates for Thursday, Friday and Saturday are the same as renting for one day as the shop is closed on Fridays.

Prices: Rental of mask and snorkel is Dhs.10 for 24 hours, boots and fins are an additional Dhs.10

Fujairah

Beach Hut, The

Location → Sandy Beach Motel · Al Aqqa | 09 244 5050
Hours → 08:00 - 17:30
Web/email → www.sandybm.com   Map Ref → UAE-E2

Snoopy Island, the 'house' reef, is just off their private beach and is an excellent site to enjoy the underwater world. Equipment is available for sale, alternatively rent a full set for the day for Dhs.50. You can also try kayaking or windsurfing.

Scuba 2000

Location → Al Badiyah Beach · Fujairah | 09 238 8477
Hours → 09:00 - 19:00 Various Timings
Web/email → www.scubauae.com   Map Ref → UAE-E2

Offers snorkelling either directly from the beach or with a boat ride, usually to Snoopy and Sharque Islands, or Al Badiyah Rock, costing Dhs.50, inclusive of gear. The centre also has other water sports facilities, including diving, jet skis, pedal boats and canoes.

Khor Fakkan

Oceanic Hotel

Location → Beach Rd · Khorfakkan | 09 238 5111
Hours → Call for timings
Web/email → www.oceanichotel.com   Map Ref → UAE-E2

Boat rides to Sharque Island are arranged, including gear, for Dhs.60. Alternatively, snorkel and swim from the beach and hire equipment for Dhs.30 an hour. These prices apply to hotel residents, and visitors also have to pay an entrance fee of Dhs.45 per adult and Dhs.25 per child.

Squash

Squash is a great fitness sport, especially in the hot summer months when the heat and humidity drive you inside. Courts are available for hire, mainly through the hotel sports clubs and private clubs. The squash league provides the best opportunities for competitive playing and meeting new players.

Prices: Court hire about Dhs.25 per person per session; coaching about Dhs.100 for 30 - 40 minutes

Abu Dhabi

Abu Dhabi Squash League

Location → Various locations | 02 622 4292
Hours → 18:30 Wed
Web/email → na   Map Ref → na

The league consists of three divisions with five teams in each division. Several tournaments are run throughout the year. The squash season runs from October to May, with a break for Christmas and Ramadan, and finishes with a dinner dance and presentation.

Annual membership: Dhs.1,000 per team of seven players
Contact: Chairman Medhat Al Hammami on the above number

Dubai

Dubai Squash League

Location → Dubai & Sharjah | 04 343 5672
Hours → Timings on request
Web/email → meshrakh@emirates.net.ae   Map Ref → UAE-C2

Approximately 400 competitors play at over 30 clubs each season. Matches are held every Monday for the Dubai and Northern Emirates Premier Series. The Open Squash League also

A TRADITION OF HOSPITALITY

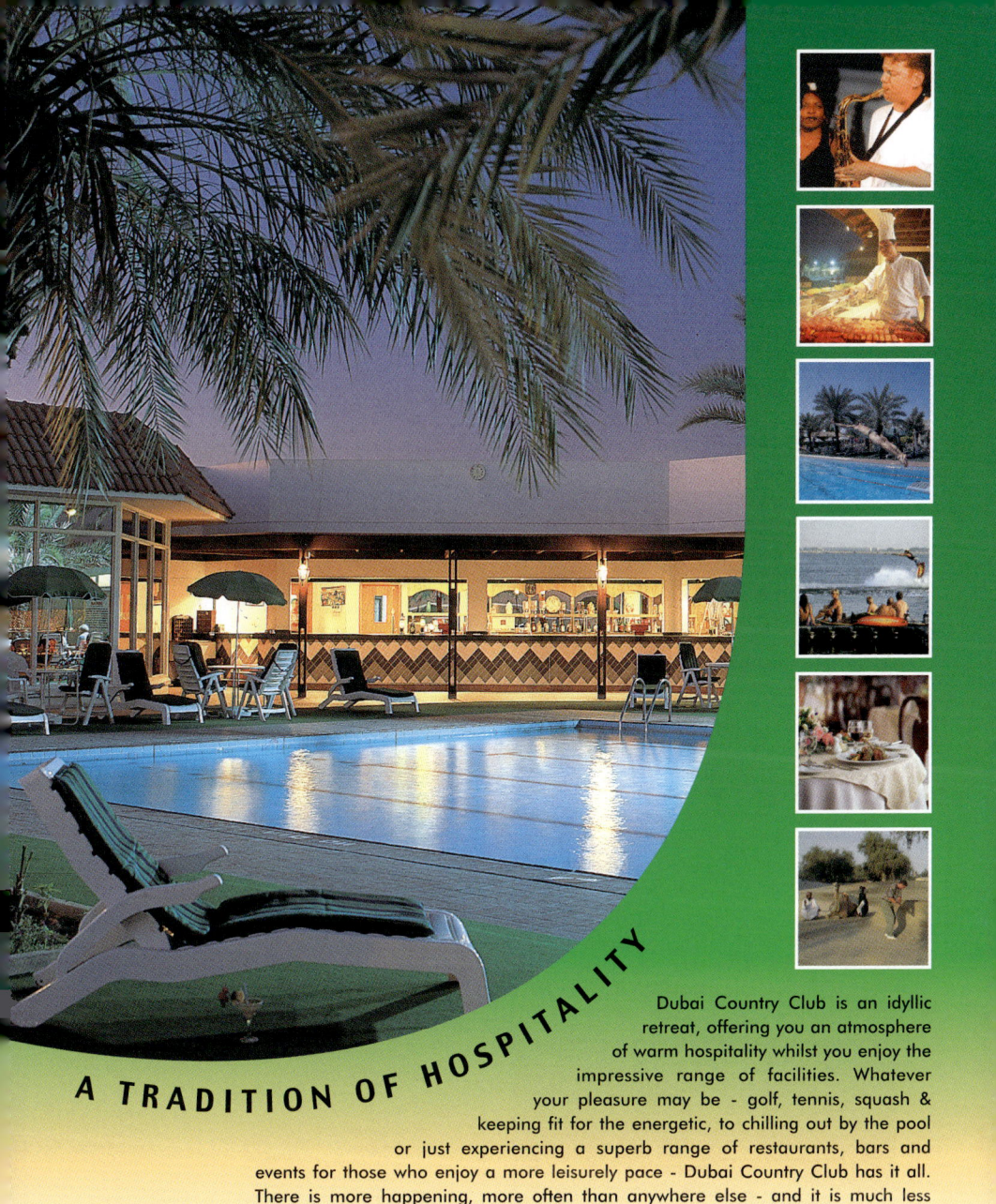

Dubai Country Club is an idyllic retreat, offering you an atmosphere of warm hospitality whilst you enjoy the impressive range of facilities. Whatever your pleasure may be - golf, tennis, squash & keeping fit for the energetic, to chilling out by the pool or just experiencing a superb range of restaurants, bars and events for those who enjoy a more leisurely pace - Dubai Country Club has it all. There is more happening, more often than anywhere else - and it is much less expensive than you would think.

The Dubai Country Club is for everyone to enjoy and if you are looking for a warm, friendly atmosphere with plenty of social activity, then this is the club for YOU!

THE DUBAI COUNTRY CLUB
P.O.BOX: 5103, DUBAI, UAE TEL: +971 4 3331155 FAX: +971 4 3331409
E-mail: dcc@emirates.net.ae - Website: www.dubaicountryclub.com

meets on Monday evenings. Mini tournaments are often arranged.

Contact: *For more information, contact Shavan Kumar (04 343 5672), Chris Wind (04 333 1155) or Andy Staines (04 339 1331)*

Jumeirah Beach Club	
Location ➔ Nr Jumeirah Beach Park · Jumeira	04 344 5333
Hours ➔ See below	
Web/email ➔ www.jumeirahbeachclub.com	Map Ref ➔ 12-E1

A junior squash clinic is run on Wednesdays, 16:00 – 17:30, for children aged 12+, priced at Dhs.25 for members and Dhs.35 for non-members. Individual coaching sessions can also be arranged, priced at Dhs.85 and Dhs.100, respectively.

Swimming

Other options ➔ Beaches [p.122]

The location of Abu Dhabi and Dubai on the Arabian Gulf means easy access to water that's relatively clean and at pleasant temperatures for most of the year. However, during the three hottest months of the summer, the water near the beach is often hotter than a bath!

Most hotels have swimming pools that are open for use by the public for a day entrance fee. This charge varies, but ranges from Dhs.25 - 50 weekdays, rising at weekends (the beach clubs tend to be more expensive). Swimming lessons are widely available from health and beach clubs, as well as from dedicated swimming coaches. Pools are usually cooled for the summer months.

Swimming off the beaches is also possible, whether it's a public beach, beach club or one of the beach parks. Remember to be modest in your choice of costume and keep an eye out for jellyfish, etc, especially on the East Coast.

Having a Splashing Time

If children have not learned to swim before they start school, they will probably be swimming by the end of the first term as many of the schools have pools. The combination of good weather and swimming pools being readily available in gardens, compounds and beach clubs means most children learn to swim at a young age.

Warning: *Be aware of the strength of the tides and currents, in 1999, 100 people drowned off the UAE's coast, due in part to the combination of strong rip tides and lack of swimming ability*

Abu Dhabi

Abu Dhabi Health & Fitness Club	
Location ➔ Sheikh Tahnoon Rd · Abu Dhabi	02 443 6333
Hours ➔ 07:00 - 23:00	
Web/email ➔ na	Map Ref ➔ 3-D3

One hour lessons for children are available for members and non members in the afternoons during the week and all day during weekends.

Prices: *Dhs.340 (members); Dhs.340 (non members) for eight lessons*

Dubai

Pharaohs' Club	
Location ➔ Pyramids · Umm Hurair (2)	04 324 0000
Hours ➔ 07:00 - 22:00 Fri 09:00 - 21:00	
Web/email ➔ www.pyramidsdubai.com	Map Ref ➔ 15-C1

A full range of swimming classes are available in the beautiful pool at Pharaohs' Club. Babies as young as two months can benefit from the gentle 'Water Babies' classes, which are run on various days according to age group. Classes for older children take place in the afternoons, according to level. For detailed information and a class schedule, contact the club on the above number.

Swimming for Babies	
Location ➔ Various locations	050 633 0188
Hours ➔ Various timings	
Web/email ➔ na	Map Ref ➔ na

Dr Jehanne Al Rustom gives swimming lessons for babies and recommends that the best time to start is before six months of age. Other classes offered include distance swimming, personal survival, water exercise for pregnant ladies and swimming for children with special needs.

Location: *Lessons given by this highly qualified instructor are available at the Jumeirah Beach Club, Dubai and an indoor pool in Sharjah*

Tennis

Other options → Annual Events [p.22]

Not surprisingly, given the climate and the lifestyle, tennis is very popular amongst the expatriate population of the UAE. Children start lessons as young as four, initially learning good hand eye coordination and ball control, as well as having fun, of course!

Most of the hotels will be able to arrange coaching on request. Lessons can be arranged for individuals or in groups and fees will vary from club to club, with some possibly asking for an additional entrance fee. There are also organisations set up solely for tennis coaching. Group lessons cost from Dhs.25 upwards per person per hour, and the numbers in a group can vary from 3 - 8 people. Expect to pay up to Dhs.100 per hour for private tuition, although rates vary so it can be worth shopping around.

> **Anyone for Tennis?**
> If you are just starting off a young child with tennis lessons, ask around his/her class to see if any other children are interested. If you approach a coach as a group not only will you benefit from discounted rates, but your child will be playing with friends and the mums can help each other out with lift sharing.

For those interested in professional tennis, Dubai has firmly established itself on the international tennis circuit with the US$1,000,000 *Dubai Duty Free Tennis Open*, held in the middle of February each year at Dubai Tennis Stadium. For further information, check out Annual Events in the Home Sweet Home section [p.22].

Ball Girls and Boys!

Abu Dhabi

E-sports

Location → Various locations	050 698 0048
Hours → Call for timings	
Web/email → www.e-sportsdubai.com	Map Ref → na

Based at the Abu Dhabi Golf Club, E-sports coaches young tennis players from age 4 onwards.

Dubai

Active Sports

Location → Various locations	04 288 2773
Hours → Call for timings	
Web/email → valkclm@emirates.net.ae	Map Ref → na

Thursday morning tennis tuition at Safa Park, and other venues through the week for children between the ages of 4 - 12.

Aviation Club, The

Location → Nr Tennis Stadium · Al Garhoud	04 282 4122
Hours → 06:00 - 23:00	
Web/email → www.aviationclubonline.com	Map Ref → 15-D1

The Clark Francis Tennis Academy at The Aviation Club offers a variety of courses, lessons and activities for all ages and abilities. The club boasts a range of facilities including six floodlit Decoturf tennis courts.

Prices: Individual classes start at Dhs.150 per person (Dhs.600 for five lessons)

Dubai Country Club

Location → Nr Bu Kidra Interchange · Al Awir Rd	04 333 1155
Hours → 08:00 - 22:00	
Web/email → www.dubaicountryclub.com	Map Ref → 6-A2

Dubai Country Club offers coaching for youngsters Thursdays to Mondays, either individually or in groups of up to three, for ages four and upwards.

Dubai Tennis Academy

Location → American University · Al Sufouh	04 397 5828
Hours → Timings on request	
Web/email → na	Map Ref → 2-C2

The Academy offers professional coaching all year round for aspiring players, which includes private lessons, group clinics, competitions, school holiday sports camps and ladies' tennis mornings. They run group lessons for children, split by age and ability: 4 – 8; 6 – 12 and 8 – 18 years.

Contact: The above or 050 6556152 for more information

LG InSportz

Location → Jct 3, Shk Zayed Rd · Dubai
Hours → 09:30 - 21:30
04 347 5833
Web/email → www.insportzclub.com
Map Ref → 12-B2

Tennis can be played all year round at this air conditioned indoor venue. Insportz have five indoor courts. Costs are Dhs.40 per person per hour. Bookings are required one day in advance.

Pharaohs Club

Location → Pyramids · Umm Hurair (2)
Hours → 07:00 - 22:00   Fri 09:00 - 21:00
04 324 0000
Web/email → www.pyramidsdubai.com
Map Ref → 15-C1

The resident coach, Tariq, teaches children from age four upwards in individual or group lessons.

SuperSports

Location → Various locations
Hours →   Call for timings
050 340 7724
Web/email → na
Map Ref → na

Professional coaching services for children age 3+, starting with basic ball skills and hand eye co-ordination, and working through to skills training and match play. They operate from a number of hotels and beach clubs, and will also come to compounds. For more information, contact Fransua on the above number.

Prices: Individual lessons at the hotels are charged at Dhs.180 for an hour, discounted for beach club members. Group lessons attract various rates depending on the number in the group and the duration (45mins/1hour). For a group of 4, the fee is Dhs.60 per student for an hour, or Dhs.50 for 45 minutes, again with discounts for students who are beach club members

Trekking

There are some wonderful hikes in the spectacular mountains and wadis of the UAE, and even in the high Hajar Mountain range, that are suitable for children over six years. Water, good walking boots and suncream are essential. Routes are generally spread by word of mouth, but unless you are sure of the way, it is advisable to go in an organised party. The tour operator Desert Rangers (see Tour Operators [p.140]) will organise trips to suit the group, taking into consideration age, fitness and the level and length of trek required. For details of interesting hikes refer to the *Off-Road Explorer*.

Dubai

Desert Rangers

Location → Dubai Garden Centre · Shk Zayed Rd
Hours → 08:30 - 14:30
04 340 2408
Web/email → www.desertrangers.com
Map Ref → 12-A2

Visit quiet hidden wadis, abandoned villages, waterfalls and rock pools. Trips can be designed to suit the group, taking into consideration age, fitness and the level and length of trek required. Age Range 6+.

Triathlon

Abu Dhabi

Abu Dhabi Triathlon Club

Location → Various locations
Hours →   Timings on request
050 311 5346
Web/email → www.abudhabitriclub.com
Map Ref → na

An informal but well represented group of people who train and race together. Anyone interested in joining should send an email to the club via the website, or contact Kevin on the above number.

Other contact information: http:\\sports.groups.yahoo.com \group\abu_dhabi_tri_club

Dubai

Dubai Triathlon Club

Location → Various locations
Hours →   Timings on request
050654 7924
Web/email → www.dubaitriclub.com
Map Ref → na

Between October and April there's a busy calendar of triathlons, biathlons and aquathons in Dubai and Abu Dhabi. No membership is required and all enthusiasts are welcome to send their email address to be registered on the UAE database.

Contact: For more information on up and coming events contact Rory McRae (050 654 7924) or Adrian Hayes (050 622 4191)

Wadi & Dune Bashing

Other options → Annual Events [p.22]

Children will love discovering the wilderness of the desert and rough terrain of the wadis in various locations around the UAE. Exploring is best done between October and May when the weather is cooler. Desert and mountain areas in the Northern Emirates are still inhabited by Bedouin and hill tribes who still live their daily lives in the traditional way, as do the fishermen in the coastal settlements.

Wadi Bashing, as the name suggests, is pretty bumpy and so children and adults should be strapped in to a sturdy, well serviced 4 wheel drive vehicle (4 WD) and if you're not on an organised trip it is advisable to travel in convoy. Bouncing over rocks and boulders in difficult terrain, traversing streams can be exhilarating, but be prepared to get stuck.

The Hajar Mountains, which run from the tip of the Mussandam, down the eastern coast of the UAE into Oman, offer spectacular drives amid rugged mountain scenery. Wadi Bih is probably the most popular route that cuts through the Hajar Mountains, linking Ras Al Khaimah and Dibba. The track tends to be passable all year, except after heavy rainfall. The wadi itself takes over two hours of slow, continuous driving, so allow a full day for the round trip.

It is advisable to plan the route and requirements in advance and be prepared to make several stops for younger travellers to stretch their legs.

For a less taxing terrain, on both your vehicle and backside, sand dunes offer an equally exhilarating trip with forever-shifting sands creating an endless variety of landscapes. Inland from all the major coastal settlements, the dunes provide peaceful and scenic picnic and camping sites, some completely devoid of vegetation and others with small woody copses and oases. Camel farms are interesting places to stop, and spotting camels and donkeys along the route can keep little minds active.

Fossil Rock and its surroundings is a wonderful area for dune bashing, camping and collecting fossils, or a stop at Big Red on the way to Hatta offers fun for desert drivers and sand boarders. Other interesting camping and dune driving sites can be found just off the main road between Dubai and Al Ain, after the third major junction and before Al Ain.

Getting stuck is inevitable so it is a good idea to get some desert driving experience to prepare yourself for such sticky situations! Tour companies offer desert driving courses, or for an even easier option take one of their organised tours. See Tour Operators [p.140].

The real test of adventure is a trip to Liwa some 250 km south of Abu Dhabi by road. This fertile oasis is set on the edge of the Rub Al Khali desert (or Empty Quarter as it is often known), amongst some of the largest dunes in the world. There are various ways of reaching the Liwa crescent, but allow a minimum of two nights camping to explore and enjoy the solitude and splendour of these enormous dunes.

Children of any age can enjoy these trips but it's not ideal to bounce babies' heads about in the backs of cars. Ensure car seats are fitted firmly and correctly, and easier routes may be more suitable if little ones are in the party. Of course toddlers may also complain vehemently about being bumped around, but you're just as likely to hear squeals of delight, depending on the child. Choosing shorter trips initially is probably be a safer plan.

> **Flash Floods**
>
> Warning – A wadi is technically a dry riverbed. However, when there is a heavy rainfall, a wadi is not the place to be – flash floods do occur. Water builds up in the mountains and gushes down the valley as a wall of water, taking boulders, palm trees and even vehicles with it. Never camp or picnic in a valley if there has been, or is, any sign of rain in the mountains.

For further information and tips on driving off-road, including stunning satellite imagery with 20 superimposed routes, detailed route descriptions and striking photos, refer to the *Off-Road Explorer*. This practical guidebook also includes a useful Off-Road Directory.

Walks

While the layout of most cities in the UAE doesn't encourage walking, there are a few places, in addition to the parks and beaches, suitable for a family walk.

Strolling along the Corniche and Breakwater in Abu Dhabi is a popular pastime, even more so in the winter months when the temperatures are perfect for the outdoors.

In Dubai, the waterfront areas on either side of the Dubai Creek, the Jumeira Beach Corniche, Al Mamzar and the area around the Hyatt Regency Hotel have paved walkways suitable for a walk with prams, as well as adequate nearby parking. The interconnected maze of covered streets that make up the Spice and Gold Souks in Deira are also worth a visit for their sights, colours and aromas, as is the smaller souk area alongside the Creek in Bur Dubai.

If you want a break from the bigger cities, head north to Sharjah. From the Sharjah Fish Souk, walk along the Creek to the Corniche and into Ajman. Alternatively, there are corniche areas adjacent to the beaches in Khorfakkan and Kalba. Parking is readily available and there are swings and grass areas to keep the kids entertained.

Head a few kilometres into the mountains to Rifaisa Dam (behind the town of Khorfakkan) and take the track linking one side of the dam to the other. Legend has it that a village lies buried at the bottom of the dam and when the water is clear you can see the remains of the buildings.

Water Parks

Other options → Amusement Parks [p.86]

Although at present, Abu Dhabi doesn't have a water park, a visit to one of the water parks in Dubai or the Northern Emirates is a great way to spend a couple of hours or even the whole day. Note that the opening times during the summer months are usually different from the winter timings - places generally open later in the summer or for Ramadan. Check before you leave home to avoid disappointment.

Dubai

SplashLand
Location → WonderLand · Umm Hurair (2)   04 324 3222
Hours → 10:00 - 19:00
Web/email → www.wonderlanduae.com   Map Ref → 15-C1

A fun filled world of water, offering fun for all ages. Whilst parents relax by the pool, the nine water rides will keep the rest of the family entertained, with rides and activities accommodating the older and more adventurous as well as the younger tots.

Prices: Dhs.45 per adult; Dhs.35 per child (under 12); free entry for under 4 years of age

Timings: Timings vary according to season. Call for details on specified days for ladies, families, schools and special offers

Refer to the review on WonderLand Theme & Water Park in Amusement Parks (Activities, p84)

Wild Wadi Water Park
Location → Wild Wadi · Umm Suqeim   04 348 4444
Hours → Timings on request
Web/email → www.wildwadi.com   Map Ref → 3-A1

Created around the adventures of Juha, a seafaring friend of Sinbad, the park tells the story of his shipwreck and discovery of a lush oasis and has an array of 24 interconnected rides set over 12 acres, which run for 1.7 km. If you dare, try the legendary 'Jumeirah Sceirah' slide, which hurtles you earthwards at speeds of up to 80 km per hour!

Entrance fees: Adults Dhs.99; children Dhs.80, subject to change

Umm Al Quwain

Dreamland Aqua Park
Location → 17km North of UAQ on RAK Rd · UAQ   06 768 1888
Hours → 10:00 - 20:00
Web/email → www.dreamlanduae.com   Map Ref → UAE-D1

One of the largest aqua parks in the world. Discover the pleasure of the breathtaking water rides, the power of the wave pool, the temptation of Crazy River and the gigantic waterfalls. Most rides are suitable for ages six upwards, and there is a 'Tots' Tub' for the little ones.

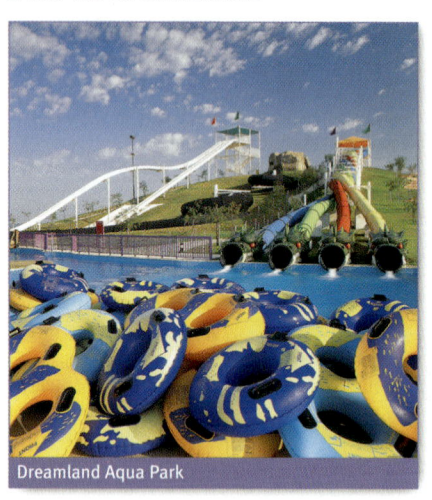

Dreamland Aqua Park

Water Skiing

Other options → Beach Clubs [p.119]

Depending on their confidence in and around water, children can learn to water ski from 5 years of age. Training skis are necessary – these are short skis that are joined together (but not fixed), with the aim of keeping the skiers legs together from the start. These can be purchased from Al Boom Marine (04 289 4858) in Dubai.

Al Soufouh Marina, Dubai, Hamriya and Umm Al Quwain creeks and the lagoons between Dubai and Sharjah all provide calm sheltered waters with areas suitable for launching boats from the beach – perfect for water skiing. On the East Coast, water-skiing depends on the weather, since the coastline is more exposed and there are no lagoons to shelter from the swell. Many of the beach clubs have water skiing facilities for hire.

Fundamentally fun!

JUMEIRAH INTERNATIONAL

Wild Wadi is the coolest choice for a fun day out. At Wild Wadi you can enjoy your day exactly the way you like it. We've got 23 rides and attractions that can relax you or get your adrenalin pumping. And you can meet Juha, Ali, Shahbandar and the rest of the Wild Wadi gang. So come and have a fundamentally fun time!

Tel: 04 348 4444   www.wildwadi.com

Wild Wadi
WATER PARK DUBAI
You just can't get enough!

Wild Wadi is a trading name of Jumeirah Beach Resort LLC. Company with Limited Liability. Registration Number 45069. Share Capital Dhs. 300,000 fully paid up.

Abu Dhabi

Al Jazira Hotel and Resort

Location → Ghantoot Area
Hours → Timings on request   02 562 9100
Web/email → na   Map Ref → na

Fascinated by the thought of doing dazzling acrobatics on water, but don't want to be seen trying it at your local club? Drive up to Al Jazira for the perfect opportunity to escape and learn how to ride the water professionally.

Costs: Water skiing and wakeboarding Dhs.50 for 10 minutes. Five coaching sessions plus one free, Dhs.400

Dubai

Dubai Water Sports Association

Location → Jadaf · End of Dubai Creek
Hours → 08:00 - 17:00   04 324 1031
Web/email → dwsa@emirates.net.ae   Map Ref → na

Devoted primarily to the promotion of water skiing and wakeboarding, the association has two tournament ski boats, a slalom course and a full sized jump for hire. Monday is for kids' coaching from 15:30 until dusk.

Prices: Daily entrance fees for non-members, Dhs.15 weekdays, Dhs.25 Fridays and public holidays (free entrance on the first visit). Ski tow Dhs.45 for 10 - 15 minutes for non-members

Pavilion Marina & Sports Club, The

Location → Jumeirah Beach Htl · Umm Suqeim
Hours → 06:30 - 22:30   04 348 0000
Web/email → www.jumeirahinternational.com   Map Ref → 12-A1

All levels, sizes and ages are catered for when it comes to skiing, and lessons are given to those wanting to learn or to improve on their technique. Other activities available include wakeboarding and kneeboarding – for which lessons are also available.

Water Sports

The UAE offers ideal conditions for water sports most of the year round. The lagoons, creeks and harbours have designated areas for water skiing and jet skiing, while the mangroves are perfect for kayaking or canoeing, the East Coast for snorkelling and diving and the Arabian Gulf coast is ideal for sailing. The sea is generally safe and unpolluted, ideal for swimming and snorkelling.

However, all children, even those who can swim, are very vulnerable in and around water and should be supervised continuously. Many of the beach clubs, hotels and tour operators have water sports facilities, including equipment available for hire.

For all water sports activities, a child's participation depends on his or her swimming ability and confidence in the water.

See also: Canoeing [p.91]; Diving [p.93]; Fishing [p.95]; Jet Skiing [p.101]; Kitesurfing [p.101]; Sailing [p.108]; Snorkelling [p.109]; Swimming [p.112]; Water Skiing [p.116] and Windsurfing [p.118]

Windsurfing

Other options → Water Sports [p.118]

Available off the beach at many of the hotels, this is a sport for almost any age and the flat waters of the Gulf make the ideal place to practice balance.

Dubai

Fun Sports

Location → Various locations, see below
Hours → 09:00 - 17:00   04 399 5976
Web/email → www.funsport-dubai.com   Map Ref → na

Fun Sports is one of the leading water sports companies in Dubai - for information, refer to their review under Jetskiing [p.101].

Jebel Ali Sailing Club

Location → Al Sufouh
Hours → 09:00 - 20:00 Thu & Fri 09:00 - 22:00   04 399 5444
Web/email → www.jebelalisailingclub.com   Map Ref → 2-C1

For children aged ten and above, JASC offers courses to learn the basics of windsurfing. For teens, typically 15+, they have just started the 'Team15' coaching where they focus on learning tricks, racing, and other cool stuff. Children who complete the course get certificates and log books.

Prices: Dhs.350 for members, Dhs.450 for non-members
Timings: Thursday mornings, 10:00 – 13:00

Yoga

Children's yoga helps build focus and self esteem, as well as physical flexibility. Most health clubs have regular yoga classes, so contact your local health club for more information. Although children's yoga has not yet made a sizeable impact in the UAE, the House of Chi and House of Healing in Dubai offers regular classes from prenatal through to Mother & Child.

Contact: House of Chi and House of Healing Tel: 04 397 4446; www.hofchi.com

Beach, Health & Sports Clubs

Beach Clubs

Although enjoying the same stretch of beach, you will find that prices vary dramatically from club to club and you should check out the facilities, annual fees and one-off membership charges of several clubs, before making your decision. Some clubs are decidedly more child-oriented, with excellent indoor and outdoor facilities, and scheduled entertainment programmes. Others may offer families nothing more than swimming pools, a clean, swept beach and safe shallow waves for children to enjoy (plus the standard restaurant/bar options you would expect) – but for a much reduced annual fee.

Abu Dhabi

Abu Dhabi Marina 'The Yacht Club'

Location → Nr Le Meridien Htl · Al Meena | **02 644 0300**
Hours → Timings on request
Web/email → www.abudhabimarina.com Map Ref → 4-C2

The club has its own private beach and marina as well as two pools of which the second, and smaller, complements the children's play area. The squash and tennis courts can be used by members or you can join on a cheaper membership that excludes these activities.

Costs: Non-members daily entrance Dhs.50; peak times Dhs.100

Abu Dhabi Tourist Club

Location → Nr Le Meridien Htl · Tourist Club Area | **02 672 3400**
Hours → 08:00 - 24:00
Web/email → adclub@emirates.net.ae Map Ref → 4-B3

Offering a range of activities for all ages, including children's play areas, bowling alley, library, billiard and snooker room, football, martial arts, badminton, tennis, volleyball, basketball, table tennis and a theatre for children's events and stage shows. Water sports include water skiing and windsurfing.

Club, The

Location → Club, The · Al Meena | **02 673 1111**
Hours → See timings below
Web/email → www.the-club.com Map Ref → 4-A3

This is a social, sporting and cultural centre for over 80 nationalities. Facilities include a 25 metre temperature controlled pool, family beach, separate adults only beach, diving, sailing, tennis, squash, badminton, snooker, children's clubs & activity session, exercise classes, library, car valet and laundry!

Membership: Membership is by application and access restricted to members and their guests

Luxurious Beach Club

Palms Resort

Location → Sheraton Abu Dhabi · Corniche Rd | **02 677 3333**
Hours → 07:30 - 22:30
Web/email → sheraton@emirates.net.ae | **Map Ref** → 4-C4

Activities range from sailing and windsurfing to water skiing, catamaran, fishing, island and sightseeing cruises, banana rides, tennis, squash and table tennis. There's also a swimming pool, children's pool, play area and activity club and a spacious gym overlooking the beach.

Dubai

Caracalla Spa & Health Club

Location → Le Royal Meridien · Marsa Dubai | **04 399 5555**
Hours → 08:00 - 22:00
Web/email → www.leroyalmeridien-dubai.com | **Map Ref** → 11-C1

Different levels of membership include different facilities: Gold is for the full club and includes the use of the pool and beach; while Silver is for fitness and includes the gym, sauna, steam room, jacuzzi, tennis and squash courts.

Entrance Fees: Non-members are charged Dhs.150 (off peak), for use of the pool and beach only.

Club Mina

Location → Le Meridien Mina · Al Sufouh | **04 399 5555**
Hours → 07:00 - 21:00
Web/email → club@lemeridien-minasiyahi.com | **Map Ref** → 11-C1

The Club offers the requisite swimming pools; long white sandy beach and children's indoor play area. There is also a gym, an extensive climbing frame for older children as well as a variety of games and water sports for different ages.

Prices: Day member Saturday to Thursday, adults Dhs.100, children Dhs.40; Fridays & public holidays, adult Dhs.150, children Dhs.60. The Penguin Club is free to health club members and hotel guests

Jumeirah Beach Club

Location → Nr Jumeira Beach Park · Jumeira | **04 344 5333**
Hours → Call for information
Web/email → www.jumeirahbeachclub.com | **Map Ref** → 12-E1

Membership at this impressive club offers spectacular landscaping winding through tropical gardens, beautiful beachfront, countless amenities and fitness options along with special programmes for children. The annual fees and registration cost, however, reflect the club's exclusivity.

Jumeirah Health & Beach Club, The

Location → Sheraton Jumeirah Beach · Marsa Dxb | **04 399 5533**
Hours → 07:00 - 22:00
Web/email → sherjum@emirates.net.ae | **Map Ref** → 11-B1

Offering a range of facilities, including a temperature controlled pool, squash courts, floodlit tennis courts, volleyball and water sports, sauna, steam room, massage and beauty salon and children's play area. The gym is equipped with treadmills, bicycles, rowing machines, and steppers.

Prices: Every Friday visitors can use all the facilities (except the gym) for Dhs.50 per person, which includes a light lunch

Timings: Beach 08:00 - 19:00; pool 07:00 - 19:00. Weekends and public holidays 07:00 - 20:00

Metropolitan Resort & Beach Club

Location → Metropolitan Resort · Marsa Dubai | **04 399 5000**
Hours → 08:30 - 20:00
Web/email → www.methotels.com | **Map Ref** → 11-C1

The sports amenities are basic additions to the main attractions of the pool and beach. Water sports, such as jet skiing, water skiing, windsurfing and charter fishing are run by Fun Sports and are available at an additional cost.

Entrance fees: Non-members Dhs.100 per adult, Dhs.50 per child

Oasis Beach Club

Location → Oasis Beach Hotel · Marsa Dubai | **04 315 4029**
Hours → 07:00 - 21:00
Web/email → www.jebelali-international.com | **Map Ref** → 11-B1

Facilities include a children's pool, gym, steam bath and sauna, outside floodlit tennis court, archery, pétanque, beach volleyball and soccer court, while water sports include water skiing, rings and banana rides, catamarans, snorkelling and much more.

Prices: Dhs.60 weekdays; Dhs.80 on Fridays and public holidays

Ritz-Carlton Beach Club

Location → Ritz-Carlton Dubai · Marsa Dubai | **04 399 4000**
Hours → 06:00 - 22:00
Web/email → www.ritzcarlton.com | **Map Ref** → 2-C1

Three swimming pools, a large water slide, a private beach and a range of water sports are all on offer at this luxurious club. The leisure facilities are extensive and include tennis, squash, aerobics studio, state-of-the-art gym and a Ritz-Carlton Kids Club.

Jazira

Al Diar Jazira Beach Resort

Location → Ghantoot Area	02 562 9100
Hours → 07:00 - 21:00; Fridays 07:00 - 00:00	
Web/email → jazbeach@emirates.net.ae	Map Ref → UAE-B3

Situated between Abu Dhabi and Dubai, this resort is well worth the trip out of the city. There is plenty for the whole family, including a beach, water sports centre, health club, pool and golf. There's also a beach party on Fridays with free camel rides for the adventurous.

Prices: Dhs.100 per person

Jebel Ali

Club Joumana

Location → Jebel Ali Htl · Jebel Ali	04 804 8058
Hours → 06:00 - 21:00	
Web/email → www.jebelali-international.com	Map Ref → 10-A1

In addition to the gym, jacuzzi, sauna, squash and tennis courts, and numerous other sporting facilities, membership allows access to the hotel's private beach, freshwater pools and a seawater and children's pool. The Golf Course is a 9 hole par 36 course.

Prices: Dhs.80, contact the club for full membership details

Health Clubs & Sports Clubs

There are numerous family orientated clubs, which offer a choice of activities and a comprehensive range of sports facilities and coaching. The beach clubs in particular are very popular with families, especially at weekends. Here you can swim, play sports and laze in the sun in peace and relative quiet whilst the children play, or follow organised entertainment programs. The list of clubs in the UAE is endless. Families may wish to visit the various venues at their leisure to find one that suits their requirements and budget.

Membership fees are paid annually and range from Dhs.500 to almost Dhs.18,000! It really is worth shopping around before you commit. Some clubs also charge a non-refundable, one off joining fee. A family usually consists of two adults and two children, with an additional fee per extra child. The definition of child varies between clubs, based on age.

Clubs also vary on their policy of allowing non-member participation in activities and sports programmes. Usually non-members or member's guests are charged an extra fee for the activity, in addition to an entry fee to the club.

Abu Dhabi

Abu Dhabi Health & Fitness Club

Location → Golf & Equestrian Club · Al Mushrif	02 443 6333
Hours → 08:30 - 22:00	
Web/email → www.adhfc.com	Map Ref → 3-D3

This club includes two extensively equipped gyms, squash, volleyball and tennis courts, 2 lane bowling alley (Dhs.60 per hour), exercise classes, crèche, and much more. Regular competitions and tuition programmes are held and coaching is available in tennis, horse riding and swimming.

Prices: Daily guest rate: Dhs.100 for use of all facilities; Dhs.50 for use of pool and gym only

Women only: Monday and Wednesday 08:00 - 11:00

Bodylines

Location → Beach Rotana · Umm Al Nar St	02 644 3000
Hours → 06:00 - 23:00	
Web/email → beach.hotel@rotana.com	Map Ref → 4-C2

Facilities include squash and tennis courts and a gym with male and female changing rooms, each containing their own sauna and steam room. Massages and aerobics are also offered. A separate supervised swimming pool with a roof is available for children.

Entrance fees: Non-members: weekends, adults Dhs.75, children Dhs.50; weekdays, adults Dhs.50, children Dhs.30

Skyline Health Club

Location → Baynunah Tower · Corniche Rd West	02 632 7777
Hours → 07:00 - 22:00	
Web/email → na	Map Ref → 5-A3

The Skyline Health Club, situated on the 29th floor of the Hilton Baynunah Tower, is one of the most prestigious and exclusive health clubs in Abu Dhabi. The club offers a state of the art gym, exercise studio, sauna, steam room, massage and Abu Dhabi's largest indoor temperature controlled swimming pool. A qualified instructor provides swimming lessons for different age groups, as well as special sessions for mums and toddlers. In addition, there is a Kids Club for children aged 5 - 12 years every Monday and Thursday.

Dubai

Al Nasr Fitness Centre

Location → Al Nasr Leisureland · Oud Metha   04 337 1234
Hours → 09:00 - 22:00
Web/email → alnasr@emirates.net.ae   Map Ref → 13-E4

This leisure and sports complex houses a great variety of activities for the whole family. Utilise the children's pool or the regular pool with water slide, the fitness centre or try your hand at bowling, ice skating, tennis, squash or video games.

Aviation Club, The

Location → Nr Tennis Stadium · Al Garhoud   04 282 4122
Hours → 06:00 - 23:00
Web/email → www.aviationclubonline.com   Map Ref → 15-D1

The club's amenities include a par 3 golf course, tennis, squash and basketball courts, volleyball, plus a glassed-in gym overlooking the large swimming pool. There is also a range of fitness classes, a steam room, plunge pool, sauna and healthy café.

Dubai Country Club

Location → Nr Bu Kidra Interchange · Al Awir Rd   04 333 1155
Hours → 08:00 - 22:00
Web/email → www.dubaicountryclub.com   Map Ref → 6-A2

The Country Club focuses on family fun with activities for all ages including squash, tennis, circuit training, aerobics, rugby, badminton, basketball, netball, bridge, karate and water skiing. Coaching is available in tennis, golf, squash and swimming. The club also has a very active social scene.

Prices: Annual membership fee for a family (parents, plus an unlimited number of children under 18) Dhs.4,650. Joining fee of Dhs.700

Dubai Creek Golf & Yacht Club

Location → Nr Deira City Centre Mall · Al Garhoud   04 295 6000
Hours → 06:30 - 19:00
Web/email → www.dubaigolf.com   Map Ref → 15-D1

This internationally renowned golf club offers a junior golf programme and has facilities including four tennis courts, gym, large swimming pool and marina club.

Prices: Social family membership per year (including two children and sports facilities, excluding golf) Dhs.6,500

Dubai Creek Golf & Yacht Club

Jumeirah Beach Club

Location → Nr Jumeira Beach Park · Jumeira   04 344 5333
Hours → Sat & Wed 08:00
Web/email → www.jumeirahbeachclub.com   Map Ref → 12-E1

Extensive leisure facilities including tennis courts, squash courts, steamroom, sauna, waterslides, gymnasium and two swimming pools are available. Water sports include jet skiing, windsurfing, water skiing, snorkelling and aqua bikes. Coaching is available in tennis, squash and swimming.

Prices: Family membership fee for two adults and two children (3 - 18 years), Dhs.12,800 plus Dhs.1,400 per extra child. Joining fee: Dhs.4000

Pharaoh's Club

Location → Pyramids · Umm Hurair (2)   04 324 0000
Hours → 07:00 - 22:00   Fri 09:00 - 21:00
Web/email → www.pyramidsdubai.com   Map Ref → 15-C1

Alongside squash and tennis courts, Pharaohs offers two well equipped gyms, two pools, a sunken pool bar, and a climbing wall to suit beginners and experienced climbers. The children can enjoy purpose built facilities, both indoor and out.

Beaches & Parks

Beaches

Other options → Beach Clubs [p.119]

A trip to the beach is a super way to keep the kids entertained for a few hours. Whether they swim in the clear waters of either coast, go beachcombing or build an enormous sandcastle, they're sure to come away happy and tired! Public beaches usually have limited facilities but no entrance charge, and beach parks are generally better equipped, cleaner and less crowded, although there is a small entrance fee. While there is a limited choice of public beaches in Abu Dhabi, Dubai has several options. The lagoon beach at Al Mamzar (Map UAE-C2) has a cordoned-off swimming area, chalets and jet skis for hire. Jumeira Beach Corniche (Map 13-B2) is packed with sun-worshipping tourists. There are smaller, quieter beaches near the Dubai Offshore Sailing Club (Map 12-C1), Wollongong University (Map 12-B2) and the Jumeirah Beach Hotel (Map 12-A1). The stretch of beach running between the Metropolitan Resort & Beach Club (Map 11-C1) and the Sheraton Jumeirah (Map 11-B1) is popular with walkers and hotel residents. The 10km beach past the Jebel Ali Hotel (Map 10-A1) is a great spot for camping and barbecues, although beach regulations are gradually becoming stricter, with dogs, driving, barbecues, camping and large parties all on the list of 'don'ts'. However, the quieter beaches are not strictly patrolled. Contact the Public Parks and Recreation Section (04 3367633) for clarification. Also be especially careful of rip tides when swimming off the public beaches, where there are no lifeguards.

Beware the Jellymonsters

There is very little sea life that will harm you on the Arabian Gulf coast, but look out for coloured jellyfish at certain times of the year (September/October in particular) and the odd stingray basking in the shallow waters. Stamp your feet as you walk into the sea and most rays will glide out away from the shore. Take greater care on the East Coast and the Indian Ocean, since in addition to jellyfish and rays, camouflaged stonefish and sea urchins live in the rocky seabed. In the Mussandam area watch out for cone-shells (identified by their diamond shaped pattern). All of these creatures can cause serious problems.

Beach Parks

Other options → Parks [p.124]

A visit to a beach park is a must, with vast stretches of white sand, hundreds of palm trees and warm, calm, turquoise waters. Generally, beach parks get pretty congested over the weekends, although certain parks, such as Al Mamzar in Dubai, cover such large areas that there is plenty of space to go round. Regarding dress codes, it is acceptable to wear swimsuits, bikinis (top and bottom halves please!), or swimming trunks for men, but it's wise to cover up somewhat if you leave the actual beach. Lifeguards are usually on duty during the day but rip tides can carry swimmers away from the shore and fatalities have occurred in the past. A raised red flag means it is unsafe to swim, and you are strongly advised to heed the warning. Like the green parks, beach parks open at 08:00 and stay open throughout the day and into the evening. Check for special timings during summer, Ramadan and on public holidays.

Dubai

Al Mamzar Beach Park

Location → Nr Hamriya Port · Al Hamriya **04 296 6201**
Hours → 08:00 - 22:30
Web/email → www.dm.gov.ae **Map Ref** → UAE-C2

One of Dubai's largest parks, Al Mamzar stretches over 99 hectares and features grassy lawns, five clean beaches and safe play areas. A trip up the tower gives birds-eye views of the surrounding areas and will help work up your appetite for a snack from the restaurant or coffee shop. To get around this vast park, take a train tour (Dhs.2) or hire a shaded bicycle from the main entrance. Air conditioned chalets on the mouth of the lagoon are available for daily rental, providing families with a place to relax and prepare food in comfort.

Prices: Dhs.5 per person; Dhs.30 per car (including all occupants); pool fees Dhs.10 per adult, Dhs.5 per child

Note: Wednesdays are for ladies and children only (boys up to the age of 8)

Al Mamzar Beach Park

Jumeira Beach Park

Location → Nr Jumeirah Beach Club · Jumeira	04 349 2555
Hours → 08:00 - 22:30	
Web/email → www.dm.gov.ae	Map Ref → 3-D1

The long, shady stretch of beach and well established gardens and grassy areas ensure that this is a popular and well used park. Barbecue pits and a volleyball court are available for public use. Saturday is for women and children only. Lifeguards are on duty between 08:00 - 18:00; and swimming is not permitted after sunset.

Prices: Dhs.5 per person, Dhs.20 per car
Age Range: All ages

Parks

Other options → Beaches [p.122]

For more than half the year the weather in the UAE is simply perfect, and luckily there is no shortage of grassy parks and beaches where families can congregate to take advantage of the clear, sunny skies. Both Abu Dhabi and Dubai have a number of immaculately clean and beautifully maintained parks, offering a welcome escape from the concrete jungle of city life. The green parks get very busy at weekends, with people having picnics, playing sports or just chilling out under a shady tree – you can even barbecue in the specially provided areas, but remember to take your own wood/charcoal, utensils and food! Regulations vary with each park, with some banning bikes and roller blades, or limiting ball games to specific areas; some rules, however, apply to all parks, such as no pets, no littering and no taking plant cuttings. The standard timings for parks are from 08:00 until well after sunset, but it's a good idea to check with each particular park before setting out, since most have ladies' days and timings can vary during summer, Ramadan and on public holidays. Entrance to the smaller parks is free, and the larger parks charge Dhs.5 per person.

Abu Dhabi

Al Mushrief Children's Garden

Location → Nr Choueifat School · Airport Rd	02 446 4848
Hours → 15:00 - 22:00	
Web/email → na	Map Ref → 3-C3

For women and children only (10 years and below), this grassy park, away from the heart of the city but not too far out, has play areas and amusement park rides, plus plenty of space for kids to run wild. Pack a picnic or get something from the park cafeteria.

Prices: Dhs.1 (entrance fee); Dhs.2 (per ride)

Capital Gardens

Location → Opp City Centre Bld · Shk Khalifa Bin Zyd St	na
Hours → 14:30 - 22:30 09:00 - 22:00	
Web/email → na	Map Ref → 13-D3

These perfectly manicured gardens in the heart of the city are the ideal retreat for the whole family. Each little cove of the garden has a small selection of rides including swings, slides and a merry-go-round. A large pond in the middle of the lawn erupts into impressive fountain bursts periodically during the day. Vending machines provide refreshments, and an enclosed cafeteria stocks a range of snacks and drinks.

Prices: Adults Dhs.1; Kids free

Khalidiya Children's Garden

Location → Opp THE One · Khalidiya	na
Hours → 15:00 - 22:00	
Web/email → na	Map Ref → 5-C3

This park for women and children only features jungle gyms, slides, swings, seesaws, fountains, some shaded seating areas with flowering bushes and several small amusement park rides for the tots. A new canteen will open after summer 2004.

Prices: Dhs.1 (entrance fee); Dhs.2 (per ride)

Al Ain

Ladies Park

Location → Zayed Al Awwal St	03 681 3910
Hours → 15:30 - 22:30 Fri 10:00 - 22:30	
Web/email → na	Map Ref → 2-B4

Also known as Basra Park, this tranquil and attractive garden is for women and children only (boys up to the age of 10 years are allowed in). Abundant greenery attracts a large number of birds in winter. There are a couple of small play areas with swings, slides and climbing frames and toilet facilities are also available. A small dry wadi with wooden bridges runs through the middle of the park, where you can find a small snack bar.

Prices: Dhs.1 Adults; children under 10 enter for free

> ### Sun Protection
> *As lovely as it is having year-round sunshine, remember that the sun's rays are harmful. Make it a family habit to wear hats and pile on the sunscreen whenever you're outdoors.*

Public Garden

Location → Zayed Bin Sultan St · Al Mutawaa | **03 765 8122**
Hours → 16:00 - 23:00 Fri 10:00 - 23:00
Web/email → na | **Map Ref** → 7-C4

The main park in the city, the Public Garden is a tranquil and relaxing spot amid the hustle and bustle of town. Play areas for younger children offer seesaws, swings and slides. For the older kids, there's a small amusement arcade tucked away by the back entrance.

Prices: Dhs.1 (children under 12 yrs free)

Dubai

Al Khazzan Park

Location → Nr Shk Zayed Rd · Al Satwa | **04 223 0000**
Hours → 08:00 - 23:00
Web/email → na | **Map Ref** → 12-E2

The highlight of this park is the large grassy area away from the road where there's loads of room for games. Other amenities are limited, as is the parking, so it's better suited to people living in the area.

Prices: Entrance is free. Bikes, barbecues and footballs are not allowed

Creekside Park

Location → Nr Wonderland · Umm Hurair (2) | **04 336 7633**
Hours → 08:00 - 23:00
Web/email → www.dm.gov.ae | **Map Ref** → 15-C1

Here you can enjoy a day in the country with acres of gardens, fishing piers, barbecue sites, children's play areas, restaurants and an amphitheatre. What makes this park unique is the cable car running alongside the Creek, plus Children's City, a huge, interactive museum for children (located near gate 1).

Prices: Dhs.5; Cable car – Adults Dhs.25; children Dhs.15. Children's City: adults Dhs.15; children Dhs.10. Wednesdays are for women and children only (boys up to the age of six years)

Mushrif Park

Location → Al Khawaneej Rd | **04 288 3624**
Hours → 08:00 - 23:00
Web/email → www.dm.gov.ae | **Map Ref** → na

The largest park in Dubai, Mushrif Park is a little out of town, but popular nevertheless. It is also pretty big, but you can take your car in. Wander around the miniature houses, take the train (afternoons only Dhs.2 a ride), and visit the camel and pony areas or the children's play areas. Separate swimming pools are available for men and women.

Prices: Dhs.3 per person; Dhs.10 per car
Swimming pools: Dhs.10 per adult; Dhs.5 per child (a membership scheme is available)

Rashidiya Park

Location → After Dubai Intl. Airport · Rashidiya | **na**
Hours → 07:30 - 23:00
Web/email → www.dm.gov.ae | **Map Ref** → na

This is a surprisingly pretty park with brightly coloured children's play areas that are mainly used by local residents (although it would also suit mothers with pre-school children). Shaded grassy areas are ideal for picnics. Saturdays to Wednesdays are for ladies and children only.

Age Range: All ages

Safa Park

Location → Nr Union Co-op · Al Wasl Rd. | **04 349 2111**
Hours → 08:00 - 23:00
Web/email → www.dm.gov.ae | **Map Ref** → 3-D2

This large park is great for everyone, offering everything from arcade games to a Ferris wheel (weekends only), plus grassy expanses dotted with small play areas and barbecue sites. It also has a jogging track, tennis courts, volleyball, basketball and football pitches. Bicycles can be hired inside, but personal bikes are not allowed.

Prices: Dhs.3 per person, free for children under three years. Bike hire: Dhs.100 deposit; Dhs.20 - 30 for one hour. Tuesday is ladies day, with boys aged up to about seven admitted

Basketball

Umm Suqeim Park

Location → Nr Jumeirah Beach Htl · Umm Suqeim | 04 348 4554
Hours → 07:30 - 23:00   Thu & Fri 07:30 - 23:30
Web/email → parks@dm.gov.ae   Map Ref → 3-A1

This small but pleasant park for ladies and children only (boys are allowed up to the age of nine) is located across a quiet road from Umm Suqeim beach. It features grassy lawns and several play areas, and is generally quiet except for during weekends. A popular hangout for mothers and children, although dads are allowed in on Fridays and holidays. There is no entrance fee.

Expand Your Horizons

Art Classes

Other options → Arty Parties [p.151]

Many people develop their artistic talents whilst living in the UAE, and the opportunities are extended to children through a variety of after-school clubs, art centres and specialist outlets.

Abu Dhabi

Craft Corner

Location → Abu Dhabi | 02 622 2563
Hours → Timings on request
Web/email → CCAbuDhabi@aol.com   Map Ref → na

Craft Corner offers a variety of quality craft supplies at affordable prices. They also offer craft classes in a relaxing environment where everyone receives individual attention. Classes change monthly so make sure to request a calender.

Cultural Foundation

Location → Opp New Etisalat · Shk Zayed 1st St | 02 619 5357
Hours → 10:00 - 12:00 18:00 - 20:00
Web/email → www.cultural.org.ae   Map Ref → 5-A3

Classes include silk painting, watercolours, oils, ceramics, sculpture, Arabic calligraphy etc. Classes are held throughout the week and some of the finished art, especially the sculptures produced by students are good enough to be featured at exhibitions.

Ladies Art Group, The

Location → Cultural Foundation · Shk Zayed 1st St | 02 619 5313
Hours → Saturday Morning
Web/email → na   Map Ref → 5-A3

Members' abilities range from complete beginners to trained experts. They paint in all mediums from watercolours and acrylics to oils and pastels, and usually provide their own materials, although basic supplies are available for beginners. All are welcome to join irrespective of level of artistic ability.

Contact: Delma Corner at the Cultural Foundation

Dubai

Book Worm

Location → Behind Park & Shop · Jumeira | 04 394 5770
Hours → Thursday mornings
Web/email → na   Map Ref → 12-D2

This children's bookshop offers story reading and arts and crafts classes (run by an art teacher) for 2 – 10 year olds usually on Thursday mornings. Places are limited and you need to call to reserve, and pay in advance.

Creative Modern Center

Location → Opp Audio Workshop · Al Rashidiya | 04 285 9925
Hours → 08:30 - 13:00 16:00 - 19:30
Web/email → mdrnart@emirates.net.ae   Map Ref → na

Offering the chance to be creative in an arty atmosphere, a variety of courses are provided, including painting, drawing, calligraphy, sculpture, fabric painting, flower arranging, ceramic flower making and cookery. Classes are also given in arts and crafts, photography, pottery, ballet, swimming and taekwondo.

Dubai International Art Centre

Location → Behind Jumeira Plaza · Jumeira | 04 342 2645
Hours → 08:30 - 19:00   Thu 8:30 - 16:00
Web/email → artdubai@emirates.net.ae   Map Ref → 4-B1

The Centre runs three terms of children's classes in September, January and April. An ever changing variety of classes are offered for children from four years and above, including ceramics, creative arts, drawing, arts and crafts and an introduction to painting.

Annual membership fees: Dhs.250 allows members to sign up for some of the many classes on offer each term. Family membership Dhs.350; student membership Dhs.50

Elves & Fairies

Location → Jumeirah Centre · Jumeira **04 344 9485**
Hours → 09:30 - 13:30 15:30 - 20:30
Web/email → jmeadows@emirates.net.ae **Map Ref** → 13-B1

These are the specialists in stencils, rubber stamps and face painting. They also sell special paints, glazes, colourwash, varnishes and brushes, as well as cross stitch, mosaics and decoupage. Regular workshops are run for children and adults on all things crafty.

Emirates Hobbies Ass. Art and Crafts

Location → Street 51, Villa 16, beh Zoo · Jumeira **04 342 1510**
Hours → 09:00 - 13:30 16:00 - 21:00
Web/email → helenart@emirates.net.ae **Map Ref** → 12-D1

The unique and colourful look of NBM Arts and Crafts building lends itself to the art related activities you'll find inside. On offer are a variety of arts and crafts workshops for children and adults. Students and artists have access to a full range of art supplies, as well as knowledgeable staff to guide them with their art projects and purchases.

Clubs & Associations

Abu Dhabi

Club, The

Location → Club, The · Al Meena **02 673 1111**
Hours → See timings below
Web/email → www.the-club.com **Map Ref** → 4-A3

Activities include ballet, pool fun, Arts & Craft, Energy Zone, swimming, tennis, football, karate and squash. Alternatively try out the shaded pools with play area or children's book, CD ROM and DVD section in the Library. They also have a crèche, for toddlers 18 months and over.

Cultural Foundation

Location → Opp New Etisalat · Shk Zayed 1st St **02 619 5357**
Hours → 10:00 - 12:00 18:00 - 20:00
Web/email → www.cultural.org.ae **Map Ref** → 5-A3

Offering numerous activities and facilities for children and adults, including computer lessons and painting. In addition, there's a cinema, plus various exhibitions, theatre performances and lectures held throughout the year.

Rainbows, Brownies, Guides, Young Leaders & Rangers

Location → Various locations **02 642 1777**
Hours → Call for timings
Web/email → pchuuat@emirates.net.ae **Map Ref** → na

Various groups for girls of different age ranges include Rainbows (5 – 7), Brownies (7 – 10), Guides (10 –14), Young Leaders and Rangers (14 – 26).

Contact: For more information on the Abu Dhabi packs contact Barbara Welsby on 02 642 1777; Mary Dunn on 04 348 9849 for the Dubai packs; Jane Henderson on 04 394 5331 for the Jumeirah packs and Liz Smith on 04 395 4640 for the UAE Senior Section

Dubai

Scouts Association (British Groups Abroad)

Location → Various locations **04 349 3982**
Hours → See timings below
Web/email → na **Map Ref** → na

The Scouts Association has sections for boys of different ages: Beavers (age 6 – 8), Cubs (8 – 10 ½), and Scouts (boys and girls) (10 ½ - 14). Explorer Scouts (14 ½ - 18) is a new group, currently only available in Abu Dhabi.

Contact: For more information contact Mrs Susan Jalilhi, District Commissioner UAE, on the above number who will point you in the right direction

Dance Classes

Other options → Music Lessons [p.132]

Every little girl, and some boys (Billy Elliot included), dreams of being a dancer and the UAE is the perfect place to make those dreams come true. Ballet, in fact, is a serious business round here. Disciplines are taught and performance days are proud affairs! Scottish dancing is also very popular for little girls while there are all manner of dancing styles from many cultures to be studied. It is great for children to start any of these classes with a friend and then, if their interest sustains, you have the added benefit of the possibility of lift sharing with another mum.

Abu Dhabi

American Arabian Gulf Squares

Location → Various locations **02 445 2490**
Hours → Timings on request
Web/email → na **Map Ref** → na

The steps are easy to learn, it's excellent exercise and it's enjoyable. Beginners are taught with the help of experienced dancers and there's a separate session for the advanced group. At present it's free to join. For information on timings and classes, call Denise Smith.

Tap Dancing	
Location → Corniche Social Club · Abu Dhabi	02 642 1777
Hours → 10:00 - 12:00 Timings on request	
Web/email → na	Map Ref → 4-C4

Tap dancing is suitable for children aged four and above, and there are three classes available according to age groups. It's for children 4 years and above. The younger ones dance for 30 minutes and the older ones for 45 minutes. Classes are run at the Corniche Hospital -Social Club.

Prices: Dhs.25 per session

Dubai

Ballet Centre, The	
Location → Behind Jumeira Plaza · Jumeira	04 344 9776
Hours → 09:00 - 12:30 15:00 - 18:30	
Web/email → na	Map Ref → 13-B2

The Centre offers a Royal Academy of Dancing ballet syllabus and examinations for children from the age of three upwards. Older children can learn jazz, tap, Irish dancing and Scottish Highland dancing. Modern dance classes are also available.

Dance Centre, The	
Location → Various locations	04 286 8775
Hours → 09:00 - 17:00 Summer closed	
Web/email → www.dance-centre-dubai.com	Map Ref → na

The Centre offers classes in ballet, tap, jazz and modern dance to children of all ages. It is affiliated to the Royal Academy of Dance in London and so is able to enter students for their RAD graded examinations each year.

Contact: For further information contact the above number or 050 624 2956

Indian Classical Dances	
Location → Nr MMI & Pioneer Bld · Al Karama	04 335 4311
Hours → 16:30 - 20:00	
Web/email → www.nrityaupadesh.com	Map Ref → 4-D4

Mrs Geetha Krishnan, a reputed Bharatnatyam and Kuchipudi teacher, holds classes for anyone aged five years and up. She also choreographs classical and folk dances and is available for event organising on a freelance basis.

Drama Groups

Over recent years, opportunities in the Emirates to see professional theatre have very much increased thanks to Streetwise Fringe and other visiting companies. For the little performers there is of course the ubiquitous school plays. In addition to the schools, a few organisations provide theatre style entertainment for, and in some cases by, youngsters in the Emirates. Check the daily newspapers for details of performances by visiting groups, or visit www.expatwoman.com, www.godubai.com or www.ibuytickets.com.

Abu Dhabi

Abu Dhabi Dramatic Society (ADDS)	
Location → Club, The · Al Meena	02 673 1111
Hours → Timings on request	
Web/email → www.the-club.com	Map Ref → 4-A3

This friendly society is perfect for the budding thespian, but if you don't fancy being centre stage, there's always plenty to do behind the scenes. Performances take place throughout the year. You must be a member of The Club to join ADDS.

See also: The Club – Clubs & Associations [p.119]

Dubai

Dubai Drama Group	
Location → Country Club · Al Awir Rd	04 333 1155
Hours → Timings on request	
Web/email → www.dubaidramagroup.org	Map Ref → 6-A2

Matinee and early evening performances are held regularly, with information and booking details are found on the website. Annual membership for anyone interested in taking to the stage or helping out behind the scenes is just Dhs.50, which also entitles you to a monthly newsletter.

Musical Youth Theatre, The Ballet Centre	
Location → Ballet Centre, The · Jumeira	04 344 9776
Hours → Timings on request	
Web/email → balletct@emirates.net.ae	Map Ref → 13-B2

This group is comprised of around 50 children who throughout the year practice dance, music and drama, leading to an annual public performance.

The Dance Centre

Ballet
Modern
Jazz
Tap
Irish Dancing
G.C.S.E. Dance

Classes in Jumeirah, Umm Suquiem, Jebel Ali & Mirdif. For further information contact:
04 2868775 or 050 6242956; email: donnad@emirates.net.ae; www.dance-centre-dubai.com

In addition to the limelight, children can also take a look behind the scenes, with education in stage make-up, costume and set design.

Language Schools

Other options → Education [p.40]

There's a wide choice of language schools in the Emirates, offering a mixture of language teaching, as well as courses in anything from secretarial skills to computer training. Most cater for all ages with courses designed specifically for children. The following are the main options.

Abu Dhabi

Alliance Française
Location → Choitram Building · Khalidiya | 02 666 6232
Hours → 09:00 - 13:00 16:00 - 20:30 Thu 09:00 - 13:30
Web/email → www.chez.com/alliancead   Map Ref → 4-D3

The centre offers morning, afternoon and evening classes for anybody wishing to learn French. Various teaching methods are used to facilitate comprehension and enrich written and oral expression. There is a summer school from July each year, where children aged seven and over are welcome to learn and speak French.

Summer School timings: 1½ hour sessions run 3 times a week (beginners only)

American Language Center
Location → Shk Hamdan Bin Mohd. St | 02 627 2779
Hours → 08:00 - 13:00 17:00 - 21:00 Thu 09:00 - 13:00
Web/email → alc@emirates.net.ae   Map Ref → 4-D3

The ALC runs various English courses each month. Courses include TOEFL preparation and all levels of general or specialised English teaching. Classes are tailor-made to suit student requirements. They also run a summer school for children in the summer months.

Berlitz
Location → Opp Burger King · Khalidiya | 02 667 2287
Hours → 08:00 - 21:00
Web/email → berlitz@emirates.net.ae   Map Ref → 5-B3

The institute offers classes in many languages, from Japanese to Portuguese, for both adults and children. The Berlitz method of teaching is an interactive experience with an emphasis on oral comprehension with the use of videos and CD-ROMs.

British Council
Location → Al Nasr St · Khalidiya | 02 665 9300
Hours → 08:30 - 13:30 16:30 - 19:00
Web/email → www.britishcouncil.org/uae Map Ref → 4-D3

The Council offers courses in the English language for children at all levels and for all needs and interests. They provide classes for young learners aged 6 - 16, and very young learners from age three upwards. They teach Arabic to non-native speakers.

ELS Language Center
Location → Al Khalidiyah | 02 666 9225
Hours → Sat - Wed 08:30 - 13:00 17:00 - 19:00; Thu & Fri closed
Web/email → www.els.com   Map Ref → 5-B3

Operating with the full recognition of the UAE Ministry of Education, the centre provides educational counselling to assist those interested in studying abroad. Tuition is available for individuals or groups in TOEFL preparation courses, children's programs and business and technical English.

Dubai

ACI (Italian Cultural Association)
Location → Various | 050 770 4670
Hours → Various timings
Web/email → rosanna@aci-dubai.com   Map Ref → na

Amongst other things, ACI run Italian school for children. The courses are held on Thursday mornings, 10:30 – 12:30, for children age 3 - 16. A class for children who speak Italian as a second language has also been set up.

Contact: For more information on courses for adults, contact Rosaria Sessa on 050 657 7916, or email her at the above address

Alliance Française
Location → Umm Hurair (2) | 04 335 8712
Hours → 09:00 - 13:00 16:00 - 20:00
Web/email → afdxb@emirates.net.ae   Map Ref → 15-C1

For further information refer to Alliance Française – Abu Dhabi review [p.130]

Berlitz
Location → Nr Dubai Zoo · Beach Rd, Jumeira | 04 344 0034
Hours → 08:00 - 20:00 Thu 08:00 - 14:00
Web/email → www.berlitz.co.ae   Map Ref → 13-A1

Refer to Berlitz – Abu Dhabi review for details.

British Council

Location → Nr Maktoum Bridge · Umm Hurair (2)	04 337 0109
Hours → 08:00 - 20:00	
Web/email → www.britishcouncil.org/uae	Map Ref → 14-A4

Refer British Council – Abu Dhabi review for details.

Dar El Ilm School of Languages

Location → Exhibition Hall 4 · Trade Centre 1&2	04 331 0221
Hours → 09:00 - 19:00 Thu 09:00 - 13:00	
Web/email → darelilm@emirates.net.ae	Map Ref → 4-A3

For children, courses are offered in Arabic, English, French, German, Italian and Spanish. DEI also provides tuition for those with a specific requirement, such as schoolwork. There is also a summer school. For adults, courses include English, French, German, Italian, Portuguese and Spanish. They teach all levels, from basic beginners to advanced.

Prices: Course prices start from Dhs.1,200

Polyglot Language Institute

Location → Al Masaeed Bld · Deira	04 222 3429
Hours → 09:00 - 13:00 16:30 - 21:00	
Web/email → www.polyglot.co.ae	Map Ref → 14-B2

Classes for older children and adults are offered in English, French, Arabic, German, Italian and Spanish. They also run courses in computing. The summer school classes are aimed at primary/junior school age.

Libraries

Other options → **Books & Stationery [p.70]**

Abu Dhabi

Club, The

Location → Club, The · Al Meena	02 673 1111
Hours → See timings below	
Web/email → www.the-club.com	Map Ref → 4-A3

Members can enjoy a range of fiction and non-fiction titles with a separate children's area. A CD ROM section, Internet access and a DVD library are also featured here.

Timings: Sat, Sun, Tue & Wed 10:00 – 19:00; Mon 11:00 – 21:00; Thu 10:00 – 18:00; Fri closed

Daly Community Library

Location → St Andrews Centre · Al Mushrif	02 446 4752
Hours → See timings below	
Web/email → na	Map Ref → 3-C3

Daly Community Library was opened in 1978 and now has nearly 7,000 books, covering fiction and non-fiction for adults and children. Books are ordered from the UK and new publications, including best sellers, are added each month.

Prices: Adults Dhs.100 annually, plus Dhs.75 initial joining fee; children (under 14) Dhs.50 annually, plus Dhs.40 initial joining fee

Timings: Wednesdays 12:00 - 14:00 & 17:00 - 18:30; Thursdays 11:00 - 13:30; Sundays 15:30 - 19:30

National Library

Location → Shk Zayed 1st St	02 619 5278
Hours → See timings below	
Web/email → www.cultural.org.ae	Map Ref → 5-A3

Responsible for collecting, keeping and organising all national literary information, the National Library has over 10,000 titles in the Children's Library, in Arabic, English, French and German.

Annual Membership: Fill in an application form with 2 photos and a passport copy. Dhs. 400 for the National Library; Children's membership is free (may borrow 3 Arabic books or 2 foreign books at a time)

Timings: 08:00 – 14:00 & 17:00 – 22:00; Thu 09:00 – 12:00 & 17:00 – 20:00; Fri 17:00 – 20:00

Dubai

Alliance Française

Location → Umm Hurair (2)	04 335 8712
Hours → 09:00 - 13:00 16:00 - 20:00	
Web/email → afdxb@emirates.net.ae	Map Ref → 15-C1

The multimedia library has over 10,000 books (including a children's section), plus 50 daily, weekly and monthly French newspapers and magazines, 1,800 videotapes, 100 CD ROMs and soon a collection of DVDs.

Annual Subscription: Dhs.650 (books only Dhs.350 per year, videos only Dhs.550 per year). Alliance Française students are allowed free access

Archie's Library

Location → Nr BurJuman · Al Karama	04 396 7924
Hours → See timings below	
Web/email → abcl180@hotmail.com	Map Ref → 13-E3

They have 45,000 books, all in English and you don't have to buy a single one. Fiction, non-fiction, classics, cookery, health and fitness, management and a vast selection of books and comics for children are available. The reading charge varies between Dhs.1 – 4. Archie's also caters to magazine buffs, offering a wide selection of the latest issues.

Annual subscription: Dhs.100 deposit and Dhs.75 (may borrow 4 books for ten days). Dhs.50 renewal fee

Timings: Sat – Thu 10:00 – 14:00 & 17:00 – 22:00; Friday & Public holidays 17:30 – 22:00

British Council Library

Location → Nr Maktoum Bridge · Umm Hurair (2) | **04 337 0109**
Hours → 09:00 - 20:00
Web/email → www.britishcouncil.org/uae   Map Ref → 14-A4

The library service includes a general lending library with particular emphasis on management and accountancy, a video library containing over 400 videos, a self access centre and CD-ROM access for learning, as well as a substantial fiction section of both classics and modern literature.

Annual subscriptions: Children under 12 years, Dhs.120 for new members and Dhs.100 for renewals, for books only. For adults, the charge is Dhs.350 for videos and books. The new Internet section in the library has eight terminals, which are available to members and non members with a scale of charges: 10 hours free to members then Dhs.10 per hour thereafter or Dhs.350 for annual use or Dhs.700 for the year, for the whole family

Old Library, The

Location → Int Art Centre · Jumeira | **04 344 6480**
Hours → 10:00 - 12:00 16:00 - 18:00
Web/email → orford@emirates.net.ae   Map Ref → 4-B1

The Old Library is run by volunteers as a non profit making service and they are always in need of new librarians, so do volunteer if you would like to help. Members are issued tickets, which they exchange for books.

Annual subscriptions: Family Dhs.80 (five books at a time); single Dhs.50 (two books at a time); children Dhs.20 (two children's books at a time). Six monthly subscriptions are also available

Music Lessons

Other options → Dance Classes [p.127]

If you are interested in encouraging your child's interest in music then a good place to start would be with the school music teacher, who will probably be able to advise you regarding which instrument to start with, and suggest an up to date list of private tutors. Alternatively keep your eye on the supermarket notice boards, the Green Pages at the back of Connector or write in

to www.expatwoman.com for other mums' recommendations. Typically, children start to learn the recorder from age 5 at school, at which time they are also introduced to, and have the chance to try a variety of musical instruments. A child can start piano lessons from age six and guitar from seven, although to some extent it will depend on their size and manual dexterity.

Abu Dhabi

Beethoven Institute of Music

Location → Al Nasr St | **02 632 7588**
Hours → Timings on request
Web/email → na   Map Ref → 4-E3

The institute offers lessons in the piano, organ, guitar and drums, with the emphasis on quality teaching and playing, which is also interesting and enjoyable. Children can start as young as six and summer courses are also held. For more information, call the above number or 02 633 9195.

Gymboree Play & Music

Location → Khalidia Palace Htl | **02 665 8882**
Hours → 08:00 - 18:00
Web/email → www.gymboree.com   Map Ref → 5-E3

Gymboree has 25 years of experience in parent child interactive and developmentally appropriate classes around the globe. Their music classes cover 16 different styles and types of music for ages 6 months - 4 ½ years.

International Music Institute

Location → Zayed 2nd St · Khalidiya | **02 621 1949**
Hours → 09:30 - 12:00 15:00 - 20:00
Web/email → zhuli@emirates.net.ae   Map Ref → 5-A3

The International Music Institute offers an assortment of musical lessons from age 5 upwards. Call the above number for more information.

Royal Music Academy

Location → Nr Eldorado Cinema · Elektra Street | **02 674 8070**
Hours → 09:00 - 12:00 16:00 - 21:00
Web/email → vinsylauh@hotmail.com   Map Ref → 4-D3

The Royal Music Academy offers tuition in instruments including the guitar, drums, violin, piano and keyboards. Watercolour, pencil drawing and dance classes are also offered, as well as summer camps for children during holidays;

activities include swimming, ice skating, arts and crafts, painting and camping.

Dubai

Crystal Music Institute

Location → Al Karama | 04 396 3224
Hours → 08:30 - 12:00 15:30 - 21:00
Web/email → www.crystalmusicdubai.com | Map Ref → 13-E3

Courses are mainly for children and are available for a variety of instruments, including piano, electric organ, guitar and violin. Classical Indian singing (Carnatic and Hindustani vocal), Bharatnatyam and Western dance, and arts and crafts are also offered.

Dubai Music School

Location → Stalco Bld, Zabeel Rd · Al Karama | 04 396 4834
Hours → 09:00 - 13:00 15:00 - 20:00
Web/email → www.glennperry.net | Map Ref → 13-E4

DMS was founded by pop star and producer Glenn Perry to encourage the artistic potential of aspiring musicians. One to one classes are offered in guitar, piano, organ, violin, brass, drums, singing and composing for beginners and serious amateurs. DMS also has centres in Deira and Sharjah, and transport can be arranged.

Costs: Monthly prices range from Dhs.200 – Dhs.395, plus a Dhs.50 registration fee

Dubai Wind Band

Location → American School of Dubai · Al Wasl | 04 394 1011
Hours → Tue 19:30 - 21:00
Web/email → na | Map Ref → 13-A2

This group consists of over 50 woodwind and brass musicians. All levels and ages are welcome. Typically, children develop an interest in playing an instrument through school and come to this group once they have attained a certain level of competence.

Contacts: For additional information contact Peter Hatherley-Greene on the above number or 050 651 8902

Gymboree Play & Music

Location → Al Mina Rd – Satwa · Dubai | 04 345 4422
Hours → 08:00 18:00
Web/email → www.gymboree.com | Map Ref → na

Refer to Gymboree Play & Music – Abu Dhabi for details.

Vocal Studio

Location → Trade Centre 1&2 | 04 332 9880
Hours → Timings on request
Web/email → doremivs@emirates.net.ae | Map Ref → 13-A3

The centre offers a range of singing related activities for adults and youngsters as well as exam preparation. The different groups include the Dubai Youth Choir (ages 9 - 11), the Viva la Voce Vocal Ensemble (ages 14 - 18), and the Dubai Woman's Chorus for adult women.

Summer Camps & Activities

Every summer there is a mass exodus of expatriate women and children from the UAE. But there's a lot of indoor entertainment on offer particularly in Dubai and if you're resourceful, and decide to make the most of the facilities available, it's entirely possible to spend an enjoyable summer here. In the last few years, more and more families seem to be staying in the UAE for longer, and consequently there are also more little friends to play with. If you do decide to stay for a few weeks of the school holidays, summer camps and courses can be a great help.

Language schools often hold summer schools which are tailored to keep the kids occupied during the hot months. Some schools may even combine lessons with other activities such as art. Both the British Council and Alliance Française offer this facility. Refer to Language Schools [p.130] for further details.

Tour Operators offer a great variety of activities for kids, although they may be subject to change during the hotter months – it's best to check what's on offer. Refer to Tour Operators [p.140] for more information.

Dubai Summer Surprises is well worth the trip up north from Abu Dhabi. From June to September events are mostly scheduled in shopping malls, entertaining families in climate controlled facilities. Keep an eye out for updates of coming events in the local newspapers or alternatively check out the website – www.mydsf.com.

Most activities are held either in the morning or the afternoon. Bookings can be made in advance for courses which are set for a fixed period of time or

> **Undercover Mums**
>
> If you are at all unsure about how your children are being cared for on any of the courses (and after all, some of them are long days for little ones), feel free to drop in impromptu, and check for yourself.

for the camps on a daily, weekly or monthly basis. Children can learn a new language, learn about computers, take up a new sport or explore their creative talents.

Dubai

Dubai Country Club

Location → Nr Bu Kidra Interchange · Al Awir Rd 04 333 1155
Hours → 08:00 - 22:00
Web/email → www.dubaicountryclub.com   Map Ref → 6-A2

The Dubai Country Club camps are run most school holidays. The facilities are excellent for families and the courses make full use of them, incorporating sports (squash, tennis, golf, swimming and water skiing), arts & crafts and dance. The children are split into groups by ages 5 – 11.

Dubai International Art Centre

Location → Jumeira 04 342 2645
Hours → 08:30 - 19:00   Thu 8:30 - 16:00
Web/email → artdubai@emirates.net.ae   Map Ref → 4-B1

Children can choose from a large range of classes including painting on ceramic pots, mirror painting, theatre masks, drawing, sketching and other arts and crafts, etc. Open 08:30 – 19:00 in winter, but closing at 16:00 in summer.

Dubai Summer Surprises

Location → Various locations 04 223 5444
Hours → June - September
Web/email → www.mydsf.ae   Map Ref → na

Promising 'Big Fun for Little Ones', DSS aims to keep families entertained in climate controlled facilities during the hotter months of the year. Events are mostly centred around the shopping malls, although the Modesh Fun City is normally held at the Dubai Airport Expo Centre. For more information call the above number or 600545555.

Dubai Tennis Academy

Location → American University · Al Sufouh 04 397 5828
Hours → Timings on request
Web/email → na   Map Ref → 2-C2

Dubai Tennis Academy runs a summer sports camp for children aged 6 – 16, offering a wide range of activities including basketball, cricket, tennis, swimming, soccer and fun Australian games. Contact the above number or 050 655 6152 for more information.

Futurekids

Location → City Tower 1 · Shk Zayed Rd 04 331 8248
Hours → 09:00 - 18:00   Sat 09:00 - 13:00
Web/email → www.futurekids.com   Map Ref → 4-B3

Futurekids offers computer courses during the summer to children aged 4 – 14. They combine the latest technology themes that kids love, to ensure that they have fun while they learn.

LG InSportz

Location → Jct 3 · Shk Zayed Rd 04 347 5833
Hours → 09:30 - 21:30
Web/email → www.insportzclub.com   Map Ref → 12-B2

Offered as an indoor mixed sports holiday camp, Insportz provides weekday games and instruction in cricket, basketball, tennis and more. Classes run from the end of June to the end of August, and are suitable for ages 5 – 14.

Sports United

Location → Various Locations 050 656 2457
Hours → Call for timings
Web/email → na   Map Ref → na

In existence since 1996, this summer camp runs over several weeks. There's a daily program of events, covering a range of sports, visits and activities for children aged 5 –12 years. Contact David on the above number for more information.

Holiday Fun

Wafi City

Location → Wafi City · Umm Hurair (2)
Hours → 10:00 - 22:00   Fri 13:00 - 22:00
Web/email → www.waficity.com   **Map Ref** → 15-C1

Based in the self contained Kids Area at Pharaohs, with contributions from the Pyramids, Encounter Zone, PMI (Popular Music Institute) and Microsoft, children can enjoy all sorts of arts, crafts and sports, music and computers, as well as outings to Encounter Zone.

Museums, Heritage & Culture

Museums – City

Other options → Museums – Out of City [p.136]

While your children might not opt for a museum as their first choice there are a number of fun, interactive exhibits guaranteed to change their minds. You and your kids can also discover the local history and heritage of the region. The following are some of the more interesting sites for children. For opening hours during Eid and public holidays, call the venue before you set off from home. Opening hours during summer can also vary, so check in advance.

Abu Dhabi

Al Maqtaa Fort

Location → Al Maqtaa
Hours → na
Web/email → na   **Map Ref** → 1-C3

Heavily renovated, this fort is one of the few remaining examples of its kind in Abu Dhabi. Originally built over 200 years ago, this fort stands on the edge of the island, and its original purpose was to fend off bandits and unwelcome visitors.

Cultural Foundation

Location → Opp New Etisalat · Shk Zayed 1st St   **02 619 5357**
Hours → 10:00 - 12:00   18:00 - 20:00
Web/email → www.cultural.org.ae   **Map Ref** → 5-A3

The Cultural Foundation, located within the famous old fort, spreads over 14 hectares and is a remarkable monument to the desire to enrich knowledge and preserve heritage. It includes a library, a theatre, an exhibition centre and a children's activity centre. Log onto the above website for further information.

Heritage Village

Location → Breakwater
Hours → na
Web/email → na   **Map Ref** → 5-D4

The Heritage Village is a reconstruction of a mosque, souk, ruler's palace and houses as they would have been in Abu Dhabi only 50 years ago. Other exhibits include a Bedouin encampment, traditional farming in an oasis and the life of a coastal fisherman, trader or pearl diver.

Dubai

Bastakiya

Location → Nr Diwan & Al Faheidi R/A · Bur Dubai
Hours → na
Web/email → na   **Map Ref** → 14-A2

One of the oldest heritage areas in Dubai, Bastakiya is great for all ages to wander around in the cooler months. Amble down alleyways, admire the windtowers, step into a converted house (now an art gallery), and picture yourself living in a bygone era.

Dubai Museum

Location → Al Fahidi Fort · Bastakiya, Bur Dubai   **04 353 1862**
Hours → 08:00 - 20:30   Fri 14:30 - 20:30
Web/email → www.dubaitourism.ae   **Map Ref** → 5-A2

Built in the 1800s as a fort for sea defence, Al Fahidi Fort was renovated in 1970 to house the museum and recently expanded underground. Displays include everything from everyday artefacts to a presentation on the discovery of oil and a reconstruction of a 1950s souk. Facilities include toilets, but there's no café.

Prices: Adults Dhs.3; child 5 - 9 years Dhs.1.5; under 5's free
Age Range: 4+

Heritage & Diving Village

Location → Al Shindagha   **04 393 7151**
Hours → 07:30 - 14:30   16:00 - 22:00 Fri 16:00 - 22:00
Web/email → www.dubaitourism.ae   **Map Ref** → 5-A1

A glimpse of Dubai's traditional culture and lifestyle is captured in these two centres, with displays focusing on the maritime past, pearl diving and architecture. Camel, donkey and horse rides are available on certain afternoons and facilities include shops, toilets and two Arabic restaurants. There is no entrance fee.

Timings: Sat - Thu 08:00 - 22:00; Fridays 08:00 - 11:30 & 16:00 - 22:00

Shk Mohammed Centre for Cultural Understanding

Location → Bastakiya · Bur Dubai | 04 353 6666
Hours → 09:00 - 17:00
Web/email → smccu@emirates.net.ae | Map Ref → 14-A2

This unique centre was mainly created to help visitors and residents understand the traditions and customs of the UAE. To achieve this various activities are organised, such as mosque tours and visits to the home of a UAE national for a traditional local lunch.

Age Range: 8+

Museums – Out of City

Other options → Tour Operators [p.140]

Ajman

Ajman Museum

Location → Opp Etisalat · Ajman Town Centre | 06 742 3824
Hours → 09:00 - 13:00 16:00 - 19:00
Web/email → ajmuseum@emirates.net.ae | Map Ref → UAE-C2

This unique museum situated in the old fort features various rooms displaying life as it was in the past, including activities like pearling, fishing, farming, cooking, desert life, popular games, medicines, and more. There are also good examples of a traditional date store, a well and a windtower, as well as other displays of weapons, archaeology, and the history of the police force. The fortress guidebook (Dhs. 5) is an easy to understand reference to the exhibits and to life as it was in the past.

> **Make a scrapbook!**
> Instead of cluttering up bedrooms with endless leaflets and tickets acquired on various outings, encourage your kids to make a scrapbook of all the places they have visited. As time spent in the UAE is often transient, this scrapbook will be an excellent souvenir of a child's stay here.

Prices: Adults: Dhs. 4; Children under 6 years: Dhs. 2; Dhs. 1 for students

Evening timings: 17:00 – 20:00 (summer); 16:00 – 19:00 (winter)

Age range: 4+

Al Ain

Al Ain Museum

Location → Al Muraba R/A | 03 764 1595
Hours → 08:00 - 13:00 15:30 - 17:30
Web/email → www.aam.gov.ae | Map Ref → 2-D4

This interesting museum is situated on the edge of the main Al Ain Oasis, on the same site as the Eastern Fort. The well presented displays of everyday life in the days before oil was found are fascinating, particularly in contrast to the gleaming, modern cities we see before us today. There is also a wonderful selection of photographs taken of Al Ain, Abu Dhabi and Liwa in the 1960s, as well as archaeological displays from the nearby Hili Gardens and the Garn Bint Saud Tombs.

Prices: 50 fils

Timings: 08:00 - 13:00 & 16:30 - 18:00 Sunday - Wednesday; 08:00 - 12:00 & 15:30 - 17:30 Thursday; 09:00 - 11:30 & 15:30 - 17:30 Friday; closed Saturday

Fujairah

Fujairah Heritage Village

Location → Nr Fujairah Fort | 09 222 7000
Hours → 07:00 - 13:30
Web/email → na | Map Ref → UAE-E2

Set around the ruins of an old fort, this 6,000 square metre village opened in 1996 and depicts life before the discovery of oil. The large walled area displays houses, fishing boats and simple dhows constructed from palm leaves (barasti), plus clay, stone and bronze implements and hunting and agricultural tools. It is a bit off the beaten track, behind the town towards the mountains, not far from the hospital and opposite Ain Al Madhab Garden. No café or toilets are available.

Prices: Dhs.5.

Age Range: All Ages

Fujairah Museum

Location → Opp Ruler's Palace | 09 222 9085
Hours → 08:30 - 13:30 16:30 - 18:30 Fri 14:00 - 18:30
Web/email → na | Map Ref → UAE-E2

Fujairah Museum offers an insight into the history and heritage of the UAE. Visible from the museum is the old castle in Fujairah, which is also fun for children to explore. It's nearly 300 years old and due to its strategic position was once used as the headquarters for ten rulers of Fujairah. The museum was enlarged during the summer of 1998 to permit more finds to be displayed. Pushchair access is suitable for a quick look around and there are toilets, but no café.

Entry fee: Adults Dhs.3; children Dhs.1
Age Range: All Ages

Hatta

Hatta Heritage Village

Location → Hatta town · On road to Hatta Pools | na
Hours → 08:00 - 19:30 Fri 15:00 to 21:00
Web/email → na   Map Ref → UAE-D3

Constructed around an old settlement, Hatta Heritage Village is a recreation of a traditional mountain village set amongst an oasis of palm trees. Here you can explore narrow alleyways and houses made of mud and palm fronds, discover traditional life and folklore, and take a camel ride. The Village is located to the left of the main town towards the mountains and there is no entrance fee.

Age Range: All ages

Kalba

Al Hisn Kalba

Location → Fujairah | 09 277 4442
Hours → 09:00 - 13:00 17:00 - 21:00
Web/email → www.shjmuseum.gov.ae   Map Ref → UAE-E2

If you go on a family outing to the East Coast don't turn back at Fujairah, as just to the south lies the southern most tip of the UAE's Indian Ocean coastline. This is the home of the oldest mangrove forest of Arabia, set in the beautiful tidal estuary of Khor (creek) Kalba.

As you drive along the coast road in Kalba town, the recently restored house of Sheikh Sayed Al Qassimi overlooks the sea. It's located at the end of a large grassy expanse with swings and small rides. On the opposite side of the road (look for the fort) is Kalba's Al Hisn Museum, which offers a limited display of weapons.

Hatta Dam

To the left of the main village, across a major wadi is the 50 metre high Hatta Dam. Built in 1989 to control the flow of water from the mountains and wadis to the village, it's an impressive sight.

To visit the dam, turn right at the Hatta Fort Hotel roundabout, at the next roundabout turn left, over several speed humps and just before the school, turn right onto a gravel track. Follow the track and the dam is to your front left.

It's a good place to break the journey, although the museum has no toilets or café. Pushchair access is limited since there are lots of steps making it difficult for toddlers and babies in arms. There is no entrance fee.

Timings: 09:00 - 13:00 & 17:00 - 21:00; Friday 17:00 - 20:30; Monday closed; Wednesday pm ladies and children only

Ras Al Khaimah

National Museum of Ras Al Khaimah

Location → Old town - behind Police HQ · | 07 233 3411
Hours → 10:00 - 17:00
Web/email → www.rakmuseum.gov.ae   Map Ref → UAE-D1

Located in the old fort, which was a former house of the present Ruler, the National Museum of Ras Al Khaimah has a Natural History Room as well as a large gun display. It's not the most exciting venue for kids and unfortunately the site is difficult for pushchairs but if you're travelling through Ras Al Khaimah at least it's an option for a quick stop. Facilities include toilets and a small bookshop.

Prices: adults Dhs.2; children Dhs.1. To visit with your camera Dhs.5

Sharjah

Discovery Centre

Location → Opp Sharjah Airport · Al Dhaid Rd | 06 558 6577
Hours → See timings below
Web/email → sdc@shj.gov.ae   Map Ref → UAE-C2

This colourful scientific park provides everything children love to see and do in safe, supervised surroundings. Based on theme areas including Sports, Body and Water Worlds, as well as Build and Drive Towns, children can touch, experiment, run and have lots of fun. There's also a supermarket, bank, café, shop, TV studio and a chance to put on wings and fly around the world!

There's much to do and learn in this active environment so allow at least two hours per visit and go early to avoid the crowds. A soft play area is available for the very young and pushchair access is excellent.

Prices: children under 2 years free; ages 2 - 12 mornings Dhs.4, evenings Dhs.7; 13 years and above mornings Dhs.5, evenings Dhs.10. For families (maximum two adults, three children) mornings Dhs.15, evenings Dhs.30

Timings: Wednesday, Thursday and Friday general public 15:30 - 20:30. July and August evening hours 16:30 - 20:30

School groups only: Saturday and Monday 09:00 - 14:00 (mixed groups). Sunday and Tuesday 09:00 - 14:00 (girls only)

Sharjah Archaeological Museum

Location ➔ Nr Cultural R/A | **06 566 5466**
Hours ➔ 09:00 - 13:00 17:00 - 20:00
Web/email ➔ www.archaeology.gov.ae   **Map Ref** ➔ UAE-C2

This hi-tech museum offers an interesting display of local artefacts and antiquities. Linked to a conference centre and used as an educational venue for schoolchildren, the museum has installed computers in each display hall to provide in depth information on the archaeological pieces displayed.

Segregated into separate interconnecting halls by subject matter and chronology, you are guided by a series of films explaining what's on display. Seasonal displays highlight the latest discoveries from excavation sites in the Emirates. Well worth a visit for archaeology and history lovers. There is no entrance fee.

Sharjah Desert park

Location ➔ Sharjah Natural History Museum | **06 531 1999**
Hours ➔ See timings below
Web/email ➔ shj_museum@hotmail.com   **Map Ref** ➔ UAE-C2

Approximately 20 minutes drive from Sharjah, this site consists of Arabia's Wildlife Centre, Children's Farm and the Natural History Museum, all within easy walking distance of each other. These state of the art facilities provide an enjoyable and educational day out with something to interest all ages. Facilities include picnic areas, cafés, shops and toilets.

Prices: Adults Dhs.15; family Dhs.30; under 12's free; schools Dhs.2 per head

Timings: Sat - Wed 09:00 - 19:00; Thursday 11:00 - 19:00; Friday 14:00 - 19:00; Monday closed. The Children's Farm is closed daily between 12:00 - 16:00

Saturdays and Wednesdays school groups only 09:00 - 14:00 (boys only). Sundays and Tuesdays school groups only 09:00 - 14:00 (girls only)

Sharjah Fort (Al Hisn)

Location ➔ Al Hisn Ave, Bank St | **06 568 5500**
Hours ➔ 09:00 - 13:00 16:00 - 20:00
Web/email ➔ na   **Map Ref** ➔ UAE-C2

This large fort is an exciting place for children to explore. Various weapons from 'khanjars' (short daggers) and knives, to swords are on display, plus many photographs of Sharjah city and its people. Al Muhalwassa Jail comes equipped with iron chains, manacles and the old flogging pole. Toilets are available, but there's no café and pushchair access is limited to the ground floor.

Sharjah Heritage Museum

Location ➔ Sharjah Arts Plaza Area | **06 569 3999**
Hours ➔ 09:00 - 13:00 16:00 - 20:00 Fri 16:30 - 20:30
Web/email ➔ www.sharjah-welcome.com   **Map Ref** ➔ UAE-C2

At the Heritage Museum, a family home as it was 150 years ago has been set up in the original two storey home of the Al Naboodah family. Three generations of the family lived here until 1972. The house has since been reconstructed in the typical local style with all rooms looking onto a central courtyard. This museum is worth a visit to see the practicalities of how people coped with the climate and the materials available in former times. The traditional games in the Children's Room are of interest, in particular the camels made from starfish — no computer games here!

Sharjah Natural History Museum

Location ➔ Jct 8 - Sharjah - Al Dhaid Rd - Sharjah | **06 531 1411**
Hours ➔ See below
Web/email ➔ shj_museum@hotmail.com   **Map Ref** ➔ UAE-C2

A trip through the five exhibit halls of this contemporary museum exposes you to the secrets and mysteries of the earth. You'll travel through time, experiencing humankind and our environment, past and present. Aimed at children, a bellowing camel, erupting volcano and a real meteor from outer space are just a few of the many popular exhibits. It also houses the Arabian Wildlife Centre and a children's farm, where donkeys, camels and goats can be fed and petted. Picnic areas are available, as well as cafés and shops. Don't miss the weekly quiz, where kids can earn gift shop vouchers for correct answers.

Age range: All ages, but particularly interesting for children aged 8+

Sharjah Science Museum

Location ➔ Nr TV station · Halwan | **06 566 8777**
Hours ➔ See timings below
Web/email ➔ www.shjmuseum.gov.ae   **Map Ref** ➔ UAE-C2

A world of discovery and illusions with 45 fun filled and hands on exhibits including a planetarium and daily presentations on cryogenics and electricity. The Learning Centre, which has a Discovery Area, Science Lab and 15 station Computer Centre offers programmes including computer basics and the Internet. Prior booking is required for school visits and parties, and times are restricted to normal opening hours. School programmes are available for nursery infants to Grade 12 students and the under 5s have their own play area. Call the museum for further information on organised activities during the summer months for children over 8 years. Other facilities include a science shop, café and toilets and there's also good pushchair access.

Prices: adults Dhs.3 morning, Dhs.5 afternoon; ages 2 - 12 Dhs.1 morning, Dhs.2 afternoon; under two free; families Dhs.8 morning, Dhs.15 afternoon

Timings: Sat - Tue 09:00 - 14:00; Wed - Fri and public holidays 15:30 - 20:30. June, July, August evening opening at 16:30

Zoos

Certain zoos in this region are desperately in need of a complete overhaul, and sadly in the meantime the animals have to make do with less than ideal conditions. Some are better than others though, and it is often worthwhile to travel a little further out of town to the good zoos.

Al Ain

Al Ain Zoo & Aquarium

Location ➔ Nr Traffic Police · Zoo R/A | 03 782 8188
Hours ➔ See timings below
Web/email ➔ na | Map Ref ➔ 7-B2

Opened in 1969, this zoo is the largest in the region and home to over 2100 mammals and hundreds of birds. Although basic, it has plenty of space for most of its residents, which are mostly from the Middle East, Africa and India. A breeding programme exists for rare or endangered animals.

Prices: Dhs.2 (children under four years free)

Timings: 07:00 - 17:30 winter; 08:00 - 17:30 summer; Saturday closed

Dubai

Dubai Zoo

Location ➔ Beach Rd, Jumeira | 04 349 6444
Hours ➔ 10:00 - 17:00
Web/email ➔ na | Map Ref ➔ 4-A1

For years there has been talk of relocating this zoo, possibly to Mushrif Park, to give the animals better living conditions. In the meantime, Dubai Zoo is still languishing in the 1800s. If you wish to see caged animals and birds, they're all here. There is a minimal fee.

Age Range: All Ages

Sharjah

Arabia's Wildlife Centre

Location ➔ Sharjah Natural History Museum | 06 531 1411
Hours ➔ 09:00 - 17:30 Thu 11:00 - 17:30 Fri 14:00 - 17:30
Web/email ➔ shj_museum@hotmail.com | Map Ref ➔ UAE-C2

Your journey through this impressive collection of animals starts with the reptiles, fish, insects and birds. Unusually for these parts, all the zoo inmates are housed in surroundings that are as spacious and natural as possible. Take a quick break at the café overlooking the flamingo lake and ibex mountain, before heading on to see the baboons, wolves, hyena, cheetahs and the rare and captivating Arabian Leopard.

Prices: adults Dhs.15, children under 12 have free entrance (unless in a school group when there is a Dhs.2 charge per child)

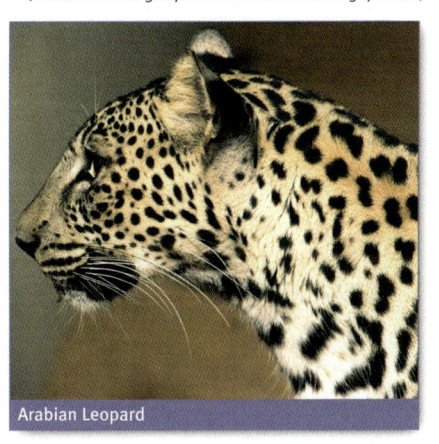

Arabian Leopard

Children's Farm

Location ➔ Sharjah Natural History Museum | 06 531 1127
Hours ➔ 09:00 - 18:30 Thu 11:00 - 18:00 Fri 14:00 - 17:30
Web/email ➔ na | Map Ref ➔ UAE-C2

Just before the Wildlife Centre you'll find the Children's Farm, where little ones can pet and feed domestic animals including cows, horses, donkeys, camels, goats and sheep. (Bags of food cost Dhs.2 each). Pony rides are available in the afternoons, at Dhs.5 per child. This is a great opportunity for kids to get up close and personal with friendly farm animals. Other attractions include a cross section of a beehive (behind glass!), watching quail eggs hatching, and tasting the locally produced cheese. There is no entrance fee.

Age Range: All Ages

Tour Operators

There is a huge choice of tour operators here in the UAE, offering a range of sightseeing and desert safari trips. Desert safaris are highly popular, because whether you choose the half day, overnighter or even two day trip, it usually includes camel riding, dune driving, henna painting, belly dancing and an Arabian style barbecue. Additional activities that can be arranged include sand boarding, sand skiing and dune buggying. These trips will be a real treat for kids and should definitely be on the 'to do' list when you have guests in town. Listed below are the operators that also offer school outings with overnight camps – generally they are the largest and most reputable tour operators in Dubai and Abu Dhabi. Each company may offer slightly varied packages, although the basic tour will be the same. Soft drinks and water are usually included in the price. Many tour companies will also arrange children's parties. For more information on individual tour operators refer to the Out of Town Parties section in Birthday Parties [p.151].

Travel Agents

Abu Dhabi	
Abdul Jail Travel Agency	02 622 5225
Abu Dhabi Travel Bureau	02 633 8700
Advanced Travel & Tourism	02 634 7900
Al Toofan Travel & Tours	02 631 3515
Emirates Holidays	800 5252
Salem Travel Agency	02 627 4424
Thomas Cook Al Rostamani	02 672 7500
Al Ain	
Al Mahboob Travel	03 751 5944
Al Rumaithy Travel & Tourism	03 765 6493
Emirates Travel Express	03 765 0777
Gulf Travel Express	03 766 6737
Dubai	
Airlink	04 282 1050
Al Futaim Travel	04 228 5470
Al Naboodah Travel	04 294 5717
Al Tayer Travel Agency LLC	04 223 6000
Belhasa Tourism Travel & Cargo Co.	04 391 1050
DNATA	04 295 1111
Emirates Holidays	800 5252
Kanoo Travel	04 393 5428
MMI Travel	04 209 5527
SNTTA Travel & Tours (L.L.C.)	04 282 9000
Thomas Cook Al Rostamani	04 295 6777
Turner Travel & Tourism	04 345 4504

Weekend Breaks

Other options → Camping [p.90]

Even a short break is usually enough to escape the chaos of city life and recharge your batteries. With distances between various locations in the UAE being relatively short, it's easy to hop in the car and travel to new surroundings within a few hours. The hotels here are among the world's finest and most make a special effort to make kids feel welcome, and with such a wide choice and such high standards, your only problem will be choosing just one! Remember, virtually all hotels will offer discount on their published room rates, so have your negotiating skills on hand when you phone for prices. And of course, during off peak times you can bag some fabulous, all inclusive weekend packages at many of the top hotels.

Visa Formalities

If you're crossing a border, even if it's just into Oman, check with the relevant authorities about visa requirements – rules have been known to change overnight in this part of the world, and you don't want your holiday to end before it begins just because you don't have the right stamp in your passport!

For those who just don't feel like they've had a break until they've actually made a border crossing, the Sultanate of Oman is within easy driving distance and has plenty of worthwhile attractions, both for happy campers and hotel junkies. The *Oman Explorer* gives you the inside info on getting there and what to see and do. But if your travel bug just won't be satisfied unless you go even further, pop in to see your friendly travel agent – the UAE is surrounded by great holiday destinations that the whole family will love, and that won't break the bank. India, Jordan, Cyprus, the Maldives, Bahrain, Kish Island and Turkey are all destinations close enough to make a short break feasible. The travel agents listed in the table can offer good advice, exciting itineraries and reasonable prices according to your requirements.

Abu Dhabi

Hilton Abu Dhabi

Location → Corniche Rd West		02 681 1900
Hours → na		
Web/email → www.hilton.com		Map Ref → 5-D3

This is the largest and oldest hotel in Abu Dhabi, located at the quiet end of the corniche. It has all the usual five star comforts and amenities, including a health club and private beach.

Al Ain Hilton

Hotel InterContinental Abu Dhabi

Location → Bainuna St | 02 666 6888
Hours → na
Web/email → www.intercontinental.com | Map Ref → 5-D3

Located on a beautiful beachfront with private marina, this is an ideal location for a weekend getaway from Dubai. The lush green surroundings, clean beach and impressive swimming pool will help you ease into a state of total relaxation. Activity addicts are spoilt for choice – tennis, squash, scuba diving, water skiing, windsurfing and sailing are just some of the sporty pastimes available here.

Khalidia Palace Hotel

Location → Al Ras Al Akhdar | 02 666 2470
Hours → na
Web/email → www.khalidiapalacehotel.co.ae | Map Ref → 5-E3

Khalidia Palace Hotel is located at the western end of the corniche. The 120 rooms are cheerfully decorated with all the usual conveniences. Facilities are extensive and child-friendly, with three swimming pools and a bouncy castle. There are plenty of places to eat, although alcohol is not served in this hotel.

Le Meridien Abu Dhabi

Location → Le Meridien · Al Meena | 02 644 6666
Hours → na
Web/email → www.lemeridien-abudhabi.com | Map Ref → 4-B3

All rooms at Le Meridien overlook the beautifully maintained gardens, swimming pools, including a special children's pool, and beach. Various activities are available for those with the energy, including water sports, tennis, squash and basketball, plus there's a health spa, and an excellent range of restaurants.

Sheraton Abu Dhabi Resort & Towers

Location → Nr Corniche Hosp · Corniche Rd East | 02 677 3333
Hours → na
Web/email → www.sheraton.com | Map Ref → 4-C4

This hotel combines a picturesque location and gardens with a wealth of leisure and sports facilities, including a relaxing pool and health spa to tennis, squash, sailing and diving. The restaurants offer cuisine ranging from Mexican and Italian to Chinese or Iranian.

Ajman

Ajman Kempinski Hotel & Resort

Location → Ajman Corniche | 06 745 1555
Hours → na
Web/email → www.ajman.kempinski.com | Map Ref → UAE-C2

Just a short drive from downtown Dubai, this resort hotel is ideal for a quick break from the city. It features rooms with idyllic sea views, an impressive pool area, and half a kilometre of private beach. There is a well equipped health club, a Wellness Centre and a host of activities to keep the whole family busy, including tennis, diving, bowling and watersports.

Al Ain

Hilton Al Ain

Location → Sarug St | 03 768 6666
Hours → na
Web/email → www.hilton.com | Map Ref → 2-E4

The main attraction here is the comprehensive range of sports and leisure activities, ranging from 9 hole par 3 golf, squash or tennis to the leisure pool complex complete with water slide and play area! When hunger sets in, there are plenty of different cuisines to choose from.

Hotel InterContinental Al Ain

Location ➜ Al Khubeirah
Hours ➜ na
Web/email ➜ www.interconti.com
03 768 6686
Map Ref ➜ 2-E4

This is a families' heaven, with three swimming pools, squash and tennis courts, horse riding, a gym with crèche, co-ordinated children's activities and much more. At this hotel, there truly is something for everyone, and it's only 80 minutes drive from Dubai.

Barka

Al Sawadi Resort

Location ➜ Barka
Hours ➜ na
Web/email ➜ www.alsawadibeach.com
+968 89 5545
Map Ref ➜ Oman

Just a few hours drive from Dubai and 40 minutes from Muscat, this resort is miles away from the daily routine. Manicured lawns and spacious, comfortable rooms and chalets are offered alongside a variety of activities for children and adults. Dining is casual with reasonably varied and priced food.

Dubai

North Star Expeditions LLC

Location ➜ Various locations
Hours ➜ Timings on request
Web/email ➜ norstar@emirates.net.ae
04 332 8702
Map Ref ➜ na

North Star Expeditions offer adventure tours to the Mussandam lasting from one to several days. Diving and 4 wheel drive mountain safaris are also available. Guests can stay at either the Khasab Hotel or the company's 16 bed self-catering villa. Suitable for teenagers.

Palace at One&Only Royal Mirage, The

Location ➜ Al Sufouh
Hours ➜ na
Web/email ➜ www.oneandonlyresorts.com
04 399 9999
Map Ref ➜ 2-C1

This graceful, sandy walled hotel is very different to Dubai's normal glass and chrome sky-rises and is equally as stunning inside as outside. Each of the elegant guest-rooms has a private balcony with views of the sea and gardens. Comprehensive facilities include swimming pools, tennis, a children's centre, water sports, health and beauty centres, plus a diverse selection of restaurants.

Ritz-Carlton Dubai

Location ➜ Marsa Dubai
Hours ➜ na
Web/email ➜ www.ritzcarlton.com
04 399 4000
Map Ref ➜ 2-C1

With its Arabic/Mediterranean design, this luxurious hotel is one of the few low-rise hotels in Dubai. Facilities are world class, from the various food outlets and subterranean health spa to the large beach, extensive water sports facilities and state of the art gym. The kids' club is ideal for children up to 12 years.

Ritz-Carlton Dubai

Fujairah

Al Diar Siji Hotel

Location ➜ Nr Etisalat Bld
Hours ➜ na
Web/email ➜ www.aldiarhotels.com
09 223 2000
Map Ref ➜ UAE-E2

The rooms of this elegant and relaxed hotel offer views of the mountains and Indian Ocean. Facilities include a pool, gym, tennis courts and six lane bowling alley, plus beach club.

Fujairah Hilton

Location → North end of the Corniche	09 222 2411
Hours → na	
Web/email → shjhitwsal@hilton.com	Map Ref → UAE-E2

The Fujairah Hilton is an ideal retreat for a family break, offering top quality rooms and facilities. In addition to the pool and the beach, there's also a playground on site, as well as tennis, basketball and watersports. The Friday Fish Market brunch has an excellent reputation.

Sandy Beach Motel

Location → Btn Dibba & Khorfakkan · Al Aqqa	09 244 5555
Hours → na	
Web/email → www.sandybm.com	Map Ref → UAE-E2

The Sandy Beach Motel offers basic accommodation in hotel rooms or self-catering chalets with lovely views across the Gulf of Oman. Snorkelling and diving are available, plus there's a long beach, pool and children's play area. The restaurant has a varied menu and there are also two bars.

Hatta

Hatta Fort Hotel

Location → 110Km from Dubai	04 852 3211
Hours → Timings on request	
Web/email → www.jebelali-international.com	Map Ref → UAE-D3

Just over an hour's drive from Dubai, the Hatta Fort Hotel is an oasis of tranquillity. Each of the 50 chalet style rooms are spacious, comfortable and thoughtfully equipped. The hotel's restaurants, swimming pool and terraces offer breathtaking views of the mountains, while there's plenty going on if it's activity you're looking for. Check with the hotel about their excellent rates during the summer.

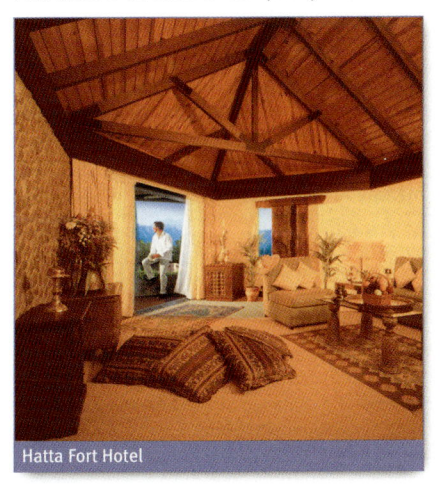

Jazira

Al Diar Jazira Beach Resort

Location → Ghantoot Area	02 562 9100
Hours → na	
Web/email → jazbeach@emirates.net.ae	Map Ref → UAE-B3

Jazira is situated halfway between Dubai and Abu Dhabi on a manmade island, right in the middle of nowhere. Rooms and self catering chalets have views over the pool, lawns and beach.

Jebel Ali

Jebel Ali Golf Resort & Spa

Location → Jct 13 · Sheik Zayed Rd	04 883 6000
Hours → na	
Web/email → www.jebelalihotel.com	Map Ref → 10-A1

Set in luxurious tropical gardens a mere 30 minutes drive from Dubai, the Jebel Ali Hotel is truly a self-contained resort. The 128 acre grounds are packed with exciting things to see and do, including camel rides, tennis, golf, horse riding. The Peaco Children's Club is a supervised play centre with loads of activities for little ones.

Khasab

Khasab Hotel

Location → Nr Khasab Airport · Mussandam	+968 83 0271
Hours → na	
Web/email → na	Map Ref → Oman

Khasab Hotel is the only hotel in the area and has 15 rooms, a small restaurant, bar, lounge and swimming pool. Furnishings are dated, but rooms are clean and have en suite bathrooms. Meals are generally eaten by the pool and the atmosphere is relaxed and friendly. Rates are very reasonable.

Hatta Fort Hotel

Khor Fakkan

Oceanic Hotel

Location ➔ Beach Rd · Khorfakkan	09 238 5111
Hours ➔ na	
Web/email ➔ www.oceanichotel.com	Map Ref ➔ UAE-E2

With its star-shaped architecture and rooftop restaurant, the Oceanic Hotel is prominent at the north end of Khorfakkan bay. The hotel prides itself on offering a range of outdoor activities and water sports, and also boasts its own sandy beach and lush gardens. The two restaurants serve international food. Take note that Khorfakkan is part of the emirate of Sharjah, so no alcohol is served.

Liwa

Liwa Resthouse

Location ➔ Mezirah	02 882 2075
Hours ➔ na	
Web/email ➔ na	Map Ref ➔ Oman

The Liwa Resthouse is popular with expats in the winter and offers 21 clean and comfortable rooms. Prices vary from Dhs.165 – 330 (children under eight years stay for free). Meals are served in a large dining area near reception, and a recreation room offers various amusements, plus table tennis and snooker. It is a little hidden away, but on arrival at Mezirah, follow the sign for the police station and the hotel is on a hill just behind the station.

Muscat

Al Bustan Palace InterContinental Muscat

Location ➔ Mutrah	+968 79 9666
Hours ➔ na	
Web/email ➔ www.intercontinental.com	Map Ref ➔ Oman

This luxury retreat is widely regarded as one of the best hotels in the Middle East, and offers an opulent getaway for those who love the VIP lifestyle. Families are well looked after, particularly during the daytime when there are lots of outdoor activities for kids. Things get a bit more formal in the evenings, but if they prefer, kids can watch DVDs and get room service while the grown-ups head for one of the many restaurants. A babysitting service is available, if required.

Grand Hyatt Muscat

Location ➔ Shati Al Qurm	+968 64 1234
Hours ➔ na	
Web/email ➔ www.hyatt.com	Map Ref ➔ Oman

This spectacular hotel is located in Muscat's diplomatic enclave, amid quiet white villas and embassies. A touch of Omani culture gently influences the décor of the 280 rooms, most of which have balconies overlooking the landscaped pool garden. There is a swimming pool and lazy river, as well as a special pool just for kids. A babysitting service is available.

Holiday Inn Muscat

Location ➔ Al Khuwayr, Muscat	+968 68 7123
Hours ➔ na	
Web/email ➔ mcthinn@omantel.net.om	Map Ref ➔ Oman

This unassuming hotel is comfortable and convenient and covers the needs of most potential guests. The large swimming pool and attached paddling pool will keep splash happy kids occupied for hours, and when they get tired of the outdoors, the satellite TV in the rooms will do the same! Five food outlets cater to most tastes and the Tex Mex restaurant features a live band every night. As club membership is open to non-residents, the facilities can get particularly crowded on Fridays.

Hotel InterContinental Muscat

Location ➔ Shati Al Qurm	+968 60 0500
Hours ➔ na	
Web/email ➔ www.interconti.com	Map Ref ➔ Oman

At this hotel, the stunning sea and mountain views, combined with the relaxing palm garden, make a tranquil getaway spot. And while Mum and Dad are chilling out, kids can let off steam in the pool, on the beach, in the fitness centre or on the sports court!

Mercure Al Falaj Hotel

Location ➔ Ruwi	+968 70 2311
Hours ➔ na	
Web/email ➔ www.omanhotels.com	Map Ref ➔ Oman

This comfortable and welcoming hotel incorporates Various food and beverage outlets including a pub, coffee shop and Japanese and Korean/Chinese restaurants. Outside, there are two swimming pools, tennis and squash facilities and even mini-golf, to keep the youngsters entertained.

MacKenzie Associates
SPECIALIST DECORATION

MURALS • SPECIALIST PAINTING • CREATIVE COMMISSIONS

PO Box 34275 Dubai UAE • Tel 04 336 4710 • Fax 04 336 4710

Radisson SAS Muscat	
Location → Al Khuwayr	+968 68 5381
Hours → na	
Web/email → www.radisson.com	Map Ref → Oman

Many of the rooms here have beautiful views of the sea and mountains, even the hotel is not far from the city and airport. There are plenty of options foodwise, while facilities include a health and fitness centre, outdoor pool set in landscaped gardens, plus a beach club with water sports only minutes away.

Sheraton Oman Hotel	
Location → Ruwi, Muscat	+968 79 9899
Hours → na	
Web/email → sheraton@omantel.net.om	Map Ref → Oman

Comfortable and elegant, the Sheraton Oman Hotel offers guests a variety of facilities, and the quality expected from a Sheraton hotel. Kids will love the cable TV, the large swimming pool outside and the fitness and tennis facilities. Babysitting and cots available.

Nizwa

Falaj Daris Hotel	
Location → Nr Toyota Showroom ·	+968 41 0500
Hours → na	
Web/email → sdhnizwa@omantel.net.om	Map Ref → Oman

A weekend jaunt to the Falaj Daris is a 'must do' for those adventurous folk exploring Oman's interior. The hotel is built in traditional style around a lush green courtyard and swimming pool. Standards are high and facilities include a gym, lounge bar and restaurant.

Ras Al Khaimah

Al Hamra Fort Hotel	
Location → Opp RAK Ceramics	07 244 6666
Hours → na	
Web/email → www.alhamrafort.com	Map Ref → UAE-D1

Built on an island in the style of an Arabian fort, the surroundings here are peaceful and luxurious. All rooms offer sea views and large balconies, and there is a good range of both water sports and dry land activities, plus a choice of four restaurants.

Ras Al Khaimah Hotel	
Location → Nr RAK Corniche	07 236 2999
Hours → na	
Web/email → na	Map Ref → UAE-D1

An hour's drive from Dubai, the Ras Al Khaimah Hotel offers views of the corniche and mountains. The rooms are well furnished and the food outlets have a range of good quality, good value cuisine. Various leisure activities are available, plus there's a beauty salon and Internet café. Alcohol is not served in the hotel.

Sohar

Sohar Beach Hotel	
Location → Left from Salan R/A (blue dome)	+968 84 1111
Hours → na	
Web/email → soharhtl@omantel.net.om	Map Ref → Oman

Appealingly designed to resemble an Omani fort, this small hotel has 41 rooms surrounding a central pool area. The atmosphere is intimate and relaxed and even when fully occupied the hotel is remarkably quiet. Limited food and beverage outlets provide a basic range of meals and snacks.

Umm Al Quwain

Flamingo Beach Resort	
Location → Right at Horsehead R/A	06 765 1185
Hours → na	
Web/email → www.flamingoresort.ae	Map Ref → UAE-C1

This resort has a pleasantly self contained atmosphere helped by the shallow, calm waters of its lagoon. The old Tourist Clubhouse is surrounded by 52 rooms, which overlook the pool, terrace and new restaurant. At dusk try crab hunting, or go on a conventional fishing trip. Many other water activities are also available.

Escape the rat race and enjoy the serenity

The Authoritative Guidebook on Abu Dhabi & Al Ain

Capitalising on all things cultural and cool in our capital, the 4th edition of the Abu Dhabi Explorer is packed with more than a few excuses to improve your get up and go. Let's just say with this book life's a walk in the park, or a stroll down Abu Dhabi's Corniche.

- General Information & UAE Overview
- Resident tips & advise
- New, informative business section
- 250 independent restaurant, bar & cafe reviews
- Exploring - museums, heritage, parks & beaches
- Shopping - what to buy and where to buy it
- Activities - sports, leisure, clubs & kids
- 36 fully referenced photographic maps

Passionately Publishing...

EXPLORER

Phone (971 4) 335 3520 • Fax (971 4) 335 3529 • Email Info@Explorer-Publishing.com

Insiders' City Guides • Photography Books • Activity Guidebooks • Commissioned Publications • Distribution

www.Explorer-Publishing.com

FLYING ELEPHANT
...We put the FUN in function.

Corporate Family Days
Theme Decoration • Birthday Parties

Tel: 04 347 9170   www.flyingelephantuae.com

Birthday Parties

EXPLORER

Birthday Parties

Birthday Parties	151	Karting	158	Parties at Home	163
		Museums	159	Birthday Cakes	165
Indoor Venues	**151**	Play Centres	159	Organisers & Entertainers	167
		Sporty Parties	161	Party Accessories	167
Amusement Centres	151				
Arty Parties	151	**Outdoor Venues**	**161**	**Theme Parties**	**170**
Bowling	152				
Cinema	153	Beaches	161		
Clubs, Hotels &		Paintballing	161	**Out Of Town Parties**	**170**
Restaurant Venues	153	Parks	162		
Fast Food	156	Sporty Parties	162		
Ice Skating	158	Water Parks	163		

MUST HAVE

Whether you are brave enough to hold your child's birthday party at home or have taken the (slightly) easier option of a hiring a geared up location, Park 'n Shop is the place to get your birthday cake. Not all private venues provide a birthday cake, and even if they do you can still opt to bring your own and Park 'n Shop have a fabulous range of cakes, whether you want Finding Nemo, Winnie the Pooh or your own picture. See [p.166]

MUST SEE

If you want to see a really big smile on your birthday girl or boy's face then children's entertainers Flying Elephant will deliver. The expert party organisers will arrange the perfect theme party, and have a handle on all the important details such as personalised balloons and decorations. See [p.167]

My girl lollipop!

Birthday Parties

Birthday parties are so much fun, but parents know all too well that the weeks of planning beforehand can cause frayed nerves and frazzled tempers. You may find yourself fretting over which venue to choose, what activities are popular for a certain age, what to feed a large group of fussy eaters and, of course, how skinny your wallet will be after forking out for the party of the year! Well, mums and dads, you can relax, because all the information you'll ever need to throw the perfect bash is right here at your fingertips. This section has been split into Indoor and Outdoor Parties, since the weather in Dubai can be either gloriously sunny or too hot to handle, depending on the time of year. You'll also find out who to call for the tastiest cakes, the funniest entertainers, the funkiest decorations and the coolest activities.

Basic Party Survival Tips!

- Keep the party short – maximum two hours
- Limit the number invited. For crowds, use an outdoor venue like a park
- If the party is at home and you have a garden, use it
- Keep a camera (and spare batteries) handy (but away from inquisitive hands)
- Remember, activities are as important as the food
- Keep the food simple. Don't over-produce
- When each child arrives with a present keep it to one side and then open them all together so as not to disrupt the flow of the party
- Plan the party in advance and keep a time and activity schedule card with you – it will give you the illusion of control!
- For party games fill a box with everything you'll need for each game or activity and put it where the action will take place
- Don't over stimulate. Plan a mix of active and quieter activities
- Blow a whistle to keep control and to remind children to have a drink
- Arrange a few backup games in case they go through everything with terrifying speed
- Keep party bags at the front door, so you won't forget to hand them out when kids leave

Birthday Party Summary

- Choose from various venues, see list below
- The total cost is based on the average birthday package per child. Costs listed are approximate and will depend on the individual's requirements
- Birthday cakes are not included in the package, although a cake can usually be supplied or you can take your own.
- Most parties listed are for two hours duration
- Generally food and birthday decorations are included in the package
- Most venues ask for a non refundable booking deposit
- Refer also to the Fast Food birthday party table [p.157]. Parties at these outlets generally cost between Dhs.10 - 20 per head, for a group of 10 - 20 children

Indoor Venues

If your child's birthday falls during the summer months, keep your party guests out of the blazing heat by choosing one of the following indoor options. Most of the listed venues offer special birthday packages, often including meals, entertainment, decorations and even a cake! The fast food table [p.157] summarises the contact details and guideline costs for these venues.

Amusement Centres

Other options → Amusement Centres (Activities) [p.83]

Many amusement centres organise birthday parties on request, and these are generally planned for a time span of two hours (long enough for the children as well as the parents!) For further information on individual amusement centres, refer to the Activities Section [p.83].

Arty Parties

Other options → Art Classes [p.126]

If the usual run of the mill party format is a bit 'been there, done that' for your youngster, and you're looking for fresh ideas, then why not try an 'arty-party'? Outlets such as Café Ceramique and

Brush & Bisque It allow children to select ceramic objects (anything from mugs to money boxes) and paint them in their own designs. Not only will your party guests enjoy an afternoon of artistic expression, but their finished items, once fired, will make great party mementoes.

Abu Dhabi

Café Ceramique

Location → Nr Choitrams 26th St Khalidiya
Hours → 08:00 - 24:00
Web/email → www.café-ceramique.com
02 666 4412
Map Ref → 9-C1

With a separate room for parties, this large café offers a 'paint and play' concept, which includes pottery painting, sand art, games, music and dancing. Party packages include decorations, invitations and a special memento for the birthday boy or girl.

Prices: Dhs.50 - 75 per child (minimum 12 children)

Dubai

Brush & Bisque It

Location → Jumeirah Plaza · Jumeira
Hours → 10:00 - 22:00   Fri 14:00 - 22:00
Web/email → bisqueit@emirates.net.ae
04 349 8899
Map Ref → 12-A1

Encourage artistic potential at a private party at the Brush & Bisque It ceramics studio. Choose pieces for all the children to paint, or book an instructor to teach them mosaic, collage and more. Take your own food or order from the nearby Dome Café.

Prices: From Dhs.25 per child

Feeding time at the Zoo

Café Ceramique

Location → Town Centre · Jumeira
Hours → 08:00 - 24:00
Web/email → www.café-ceramique.com
04 344 7331
Map Ref → 12-E1

See the Abu Dhabi review for further details.

Bowling

Other options → Bowling (Activities) [p.88]

Bowling is about much more than simply strapping on a pair of multi-coloured, white soled shoes – it encourages physical activity and team work, and since your average child doesn't go bowling that often, it scores high points for novelty value! You can pretty much guarantee that a bowling alley birthday party will be a great success, whether you have six guests or a whole class full.

Abu Dhabi

Khalifa International Bowling Centre

Location → Nr Zayed Sports Complex
Hours → See below
Web/email → na
02 403 4648
Map Ref → 2-B1

This modern bowling alley boasts 40 lanes. Birthday parties are welcomed and lanes will be booked for you. While food is not included in the price, you can easily arrange this separately with the in-house restaurant.

Prices: Dhs.7 per child. Dhs.5 each for a pair bowling shoes. Special discount rates given according to the number of children
Timings: 12:00 - 24:00, Thu 10:00-24:00, Fri 14:00 - 24:00

Dubai

Al Nasr Leisureland

Location → Beh American Hospital · Oud Metha
Hours → 09:00 - 23:00
Web/email → www.alnasrleisureland.co.ae
04 337 1234
Map Ref → 13-E4

Parties at this eight lane alley are great for large numbers. Remember to book ahead, and ask your party guests to wear socks and trainers. Bowling shoes are available free of cost.

Prices: Dhs.7 entrance per child plus Dhs.25 each for food

Thunder Bowl

Location ➔ Nr Defence R/A, · Trade Centre 1 & 2 | **04 343 1000**
Hours ➔ 09:00 - 24:00
Web/email ➔ tb@emirates.net.ae   Map Ref ➔ 12-E2

A typical party at Thunder Bowl includes an hour of bowling followed by a meal upstairs. The general package includes bowling, balloons, invitations, two tokens for the video games, and the meal. Trainers and socks are the recommended footwear.

Prices: Dhs.35 per child (1 hour); Dhs.45 (1½ hours)

Cinema

A birthday party at the movies is a special treat for slightly older kids and their friends, depending of course on what films are being screened at the

Cinemas

Arabic (Abu Dhabi)
Century Cinemas	02 645 8988
Cinestar Marina Mall	02 681 8484
Grand Cineplex	02 633 3000

Asian (Abu Dhabi)
Eldorado	02 676 3555
National	02 671 1700

English (Abu Dhabi)
Century Cinemas	02 645 8988
Cinestar Marina Mall	02 681 8484
Cinestar Gold Class	02 681 8484
Grand Al Mariah	02 678 5000
Grand Cineplex	02 633 3000

Arabic (Dubai)
Century Cinemas	04 349 8765
Cinestar	04 294 9000
Grand Cineplex	04 324 2000
Grand Metroplex	04 343 8383

Asian (Dubai)
Al Nasr	04 337 4353
Donya	04 881 2838
Galleria	04 209 6469
Lamcy	04 336 8808
Plaza	04 393 9966
Rex Drive-in	04 288 6447

English (Dubai)
Century Cinemas	04 349 8765
Cinestar	04 294 9000
Grand Cineplex	04 324 2000

time. It is also an activity that busy parents will love, as it requires very little planning other than standing in the ticket line and making sure everybody has popcorn! Combine a movie party with a sleepover or a fast food dinner, for a truly memorable birthday. The cinema listings table shows where you are likely to find English, Arabic or Asian films, but to find out exactly what films are showing, call the cinemas directly, log on to their websites, or see the local press.

> **Movie babies**
>
> For mothers with young babies, Cinestar Dubai has a 'babes in arms' session showing the latest film release every Tuesday morning at 9:30. The lights are left on and the sound level is decreased.

Clubs, Hotels & Restaurant Venues

Other options ➔ Eating Out [p.177]

Most food and entertainment venues can make arrangements for birthday party groups, so check with your favourite restaurant, health club or hotel for what special activities or menus they can offer. Generally outlets have indoor and outdoor options, so you can party in the sunshine during winter, and in the air-conditioning during summer!

Abu Dhabi

Club, The

Location ➔ Club, The · Al Meena | **02 673 1111**
Hours ➔ 08:00 - 01:00 Fri 08:00 - 24:00
Web/email ➔ www.the-club.com   Map Ref ➔ 4-A3

For a tailor made birthday party, The Club lets you choose the menu, cake, setting (ie, the main hall, the family play area or even the beach), and the activities (bouncy castle, disco set-up, etc).

Prices: Vary depending on the package. Contact the club

Chili's

Location ➔ Grand Al Mariah Cineplex | **02 671 6300**
Hours ➔ See timings below
Web/email ➔ www.chilis.com   Map Ref ➔ 8-B2

Chili's offers a range of kiddie meals, including soft drinks. The recommended time for parties is from 16:00 to 19:30 daily, when the restaurant is quiet. Call in advance for bookings.

Prices: Dhs.11 per child
Timings: 11:00 - 23:00 Thu 11:00 - 24:00 Fri 13:00 - 23:00

Fuddruckers

Location → Marina Mall · Breakwater
Hours → 08:00 - 24:00
Web/email → www.marinamall.ae
02 681 8160
Map Ref → 5-A2

The special party room at Fuddruckers has plenty to keep the kids entertained. Face painting, organised games, a clown and food are all included in the price. A birthday cake and video coverage can be provided on request.

Prices: Dhs.20 per child

Hilton Abu Dhabi

Location → Corniche Rd West
Hours → On request
Web/email → www.hilton.com
02 681 1900
Map Ref → 5-D3

Coconut Bay at the Hilton is a party destination with an endless list of activities on offer – clowns, bouncy castles, magicians, handicrafts, sports, music, games – everything a little one's heart desires! There is also the beach, the pool and a children's animal farm.

Prices: Contact the hotel and ask for the Banqueting and Conference Centre for further details

Hilton Baynunah Tower

Location → Corniche Rd West
Hours → On request
Web/email → www.hilton.com
02 632 7777
Map Ref → 5-A3

Parties are held in the Al Dhafra Hall, The price includes room decoration, balloons, streamers, TV/ video and one hour of swimming in our indoor swimming pool situated on the 29th floor of the residence.

Prices: Various party menus from Dhs.35 - 45

Le Meridien Abu Dhabi

Location → Le Meridien · Al Meena
Hours → Various timings
Web/email → www.lemeridien-abudhabi.com
02 644 6666
Map Ref → 4-B3

A tasty menu just for the kids comprises mini pizzas, hamburgers, chicken nuggets, desserts, soft drinks and juices. Also on offer is a bouncy castle and face painting for 2 hours. The lush gardens are home to a splendid pool, and there is also the beach facilities, both are available for use by your party.

Prices: Dhs.70 per child, minimum 30 children
Supervision fees are an additional cost.

Marina Mall

Location → Breakwater
Hours → 10:00 - 22:00 Fri 14:00 - 22:00
Web/email → www.marinamall.ae
02 681 8300
Map Ref → 5-D4

Party packages include food, free dining area for two hours, invitation cards, balloons, paper crowns, games, face painting and a gift for the birthday boy or girl. The fast food outlets also cater for children's parties.

Prices: Dhs.17 per child, minimum 20 children

Sheraton Abu Dhabi Resort & Towers

Location → Nr Corniche Hosp · Corniche Rd East
Hours → 07:00 - 22:00
Web/email → www.sheraton.com
02 677 3333
Map Ref → 4-C4

You'll find indoor and outdoor activities galore at Bizziwizz Kids' Club – from pirates' picnics to treasure hunts, arts and crafts to sporty games, they've got birthday party fun covered! The Club is ideally suited to kids aged 4 to 13 years.

Prices: Vary depending on choice of activity. Check with club

TGI Friday's

Location → Tourist Club Area
Hours → 11:00 - 01:00
Web/email → tgiauh1@kfcuae.co.ae
02 674 4500
Map Ref → 7-E1

At this vibey venue, each guest can choose their own meal from the varied children's menu. Balloons, colouring in menus and crayons are provided for entertainment. A cake can be arranged, or you can bring your own.

Prices: From Dhs.11 per child (for food) not including soft drinks

Explorer Food Reporter!

A Star Studded Dining Experience For The Whole Family

PLANET HOLLYWOOD

Great American food, authentic Hollywood memorabilia and the biggest stars performing for you on the big screen

Funfilled exciting activities for kids every month and an awesome WILD BRUNCH every Friday

Birthday Parties with games, decorations, fun food and beverages and everything to make your party special.

Dance the night away at our **Disco Parties** with your own DJ

ENCOUNTER ZONE

Experience the chills, thrills and frills of ultimate entertainment!

Visit 2 of Encounter Zone's Famous Theme areas, Galactica and Lunarland! Fun for All Ages

- Get the Thrill run down your spine in the CHAMBER (Live Horror Show)
- Get the Chill in MAX FLIGHT (Virtual Reality Roller Coaster)
- Get frilled in the CRYSTAL MAZE (Same as the TV Game show)
- Get your guts going in GALACTICA EXPRESS

Celebrate your Birthday in deep space and make it the most memorable one you've ever had!

Ultimate Venue: Moonbase
Great Alien theme parties with special customer service member assigned to take care of your every need. Your choice of cake design & flavour and menu selection from our food court.

For more information, please call - tel : 04 324 4777, fax : 04 324 5757
e-mail us at phsales@emirates.net.ae / ezone@emirates.net.ae or
log on to www.planethollywood-dubai.com

WAFI CITY

Dubai

Chili's

Location → Merdian Fairways · Al Garhoud | 04 282 8484
Hours → 11:00 - 23:00   Thu 11:00 - 01:00   Fri 13:00 - 23:00
Web/email → www.chilis.com | Map Ref → 13-B1

Refer to the Abu Dhabi review [p.153] for further details.

Fudd's Playland

Location → Fuddruckers · Al Garhoud | 04 282 7771
Hours → 07:30 - 23:00
Web/email → fudxbger@eim.ae | Map Ref → 15-D1

A two hour party includes face painting, a clown, food, organised games, decorations and music in the soft play area, and the latest Disney videos are shown in the kids' theatre downstairs. Suitable for children aged one to ten (minimum group of 20).

Prices: Dhs.20 per child

Hard Rock Café

Location → Hard Rock Café · Jct 5 Shk Zayed Rd | 04 399 2888
Hours → 12:00 - 01:00
Web/email → www.hardrock.com | Map Ref → 11-C2

Hard Rock Café knows how to host a rockin' rollin' party – guests can choose from the Lil' Rock birthday menu, and each child gets a colouring book, crayons and balloons. The birthday brownie, a cake with a difference, should be ordered in advance.

Prices: Dhs.25 per child

Pharaoh's Club

Location → Pyramids · Umm Hurair (2) | 04 324 0000
Hours → 07:00 - 22:00   Fri 07:00 - 21:30
Web/email → www.pyramidsdubai.com | Map Ref → 15-C1

Birthday parties at Pharaoh's are held either in the children's club, around the lazy river, or on the climbing wall. There are various packages, all of which include food, decorations and service. Additional entertainment (clown, magician, bouncy castle, etc) can be arranged.

Prices: Dhs.50 - 75, depending on the package.

Planet Hollywood

Location → Wafi City · Umm Hurair (2) | 04 324 4777
Hours → 12:00 - 24:00
Web/email → www.planethollywood-dubai.com | Map Ref → 15-C1

Lights, camera, action! Let your birthday guests delve into the fascinating world of movies in a star studded setting. Planet Hollywood has various party options and will arrange just about anything you have in mind. They also have complimentary climbing frames for the younger ones to play on. The basic package includes food and an entertainer.

Prices: Dhs.25 - 35 for the basic party package

Party time at Planet Hollywood

Sinbads Club

Location → Jumeirah Beach Htl · Umm Suqeim | 04 348 0000
Hours → 08:00 - 20:00
Web/email → na | Map Ref → 12-A1

Fully supervised parties can be arranged at Sinbad's and the great adventure playground, with its huge maze of climbing frames and slides. Food and games are included with musicians, face painting, water rides and a birthday cake (all optional extras.) Call for more info.

Prices: Various party menus from Dhs.40 - 60; Supervision fees start at Dhs.150

TGI Friday's

Location → Shk Zayed Rd | 04 331 8010
Hours → 11:00 - 01:00
Web/email → tgifdxb@kfcuae.co.ae | Map Ref → 13-B3

Refer to the Abu Dhabi review [p.154] for details.

Fast Food

Fast food outlets certainly have birthday parties down to a fine art – they'll have your group fed, entertained, filmed and all played out within two hours! All the various fast food chains are available at different locations throughout the Emirates, although not all outlets are suitable for parties, so phone ahead for more info.

Fast Food Outlets

American Fried Chicken
Dubai	Hamarain Centre	04 262 4411

Burger King
Abu Dhabi	Hamdan Street	02 633 2338
	Tourist Club Area	02 666 2526
Dubai	Al Diyafah Street	04 345 5941
	Beach Centre	04 344 7001

Chicken Tikka Inn
Dubai	Nr Nasser Square	04 222 5683

Hardee's
Abu Dhabi	Tourist Club Area	02 672 2345
	Airport Road	02 642 2944
Dubai	Al Diyafah Street	04 398 7616
	Lamcy Plaza	04 334 8324

Kentucky Fried Chicken
Abu Dhabi	Hamdan Street	02 627 7665
	Tourist Club Area	02 674 4600
Dubai	Al Faheidi Street	04 353 4337
	Rashidiya	04 285 6900
	Al Rigga Street	04 223 2536

McDonald's
Abu Dhabi	Al Falah Plaza	02 642 4770
	Al Mariah Cinema	02 676 6500
Dubai	Al Bustan Centre	04 263 3619
	Al Ghurair Centre	04 223 6817
	Al Khaleej Centre	04 359 9141
	Holiday Centre Mall	04 331 3221

Pizza Corner
Dubai	Khalid Bin Walid Street	04 228 4330

Pizza Hut
Abu Dhabi	Hamdan Street	02 627 7667
	Airport Road	02 446 1900
Dubai	Al Diyafah Road	04 345 1225
	Al Rigga Street	04 223 2511

Pizza Inn
Abu Dhabi	Hamdan Street	02 679 1919
Dubai	Muraqabbat Street	04 273 7360
	Shk Hamdan Colony	04 396 8256

Subway
Abu Dhabi	Tourist Club Area	02 645 2100
Dubai	Mercato Mall	04 342 0550
	Town Centre	04 344 0111
	Al Ain Centre	04 355 1221

Pizzaland
Abu Dhabi	Meena Road	02 673 3220
Dubai	Al Rigga Road	04 222 5666
	Umm Suqeim	04 348 4911

Burger King

Burger King offers a choice of three menus, each come a toy, decorations, face painting, balloons and two hours of video coverage. A mascot and supervision can also be arranged. All you need to bring is the cake and the kids!

Prices: Dhs.15 per child

Hardee's

Hardee's offers various party packages with some or all of the following options: invitations, games, singing, dancing, food, face painting, story telling, magic show and birthday cake! They will also provide video coverage and a special gift for the birthday child.

Prices: Dhs.15, Dhs.18 or Dhs.20 per child, depending on package

Kentucky Fried Chicken

Parties can be held at any time at KFC, but book early for a weekend bash. The menu can be pre-arranged and the cost includes food, video coverage, five games and gifts.

Prices: Dhs.15 per child, minimum 20 children

McDonald's

Order Happy Meals for each of your birthday guests (minimum of 15 kids) and McDonald's will throw in the party decorations, a few party games, an appearance by Mr Hamburger, party bags for all and a special gift for the birthday child.

Prices: Dhs.10 per Happy Meal

Pizza Hut

Birthday party guests can enjoy two slices of pizza, a soft drink and five games (with gifts for the winners). Video coverage of the party is provided. There are party halls in the Sharjah, Rigga, Karama and Sharjah - Dubai Road branches.

Prices: Dhs.15 per child

Pizzaland

Parties are held in the reserved family zone where there is a small soft play area for little ones. The birthday package includes decorations gifts, fries, garlic cheese bread, pizza, salad, a soft drink and ice cream. Small and large groups welcome.

Prices: Dhs.10 per child; cake not included

Subway

For a birthday party at Subway, choose from individual meals of a sandwich, crisps or cookie, a soft drink and a gift, or go for the party platter, which has seven sandwiches cut into 21 pieces. Decorations can be arranged.

Prices: Dhs.10 per child

Ice Skating

Other options → Ice Skating (Activities) [p.100]

Ice skating rinks in Abu Dhabi and Dubai are an excellent venue at any time of the year and an obvious party option in the hotter months. All that ice can make things pretty cold, so don't forget to tell everybody to bring a jersey.

Abu Dhabi

Abu Dhabi Ice Rink

Location → Zayed Sport City · Old Airport Rd | 02 444 8458
Hours → See timings below
Web/email → na | Map Ref → 2-B1

Bring on the chills for a different party in the desert! A meal, skates and two hours of ice time are provided in the special party room, which can be decorated. Cake is not supplied but can be brought in.

Prices: Dhs.30 per child
Timings: Split into 4 sessions from 10:00 - 12:00, 12:30 - 14:30, 15:00 - 17:00, 17:30 - 19:30, 20:00 - 22:00

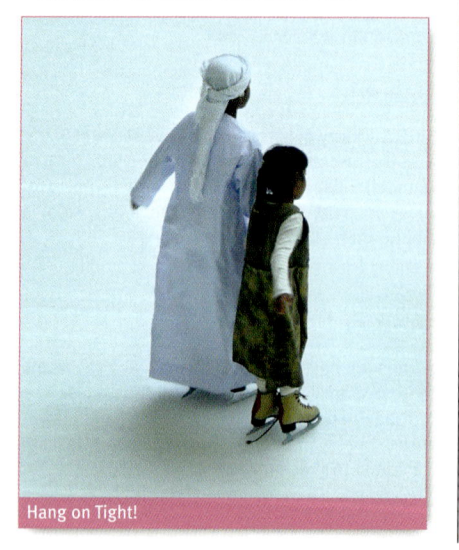

Hang on Tight!

Dubai

Al Nasr Leisureland

Location → Beh American Hospital · Oud Metha | 04 337 1234
Hours → 09:00 - 23:00
Web/email → www.alnasrleisureland.co.ae | Map Ref → 13-E4

You can host an ice skating birthday party which includes food, decorations and a sound system. The rink is not always available, so advance booking is essential.

Prices: Dhs.25 per child plus Dhs.5 hire each for a pair of skates

Galleria Ice Rink

Location → Hyatt Regency · Deira | 04 209 6550
Hours → See timings below
Web/email → www.dubai.regency.hyatt.com | Map Ref → 14-B1

You'll be spoilt for choice with all the various options available for skating parties at this popular ice rink – be sure to have a pen and paper handy when you call for more info!

Prices: From Dhs.20 per child
Timings: 10:00 - 13:30 14:00 - 17:30 18:00 - 21:00

Karting

Other options → Karting (Activities) [p.101]

Abu Dhabi

Leisure Games Centre

Location → Nr Tourist Club · Tourist Club Area | 02 679 3330
Hours → 09:00 - 12:00 17:00 - 24:00
Web/email → saeed-lgc@hotmail.com | Map Ref → 4-B3

This is a great way to let your kids get an early start on learning to drive! The Leisure Games Centre handles group bookings for birthday parties, and larger groups qualify for a discount.

Prices Dhs.30 for 10 minutes on the track.

Dubai

Emirates Karting Centre

Location → Nr Jebel Ali Hotel · Jebel Ali | 04 282 7111
Hours → 11:00 - 18:00
Web/email → www.emsf.ae | Map Ref → 10-A1

The newly renovated Emirates Karting Centre gives groups of children aged eight and upwards the opportunity to experience the thrill of racing.

Prices Dhs.30 for 10 minutes on the track.

Formula One Dubai

Location → Dubai Exiles Rugby Club · Dubai | 04 338 8828
Hours → 15:00 - 22:00
Web/email → f1dubai@emirates.net.ae | Map Ref → 15-C1

Currently operating out of a temporary outdoor racing track at the Dubai Exiles Rugby Club, Formula One Dubai is a brilliant party option for little Michael Schumacher wannabes. Call for more information about packages and discounted rates for groups.

Prices: Dhs.40 (10 min) per child (8+) ; Young adults (10 min) Dhs.50 (12+)

Museums

Other options → Museums (Activities) [p.135]

A trip to a museum makes an unusual, but fun and informative party destination for the right group of children. The advantage is that as long as you have transport, the outing can be arranged without too much fuss – just load your party guests into the car and let them expand their minds during an afternoon at one of the fascinating museums available. Abu Dhabi lacks any museums suitable for children, but it is well worth a trip to Sharjah to enjoy a day of education. Round the day off with a pit stop at a fast food restaurant, and you've just had yourself a successful party! The list of museums below offer excellent facilities for birthday parties. For alternative museums in both Abu Dhabi and Dubai refer to the Activities section [p.136].

Dubai

Children's City

Location → Creekside Park · Umm Hurair (2) | 04 334 0808
Hours → 09:00 - 21:00   Fri 15:00 - 22:00
Web/email → www.childrencity.ae | Map Ref → 15-C1

Children's City is an interactive science museum with plenty of interactive displays and activities. After a tour of the exhibits and a birthday tea party in the large café, sit back and relax while the kids let off some steam in Creek Park.

Prices: Dhs.20 per child, which includes a fast-food meal
Entrance Fee: Dhs.10 for children; Dhs.15 for adults
Timings: 09:00 - 21:30 (Sat - Thurs); 16:00 - 21:30 (Fri)

Sharjah

Discovery Centre

Location → Opp Sharjah Airport · Al Dhaid Rd | 06 558 6577
Hours → 09:00 - 14:00   Wed - Thu 15:30 - 20:30
Web/email → na | Map Ref → UAE-C2

Children aged three - 12 will have a great time in the fun and educational surroundings of this fascinating museum. Parties can be held on Wednesday, Thursday or Friday afternoons, and you can take your own food or arrange for catering inside the cafeteria.

Prices: Adults – Dhs.10; Children under 12 – Dhs.7. 20% discount for groups of more than 20.

Play Centres

Other options → Play Centres (Activities) [p.106]

Abu Dhabi

Fun Island

Location → Al Jernain Center · Shk Zayed 1st St | 02 665 9009
Hours → 10:00 - 22:00   Fri 16:00 - 22:00
Web/email → na | Map Ref → 5-A3

Fun Island, with its soft play area, tube slides, ball ponds and cruiser rollers, is great (and safe) fun for tiny tots. A birthday room is available.

Prices: Dhs.20 per child (for food); Dhs.300 for hire of the birthday room

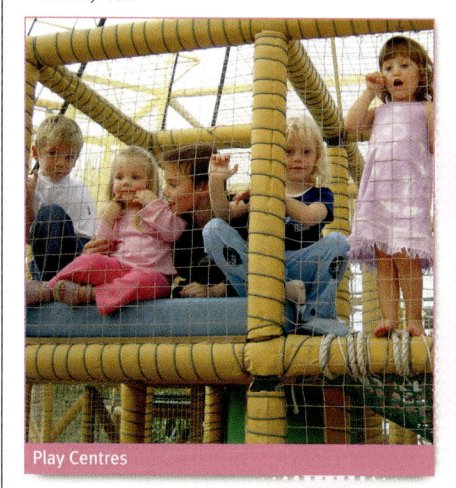

Play Centres

Gymboree Play & Music

Location → Khalidia Palace Htl · Khalidiya
Hours → 08:00 - 18:00 Closed Fri
Web/email → www.gymboree.com
02 665 8882
Map Ref → 7-A2

Gymboree organises in house and home parties in both Abu Dhabi and Dubai. All party goodies are provided including games, clowns, bouncy castles, cartoon characters (weekdays), cooking activities (weekends), face painting, and arts and crafts activities. Food is not included.

Prices: Private locations (aged 1 - 12) Dhs.1000+; Gymboree locations (aged 1 - 6) Dhs.35 minimum 15 children (weekdays), Dhs.45 minimum 20 children (weekends)

Kids Play

Location → Toys 'R' Us · Mina Rd
Hours → 10:00 - 22:00
Web/email → info@alfuttaimsons.com
02 673 2332
Map Ref → 7-B4

Situated in the same centre as Toys 'R' Us (in both Abu Dhabi and Dubai), Kids Play party packages include 75 minutes in the play zone, a private party room, food and invitations. They'll even provide staff to supervise and clean up afterwards!

Prices: Dhs.35 per child (Dhs.100 deposit required)

Dubai

Doodles

Location → Al Khaleej Centre · Bur Dubai
Hours → 09:00 - 22:00   Fri 14:00 - 22:00
Web/email → khaleejc@emirates.net.ae
04 352 2843
Map Ref → 13-E2

Doodles focuses on the very young, with a mini adventure play area for infants and a special role playing area for kids aged one to eight. A typical party lasts for three hours, with party games, face painting, a clown, helium balloons and a meal.

Prices: Dhs 40 per child (minimum 12 children)

Fun Corner

Location → Spinneys · Umm Suqeim
Hours → 09:00 - 22:00
Web/email → www.spinneys.com
04 394 1215
Map Ref → 12-C2

Fun Corner offers three party packages – the basic package includes two hours of play, a meal, invitations, balloons, party bags and a gift for the birthday child. Other packages add on activities such as games, face painting or even a complete party theme.

Prices: Dhs.40, Dhs.55 or Dhs.88 per child depending on package

Gymboree Play & Music

Location → Al Mina Rd · Satwa
Hours → 08:00 - 18:00 Closed Fri
Web/email → www.gymboree.com
04 345 4422
Map Ref → 7-A2

Refer the Abu Dhabi review for details.

Kids Play

Location → Toys 'R' Us · Al Futtaim Centre
Hours → 10:00 - 22:00
Web/email → info@alfuttaimsons.com
04 224 0000
Map Ref → 14-C3

Refer the Abu Dhabi review for details.

Lou Lou Al Dougongs

Location → Lamcy Plaza · Oud Metha
Hours → 10:00 - 22:00   Wed & Thu 10:00 - 23:00
Web/email → www.lououaldugong.com
04 335 2700
Map Ref → 13-E4

There's something for kids of all ages at this popular play centre, from the soft play area for babies to the imaginative activities for older children (mini supermarket, mini kitchen, fishing area, water play, face painting, arts studio etc). Various birthday packages are available.

Prices: Dhs.45 - 60 per child

Safe Play

Location → Jumeirah Plaza · Jumeira
Hours → 09:00 - 21:30   Wed & Thu 09:30 - 22:30
Web/email → www.dubaishoppingmalls.com
04 349 9119
Map Ref → 13-B1

This is another branch of Fun Corner and the birthday packages are similar. This venue is more suitable for younger children. Party meals are provided by the Dome café who can be relied upon to deliver a superior chicken nugget!

Prices: Dhs.40, Dhs.55 or Dhs.80 per child depending on the party package. Minimum 15 children

Toby's Jungle Adventure

Location → BurJuman Centre · Bur Dubai
Hours → 10:30 - 22:00   Fri 14:00 - 22:30
Web/email → na
04 355 2868
Map Ref → 14-A3

Your party guests can enjoy two hours of fun and excitement in Toby's Jungle Adventure, including a meal from A&W in the party area, and a surprise visit from Toby the Bear or Toby the Turtle! Bring your own cake.

Prices: Dhs.30 per child

Sporty Parties

You can easily satisfy young sports fans by improvising. Refer to the Activity section [p.82], choose your youngster's favourite sporting activity and tailor make a Sporty Party to remember.

Dubai

LG InSportz

Location → Jct 3, Shk Zayed Rd · Shk Zayed Rd | 04 347 5833
Hours → 09:30 - 21:30
Web/email → www.insportzclub.com | Map Ref → 12-B2

The air conditioned facilities at Insportz are especially suitable for summer parties when outdoor temperatures start soaring. The birthday package includes a variety of sports and two hours of supervised games. No meal is included, but you can take your own food.

Prices: Dhs.350, maximum 20 children. Dhs.15 for every additional child

Outdoor Venues

Make use of the wonderful weather between October and April to host your child's party outdoors. Whether it's a trip to the local park, a private club or the beach, there are plenty of choices to suit all requirements and budgets. Remember when choosing a destination that the distance you have to travel, either by vehicle or on foot, will limit games, props, catering and numbers. Volunteer parents may also be required to keep an eye on participants and to assist in the organisation of games. Football, rounders and tag are good team games that can be played anywhere, as long as you have enough space. For beach parties, a team sand building competition with a theme can be great fun, using natural decorations, such as shells and wood found on the beach. A competition to see who can pick up the most rubbish is a fun way to clean up at the end of the party! Remember to keep all your party guests well hydrated with regular drinks breaks, and most importantly, make it a non negotiable rule that all kids and adults are well protected from the sizzling sun, even during the cooler months, with hats and sun block all round.

Beaches

Other options → Beaches (Activities) [p.122]

The beaches of the UAE are beautiful, and beach parks have plenty of grassy areas, barbeque sections and playgrounds to keep the kids entertained. These picturesque parks are ideal for a chilled out party – just pack a picnic and let the kids run wild.

Prices: Dhs.5 - 20 per child

Building Sandcastles

Paintballing

Other options → Paintballing (Activities) [p.106]

While clearly not a first choice for pretty, pink, party princesses, paintballing will have your older, more boisterous birthday group fine tuning their battle tactics and splattering their mates with brightly coloured paint. At present there's nowhere in Abu Dhabi to cover friends in paint! However, this fun activity is available in Dubai. Paintball is suitable for kids over ten and protective clothing is provided.

Dubai

Pursuit Games

Location → WonderLand · Umm Hurair (2) | 04 324 1222
Hours → Timiings on request
Web/email → wonderld@emirates.net.ae | Map Ref → 15-C1

For a birthday that's active and good fun, book your party group in for two hours of paint balling at Pursuit Games. A minimum of six players is required, and an adult should accompany children under 12.

Prices: Dhs.70 for two hours (includes 100 paintballs). Each refill of 100 paintballs costs Dhs.50.

Parks

Other options → Parks (Activities) [p.124]

If you don't have a garden, or the thought of a wild bunch of rowdy kids stampeding through your flowerbeds gives you the cold shivers, then a party in one of Abu Dhabi's or Dubai's beautiful green parks could be the answer. Most of the parks are really child friendly, with vast lawns, playgrounds, sandpits and water features galore. Your party guests can spend the afternoon running free and making as much noise as they want while you supervise from your blanket under a shady tree. Another advantage of this option is that you can control the costs and effort involved – once you have paid the minimal park entrance fee, the catering and entertainment activities fall solely under your command. Pack lots of picnic blankets and prepare individual tubs filled with yummy goodies like biscuits, sandwiches, grapes, cucumber and carrot sticks, crisps, mini-sausages, etc, arrange the tubs on the blankets and voila! You have a birthday picnic feast. If that sounds too much like hard work, you could get outside caterers to prepare the food and you could pick it up on the way. Don't forget to take paper plates, serviettes, plastic cutlery and paper cups, and it's a good idea to pack a whole cooler full of drinks – running around in the UAE sunshine makes for seriously thirsty boys and girls. Most of the parks have kiosks and food outlets where you can stock up on refreshments if you run out. Games and activities can be planned in advance and supervised by you (it may be a good idea to enlist the help of a few other adults). Finally, don't forget to take some empty bags for collecting all your rubbish at the end of the day. Refer to the Activities section [p.124] for details on specific parks in both Abu Dhabi and Dubai.

Prices: Dhs.1 – 2 per child

Park Life

While municipality parks offer a great location for a party thanks to their lush greenery, plentiful trees and play areas they are also rather large and you can get lost – or loose party guests – in them very easily. So get friends to lend an extra watchful eye and also tie a few high flying balloons to a tree near your location so that if any children do wander off they can spot the party from a distance. Also don't set up too far from the toilets – especially after all that juice!

Sporty Parties

Abu Dhabi

Abu Dhabi Golf and Equestrian Club

Location → Al Tahnoon Street · Al Mushrif | 02 445 9600
Hours → 06:00 - 23:00
Web/email → www.adec-web.com | Map Ref → 3-D3

Get out of the city and relax as your child and friends play in the gardens and swim in the pool under the watchful eye of a lifeguard. You can select activities ranging from football to table tennis and drawing to organised games and music.

Prices: Dhs.30, 40 or 50 per child depending on the menu (minimum 25 children)

Dubai

Emirates Riding Centre

Location → Nr Golf & Racing Club · Nad Al Sheba | 04 336 1394
Hours → 08:00 - 13:00 16:00 - 19:00 Fri closed
Web/email → emrc@emirates.net.ae | Map Ref → 15-C1

For a unique birthday party activity, Dubai Equestrian Centre does pony rides for kids aged three and above. The groom leads each little rider around the square a couple of times before returning them safely to the group. Morning bookings are preferable.

Prices: From Dhs.15 per child

Jebel Ali Equestrian Club

Location → Jebel Ali Village · Jebel Ali | 04 884 5485
Hours → 08:00 - 11:30 16:00 - 19:00 Fri closed
Web/email → na | Map Ref → 10-E3

Pony rides can be arranged for a group of children. Afterwards you could take them for a picnic on the hill, or lunch at the nearby Hard Rock Café. Suitable for kids aged three and older.

Prices: From Dhs.10 per child

Jebel Ali Sailing Club

Location → Al Sufouh | 04 399 5444
Hours → 09:00 - 20:00   Thu & Fri 09:00 - 22:00
Web/email → www.jebelalisailingclub.com | Map Ref → 11-C1

Set on the beach at the mouth of the Creek, Jebel Ali Sailing Club offers activities such as sailing, kayaking, wind surfing or power boating for birthday party groups. There is also a pool, playground and party room for games. Catering is available.

Prices: Vary depending on the choice of activity. Check with club

UAE English Soccer School of Excellence FZ-LLC

Location → Various locations · Dubai | 050 476 4877
Hours → Various
Web/email → masty57@hotmail.com   Map Ref → na

For soccer mad kids, a coach can organise an hour of soccer and general ball games in your garden or local park. One coach can supervise up to 15 children.

Prices: Dhs.150 per coach

Jebel Ali

Club Joumana

Location → Jebel Ali Htl | 04 804 8058
Hours → 06:00 - 21:00
Web/email → www.jebelali-international.com   Map Ref → 10-A1

A golfing party in the beautifully landscaped grounds of Club Joumana can be an entertaining birthday option for kids over six. Pony rides are also available.

Prices: Dhs.750 for 8 - 15 children. Smaller groups can be accommodated

Water Parks

Other options → Water Parks [p.116]

Water Babies...
It is very important to take plenty of helpers to supervise water areas and limit the party numbers accordingly.

Water parks are a great way to celebrate a birthday in the outdoors. Abu Dhabi does not yet have a water park but it is well worth the trip into Dubai for a fun-filled day – even for the big kids!

Dubai

SplashLand

Location → WonderLand · Umm Hurair (2) | 04 324 3222
Hours → 10:00 - 19:00
Web/email → www.wonderlanduae.com   Map Ref → 15-C1

Celebrate your child's birthday with a splash at this water theme park with its self contained party area and wide choice of thrilling water rides. Entertainment, decorations, two hours of free play and a birthday cake are included in each package.

Prices: Dhs.45 - 65, depending on the package

Wild Wadi Water Park

Location → Wild Wadi · Umm Suqeim | 04 348 4444
Hours → Timings on request
Web/email → www.wildwadi.com   Map Ref → 12-A1

For a birthday that's wet and wild, treat your little guests to a party at Wild Wadi. The birthday package includes a full day pass and a picnic of sandwiches, crisps, chocolate, fruit, salad and juice. Recommended for juniors who are excellent swimmers. 48 hour confirmation is required and you get one free adult pass with every five children.

Prices: Dhs.120 per child; Dhs.140 per adult (excluding the free pass with every five children)

Timings: Vary depending on season. Call the above number before heading out

Umm Al Quwain

Dreamland Aqua Park

Location → 17km North of UAQ on RAK Rd · UAQ | 06 768 1888
Hours → 10:00 - 20:00
Web/email → www.dreamlanduae.com   Map Ref → UAE-D1

Birthday packages at this water adventure park are available for groups of 20 or more. After the thrill of the rides, recharge the kids' batteries with a meal from one of the fast food outlets on site. Birthday cakes are available on request.

Prices: Dhs.35 (12 years and older); Dhs.15 (11 years and under)

Parties at Home

Other options → Toys & Crafts [p.76]

Parties at home give you complete control over the food, entertainment and budget. Follow the tried and trusted formula of a few organised games, a scrumptious party tea and then playtime with their friends. If you want some party entertainment, and Dad refuses to wear a giant Scooby Doo costume, refer to the Organisers and Entertainers section for a few ideas [p.167]. There's also a section on birthday cake suppliers and outside catering, as well as party accessories (decorations, gift bags, etc), [p.167].

Party Games

To organise party games at home, you'll need music, prizes and lots of excited kids. Keep prizes small, and remember to play some games where everybody gets a prize. Below is a list of party games to get you started. If you're having a theme party, then many of these games can be modified to fit in with your particular theme.

Pin the Tail on the Donkey: Tape a picture of a donkey to the wall, blindfold each child and hand them a pre-taped tail, point them in the direction of the donkey and enjoy the hilarious results! For an alternative try pin the nose on the clown.

Pass the parcel: Wrap a prize in multiple layers of paper and get the kids to pass it around to music. When the music stops, the child holding the parcel gets to unwrap one layer. The lucky one holding the parcel when the final layer is removed wins the prize.

What's the Time Mr Wolf?: Best played outside, one child stands at the opposite end of the garden with his back to the rest of the kids, who stand together and shout "what's the time, Mr Wolf?". He replies "one o'clock" or "three o'clock" or any time he wishes, and the group of children must then pace forward one step, or three steps, or the corresponding number of steps. When he feels they are getting close, he shouts out "it's dinnertime!!!" and chases all the children back to the starting point – whoever he catches first is the next Mr Wolf.

Simon Says: The kids have to do everything that Simon says but if they do an action where Simon hasn't said it, they're out! So, "Simon says put your hands on your head", means everybody should put their hands on their heads. But "jump up and down" – anybody jumping goes out, because there was no "Simon says."

Action Songs: Really just for younger kids, who will love performing all the actions to their favourite nursery songs like 'Wheels on the Bus' and 'Old MacDonald had a Farm'.

Races: A good way to make sure everybody goes home tired! Add variety by giving them beanbags to balance on their heads, an egg to balance on a spoon, or obstacles to overcome. Or team kids up into pairs for 'wheelbarrow' races (one child holds the other's legs while he uses his hands to walk along the ground), three legged races (tape one leg of each child together), and leapfrog.

Crepe Paper Tag: Split the party into two teams, and give each child a crepe paper belt in the team colour to tie around their waist. The aim is simple – rip off the other team's belts before they rip off yours! Anyone who gets 'unbelted' sits out for the rest of the game.

Balloon Bouncing: Get everyone to lie down in a circle and throw five balloons into the middle. The aim is to keep the balloons in the air for as long as possible by bouncing them with your hands.

Crawl Through the Hoops: Put a couple of hula-hoops on someone's arm and then all join hands in a circle. Get one hoop going around the circle in one direction and the other hoop in the opposite direction. Squeeze, crawl and shake your way through them, but no unfair letting go of hands!

Treasure Hunt: Hide clues, sweets or coins around the house and garden – just remember to stipulate areas that are 'off limits', like the bathroom cupboards or the china cabinet! The one who finds the most is the winner.

Musical Games: Whether it's musical bumps (last one to sit down), musical statues (everybody stands still), or musical chairs (the last one to get to a chair), these games all start with the kids dancing round until the music stops, then performing the actions described above.

The Traffic Game: One child acts as the caller and when he shouts out a word, the other kids have to do the corresponding action, as follows: 'green' (everybody runs around); 'amber' (run on the spot), 'red' (stop), 'roundabout' (sit down with arms tucked under knees, and spin around), and 'accident' (lie on their backs, waving their arms and legs in the air).

Jack Frost: Two players are designated 'sunshines' and one 'Jack Frost'. All the kids start running around but if caught by Jack, they have to stand still until a sunshine comes to release them.

Stuck in the Mud: One or two children are selected as catchers. When caught, a child must stand still with their arms and legs spread wide. Any free child can release them by crawling through their legs.

Piñata: Make a papier mache vessel and fill it with sweets and prizes before sealing. Hang it from a tree and each child, blindfolded, gets to hit it with a plastic bat three times. Once it breaks open, everybody can dive in!

Swimming Parties at Home: If you are prepared to take on the responsibility of a swimming party, keep in mind the following safety recommendations: enlist the help of a few adult volunteers to keep their eyes on the pool at all times, and make sure the kids understand that rules such as 'no diving in the shallow end' and 'no running around the pool' are not to be broken. That said, make sure everybody has a splashing good time by filling the pool with foam noodles and inflatable toys and suggesting special water games. Just don't forget the sunblock!

Water Babies

Party Food Favourites

Here are some tasty ideas for party food:

- Sandwiches with various fillings (marmite, cheese, chocolate spread etc) – use fun cookie cutters to cut out hearts, stars or faces
- Baby tomato halves
- Cheese cubes
- Fruit kebabs
- Sausage rolls or sausages on sticks
- Savoury biscuits and cheese straws
- Strawberries and seedless grapes
- Slices of carrot and cucumber
- Jelly and custard
- And of course the birthday cake!!

Birthday Cakes

Although it is rumoured that mothers generally like to make their own personalised birthday cakes, sometimes it is very helpful to order a cake from an outside source. Most bakeries and hotel pastry shops will prepare a birthday cake. They do some great themes and the choice is down to you and your child. The following are some bakers that come well recommended. The prices indicated are for normal birthday cakes. Elaborate choices will generally incur a greater charge.

Abu Dhabi

Abela Superstore

Location → Nr Dana Plaza · Khalidiya | 02 667 4675
Hours → 08:00 - 23:00
Web/email → www.abela.com | Map Ref → 8-C2

Come to the bakery section a day before your child's special day and have a cake specially decorated with ornaments or characters such as Mickey Mouse, Donald Duck, Tweety Bird or, better still, scan your baby's picture for a truly personalised sweet.

Prices: Dhs.75 per kg (character and scaned picture cakes)

Baskin Robbins

Location → Tourist Club Area | 02 672 1879
Hours → 10:00 - 24:00 Fri 15:00 - 24:00
Web/email → www.galaice.com | Map Ref → 7-E1

If the little ones all scream for ice cream, this is the place to go. Cakes can be either all ice cream or ice cream and sponge. Creative options include a train roll cake, summer flowers and ballerina slippers. 48 hours notice is required.

Prices: Dhs.62 - 350

Mister Baker

Location → Shk Hamdan Bin Mohd. St | 02 678 0055
Hours → 07:00 - 01:00
Web/email → mrbauh@emirates.net.ae | Map Ref →7-E1

This café and bakery, dedicated to celebration cakes, offers an impressive range of possibilities. Browse the big book and choose from a wide range including Sesame Street, Jungle Book, dinosaur, guitar and doll-themed cakes. You're sure to find just the right delight. 24 hours notice is required.

Prices: Dhs.60 per kg

Miss J Café

Location → Dana Plaza · Khalidiya | 02 666 7800
Hours → 07:00 - 24:00
Web/email → na | Map Ref → 9-C1

A variety of fillings and character cake options await you at this popular café and bakery. Winnie the Pooh and Hercules are among the child focused choices here, and there is also the trendy scanned photo alternative. Be sure to order in advance.

Prices: Dhs.75 per kg (Dhs.50 for scanned picture)

Dubai

Baskin Robbins

Location → Opp Karama Post Office · Karama **04 396 9313**
Hours → 10:00 - 01:00 Fri 14:00 - 01:00
Web/email → www.galaice.com Map Ref → 13-E3

Refer to the Abu Dhabi review [p.165] for details.

Boulevard Gourmet, The

Location → Hotel Inter-Continental · Deira **04 205 7317**
Hours → 08:00 - 22:00 Fri 09:00 - 22:00
Web/email → www.interconti.com Map Ref → 14-B2

Start a feeding frenzy with yummy cakes made to order, topped with your favourite cartoon characters or caricatures painted onto marzipan. Prices vary according to the size of the cake, and special orders should be made two days in advance.

Prices: Painting: Dhs.180 per kg; Royal Icing: Dhs.105 per kg

Coco's

Location → City Centre · Deira **04 295 3777**
Hours → 08:00 - 01:00
Web/email → www.deiracitycentre.com Map Ref → 15-D1

Coco's delicious triple layer chocolate birthday cakes are freshly baked every day, and are available in two sizes: 1.5 kg and 3 kg

Prices: Dhs.60 (1.5kg); Dhs.120 (3kg)

French Bakery

Location → Defence R/A · Shk Zayed Rd **04 343 6444**
Hours → 24 hrs
Web/email → fb@lamarquise.co.ae Map Ref → 12-E2

Scrumptious cakes for children and grown ups. Count on roughly Dhs.8 per portion, so a cake for ten people would work out to about Dhs.80. Free delivery in Dubai for cakes costing Dhs200+.

French Connection

Location → Wafa Tower · Trade Centre 1&2 **04 343 8311**
Hours → 07:00 - 24:00
Web/email → na Map Ref → 13-A3

The mouth watering birthday cakes from this French style patisserie come highly recommended, and for extra fun, they can make a cake with a picture of the birthday boy or girl on it! The minimum cake size is ten portions.

Prices: Start from Dhs.80

Gift Express

Location → Jumeirah Centre · Jumeira **04 342 0568**
Hours → 08:30 - 17:30
Web/email → www.giftexpress.co.ae Map Ref → 13-B1

Choose a cake from the standard range, or order a special or unique cake (advance notice for special orders is required). Cakes can be delivered anywhere in the Emirates. Call for more info, or check out the Website.

Prices: From Dhs.120

Mister Baker

Location → Nr GPO, Zabeel Rd · Al Karama **04 336 8292**
Hours → See timings below
Web/email → na Map Ref → 13-E3

Mister Baker can bake almost any kind of cake in any flavour or size – all you have to do is choose from their catalogue and order one day in advance. They can also provide pizzas, pastry puffs and chicken/sausage rolls. Delivery available.

Prices: Cakes are Dhs.50 per kg; minimum size of 2 kg
Timings: 08:00 - 03:00 Fri 08:00 - 11:30 & 16:00 - 24:00

Park N Shop

Location → Jumeira Beach Rd · Jumeira **04 394 5671**
Hours → 07:00 - 22:00
Web/email → www.parkshopdubai.com Map Ref → 12-D2

This popular bakery will try almost any idea for cakes – just take a picture of what you have in mind, or choose from their book of designs. Prices vary depending on size.

Prices: From Dhs.100

Just a Little Bit More Icing...

Spinneys

Location ➜ Mercato · Jumeirah Beach Rd
Hours ➜ 08:00 - 23:00
Web/email ➜ www.spinneys.com
04 349 6900
Map Ref ➜ 12-E1

Spinneys can make your birthday cake in various designs, shapes and sizes – they have a catalogue for you to look through before making your selection. Try to give three or four days notice.

Prices: Start from Dhs.75 per kg. Prices vary according to design and size

Organisers & Entertainers

Whether you're looking for a bouncy castle, a clown or a magic show to add some pep to your party, or you just want to hand all responsibility for party arrangements over to the experts, this section lists the options available. Although both of these companies are based in Dubai, they cover all the emirates and will increase their fees in proportion to the distance. If you are throwing a party for a particularly sporty bunch then bare in mind that some sports coaches will come and organise an hour or two of games at your chosen location. For more information on this, see Sporty Parties [p.162].

Dubai

Balloon Lady, The

Location ➜ Jumeirah Plaza · Jumeira
Hours ➜ See timings below
Web/email ➜ balloonladyuae@hotmail.com
04 344 1062
Map Ref ➜ 13-B1

This one stop party shop offers more than balloons – they do bouncy castles, clowns, face painting, magic shows – the list is endless! For hungry party tummies, hire popcorn, candyfloss, or slush machines, or treat birthday girls to a girly hair and make up party. Call for more info.

Timings: 09:00 - 13:00   16:00 - 22:00   Fri 17:00 - 21:00

Flying Elephant

Location ➜ Warehouse · Jct 3, Shk Zayed Rd
Hours ➜ Timings on request
Web/email ➜ www.flyingelephantuae.com
04 347 9170
Map Ref ➜ 12-B2

These party professionals provide everything you need for an action packed party from bouncy castles to birthday cakes! For home parties anywhere in the Emirates, they'll provide kids' chairs and tables, decorations and catering, and can even take care of the photographs and video.

Party Accessories

Other options ➜ Elves & Fairies [p.77]

Most major supermarkets and stationery shops sell the basic party paraphernalia. However, the following list of outlets specialise in everything from decorations and cards to candles, table settings, party favours, gift wrapping and, in some cases, presents and fancy dress costumes. Toy shops also usually stock cards and wrapping paper.

In Dubai, Satwa, Karama and Bur Dubai are potential treasure chests for filling party bags, with guaranteed to delight presents for Dhs.10 or less. If you are buying in bulk and have the time, Deira wholesale souk is especially good for battery powered toys, bags of hair slides, bangles and beads, sold for next to nothing. Head for the tangle of streets between the Creek and the Gold Souk. For those residing in Abu Dhabi, the various souks are a good place to look for these knick knacks.

Abu Dhabi

Gulf Greetings

Location ➜ Marina Mall
Hours ➜ 10:00 - 23:00
Web/email ➜ na
02 681 3338
Map Ref ➜ 5-A2

Stocked up for party time, from invitations and cards to wrapping paper, toys, candles, party bag presents, posters. You name it – Gulf Greetings sells it and more! Branches are located in Abu Dhabi and Dubai, and in the bigger shopping malls.

Kids Play

Location ➜ Toys 'R' Us · Mina Rd
Hours ➜ 10:00 - 23:00
Web/email ➜ n/a
02 673 2332
Map Ref ➜ 7-B4

For parties at home, this is a good place to order helium balloons (Dhs.10 to fill four foil balloons) or if you supply your own, they will fill them for Dhs.1. Kids Play also sells individually wrapped party bags priced from Dhs.5 - 8.

Toys 'R' Us

Location → Mina Rd	02 673 2332
Hours → 10:00 - 22:00 16:00 - 22:00	
Web/email → na	Map Ref → 7-B4

These party professionals provide everything you need for an action packed party from bouncy castles to birthday cakes! For home parties anywhere in the Emirates, they'll provide kids' chairs and tables, decorations and catering, and can even take care of the photographs and video.

Dubai

Balloon Lady, The

Location → Jumeirah Plaza · Jumeira	04 344 1062
Hours → See timings below	
Web/email → balloonladyuae@hotmail.com	Map Ref → 13-B1

Having a party, need some help? As well as arranging parties at home, the shop stocks every decoration imaginable, while for theme parties you can buy masks, wigs, henna etc. Fancy dress costumes can be hired for 24 hours (prices start from Dhs.50, plus deposit).

Timings: 09:00 - 13:00 16:00 - 22:00 Fri 17:00 - 21:00

Card Shop

Location → Al Diyafah St · Al Satwa	04 398 7047
Hours → 09:00 - 13:00 17:00 - 22 :00	
Web/email → crdshp@emirates.net.ae	Map Ref → 13-C2

A great shop for birthday party accessories – they sell banners by the metre, small presents, cards, paper, ribbons, streamers, matching boxes and bags, helium balloons and party favours. Items can be custom made and they also do home visits to decorate your house.

Flying Elephant

Location → Warehouse · Jct 3, Shk Zayed Rd	04 347 9170
Hours → Timings on request	
Web/email → www.flyingelephantuae.com	Map Ref → 12-B2

Flying Elephant can supply all the accessories for your party (including the only confetti 'canon' in Dubai), as well as arranging the whole event with birthday cakes, party bags, tables, music etc. If you need balloons, they can supply anything your imagination could possibly desire!

Gulf Greetings

Location → Al Bustan Centre · Al Twar	04 263 2771
Hours → 10:00 - 23:00	
Web/email → na	Map Ref → 15-E1

Refer to the Abu Dhabi review [p.167] for details.

Kids Play

Location → Toys 'R' Us · Al Futtaim Centre	04 224 0000
Hours → 10:00 - 22:00	
Web/email → info@alfuttaimsons.com	Map Ref → 13-E3

Refer to the Abu Dhabi review [p.167] for details.

Magrudy Book Shop

Location → Magrudy Shopping Mall · Jumeira	04 344 4193
Hours → See timings below	
Web/email → www.magrudy.com	Map Ref → 13-B1

Magrudy's is definitely the place to go for that special card since the selection is varied and different. Also available are invitations, table displays, party bags and fillers, decorations and affordable presents.

Timings: 09:00 - 20:00 16:00 - 20:00 Fri 16:30 - 20:30

Papermoon

Location → Mina Rd, off Al Diyafah St · Al Satwa	04 345 4888
Hours → 09:30 - 13:00 16:30 - 21:30	
Web/email → stallion@emirates.net.ae	Map Ref → 13-C2

Papermoon offers a lovely selection of brightly coloured wrapping paper, ribbons, birthday cards and gift wrapping accessories. They also sell more unusual gifts, such as Austrian dolls, drums and even small bows and arrows from South Africa! Gift wrapping is available (Dhs.10 - 100).

Parties at Home

*I*magine a haven away from the stresses of everyday life.

A stylish space where friends can meet to enjoy superb casual dining, yet somewhere that is much more than a sophisticated Café.

A place to be inspired, where the artist in all of us is given free rein to paint beautiful, individual works of art.

Abu Dhabi, Khalidiya, Telephone 02 666 4412   **Dubai,** Town Center, Jumeirah, Telephone 04 344 7331   *Email tast4art@emirates.net.ae*
Website: cafe-ceramique.com

Café Céramique
A taste for art

Toys 'R' Us

Location → Al Futtaim Centre · Deira | 04 222 5859
Hours → 10:00 - 22:00
Web/email → info@alfuttaimsons.com   Map Ref → 14-C3

Refer to the Abu Dhabi review [p.168] for details.

Theme Parties

Kids love dressing up and theme parties are always popular, especially if the theme is carried through from the invitations to the costumes, the food and even the party games. If you are hosting a theme party, be kind to other parents and keep things simple – otherwise you may get a rather frosty greeting from the mother who has been forced to stay up all night hand sewing her child's all too intricate costume! Fortunately, there are many options available for parents who have to kit their kids out in a particular theme. If you can't beg, borrow or steal one from another mum, an easy and cheap option is to have a browse round the little backstreet shops in areas such as Satwa. You'll find plenty of Batman suits, Superman capes, Pokemon costumes and Hello Kitty masks here. If you want something a bit more unique, you can buy some fabric and have a tailor knock something up for you within a few days. If time is running out and money is no option, try the ready made costumes sold by The Balloon Lady and shops like Magrudy's, Park N Shop, and Gulf Greetings in Dubai.

Abu Dhabi

Posters

Location → Tourist Club Area | 02 672 4724
Hours → 09:00 - 22:00 Fri 17:00 - 21:00
Web/email → posters@emirates.net.ae   Map Ref → 7-E2

This eclectic novelty shop features hats, masks, wands, make up and a range of costumes for all your child's dress up needs. Stock is imported from England, and prices range from Dhs.65 for a soldier to Dhs.255 for various animal get ups.

Toys 'R' Us

Location → Mina Rd | 02 673 2332
Hours → 10:00 - 22:00
Web/email → na   Map Ref → 13-E3

You'll find some trendy brand-based costumes here for your little Barbies and Bratz, as well as some superhero masks. Selection is limited and prices and stock vary so call first to see what's available.

Dubai

Balloon Lady, The

Location → Jumeirah Plaza · Jumeira | 04 344 1062
Hours → See timings below
Web/email → balloonladyuae@hotmail.com   Map Ref → 13-B1

For theme parties, The Balloon Lady hires or sells costumes in various designs and sizes. You'll have to pay a refundable deposit and a rental fee, both of which vary according to the costume. Contact them at least a week in advance to avoid disappointment.

Timings: 09:00 - 13:00 16:00 - 22:00 Fri 17:00 - 21:00

In Disguise

Location → Near Iranian Hospital · Jumeira | 04 342 2752
Hours → 10:00 - 16:00
Web/email → disguise@emirates.net.ae   Map Ref → 13-C2

In Disguise has a huge choice of fancy dress costumes and can tailor make something special if they don't have what you're looking for. The cost for a rental varies from Dhs.50 to Dhs.200, and a refundable deposit is required.

Out Of Town Parties

A trip to the mountains, desert or beaches can be great fun for an out of town party, provided you have access to a vehicle or 4 wheel drive to transport the gang and the food. In the desert and mountains, you can set nature trails for the children where they have to find a number of non living items such as a rock, a feather, etc, which they can take home as a souvenir in a party bag. On the beach, beachcombing, tug of war and sandcastle building competitions are always popular. To keep it simple take a mat or groundsheet for seating, and a folding table or use the back flap of your car! Light a fire and have a sunset barbecue, then camp for the night. See the section on Camping in Activities [p.90]. If you are looking to be a little more extravagant, a weekend away in a hotel makes for a very special birthday outing for limited numbers (this option is fun for parents too!) For information on popular spots in family orientated hotels, refer to the Weekend Breaks section in Activities [p.140]. Most hotels have pools and sports facilities, so check first to ensure you take all the necessary equipment.

In Disguise gives you any costume you can imagine!

...and corporate mascots, and uniforms for events too!

For private parties, our fancy dress costumes always impress. There are outfits for adults and children, – for hire or sale. We also do uniforms for corporate events and giant company mascots. Call us to see what great costume ideas we've got.

BY APPOINTMENT ONLY

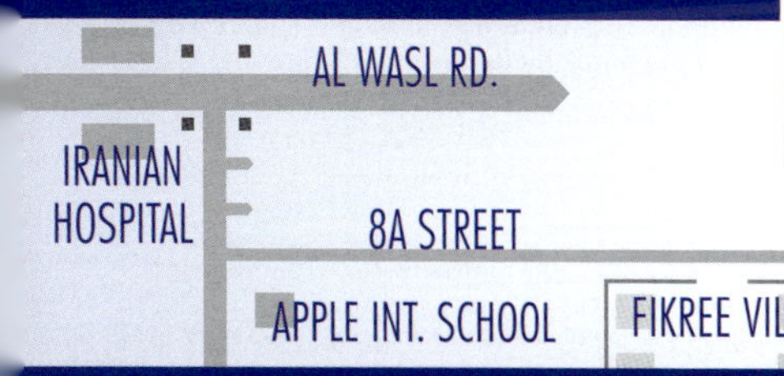

IN DISGUISE
No.41, 8a Street, Satwa
04 3422752 / 050 4556929

Email: disguise@emirates.net.ae
www.indisguise.biz

AL WASL RD.
IRANIAN HOSPITAL
8A STREET
APPLE INT. SCHOOL
FIKREE VILLAS
AL DIYAFAH ST.

Whodunnit Dinners®

we also produce:
MURDER MYSTERY DINNERS

– for groups of 10 people
set in Carter's Private Dining Room ~

- A mystery to solve • Great costumes
- 3 course meal **Plus** 1/2 bottle of wine / person

all inclusive for just **325Dhs** / person.

CALL WAFI CITY NOW ON: 04 324 0000

Book our latest 70's theme mystery!

The fun of murder mysteries – without the hassle!

The following tour operators will organise various excursions. Check with the tour operators for details on prices as these vary according to the choice of activities and the number of children in the party.

Abu Dhabi

Net Tours

Location ➔ Sheraton Resort & Towers | 02 679 4656
Hours ➔ 08:00 - 19:30
Web/email ➔ www.nettoursdubai.com | Map Ref ➔ 4-C4

Net Tours can arrange desert safari trips and outings to Wild Wadi. A safari party could include sand skiing, camel riding and a barbeque dinner with cake. A small disco set up can also be arranged.

Prices: For special party offers, call the above number

Offroad Emirates

Location ➔ 4th St btn Electra and Hamdan St | 02 633 3232
Hours ➔ See below
Web/email ➔ www.offroademirates.com | Map Ref ➔8-C1

This provider specialises in desert tours with half day desert dune and overnight safaris. Parties usually consist of families and the price depends on the number of participants and what is requested.

Timings 08:00 - 13:00 16:00 - 19:00 Sat - Wed; 8:00 - 13:00 & 16:00 - 18:00 Thurs; Fri closed

Sunshine Tours

Location ➔ Beh National Htl Bld · Old Airport Rd | 02 444 9914
Hours ➔ 07:30 - 15:00 Closed Thurs & Fri
Web/email ➔ www.adnh.com | Map Ref ➔ 2-B2

Sunshine Tours conducts afternoon desert safaris through the dunes complete with camel riding and a barbecue dinner. They can arrange a birthday cake at an extra cost, or the family can bring along their own cake.

Prices: Dhs.255 per person

Dubai

Arabian Adventures

Location ➔ Emirates Holiday Bld · Shk Zayed Rd | 04 303 4888
Hours ➔ 09:00 - 18:00
Web/email ➔ www.arabian-adventures.com | Map Ref ➔ 12-D2

Arabian Adventures will organise desert adventure parties for groups of children ten years or older – party numbers are limited to six per vehicle, but any number of vehicles can be booked. Choose from activities such as sand skiing, camel riding, etc.

Prices: Varies according to chosen activities.

Desert Rangers

Location ➔ Dubai Garden Centre · Shk Zayed Rd | 04 340 2408
Hours ➔ 08:30 - 14:30
Web/email ➔ www.desertrangers.com | Map Ref ➔ 12-A2

Desert Rangers specialise in desert parties at their camp just outside of Dubai with activities such as sand-boarding or camel-riding on the menu. Catering, including a birthday cake, can be arranged, and the camp can accommodate up to 400 kids at a time.

Prices: Vary according to chosen activities.

Dubai Travel & Tourist Services

Location ➔ Khalid Bin Al Waleed Rd · Bur Dubai | 04 336 7727
Hours ➔ 08:30 - 17:30 Fri 10:00 - 13:00
Web/email ➔ dttsdxb@emirates.net.ae | Map Ref ➔ 14-A3

This overnight dune safari stops at Ali Baba's Bedouin Village where the kids can experience camel rides before settling down to an Arabian barbecue and either a magic show or falconry exhibition. The following morning includes a visit to the Hatta Pools before heading home.

Prices: Dhs.175 per child; special group rates for parties

Net Tours

Location ➔ Al Bakhit Centre - 1st floor · Deira | 04 266 8661
Hours ➔ 08:00 - 19:00
Web/email ➔ www.nettoursdubai.com | Map Ref ➔ 7-D2

Refer to the Abu Dhabi review for details.

Orient Tours

Location ➔ Various locations | 04 282 8238
Hours ➔ 24 hrs
Web/email ➔ www.orient-tours-uae.com | Map Ref ➔ na

A birthday party at one of Orient's desert camps can be tailor made according to your requirements – choose your activities from sandboarding, camel riding, desert volleyball, a bouncy castle, a dhow trip, and many more. Catering and birthday cake can be supplied.

Prices: Varies according to chosen activities.

Be more than just a better parent!

Each month Emirates Parent Plus brings to you guidance on travel, food, crafts, health care, books, parties and games. With a dedicated focus on issues relating to parenting and everyday family life, it's a must for every home!

EMIRATES PARENT PLUS

The first family magazine in the U.A.E

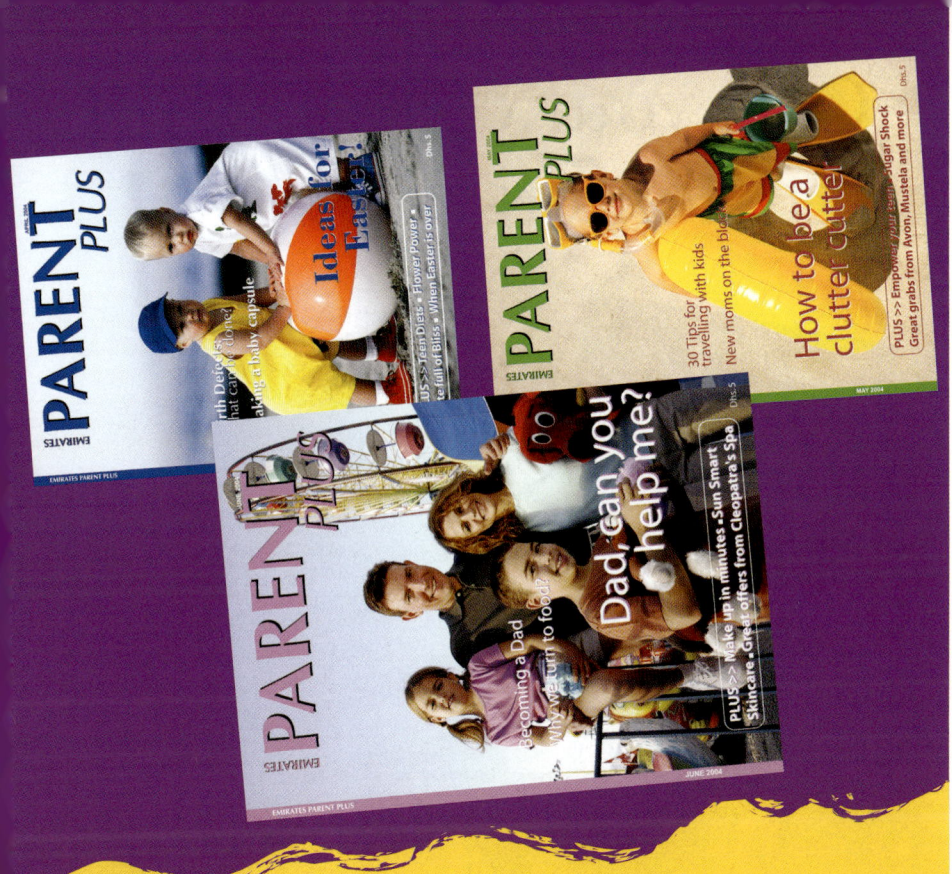

SPEAR PUBLISHING

T: +971 4 2869984 F: +971 4 2869880 P.O.Box 62870, Dubai, U.A.E.
For sale enquiries, please contact Sukaina Hussein. Mobile: 050-5159691 Email: sukaina@spearadv.com www.spearadv.com

Give your corporate customers a treat!

A great reason to get a coffee table!

A picture tells a thousand words, and this outstanding collection of stunning photography books speaks volumes. A corporate gift, festive present or interior accessory, discover UAE life through the lens of gifted photographers with an eye for the awe-inspiring.

Passionately Publishing...

EXPLORER
www.Explorer-Publishing.com

Explorer Publishing & Distribution LLC • 51 B • Zomorrodah bldg • Za'abeel road • Karama • PO Box 34275 • Dubai • UAE
Phone (971 4) 335 3370 • Fax (971 4) 335 3529 • Email Info@Explorer-Publishing.com

Going Out
EXPLORER

Going Out

Going Out	177	Restaurants	184	Cafés & Coffee Shops	193
Restaurant Listing Structure	177	Abu Dhabi	184		
Icons - Quick Reference	178	Dubai	188	Foodcourts	196
Friday Brunch	178				

MUST KNOW

For new residents to the UAE leaving behind family traditions like Sunday Lunch can compound homesickness. However you will soon come to realise that your new location can be a home away from home. It may be on a different day of the week but the famous UAE Friday Brunch is every bit as satisfying as mum's Sunday Roast. Plus the buffet style lets you choose from meat and veg or a full breakfast, as well as a whole host of international temptations. See [p.178]

MUST DO

You may not be in Paris or Rome but café culture is still very much part of the picture postcard here. From shisha pipes and Arabic coffee that will put hairs on your chest to the 'ladies that lunch' ubiquitous tea and cake, there is a scrumptious selection of cafés to satisfy your sweet tooth. They also make an extremely popular location for mother's meetings, with various mums and their tots chatting over chocolate cake on most afternoons. See [p.193]

MUST KNOW

The holy month of Ramadan, when Muslims are required to fast between sunrise and sunset, is a festive and interesting time in the UAE. Even non Muslims are not allowed to eat, drink or smoke in public, and you will find that many restaurants are closed during the day. However, for most hotel outlets it's 'business as usual', and some fast food chains still offer a takeaway service. Young children, pregnant women, the sick and the elderly are exempt from fasting.

Oh I do like to be beside the seaside....

Going Out

Eating Out

Dining out is one of the most popular pastimes in the UAE, and the choice of cuisine and cultural venues are limitless. Having a family doesn't have to stunt your social life while you are here. Children are welcomed at a large majority of restaurants and while some of the more exclusive eateries may not allow kids you will find at least one or two choices in all the hotels. Also, bringing your kids to dinner doesn't mean eating in shopping mall fast food family joints, in fact you can still enjoy fine dining delicacies and international flavours in a wide variety of restaurants, both during the day and evening.

In this cosmopolitan environment, children may learn to love samosas, shawarma, fajitas, sashimi or even mushy peas, arming you with sufficient culinary choices to please even the fussiest eaters! Limited budgets and/or time restraints can also be catered for, and takeaways are available at most outlets, from five star hotel restaurants to street side cafés. The UAE also has the famous Friday Brunch which is one of the most popular times for a family meal with a good selection of restaurants offering great value dining and a whole range of entertainment for kids.

Children generally exert, even if unintentionally, an important influence on a family decision for a meal out. Not all children are quiet and well behaved, or will sit still for long periods of time while parents relax over a three course meal plus coffee. Most children need to be entertained or they start fidgeting, and there are a number of restaurants with a games corner and others that provide colouring books to keep your kids happy while you enjoy your meal.

One thing's for sure – in the UAE, children are well liked not only by the locals, but also by a huge part of the expatriate community. When eating out, if the staff have taken a shine to your little ones, they are often whisked away (if they are willing) on a tour of the restaurant or to the kitchen to meet a work colleague. They might perhaps even be given a treat or two (which helps take the edge off their appetites). All this is with the best intentions. Parents and children that are new to the UAE might find this sort of behaviour a little uncomfortable, but remember, we live in a country where family is important and most of the staff that serve you have families and perhaps even children of their own far away in their home countries.

While this section highlights some of the most family orientated restaurants and cafés it is by no means exhaustive and there are plenty of venues that will welcome children, and although they may not have specific kid's menus or even high chairs, most will happily whip up a plate of plain tomato spaghetti or chicken and chips. Some restaurants, especially those where your bill is sizeable, won't even charge you for your children's food.

For a more extensive selection of restaurants, bars and cafés in the emirates of Dubai and Abu Dhabi, check out the latest *Dubai Explorer* and *Abu Dhabi Explorer*. While these guidebooks may not highlight specific information on what each restaurant offers for children you will find the 'kids welcome' icon by a vast array of restaurants offering all types of cuisine.

Restaurant Listing Structure

As Friday Brunch is one of the most popular family meals out, this category appears first and includes restaurants offering various cuisines. These restaurants are often good family options for other days, or evenings, but may not provide the same entertainment or children's menus as they do for Friday Brunch. So it's worth checking with the restaurant, when you make your booking, what activities they have for children.

In addition there is a selection of restaurants that welcome children and provide high chairs, a children's menu or will prepare dishes in half portions for reduced prices.

Say Cheese!

Get used to complete strangers walking up to you and asking if they can have their picture taken with your child... and not with you! Children are well liked in the UAE.

Tips and Taxes

On top of the basic bill, there is a 15 - 16% service charge. These taxes are incorporated into the customers' bill, but often indicated as being in addition to a price with a ++. This information has to be indicated somewhere on the menu. It is still unclear as to whether the latter charge is actually passed on to staff or whether it can be withheld for poor service, but when in doubt, give the servers a break.

You can also find a number of restaurants and cafes, as well as a Fast Food table, in the Birthday Parties section [p.150].

Icons – Quick Reference

For an explanation of the various symbols or icons listed against the individual reviews, refer to the Quick Reference Explorer Icons table below.

Quick Reference Explorer Icons
Explorer Recommended
NO Credit Cards Accepted
Alcohol Available
Will Deliver
Reservations Recommended
Dress Smartly
Outside Terrace
Vegetarian Dishes

Friday Brunch

One of the best times to go out for a family meal is on a Friday when a wide variety of restaurants, from Arabic and American to Seafood and Steakhouses, have a Friday Brunch serving a buffet of tasty dishes in hearty portions for fantastic value. In addition to dedicated children's menus or buffet stations, a whole feast of entertainment is served up to a well-fed audience of excited youngsters. Just beware, some of the venues encourage rowdy family fun, which may leave you feeling a little frazzled. Your kids, however, are guaranteed to have a ball. If you're looking for something a little more low key, or you're brunching with childless guests who may not be up for a side order of over excited kids with their leisurely Friday brunch, then there is still a wide variety of restaurants that have highchairs and will prepare food for kids but are not over run by families. However, not all restaurants, despite being 'child-friendly' have baby changing facilities.

Some of the beach clubs allow nonmembers entry for the Friday buffet and use of the facilities. The charge is usually over Dhs.120 per head for an adult and Dhs.60 for a child, which includes use of the pool and beach.

Abu Dhabi

Beachcombers

Location → Marina & Yacht Club · Al Meena 02 644 0300
Hours → 21:00 - 02:30 Thu 21:00 - 02:30
Web/email → www.abudhabimarina.com Map Ref → 4-C2

Not only is this a popular weekend spot to dine and dance under the stars with an interesting mix of people, but the Friday Brunch is well worth checking out. Set on the beach, it's perfect for a lazy winter Friday afternoon with more delicious food on offer than you could dream of. Adults pay Dhs.120 for the buffet while children under 12 get a 50% discount and under fives eat for free. There is a great kids' area full of fun activities including face painting, games and colouring books.

Benihana

Location → Beach Rotana 02 644 3000
Hours → 12:00 - 15:00 19:00 - 23:30
Web/email → www.rotana.com Map Ref → 4-B3

Benihana is Japanese for the masses rather than for the connoisseur. You're guaranteed entertainment and a very social atmosphere at the teppanyaki tables (book ahead) and children will be catered for with finger foods and small portions for Dhs.60 - 70 per child. The best time for familes to go is the Friday Brunch (Dhs.95 for adults, Dhs.45 for children) when there is more choice for fussy eaters, including a roast buffet. It's also likely that the face painting, balloons and colouring books will be more appreciated than sushi! High chairs are available.

Garden, The

Location → Shk Hamdan Bin Mohd. St 02 621 0000
Hours → 12:00 - 16:00 19:00 - 23:00
Web/email → www.abu-dhabi.crowneplaza.com Map Ref → 4-D3

Indulge the nature lover within you in this faux alfresco 'garden' venue, decorated with an abundance of plants and complete with waterfall! Daily theme nights cover the cuisines of the world – every evening you'll find an impressive buffet laid out, designed to confuse and delight your taste buds. House beverages are included in the price on most nights.

The Mighty Brunch on Fridays is a real family affair, where the buffet is bursting with truckloads of tasty food. Children aged seven to 12 dine for half price (free for under sevens), and there is face painting, a play area and a TV/video showing kids' films and cartoons. High chairs are available.

La Brasserie

Location → Le Meridien · Al Meena
Hours → 12:00 - 16:00 18:00 - 24:00
Web/email → www.lemeridien-abudhabi.com
02 645 5566
Map Ref → 4-B3

This established eatery, overlooking Le Meridien's lively Culinary Village, serves a good selection of French regional cuisine and has a simple yet satisfying children's menu. When the weather is cooler, the terrace is a wonderful place for an evening of laid back alfresco dining.

The popular Friday Brunch buffet (Dhs.79) serves both breakfast and lunch options and has a kiddies' corner which is free to under fives and half price for five to 12 year olds. There is also a very good outside play area with a bouncy castle, face painting and cartoons playing. High chairs are available.

La Piazza

Location → Sands Hotel · Shk Zayed 2nd St
Hours → 12:00 - 15:30 19:00 - 23:30
Web/email → www.sands-hotel.com
02 633 5335
Map Ref → 4-D3

If you love the ambience and charm of a good Italian restaurant, then this characterless venue may be a disappointment – it lacks the traditional décor, music and atmosphere that you would normally expect. However, the menu stays true to the Italian theme, with a good selection of authentic starters, main dishes and desserts that are all pleasant. The best option for families is the Friday Brunch buffet mainly because it's such good value - adults pay Dhs.75 and children under 12 eat for free! High chairs are available.

P. J. O'Reillys

Location → Shk Khalifa Bin Zyd St
Hours → 12:00 - 15:30 18:00 - 22:30
Web/email → www.lemeridien.com
02 695 0515
Map Ref → 4-D3

Known affectionately as PJ's, this welcoming Irish pub is home to a throng of happy punters all through the week. As you would expect, the décor is as Irish as it comes; but the menu offers a more diverse international selection of dishes. Happy hour runs from 12:00 to 20:00 daily, and even longer on Fridays, when the brunch is popular with the expat crowd. The buffet is served between 11:00 and 15:00 and adults pay Dhs.55 and kids get a 50% discount. Colouring books and crayons are available to keep youngsters occupied. There is no high chair in the pub, but if you call in advance they will arrange for one.

Rock Bottom Café

Location → Al Diar Capitol Hotel · Al Meena St
Hours → 12:00 - 16:30 19:00 - 03:30
Web/email → www.rockbottomcafe.com
02 677 7655
Map Ref → 4-C3

Named after the Wall Street crash, this vibrant American diner has somewhat of a split personality – go early in the evening to enjoy a quiet dinner, or hang around until later when the live music starts and the pace becomes frenetic. Then on a Friday families take over for brunch with mini burgers, chicken nuggets and spaghetti for kids. High chairs are available.

Rosebuds

Location → Beach Rotana · Umm Al Nar St
Hours → 06:00 - 16:30
Web/email → www.rotana.com
02 644 3000
Map Ref → 4-C2

This is an excellent Friday Brunch: adults can head for the seven international food stations, enjoy a full breakfast, salads or the dessert buffet with live cooking stations, and guzzle unlimited house sparkling wine. The children meanwhile can relax in their own area, which has live music, their own small buffet station (with food that should tempt any child), toys, face painting, plus a balloon-shaping clown! This area is supervised. The buffet is reasonably priced at Dhs.95 for adults, half price for children under 12 and free for under fives. High chairs are available.

Royal Orchid, The

Location → Al Salam St
Hours → 11:30 - 15:30 19:00 - 24:00
Web/email → na
02 644 4400
Map Ref → 4-C3

The spectacular entrance over a glass covered fishpond containing huge Koi carp, attention to detail and calming atmosphere keep this popular restaurant busy. The buffet comprises Thai, Chinese and Mongolian food and makes a refreshing change from all the full English breakfasts and Sunday roasts that dominate so many Friday Brunch deals. The Dhs.42 price tag is pretty attractive too, and kids can enjoy fish fingers, chicken and French fries at half price for ages six to 12, and free for under six year olds. This restaurant is a must for visitors and residents alike and one of Abu Dhabi's best kept secrets. High chairs are available.

Sevilo's

Location → Shk Khalifa Bin Zyd St | 02 626 2700
Hours → 12:00 - 15:00 19:00 - 23:30
Web/email → www.milleniumhotels.com | Map Ref → 4-D3

The cooler months are the best time to make use of the poolside terrace at this venue, complete with stunning views of the city and gardens. The varied, yet uncomplicated menu delivers classic Italian cuisine, which is freshly prepared and generally of a high standard. While Sevilo's is a pleasant, intimate eatery with great service, it also offers a satisfying Friday Brunch where children aged six to 12 eat for half price and those under six eat for free! They also have kids' movies playing and a playstation. Even better, adults pay just Dhs.79 for the buffet which includes unlimited selected beverages. High chairs are available.

Culinary Genius in the Making

Tavern

Location → Corniche Rd East | 02 677 3333
Hours → 12:00 - 01:00
Web/email → www.sheraton.com | Map Ref → 4-C4

The Tavern may not epitomise sophisticated dining, but they do cracking roast dinners which will please those in need of some 'morning-after' carb loading. The no frills approach, comfortable dining area and the limited yet familiar menu, create a relaxed, functional atmosphere with no pretension. The Friday Brunch is a bargain Dhs.44 with one free drink (12:00 to 16:00) and just Dhs.22 for kids. Early birds get the armchairs, and highchairs are in short supply, so get there as close to noon as possible.

Al Ain

Flavours

Location → Hilton Al Ain | 03 768 6666
Hours → 12:00 - 15:00 19:00 - 23:00
Web/email → www.hilton.com | Map Ref → 2-E4

This modern and imaginative fusion restaurant serves a variety of very well presented food from an extensive menu. The Friday Brunch satisfies a wide variety of tastes and there is also a dedicated children's menu, a kids' play area, and giveaways to keep the youngsters happy while the grown ups load up at the buffet table!

Le Belvedere

Location → Mercure Grand Hotel - Jebel Hafeet | 03 783 8888
Hours → 12:30 - 15:00 19:00 - 22:30
Web/email → www.mercure.com | Map Ref → 9-B4

Located in the Grand Hotel Jebel Hafeet, Le Belvedere commands a spectacular view of the surrounding countryside. Don't be put off by the drive - the view, the improbable location and the restaurant itself make the trip well worth it. A lengthy wine list complements the mainly French and Mediterranean buffet and à la carte menu. The look is contemporary and both food and service are appealing. The Friday lunch buffet is particularly popular with families at Dhs.89 and half price for children under 12 (free for kids under five). High chairs are available and bookings are recommended at weekends. You could even make full use of the hotel facilities (including two tennis courts) by staying the night.

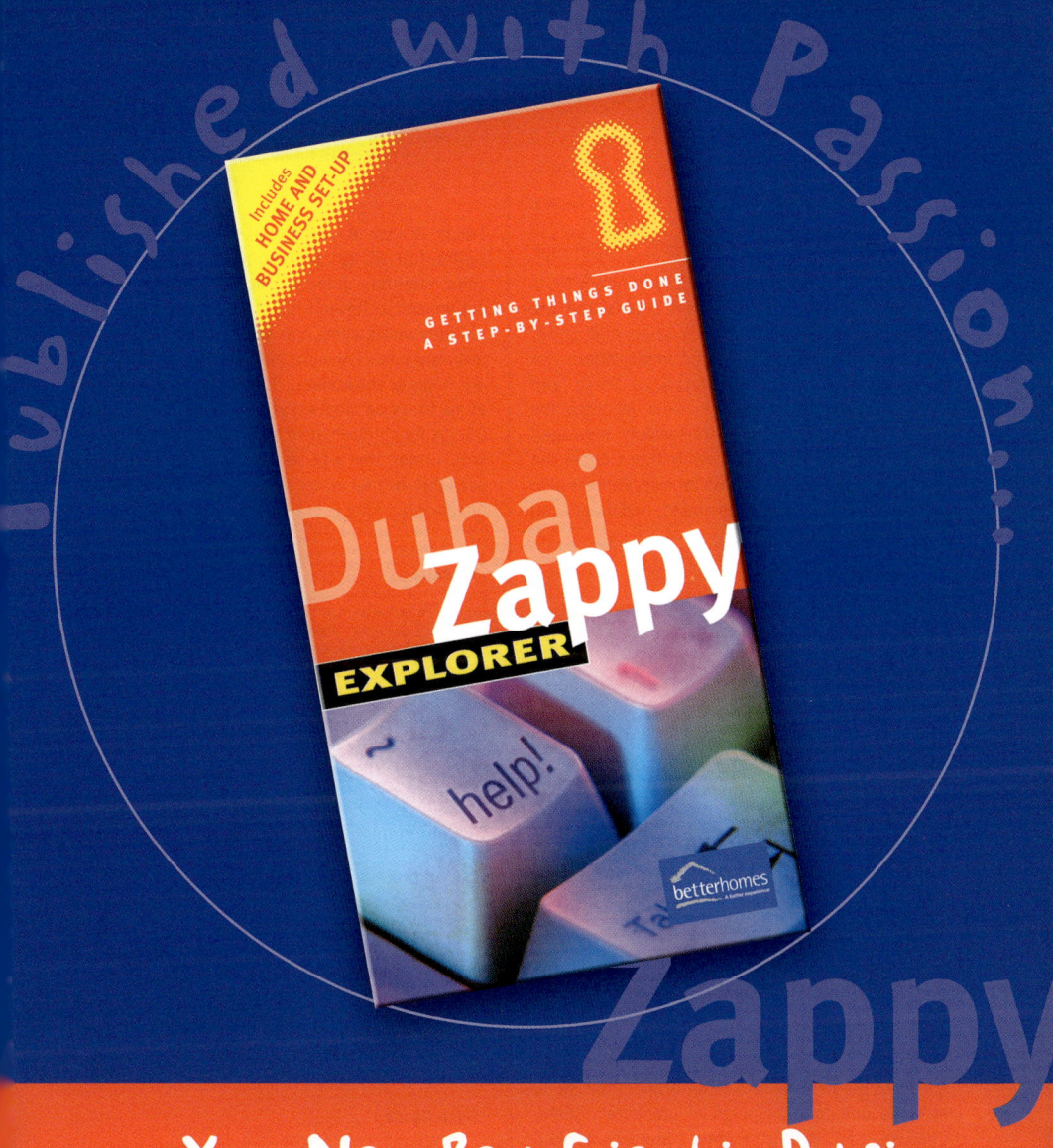

Your New Best Friend in Dubai

This step-by-step guide on life in Dubai covers everything from visas and finance to housing and transportation, health and education to telecommunications and utilities, equipping you with the inside track to this city's administrative maze. So instead of getting wound up in Dubai's red tape you can start painting the town red!

- Immigration
- Residence
- Communications
- Transportation
- Personal Affairs
- Business
- Maps

Passionately Publishing...

EXPLORER

Phone (971 4) 335 3520 • Fax (971 4) 335 3529 • Email Info@Explorer-Publishing.com

Insiders' City Guides • Photography Books • Activity Guidebooks • Commissioned Publications • Distribution

www.Explorer-Publishing.com

Dubai

Bella Vista

Location → Jumeira Rotana · Al Satwa
Hours → 11:00 - 15:30   19:00 - 23:00
Web/email → www.rotana.com
04 345 5888
Map Ref → 13-C2

Visitors and residents alike flock to the Bella Vista to enjoy its dinner buffet theme nights and the Friday Brunch, served between 11:30 and 15:00, has become a well established family affair. The food, despite its buffet status, is fresh and delicious and with unlimited drinks included the Dhs.79 price tag is very easy to swallow. Kids aged six to 12 dine for half price, while those under the age of six can pick and choose for free. There is also a children's play room, high chairs, and diners can use the pool after lunch.

Benihana

Location → Al Bustan Hotel · Al Garhoud
Hours → 12:00 - 15:00   19:00 - 23:30
Web/email → www.rotana.com
04 282 0000
Map Ref → 15-D1

Refer to Abu Dhabi review [p.178] for details. Benihana in Dubai doesn't have a Friday Brunch in their restaurant but does have a buffet station in the Fotana restarant, see review opposite for more information.

Cafe Insignia

Location → Ramada Hotel · Bur Dubai
Hours → 06:00 - 23:30
Web/email → www.ramadadubai.com
04 351 9999
Map Ref → 13-E2

More of a lunch than a breakfast, this Friday Brunch is one of the most extensive in Dubai. The menu includes unlimited helpings of omelettes, sushi, Chinese and Arabic dishes, English cooked breakfasts, tempting gateaux, plus a delicious waffle/pancake stand and much more, served in an Italian style setting. Adults pay Dhs.75 and kids aged seven to 12 get a 50% discount while children under seven eat for free. Children are well looked after by the friendly staff and the children's corner shows cartoons throughout the brunch. There is also a magician who entertains everyone for an hour and a half. The 'little chef's corner' lets kids become part of the Ramada's kitchen team by creating their own 'delicacies'.

Carter's

Location → Pyramids · Umm Hurair (2)
Hours → 12:00 - 02:00
Web/email → www.pyramidsdubai.com
04 324 4100
Map Ref → 15-C1

Friday Brunch at Carter's is a hearty traditional buffet full of all the family favourites, plus a complimentary juice on arrival. The separate supervised children's play area has videos, face painting and games, and allows parents to enjoy a leisurely meal knowing that the rest of the family are happily entertained. The buffet is served from 11:30 to 15:00 and costs just Dhs.60 for adults, Dhs.35 for children aged seven to 14 and is free for kids under the age of seven. High chairs are available but be warned they are in short supply. Advance booking is essential.

Fontana

Location → Al Bustan Hotel · Al Garhoud
Hours → 12:00 - 15:00   19:00 - 23:30
Web/email → www.rotana.com
04 282 0000
Map Ref → 15-D1

Variety is truly the spice of life at Fontana's theme nights. Sunday is seafood night; Monday, Spanish night; Wednesday, curry night and Thursday, Tex Mex (all theme nights include unlimited select beverages). The décor tunes in to each particular theme with colour and zest. The Friday Brunch is a little on the expensive side in comparison to other options. Adults eat for Dhs.119 and children aged six to 12 for Dhs.59 (under six year olds eat for free) which entitles them to the kids' buffet full of favourites including mini burgers, French fries, fish fingers and chicken nuggets. Kids are also treated to face painting and there's a playstation for older children. High chairs are available.

Gozo Garden

Location → Millennium Airport Htl· Al Garhoud
Hours → 12:00 - 15:30   20:00 - 23:30
Web/email → apothotl@emirates.net.ae
04 282 3464
Map Ref → 6-D1

This open plan café has a variety of buffet choices on Friday, which include traditional breakfast options as well as a carvery, vegetables and desserts, and is reasonably priced at Dhs.45 for adults, half price for five to 12 year olds and free for under fives. It's advisable to book if you want high chairs as they are limited. There is a small enclosed area for children with some entertainment, including cartoons, so request a table near there and you can keep an eye on your kids while you eat.

Lodge, The

Location → Al Nasr Leisureland · Oud Metha
Hours → 11:00 - 03:00
Web/email → www.thelodgedubai.com
04 337 9470
Map Ref → 13-E4

The Lodge may be infamous as a late night hotspot but after the beer as been mopped up and the smoke has cleared it actually scrubs up quite nicely for Friday Brunch. Served in the Cheers Bar, the buffet is just Dhs.40 for adults and Dhs.20 for kids and the entertainment is a little cleaner than the night before! A magician and face painters entertain while cartoons play on the TV screens. Since its comeback, The Lodge has become popular both as a late night and Friday Brunch option so booking is recommended.

Market Place, The

Location → JW Marriott Hotel · Deira
Hours → 12:30 - 15:00 19:30 - 23:30
Web/email → www.marriott.com
04 262 4444
Map Ref → 14-C3

As a good 'all you can eat' Friday buffet with a range of cuisine, from Italian and Chinese to BBQ grill plus beverages, this decent sized restaurant scores points for novelty. Firstly because the venue has a marketplace feel with strategically placed 'shop shelves' of goodies and fare piled high and secondly because they charge children, above a certain height, according to how tall they are! The kids get their own mini buffet and there is also a play area with face painting and cartoons playing. The staff are jovial and helpful, making for a relaxed atmosphere and a leisurely bite. High chairs are available.

Nad Al Sheba Club

Location → Nad Al Sheba
Hours → 07:00 - 01:00
Web/email → www.nadalshebaclub.com
04 336 3666
Map Ref → na

Nad Al Sheba offers the ultimate family Friday Brunch but be warned - it's not for the faint hearted or hungover, and you can expect over excited kids and activities galore. While it may be a bit of a full on family fest for you, your kids will absolutely love it. Held in the Millennium Grandstand Dubai Restaurant, there's enough food on offer to feed a small country and the children's buffet satisfies a hoard of hungry youngsters. Then there's the two bouncy castles and play area, jungle gyms, face painting and clowns. It's loud, and you might not want to take your childless guests there, but everything you need for kids of all ages is available including high chairs. This Friday Brunch is very popular with families, so it is advisable to book in advance.

Planet Hollywood

Location → Wafi City · Umm Hurair (2)
Hours → 12:00 - 24:00
Web/email → www.planethollywood-dubai.com
04 324 4777
Map Ref → 15-C1

The huge blue dome of Planet Hollywood in Dubai is hard to miss. Inside the famous worldwide chain, the restaurant is decorated with movie memorabilia and a whole host of famous faces and artefacts. Kids will love it because there is so much on offer to keep them amused, including play area, balloons, colouring books and crayons, and the menu is right on the money when it comes to satisfying junk food cravings. The Friday Brunch between 11:30 and 15:00 is the ultimate fun packed experience with a whole host of activities and games for children. Supervisors are on hand so that you can savour your food while your kids enjoy the entertainment. High chairs are available.

Spice Island

Location → Renaissance Hotel · Hor Al Anz
Hours → 19:00 - 23:30
Web/email → rendubai@emirates.net.ae
04 262 5555
Map Ref → 14-C3

Spice Island's 'all you can eat and drink' buffets are renowned as good nights out. However if you thought these guys could do the aforementioned buffet well, just wait until you sample their Friday offering. For three hours, between 12:00 and 15:00, you can indulge yourself in gastronomical heaven with international flavours guaranteed to satisfy the biggest of appetites. Kids can fill up at their very own buffet station before working it off in the play area, which is fully equipped with all things exciting. A clown entertains with balloon shapes and face painting, and there are also little houses, slides and seesaws as well as a TV. Children under the age of six eat for free while six to 12 year olds pay Dhs.50 for an all inclusive buffet. As for the grown ups, it's Dhs.75 for the teetotal brunch but if you're letting your hair down it's Dhs.99 for the famous 'all you can eat and drink'. High chairs are available and advance booking is imperative. It's worth requesting a table near the play area when you book so you can keep one eye on your kids and one on the prize buffet!

Restaurants

One of the most appealing aspects of the UAE, whether you're a holiday maker or a resident, is how families are genuinely welcomed and catered for. A vast number of restaurants will welcome children and while not all have children's menus most will have at least one high chair and are usually happy to create tantalising temptations for your kids. In this section a variety of restaurants with various cuisines and culinary themes have been selected, with some more geared towards kids than others. In addition, the *Abu Dhabi Explorer* and *Dubai Explorer* have a wider selection of restaurants, many of which welcome children. Look out for the 'kids welcome' icons in the Going Out sections of these books.

Chili's

Abu Dhabi

Argila

Location → Khalidia Palace Htl · Al Ras Al Akhdar | 02 666 2470
Hours → 18:00 - 02:00
Web/email → www.khalidiapalacehotel.co.ae   Map Ref → 5-E3

Located in one of the city's older hotels, Argila will give you a taste of local cuisine in the open air, or to the sounds of a local band in the large function room adjacent. Buzzing with mostly Arab and local families, this somewhat shabby restaurant offers kids plenty of space to run around until the early hours. Five private cabanas are available to rent for a meal or shisha, each with a TV. The cuisine is good, simple Lebanese and Egyptian fare, served by polite staff. There is no children's menu but the food lends itself to sharing. However, fussy eaters may not be impressed. High chairs are available.

Coconut Bay

Location → Corniche Rd West | 02 681 1900
Hours → 10:30 - 18:45
Web/email → www.hiltondubai.com   Map Ref → 5-D3

The a la carte menu at Coconut Bay is impressive, but during the cooler months the Mongolian Barbeque on Friday evenings is a hands-down winner. On other days, the extensive selection of sandwiches and the original salads make this a great place to recharge after a hard day's relaxing on the beach – the setting is ideal for a casual dinner and a few sundowners. Kids are welcome and there is a special menu for hungry little tummies. High chairs are also available.

Chili's

Location → Umm Al Nar St | 02 671 6300
Hours → 11:00 - 24:00   Fri 13:30 - 24:00
Web/email → www.chillis.com   Map Ref → 13-D3

Chili's is always packed with families of all nationalities. The atmosphere is open and friendly, and the time of day and week will dictate how busy you'll find it. Their extensive Tex-Mex menu is bursting with dishes to tantalise the taste buds, and they have a very appealing children's menu. Children are not only welcomed but made a fuss of with colouring books, crayons and balloons, and the free soft drinks refill is a guaranteed winner with thirsty kids. Staff often keep your kids amused, showering them with attention and keeping smiles on their faces. Plenty of high chairs are available. While your kids will love the high calorie treats Chili's now have low carb and guilt free options for those watching their waistlines!

Fishmarket, The

Location → Htl Inter-Continental · Bainuna St | 02 666 6888
Hours → 12:30 - 15:00 19:30 - 23:00
Web/email → www.intercontinental.com   Map Ref → 5-D3

Shop for your supper at this established seafood restaurant – hand pick your ingredients from the freshest local produce at the 'market stall', ably assisted by friendly and knowledgeable staff, and then sit back and relax while your selection is whisked off to the kitchen and transformed into a delectable feast. The ambience is warm and pleasing, and the cooking style leans towards the Far Eastern and Thai cuisines. Food is charged according to weight so children can decide on how much or how little they want and if they're not fish lovers then there are other options such as grilled chicken and french fries. High chairs are available.

Foodlands

Location → opp Al Manhal Palace · Airport Rd | 02 633 0099
Hours → 12:00 - 15:30 18:30 - 24:00
Web/email → na   Map Ref → 4-E3

Recently opened at its new location on Airport Road, Foodlands is the place to go for a reasonably priced family meal. There are two separate areas, depending on whether you are dining or just fancy a quick snack – both offer tasty Indian, Chinese, Arabic and Continental cuisine, served with a smile. There is no specific children's menu but with so much on offer kids are sure to find something they like and staff are more than willing to mix and match to cater for special requests. Parking can be a problem, so prevent road rage on busy nights by taking a taxi. High chairs are available.

Fuddruckers

Location → Marina Mall · Breakwater | 02 681 8160
Hours → 08:00 - 24:00
Web/email → fudafsab@emirates.net.ae   Map Ref → 5-A2

At Fuddruckers, you'll find the food is what you may expect from a chain restaurant in a mall, but they do serve some of the best hamburgers in town.

You get to order them the way you want, and then add toppings from a small relish bar, which also doubles as a salad bar. The children's menu, priced at Dhs.15, is packed with crowd pleasers such as chicken nuggets, hotdog bites, burgers and French fries and includes unlimited sodas and a cookie coupon. High chairs are available and there is also a play area with a padded soft area and ball pen, climbing frame, slides and small houses with mini tea tables and kitchens. However, this is sometimes closed off for private parties. A video room shows cartoons and there are video games for older children.

Il Palazzo

Location → Al Ain Palace Hotel · Corniche Rd East | 02 679 4777
Hours → 12:00 - 15:00 19:00 - 24:00
Web/email → www.alainpalacehotel.com   Map Ref → 4-D4

The walls and ceiling are rustic brick while the window view overlooks the Corniche, enhancing the ambience of this quaint Italian restaurant. The menu is regular Italian (no surprises) and offers a range of antipasti, soups, salads, pastas, pizzas, etc, and a variety of main dishes cater to different clients, not overlooking children's needs. There may not be a children's menu as such, although Italian food tends to be a favourite with kids and children's portions of pasta or pizza can be prepared. High chairs are also available

More Please, Mum!

Nihal Restaurant

Location → Nr Sands Htl · Shk Zayed 2nd St
Hours → 12:00 - 15:00 18:30 - 24:00
Web/email → nihal88@emirates.net.ae
02 631 8088
Map Ref → 4-D3

In the unique setting of the former Heritage Village, this outlet has to be one of the most picturesque places for a meal in Abu Dhabi. You enter through a fortified stone watchtower into an Arabic 'village', which has a stunning view of the Corniche at night, lit up across the water. Tables line the edge of the Breakwater, or choose the more private seating inside small wooden shelters. Main courses are mostly meat and fish, served with rice and vegetables. There is no children's menu as such but kids can have smaller portions and if all else fails, chips are on the menu! This is a great venue to eat Arabic food or just to have a drink – the perfect place to bring visitors to the UAE.

Oasis Chinese Restaurant

Location → Madinat Zayed
Hours → 12:30 - 15:30 18:00 - 24:00
Web/email → na
02 635 1545
Map Ref → 4-E2

Although Oasis is probably better known for its home delivery service, it's an ideal restaurant to take the family for a cheap and cheerful Chinese meal. The décor is 'typically' Chinese in both of the branches on either side of town. There's a choice of seating upstairs in comfortable booths, or at tables for four downstairs. High chairs are available. The extensive menu offers all the usual favourites and large portions of tasty food ensure that diners get good value for money. Although there isn't a children's menu they will prepare special requests such as fried chicken with chips, and the service is quick and efficient.

Palm, The

Location → Al Diar Capitol Hotel · Al Meena St
Hours → 12:30 - 15:30 19:00 - 11:00
Web/email → adcaphtl@emirates.net.ae
02 678 7700
Map Ref → 4-C3

Ideal for families, The Palm offers a reasonably priced buffet, packed with fresh, tasty salads, hot meals and desserts. The restaurant is moving to a new location in early 2005 and will have a dedicated children's menu as well as high chairs and colouring books.

Panda Panda Chinese Restaurant

Location → nr Jashanmal · Al Istiqlal St
Hours → 12:30 - 16:00 19:00 - 24:00
Web/email → panda@emirates.net.ae
02 633 9300
Map Ref → 4-E3

This contemporary eatery mixes modern and traditional oriental influences – the result is a convivial venue serving wholesome Chinese food in a family friendly setting. The extensive menu caters equally well to vegetarians, seafood lovers and carnivores, with the Hot and Sour soup and the Schezuan Beef both heartily recommended. Service is quick, attentive and enthusiastic, which is perfect for fidgets who will only sit still for short periods. If the prices seem high at first, remember that portions are usually generous enough to feed two and while there is no specific children's menu the staff are more than happy to prepare mini meals such as chicken balls and French fries. High chairs are available.

Pizzeria Italiana

Location → Al Diar Gulf Htl · Al Maqtaa
Hours → 11:00 - 22:30
Web/email → adglfhtl@emirates.net.ae
02 441 4777
Map Ref → 1-D3

A warm welcome awaits you at this appealing Italian café. The interior is simple and rustic, with crisp, fresh linen draped over wooden tables, and the outside terrace is good for alfresco dining. Salads, pizza and pasta dominate the menu, although there are a few interesting extras, and there is a decent enough children's menu. Both the food and the wine are very reasonably priced. High chairs are available.

Rainbow Steak House

Location → Shk Hamdan Bin Mohd. St
Hours → 12:30 - 16:00 18:30 - 24:00
Web/email → www.rainbowauh.com
02 633 3434
Map Ref → 4-D3

As the name suggests, steaks are a speciality here – there is a good range and all are cooked to perfection. They also do a good selection of seafood, as well as Chinese, Indian and continental cuisine. Lunch and dinner buffets are available daily at unbelievably low prices (Dhs.35 for lunch, Dhs.40 for dinner and just 20dhs for kids); yet the friendly, efficient service remains uncompromised. While high chairs may be the only offering for kids, children are welcomed with open arms and the buffet style avoids impatient moaning from rumbling tummies!

Any Time, is Chili's Time!

Family Time
Kids Time
Lunch Time
Party Time
Fun Time
Free Time
Dinner Time
Hang out Time

Bahrain
Egypt
Kuwait
Lebanon
Oman
Qatar
Saudi Arabia
United Arab Emirates

Chili's — Fun. Fresh. Flavorful.

Dubai Jumeirah, Deira City Centre, Garhoud, Dubai Internet City, Burjuman Centre, Al Ghurair City **Abu Dhabi** Al Mariah Cineplex **Al Ain** Al Jimi Mall **Sharjah** Sahara Centre
Opening 2004 Sharjah Mega Mall

Dubai

Aeroplane

Location ➔ Golden Tulip Aeroplane Hotel · Deira | 04 272 2999
Hours ➔ 13:00 - 15:00 19:30 - 23:30
Web/email ➔ www.goldentulip.com | Map Ref ➔ 14-B2

Upon boarding, it may appear that you've stumbled into the first class section of an Emirates aircraft. Comfortable plane seats, complete with attendant call lights, add to the authenticity for this flight themed dining experience and are sure to impress junior flyers! The menu includes a diverse and very reasonably priced selection of good quality food and there is also a children's menu. The service is a little haphazard and the flight is dry, but for kids (aged five and above) it's sure to be a fun, novel experience.

Al Areesh

Location ➔ Umm Hurair (2) | 04 324 3000
Hours ➔ 12:00 - 16:00 19:00 - 24:00
Web/email ➔ abt@emirates.net.ae | Map Ref ➔ 15-C1

For an authentic, Arabian experience, look no further! The Al Areesh dhow trip serves a delicious buffet with an attractive selection of seafood, chicken and meat. Food at this restaurant is extremely fresh and plentiful. A healthy choice of 'local' and traditional starters and desserts can be washed down with freshly made mocktails that are highly recommended. Families with young children are well catered for and private 'majlis style' rooms accommodate the larger groups. The buffet is half price for kids and there are high chairs on board.

Al Khayal

Location ➔ Jumeirah Beach Htl · Umm Suqeim | 04 406 8181
Hours ➔ 12:30 - 15:00 20:00 - 03:00
Web/email ➔ www.jumeirahinternational.com | Map Ref ➔ 4-E3

The spices of Arabia run past your senses on the Jumeira sea breeze as you enjoy sizzling meats and scrumptious salads. The belly dancing and music are a nice backdrop to the traditional Arabic foods offered. Familes occupy the lunch time and early evening tables before the place fills up with a sophisticated late night Arabic crowd, who stay late to enjoy a cappuccino and strawberry or coconut flavoured shisha. There is a children's menu, as well as Wild Wadi colouring sheets and crayons. High chairs are available.

Al Koufa

Location ➔ Nr Cyclone · Oud Metha | 04 335 1511
Hours ➔ 18:30 - 02:00
Web/email ➔ na | Map Ref ➔ 13-E4

A great place to introduce visitors to Arabic food, Al Koufa is always busy at weekends and popular with families as children are welcome all hours of the evening and can be found running about while adults relax, play dominos and listen to the Lebanese band. It is enclosed by windtowers and barasti walls made from palm leaves, and covered during the summer months to allow air conditioning. The large courtyard is filled with plastic chairs and tables. Service is genuine and the food is really good value. Tucked away in a corner is a portakabin serving ice-cream – a favourite with kids! However, there are no high chairs.

Biella Caffé Pizzeria Ristorante

Location ➔ Wafi Mall · Umm Hurair (2) | 04 324 4666
Hours ➔ 12:00 - 24:00
Web/email ➔ www.pyramidsdubai.com | Map Ref ➔ 15-C1

Biella is a casual Italian café/restaurant serving top quality wholesome food at value for money prices. The indoor and terrace facilities create a relaxed ambience and the outstanding service is prompt, efficient and knowledgeable. The menu provides a host of mouth-watering options and includes an extensive range of pizza, pasta, meat, fish and

Biella Caffé Pizzeria Ristorante

excellent vegetarian specials. Try their delicious range of non-alcoholic cocktails too. They have a children's menu with pasta and pizza and provide high chairs, making this a good place to stop when you're on a Wafi shopping trip.

Blue Elephant

Location ➜ Al Bustan Hotel · Al Garhoud | 04 705 4660
Hours ➜ 12:00 - 15:00   19:00 - 23:30
Web/email ➜ www.rotana.com | Map Ref ➜ 15-D1

The indisputable 'King of Royal Thai Cuisine', the Blue Elephant is an experience that no one in the family will forget in a hurry! With décor reminiscent of a Thai village – complete with huts, a waterfall, flowing streams and lush vegetation, a traditional warm Thai welcome and excellent food, this is a superior, authentic destination for a meal out. A special children's menu is designed to appeal to younger taste buds and the staff also hand out crayons and a colouring book. Whether for lunch or an early evening meal, the service here is impeccable and the staff are good with children. A Saturday lunch and dinner buffet has a tempting range of dishes, and reservations, especially at weekends, are essential. High chairs are available.

Boardwalk, The

Location ➜ Creek Golf Club · Al Garhoud | 04 295 6000
Hours ➜ 09:00 - 24:00
Web/email ➜ creekfnb@dubaigolf.com | Map Ref ➜ 14-C2

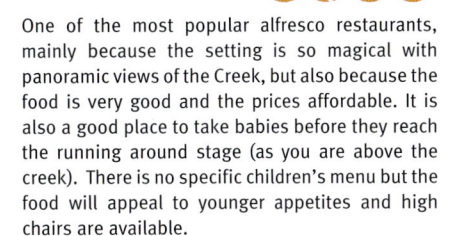

One of the most popular alfresco restaurants, mainly because the setting is so magical with panoramic views of the Creek, but also because the food is very good and the prices affordable. It is also a good place to take babies before they reach the running around stage (as you are above the creek). There is no specific children's menu but the food will appeal to younger appetites and high chairs are available.

Cactus Cantina

Location ➜ Rydges Plaza Hotel · Al Satwa | 04 398 2274
Hours ➜ 12:00 - 23:15
Web/email ➜ www.cactuscantinadubai.com | Map Ref ➜ 13-C2

Unlike many other restaurants in town, Cactus Cantina doesn't have a live band so you can enjoy a pleasant family meal without being drowned out by loud music. At the same time, it's still a lively place with a good atmosphere and constantly changing promotions. Children are more than welcome with a kids' menu of good value Tex-Mex food just for them, which doubles as a colouring sheet to be attacked with the crayons provided. Highchairs are available (but limited!).

Chili's

Location ➜ Meridien Fairways · Al Garhoud | 04 282 8484
Hours ➜ 11:00 - 23:00   Thu 11:00 - 24:00 Fri 13:00 - 23:00
Web/email ➜ www.chilis.com | Map Ref ➜ 13-B1

Refer to the Abu Dhabi [p.184] review for details.

China White

Location ➜ Century Village · Al Garhoud | 04 282 5377
Hours ➜ 12:00 - 01:00
Web/email ➜ na | Map Ref ➜ 15-D1

Nestled within Century Village, the restaurant offers an attractive outdoor terrace and a Chinese themed indoor section. A large selection of dishes will appeal to both meat eaters and vegetarians, and non MSG fare can be requested. Cantonese and Szechuan styles dominate, but at times the resulting food does not quite match the description on the menu. Alfresco dining is always a bonus for families (the sound of screaming children doesn't echo outside). China White has no children's menu, although they can prepare chicken and chips as a failsafe. High chairs are also available.

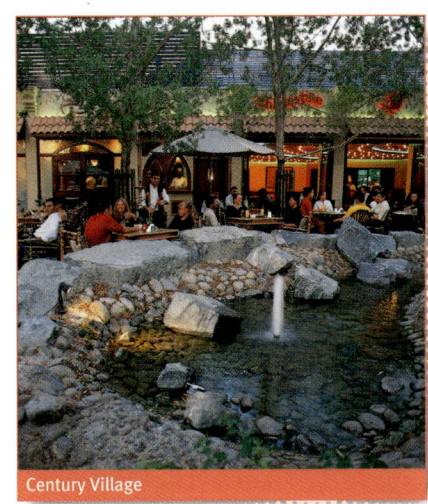

Century Village

Chinese Pavilion

Location → Beach Centre, The · Jumeira
Hours → 12:30 - 15:00 19:00 - 23:30
Web/email → na
04 344 4432
Map Ref → 13-A1

This small, friendly restaurant, tucked away in a far corner of the Beach Centre, is simply and tastefully decorated with wicker furniture and dim lighting. The menu offers a good selection, with specialities ranging from Singapore chicken to chilli dishes with crispy vegetables. On Fridays, Chinese Pavilion has special offers for lunch, which are very popular with families – rice or noodles are on the house with any dish. However, apart from high chairs there is little on offer for kids so only go if they like Chinese food.

Coco's

Location → Deira City Centre
Hours → 08:00 - 01:00
Web/email → www.deiracitycentre.com
04 295 3777
Map Ref → 15-D1

One of the biggest and best known restaurant chains in America, Coco's offers a special children's menu for the under tens, with a wide selection of good food to eat in or take away. Prices are reasonable and the surroundings are simply furnished, comfortable and quiet, and away from the bustle of the mall. The menu offers a good variety of soups, salads, sandwiches, Mexican dishes and hearty main courses, while for afternoon tea a large selection of yummy pies, cookies, cakes and cobblers are too tempting to resist. High chairs are available

Da Vinci's

Location → Millennium Airport Hotel
Hours → 12:00 - 24:00   Thu 12:00 - 01:00
Web/email → apothotl@emirates.net.ae
04 703 9123
Map Ref → 15-D1

One of the most popular Italian restaurants in Dubai, Da Vinci's has undoubtedly discovered the secrets of success. Always busy, it has just the right mix, with a genuinely homely atmosphere, a pervading smell of herbs and homemade pasta sauces, very reasonable prices and an Italian trattoria feel. There is now a kids' menu, which offers mini burgers and pizzas, macaroni, a fascinating pudding called 'swan eclair', as well as banana boats and good old ice-cream. The staff are friendly, helpful and welcoming to children, and there are plenty of highchairs. Da Vinci's has family rooms, which can be reserved to keep your flock contained. Advance reservations are always advisable.

Der Keller

Location → Jumeirah Beach Htl · Umm Suqeim
Hours → 18:00 - 23:30
Web/email → www.jumeirahinternational.com
04 406 8181
Map Ref → 12-A1

Der Keller, German for 'the cellar', gives you a warm welcome and hearty food along with an unexpected but fantastic view of the sea. The red bricked walls, carefully planned lighting and soft background music create a relaxed family atmosphere. Do try the speciality veal dishes and the sauerkraut, not to mention the fondue to share. Service here is always with a smile, but beware the Germanic sized portions – this is not a place for light eaters. Children can order from the standard hotel kids' menu, which has the usual favourites of chicken nuggets and chips, or they can have child sized portions from the restaurant's main menu. High chairs are available but there is no specific activities or entertainment for children.

Dhow & Anchor

Location → Jumeirah Beach Htl · Umm Suqeim
Hours → 12:00 - 24:30
Web/email → www.jumeirahinternational.com
04 406 8181
Map Ref → 12-A1

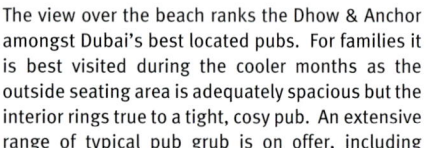

The view over the beach ranks the Dhow & Anchor amongst Dubai's best located pubs. For families it is best visited during the cooler months as the outside seating area is adequately spacious but the interior rings true to a tight, cosy pub. An extensive range of typical pub grub is on offer, including salads, curries, seafood, meat, sandwiches and simple, well executed desserts. Kids can order from the standard Jumeirah Beach Hotel children's menu, including chicken nuggets and chips, although the pub menu will more than likely have something to suit most fussy eaters. For those not in a hurry, this is a good choice for a nice, simple and reasonably priced meal. High chairs are available but push chair access is a little difficult so be prepared to tackle a few obstacles in order to get a perfect spot alfresco.

Don Corleone

Location → Metropolitan · Jct 2, Shk Zayed Rd **04 343 0000**
Hours → 12:30 - 14:30 19:00 - 23:00
Web/email → www.methotels.com **Map Ref** → 12-D2

A special find among Italian restaurants, Don Corleone is well loved for its great atmosphere and value for money menu. The setting is perfect, both for groups indoors in the cosy family atmosphere or an intimate dinner for two on the large terrace overlooking the tree lined gardens. The food is delicious, but tends to be rich. There's no entertainment or special menu for children, but the restaurant will provide smaller portions on request. Reservations are advisable, especially if you want a table on the terrace on busier evenings, and there is only one high chair up for grabs.

Eauzone

Location → One&Only Arabian Court · Al Sufouh **04 399 9999**
Hours → 19:30 - 24:00
Web/email → www.oneandonlyresort.com **Map Ref** → 11-C1

Wooden causeways take you across the Royal Mirage swimming pools to the intimate Asian influenced Eauzone restaurant that has a pleasant terrace perfect for lunch or a casual dinner, and is popular with family hotel residents. The children's menu comprises hammour fillet and fries, chicken burger, mini beef steaks and pasta dishes. The hotel's Al Koufa kids club offers swim and play for kids. High chairs are available.

Fuddruckers

Location → Beh Al Tayer Motors · Al Garhoud **04 282 7771**
Hours → 07:00 - 02:00
Web/email → fuddubaigar@emirates.net.ae **Map Ref** → 6-D1

Refer to the Abu Dhabi review [p.185] for more info.

Gardenia

Location → Towers Rotana · Trade Centre 1&2 **04 312 2210**
Hours → 06:00 - 23:00
Web/email → www.rotana.com **Map Ref** → 13-A3

The Pirates of Penzance have set up shop at the Towers Rotana, where guys in feathered hats and plastic swords serve up a mean roast beef. Kids will love the fun, fantasy style atmosphere and the children's menu will definitely please with Barbie spaghetti and Superman burgers. Grown ups will love the dessert bar, home to what may be the world's best chocolate mousse and toffee torte. For the early birds, the breakfast buffet and a Friday brunch are good options in this buffet restaurant. High chairs are available.

Go West

Location → Jumeirah Beach Htl · Umm Suqeim **04 406 8181**
Hours → 18:00 - 23:30 Thu, Fri 12:30 - 15:00
Web/email → www.jumeirahinternational.com **Map Ref** → 12-A1

Reminiscent of a Colorado steak joint with saddles, wagons and servers in plaid shirts, Go

Go West

West completes the Western experience with great North American chow. For starters, the buffalo wings are enough for two, chicken fajitas arrive sizzling with all the trimmings, and the BBQ ribs are rich and tender. The children's menu comprises chicken nuggets, burgers and fish and chips as well as unlimited soft drinks. High chairs are available as well as colouring books and crayons.

Hard Rock Café

Location → Jct 5 Shk. Zayed Rd · Al Sufouh   04 399 2888
Hours → 12:00 - 01:30
Web/email → www.hardrock.com   Map Ref → 11-C2

Hard to miss, the Hard Rock Cafe is set below a large replica of the Empire State Building, adorned with two huge guitars. The Lil' Rock Kids Club on a Friday serves up hearty portions of fun and excitement with live entertainment, face painting and a clown. For those aged under ten, there's a great Lil' Rockers menu at Dhs.20 per head, which includes children's favourite choices of burgers plus unlimited sodas. The staff are lively, very helpful and attentive. The entertainment changes throughout the week so give them a call before you go to find out what's on the menu! High chairs, colouring books and crayons are available.

India Palace

Location → Opp Sofitel City Cen. Htl · Al Garhoud   04 286 9600
Hours → 12:00 - 16:00 19:00 - 01:00
Web/email → na   Map Ref → 6-D1

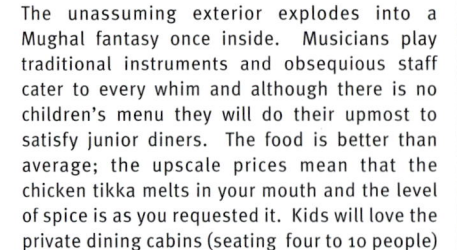

The unassuming exterior explodes into a Mughal fantasy once inside. Musicians play traditional instruments and obsequious staff cater to every whim and although there is no children's menu they will do their upmost to satisfy junior diners. The food is better than average; the upscale prices mean that the chicken tikka melts in your mouth and the level of spice is as you requested it. Kids will love the private dining cabins (seating four to 10 people) where you can summon your waiter with a bell (to then have him knock before entering). High chairs are available.

Irish Village

Location → Aviation Club, The · Al Garhoud   04 282 4750
Hours → 11:00 - 01:30 Wed & Thu 11:00 - 02:30
Web/email → www.aviationclubonline.com   Map Ref → 15-D1

The authentic atmosphere of the Irish Village (beer sticky floor and a smoky atmosphere packed with 'merry' men) means that for the hotter and more humid 6 months of the year it isn't the most family friendly of places, unless you come in for lunch or the Friday roast. However, in the cooler months the large outdoor terrace overlooking landscaped gardens provide space for kids to roam. There is a kids' menu but high chairs are limited so it's first come first served, and children are only allowed (even outside) up until 20:30.

Johnny Rockets

Location → Opp Jumeirah Centre · Jumeira   04 344 7859
Hours → 12:00 - 24:00
Web/email → www.johnnyrockets.com   Map Ref → 4-B1

This friendly '50s/'60s style venue offers superior freshly made burgers, but is best suited for a quick bite to eat due to the limited number of seats and tables. Great malt shakes, generous portions and a lively, friendly atmosphere most afternoons and evenings make Johnny Rockets a great contender to the standard burger joints in town. There are also staple children's options such as chicken nuggets and grilled cheese on toast and high chairs are available. Select one of the songs on the table-bar jukeboxes while your order is prepared before your very eyes. Kids love it, since to a particular song the staff throw down their tools to perform the infamous Johnny Rockets song and dance routine!

Nina

Location → One&Only Arabian Court · Al Sufouh   04 399 9999
Hours → 19:00 - 23:30
Web/email → www.oneandonlyresort.com   Map Ref → 11-C1

In keeping with the Royal Mirage, the décor is immersed in opulence. Dining here is akin to an evening in an Arabian palace, where the smallest detail warrants attention. The food is presented in novel tradition, and is a fusion of European and Indian ingredients. The range of food caters to a variety of tastes, and the portions are small but adequate. A children's menu is available along with high chairs but there is little else to tempt families. However, it is definitely a choice for a special occasion when you want to bring the kids along.

Plaice, The

Location → Century Village · Al Garhoud   04 286 8233
Hours → 11:00 - 01:00
Web/email → www.aviationclubonline.com   Map Ref → 15-D1

Fish and chips, the traditional way, is the concept behind this 'plaice'. Fish, more fish, and loads of hot, fresh chips are available for dining in, takeaway or delivery. Situated just to the left of the entrance to the Irish Village, it provides a quick and very casual alternative to the other restaurants in Century Village and is a great family stop off. The kiddy portions are quite large and high chairs are available.

Pizzeria Uno Chicago Grill

Location → Deira City Centre   04 294 8799
Hours → 08:00 - 24:00
Web/email → www.pizzeriauno.com   Map Ref → 15-D1

Pizzeria Uno offers a wide choice, with a menu that ranges from breakfast items to pizza, nachos, burgers, steaks and pasta. There's a kids' menu with typical selections, such as chicken nuggets, burgers and smiley potatoes. The staff are eager to please and children are made very welcome, with plenty of highchairs and colouring books with crayons.

Sea World

Location → Above Safestway · Al Wasl   04 321 1500
Hours → 12:00 - 16:00 19:00 - 23:00
Web/email → www.seaworld-dubai.com   Map Ref → 12-E2

This venue brings the novelty of a seafood market to a mass audience. The large tank in the centre of the restaurant is home to a selection of live seafood. The dining area is comfortable, with an impressive 500 seating capacity. Alternatively, there are private cabins for larger or private parties. Place selections in your trolley, add vegetables, and select your preferred cooking method. With fairly reasonable prices, this huge, family friendly restaurant is a good place to chomp crustaceans. However, there is no children's menu so kids will have to pick their own fish or suffice with chips. High chairs are available.

TGI Friday's

Location → Shk Zayed Rd   04 331 8010
Hours → 11:00 - 01:00
Web/email → tgifdxb@kfcuae.co.ae   Map Ref → 13-B3

This famous chain has typical American offerings and Hollywood memorabilia. The menu of enormous burgers, sizzling Tex Mex fajitas, speciality salads, appetisers, pasta and ribs, are more than generous in size, while the children's menu will satisfy even the hungriest tummies with chicken fingers, macaroni cheese and mini burgers. For kids a trip to TGI's will feel like a special treat, especially on the 'Friday Family Day' when the play area comes alive with face painters and games. High chairs are available.

Thai Chi

Location → Pyramids · Umm Hurair (2)   04 324 4100
Hours → 12:00 - 15:00 19:30 - 24:00
Web/email → www.pyramidsdubai.com   Map Ref → 15-C1

Duality masquerades in the form of Thai Chi, bringing two popular Far Eastern cuisines under one roof. While mood and ambience are determined by your choice of setting – formal fare, intimate Thai, or casual laid back Chinese – your choice of cuisine is interchangeable. Families may prefer the no nonsense, time conscious option of the set menus. While kids are welcome in the evenings there is no children's menu but during the day children age six to 12 can enjoy the lunch buffet at half price (children under six eat for free). High chairs are available.

Cafés & Coffee Shops

Café culture is very much alive and well in the UAE, and is especially popular with the expat mum crowd. There is an appealing array of coffee and cake haunts that also serve a tasty selection of sandwiches and salads. Full of mothers and babies, meeting for tea and biscuits is a great way to socialise with other mums. While many cafés provide little in the way of entertainment for kids, we all know it's not about whether they have clowns or not that is important, but rather whether the cakes are good! Even better, there are plenty of locations to sample.

Abu Dhabi

Café Ceramique

Location → Nr Choitrams, 26th St · Khalidiya 02 666 4412
Hours → 08:00 - 24:00
Web/email → www.cafe-ceramique.com   Map Ref → 14-B3

The novel idea of creating your own mug, plate or dish while you eat is a definite crowd pleaser, especially with artistic kids who also get to feast on macaroni cheese, chicken nuggets and hot dogs while they create. After all that hard work they can finish off with toast and maple syrup! High chairs are available and parties can be arranged. See Birthday Parties for more details [p.151].

Citrus

Location → Shk Khalifa Bin Zyd St   02 626 2700
Hours → 12:00 - 15:30 19:00 - 23:00
Web/email → www.milleniumhotels.com   Map Ref → 4-D3

Business lunchers and people watchers will enjoy this refreshingly elegant café located in the hotel foyer. The buffet and a la carte options are both packed with delicious, fresh food, and the buffet in particular is very good value for money. While there is no children's menu, the restaurant is happy to prepare dishes for kids such as chicken nuggets and chips. High chairs are available.

Havana Cafe

Location → Breakwater · Al Ras Al Akhdar   02 681 0044
Hours → 09:00 - 00:45
Web/email → www.havanagroup.co.ae   Map Ref → 5-D4

Only two minutes from the Marina Mall, this wonderful café has an outside play area for children, and is also happy to cater to their needs. Prices are reasonable and a great variety of non-alcoholic cocktails and drinks are on offer. The café overlooks the sea and so parents with children who tend to wander should take care.

THE One

Location → Nr BMW Garage · Shk Zayed 1st St   02 681 6500
Hours → 08:00 - 21:00 Fri 14:00 - 21:00
Web/email → www.theoneme.com   Map Ref → 1-C3

Surround yourself in stylish furnishings as you mull over the delights of the 'fusion' menu. This café offers all day breakfast, daily specials and a mouthwatering selection of exotic dishes. With the weekend crowd, waiting times can be a bit longer but there is plenty of reading material and the daily papers to help you bide the time. Traditional English cream teas are served in the afternoon and a kids' menu provides a few healthier options in comparison to the usual fast food offerings. Instead of chicken nuggets and chips there is a toasted breakfast muffin and kids club sandwiches. High chairs are available.

Dubai

Café Ceramique

Location → Town Centre · Jumeira   04 344 7331
Hours → 08:00 - 24:00
Web/email → www.cafe-ceramique.com   Map Ref → 12-E1

Refer to the Abu Dhabi review for details.

Dome Café

Location → BurJuman Centre · Bur Dubai   04 355 6004
Hours → 07:30 - 23:30
Web/email → na   Map Ref → 14-A3

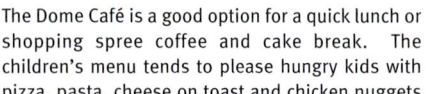

The Dome Café is a good option for a quick lunch or shopping spree coffee and cake break. The children's menu tends to please hungry kids with pizza, pasta, cheese on toast and chicken nuggets with chips and comes with a drink and ice cream. However, there are only a couple of high chairs.

Other branches: Jumeirah Plaza (04 349 0383); Bin Sougat Centre (04 284 4413)

Fiesta World Cafe

Location → Mercato Mall, Ground Floor · Jumeira   04 349 0777
Hours → 10:00 - 24:00
Web/email → www.fiestacafes.com   Map Ref → 12-E1

Tucked in a small piazza area of the mall near Spinneys supermarket, the Fiesta World Café offers a limited kids' menu, but they will adapt any of their main menu choices for smaller appetites. The range of food from this relatively small café is impressive and they try very hard to please. Choices include sushi, grills, stir-fries, pasta, pizza, sandwiches, soups, salads, burgers and breakfasts. High chairs are available.

French Connection

Location → Wafa Tower · Trade Centre 1&2
Hours → 07:00 - 24:00
Web/email → na
04 343 8311
Map Ref → 4-A3

French Connection bustles at almost any time of the day. Once you manage to tear your eyes away from the tantalising display of gateaux, pastries and breads at the entrance, you'll be struck by the trendy décor of this concept café. Stop in for a coffee and croissant, a quick snack, salads or sandwiches, or treat yourself to one of the many patisserie items. There's also a bakery section with a variety of traditional, popular and lesser known French breads, which are freshly baked twice a day – guaranteed to make your mouth water! The café has high chairs for children and although there is no selection specifically for them, children will undoubtedly find something here that appeals.

IKEA

Location → Deira City Centre
Hours → 10:00 - 22:00 14:00 - 22:00
Web/email → www.ikeadubai.com
04 295 0434
Map Ref → 15-D1

This Scandinavian self-service restaurant may seem a bit like a school canteen but it is the perfect place to grab cheap eats and take time out of a hectic Deira City Centre shopping trip. The children's menu changes regularly and is unbelievably cheap – for example, a plate of spaghetti with tomato sauce is just Dhs.4, including a drink! The restaurant can get a little crowded but is well geared up for families, with a baby food station fully equipped with little bowls, cutlery, bibs and a microwave. There is also a small children's corner with chairs and a couple of toys where your kids can watch films such as the Lion King while you savour the famous Swedish meatballs. High chairs are plentiful.

La Brioche

Location → Jumeirah Centre · Jumeira
Hours → 10:00 - 22:00
Web/email → www.binhendi.com
04 349 0588
Map Ref → 13-B1

A pleasant and popular place for families or shoppers, especially on a Thursday morning when it's generally fairly full, La Brioche offers a tempting variety of snacks and meals. Savoury filled croissants, hefty salads and pasta dishes cost from Dhs.10 - 30. For kids, dishes such as freshly made chicken nuggets come with fresh salad, fries and a fizzy drink for only Dhs.12. High chairs are also available.

Lime Tree Café

Location → Nr Jumeira Mosque · Jumeira
Hours → 07:30 - 20:00
Web/email → limetree@emirates.net.ae
04 349 8498
Map Ref → 4-B1

A tremendously popular café, the Lime Tree Café not only offers its customers a relaxing atmosphere, but also the chance to sample some of the finest cakes and sandwiches around. Their carrot cake has the reputation of being the best in Dubai, and the sandwiches are not only healthy but also incredibly tasty, with lots of choices for children. The menu offers value for money as the portions are generous and getting children to eat Lime Tree goodies requires little effort! High chairs are available but be warned: children are not allowed on the picturesque balcony.

Marks & Spencer Café

Location → Salah Al Din Rd · Deira
Hours → 10:00 - 22:30
Web/email → na
04 222 2000
Map Ref → 14-C3

This friendly café offers quick, reasonably priced snacks and soft drinks. The surroundings are quiet and relaxed, although this is a popular café with shoppers at Marks & Spencer or Toys 'R' Us. It's also next to Kids' Play, allowing parents a pleasant break while the kids run riot! The children's menu has the usual chicken nuggets, chips and beans, among other options, and high chairs are available. There are also a couple of colouring book stations with mini tables and chairs.

More

Location ➜ Nr Welcare Hospital · Al Garhoud	04 283 0224
Hours ➜ 08:00 - 22:00	
Web/email ➜ www.morecafe.biz	Map Ref ➜ 6-D1

MORE offers what Dubai has needed for a long time – a good dose of industrial chic. Wholesome dishes are prepared with fresh ingredients; the salads and catch of the day are excellent and highly recommended. Seating options are wide ranging, from a small coffee bar to lots of private tables and a couple of sofas. The place is packed with personality and they're family friendly. Half portions for kids are available and if requested, they even provide paints. High chairs are provided.

West One

Location ➜ Opp Al Hana Centre · Al Mankhool St	04 349 4500
Hours ➜ 07:30 - 21:00 Fri. Closed.	
Web/email ➜ na	Map Ref ➜ 13C-2

This refreshingly casual, café style eatery is a great place for a light meal or a quick sandwich on the run. The food is tasty and fresh, the service fast and friendly, and with a set lunch starting from Dhs.25, it's also good value. The kids menu will suffice and high chairs are available but the restaurants speciality is outside catering so they are a good option for birthday parties.

Foodcourts

Most shopping malls have a foodcourt as part of their facilities. These are a particular favourite among tired shoppers looking to rest their aching feet after an intense shopping spree. Reasonably priced meals or snacks are promptly served from numerous outlets and you will notice most of the famous fast food hamburger chains have a branch here. The range of cuisine, otherwise, is quite multicultural and diverse.

Popular with all ages and nationalities, the variety of food provides something for every palate; even the fussiest of eaters should find their nibble of choice! Moreover, the casual and relaxed environment is ideal for families, for most food courts house a play area that keeps the children occupied and high chairs are generally available. For reviews on the various shopping malls in Abu Dhabi and Dubai see the Shopping section [p.61].

Jumeirah Beach Hotel

GRAND CUISINE

Whether you choose traditional Lebanese, modern Italian, sophisticated New York grill, fragrant Vietnamese or spicy Singaporean, our goal is simple; to bring you the best ingredients and the finest cooking from around the world. FEEL THE HYATT TOUCH®

For reservations call Grand Hyatt Dubai at 04 317 2222.

GRAND HYATT DUBAI

P.O. Box 7978, Dubai, United Arab Emirates. Telephone +971 4 317 1234,
Facsimile +971 4 317 1235, e-mail dubai.grand@hyattintl.com, www.dubai.grand.hyatt.com

in the UAE since 1976

MAPS geosystems

Spatial Data Acquisition, Processing & Integration

- Aerial Photography
- Satellite Image Processing
- Ground Survey
- Utility Mapping
- Geodetic Network Rehabilitation
- Terrain Modelling
- T3D Vector Mapping
- Orthoimage Production
- Geographic Data Acquisition
- Spatial Data Integration
- GIS Implementation
- Application Service Provision

Master Reseller of QuickBird from DIGITALGLOBE
The market's highest resolution satellite imagery.

MAPS (UAE), Corniche Plaza 1
P.O. Box 5232, Sharjah, U.A.E.
Tel.: + 971 6 5725411
Fax: + 971 6 5724057

Certified to EN ISO 9001:2000
TÜV CERT — EN ISO 9001 : 2000
Deutscher Akkreditierungs Rat
TGA-ZM-30-96-00

www.maps-geosystems.com
info@maps-geosystems.com

Operations throughout Europe, Middle East and Africa with regional offices in: **Munich, Sharjah, Beirut, Lisbon, Bucharest, Dubai, Abu Dhabi, Conakry, Dakar.**

Maps & Index

EXPLORER

Maps

Map Legend	200	Street Index	204	**Dubai**		
User's Guide	200	Maps 1-5	206-215	Street Index	226	
Technical Info	200			Overview Map	227	
UAE Map Overview	202	**Al Ain**		Maps 10-15	228-239	
		Street Index	216			
Abu Dhabi		Overview Map	217			
Zones, Sectors & Streets	200	Maps 6-9	218-225			
Overview Map	201					

Map Legend

Corniche Hospital	Embassies / Hospitals
Al Meena	Areas / Roundabouts
Crowne Plaza	Hotels
Bowling City	Activities
City Centre	Shopping/Souks
National Cinema	Cafés/Cinemas
Clock Tower	Important Landmarks
Etisalat	Business
Wadi Tawia	Exploring

Map pages 1-12,15 are at a scale of 1:50,000 (1cm = 500m)
Map pages 13,14 are at a scale of 1:25,000 (1cm = 250m)

User's Guide

To further assist you in locating your destination, we have superimposed additional information, such as main roads, roundabouts and landmarks on the maps. Many places listed throughout the guidebook also have a map reference alongside, so you know precisely where you need to go (or what you need to tell the taxi driver).

To make it easy to find places and give better visualization, the maps have all been orientated parallel to the coastline of the Corniche, which runs along the northwest side of the island (not north orientated). While the overview map on this page is at a scale of approximately 1:130,000 (1cm = 1.3km), all other maps range from 1:25,000 (1cm = 100m) to 1:50,000 (1cm = 500m).

Technical Info – Satellite Images

The maps in this section are based on rectified QuickBird satellite imagery taken in 2003.

The QuickBird satellite was launched in October 2001 and is operated by DigitalGlobe™, a private company based in Colorado (USA). Today, DigitalGlobe's QuickBird satellite provides the highest resolution (61 cm), largest swath width and largest onboard storage of any currently available or planned commercial satellite.

MAPS geosystems are the Digital Globe master resellers for the Middle East, West, Central and East Africa. They also provide a wide range of mapping services and systems. For more information, visit www.digitalglobe.com (QuickBird) and www.maps-geosystems.com (mapping services) or contact MAPS geosystems on 06 572 5411.

Abu Dhabi Zones, Sectors & Streets

Abu Dhabi Island is split into two zones using New Airport Road (Sheikh Rashid Bin Saeed Al Maktoum Street) as the dividing line. The area to the east is zone 1 (east) and the area to the west is zone 2 (west). The zones are further divided into numbered square sectors which are bordered by the main streets (creating a road network that is based on a grid system).

All streets (main and secondary) that are parallel to New Airport Road are given even numbers with the numbers increasing as they move away from New Airport Road towards either coast. Those streets that are parallel to the Corniche (ie, at right angles to New Airport Road) are given odd numbers, which increase as you move away from the Corniche. At the main street intersections, blue road signs show the zone and sector names while at secondary streets, green road signs are used. And just to confuse matters, many roads have more than one name! Listed in the index are the main roads with their official or map name, their common name, their street number and their position in relation to New Airport Road or the Corniche.

Abu Dhabi Overview Map (Map Sheet Index)

Abu Dhabi Overview Map

Maps

201

Abu Dhabi, Dubai & Northern Emirates

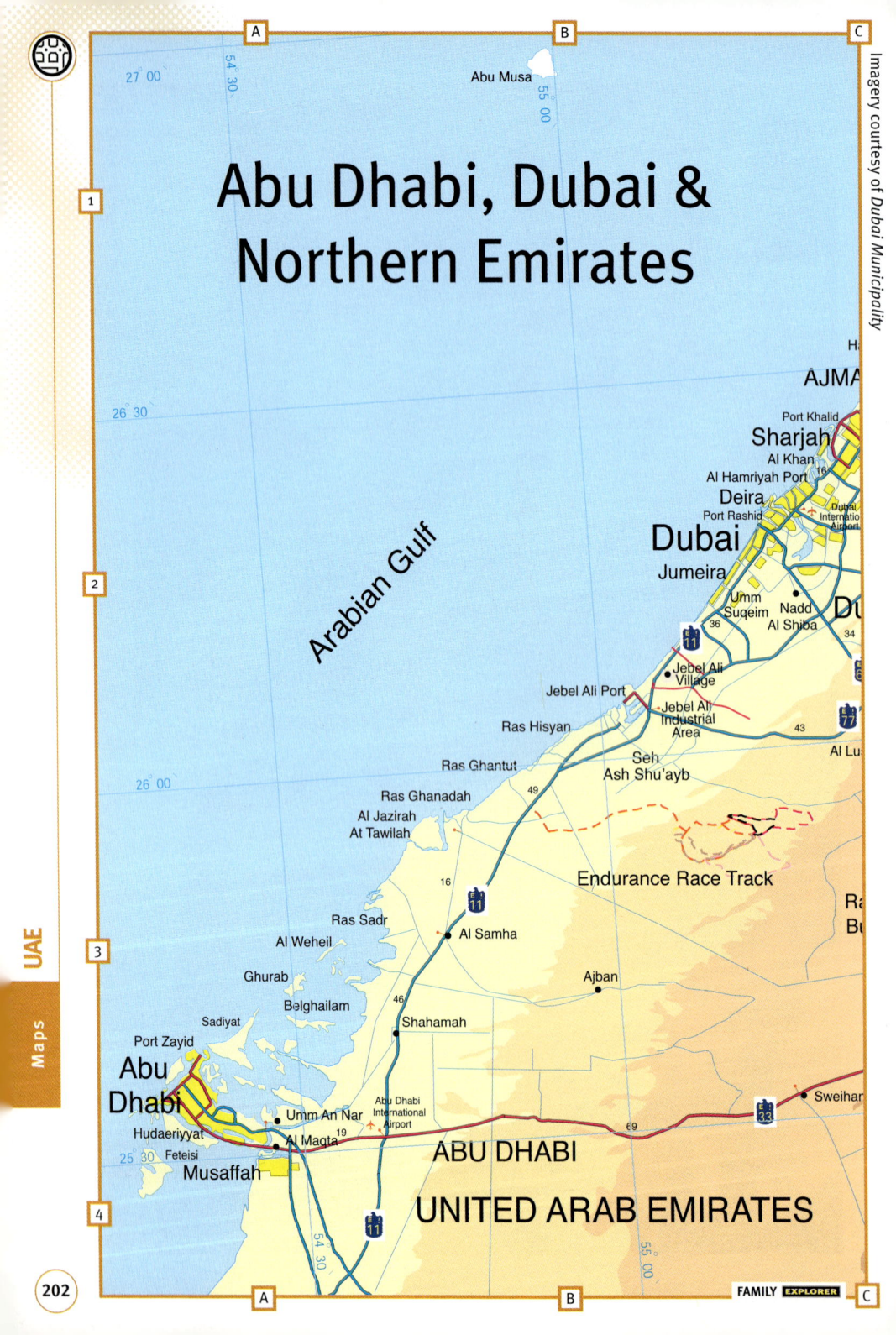

Rams
Ad Dharbaniya
Ras Al Khaimah
Musandam
(Sultanate
of Oman)
Gulf
of
Oman
Al Fulayyah
Al Jazirah
Al Hamra'
Kharran
Wadi Naqab
Ham Ham
Digdagga
RAS AL
KHAIMAH
Khatt
Wadi Sidakh
Wadi Khabb
Dibba
Al Rul
Ras Dibba
Umm Al
Qaiwain
Khor Al Beidah
Al Rafaah
Ras Al Khaimah
International Airport
Massfarah
Seh Jiri
Tawyain
Dhadnah
Umm Al
Qaiwain
Uyaynat
Sharm
Badiyah
Hoshi
Zubarah
Lulayyah
amriya
Lamhah
Wadi Khadra
Idhn
AJMAN
Biatah
Wadi Lamhah
Tayyibah
Hamadiyah
Nabgha
Ghayl
Khulaybiyah
Falaj
Al Mu'alla
Sharjah
International
Airport
Manama
Khor Fakkan
Masafi
Madha
(Sultanate
of Oman)
Qidfa
Al Dhaid
Mileilah
Dattah
Murbah
Sharjah
Al Khawaneej
Seh
Dhaid
Wadi Ashwan
Bithnah
Al Awir
Mileiha
Fujairah
Saqamqam
Fujairah
Fujairah
International
Airport
Al Gorfa
ubai
Wadi Yudayyah
Kalba
Lahbab
Daynah
Wadi Halw
Khor Kalba
AlMadam
Khatmat Milahah
Wadi Munay
Wahlah
saili
Murgham
Wadi Yudayyah
Huwaylat
Sayh
Al Madam
Al Bulaydah
Muraqqab
Masfut
Hatta
Al Wajajah
Al Maha
Resort
Al Widayyat
Jabal as
Sumayni
Wadi Hatta
Al Shuaib
Al Fayy
Shinas
aml Al
uhuth
Al Faqa
Wadi as Sumayni
SULTANATE
OF OMAN
Al Awhah
This map is not an authority
on international boundaries
Al Buraymi
Al Ain
Copyright © 2000 by Dubai Municipality

Abu Dhabi – Community & Street Index

The following is a list of the main streets in Abu Dhabi, which are referenced on map pages 1 - 5. Many roads are longer than one grid reference, in which case the main grid references have been given.

Street	Map Ref
Airport Rd	1-D4; 2-C2; 3-C1
Al Falah St	4-C2/D2
Al Istiqlal St	4-E3
Al Ittihad St	4-E3/E4
Al Karamah St	3-C3; 5-A1
Al Khaleej Al Arabi St	3-D4; 5-B1/B2/B3
Al Maktoum St	4-E1/E2/E3
Al Manhal St	4-E2; 5-A2/B2
Al Meena Rd	4-B4/C3
Al Nahyan St	3-D4
Al Nasr St	4-E3; 5-A3
Al Saada St	3-B2/C2
Al Salam St	5-C1/D2/E3
Al Sharqi St	4-E2
Bainunah St	5-C1/D2/E3
Bani Yas St (Najda)	4-D1/D2
Bateen St	5-A1/B1/C1
Coast Rd	1-E3; 2-D2; 3-D1
Corniche Rd (East)	4-D4/E4
Corniche Rd (West)	5-A3/B3/C3/D4
Defence Rd	see Haza'a Bin Zayed St (East)
Defence St	3-B4/C4
Delma St	3-D4
East Rd	3-B3/4-E1
Eastern Ring Rd	1-D3; 2-A3; 3-A1
Electra St/Rd	see Shk Zayed Second St (East)
Eleventh St	see Bateen St (West)
Eleventh St	see Haza'a Bin Zayed St (East)
Eleventh St	see Sudan St (Middle – West)
Fifteenth St	see Mohammed Bin Khalifa St (West)
Fifth St	see Shk Hamdan Bin Mohammed St (East)
First St	see Corniche Rd (East)
First St	see Corniche Rd (West)
First St	see The Corniche
Hamdan St	see Shk Hamdan Bin Mohd. St (East)

Street	Map Ref
Haza'a Bin Zayed St	4-D1/E1
Juwazat St	see Al Manhal St (West)
Khalid Bin Waleed St	5-A3
Khalidiyah St	5-C3
Khalidyah St	see Shk Zayed First St (West)
Khalifa Bin Shakhbout St	3-D3; 5-B1
Khalifa Bin Zayed St	4-D3/E3
Khalifa St	see Al Istiklal St (East)
Khubeirah St	5-D3
King Khalid Bin Abdel Aziz St	3-D3; 5-B1/B2/B3
Liwa St	4-E3/E4
Lulu St	4-D3/D4
Mohammed Bin Khalifa St	3-C3/C3/D3
New Airport Rd (Muroor Rd)	2-B3/C3; 3-B1/B2/B3/B4
Nineteenth St	see Al Saada St (East)
Nineteenth St	see Saeed Bin Tahnoun St (West)
Ninth St	see Al Falah St (East)
Ninth St	see Al Manhal St (West)
Old Passport Rd	see Al Falah St (East)
Port Rd	4-A4
Saeed Bin Tahnoon Street	3-C2/D2/E2
Seventh St	see Shk Zayed First St (West)
Seventh St	see Shk Zayed Second St (East)
Shk Hamdan Bin Mohd. St	4-C3/D3
Shk Rashid Bin Saeed	3-C2/C3/C4
Shk Zayed the First St	5-A1/B1/C1/D1
Shk Zayed the Second St	4-C3/D3/E3
Sultan Bin Zayed St	5-C1/C2
The Corniche	see Corniche Rd (East)
Third St	see Al Istiklal St (East)
Third St	see... Khalifa St
Third St	see Khalifa Bin Zayed St (West)
Thirteenth St	see Delma St (West)
Thirteenth St	see Defence St (East)
Umm Al Nar Street	4-D3

Future Developments

Scheduled for completion in early 2007, the Abu Dhabi Third Crossing or Sheikh Zayed Bridge will add to the Al Maqtaa and (Al) Mussafah Bridge. This Dhs.635 million project will cross the Al Maqtaa channel and link Abu Dhabi city to Dubai and the Northern Emirates.

Streetwise

Fellow cartographers beware! The hot gossip circulating town is that street names in Abu Dhabi will be changed in the near future. Whether this change will be drastic or not is yet to be confirmed. Watch this space!

DIGITALGLOBE™

C L E A R L Y   T H E   B E S T

61 cm QuickBird Imagery is the highest resolution satellite imagery available. We offer products and resorces to both existing GIS users and the entire next generation of mapping and multimedia applications.

Burj Al Arab, Scale 1:2500, dated May 2003 © DigitalGlobe

MAPSgeosystems

DigitalGlobe's Master Reseller serving the Middle East and East, Central and West Africa

MAPS (UAE), Corniche Plaza 1, P.O. Box 5232, Sharjah, UAE.
Tel : +971 6 5725411, Fax : +971 6 5724057
www.maps-geosystems.com

For further details, please contact quickbird@maps-geosystems.com

1

Abu Dhabi Golf Club by Sheraton

Al Ain

Dubai

Umm Al Nar

Channel St

Car Showrooms

Under Construction

Imagery courtesy of MAPS geosystems – Master Reseller for *Digital Globe*

MAPSgeosystems

Abu Dhabi

Maps

206

FAMILY EXPLORER

DIGITALGLOBE
C
D
E
1
2
3
4
Mussafah Bridge /
Al Ain Bridge
Al Diar Gulf
Hotel & Resort
Officers Club
Al Maqtaa Bridge
Al Maqtaa
Grand Mosque
Al Maqtaa Fort
Coast Rd
Eastern Ring Rd
Airport Rd
Khalifa Park
2
FAMILY EXPLORER

Imagery courtesy of *MAPS geosystems* – Master Reseller for *Digital Globe*

Qasr El Shatie

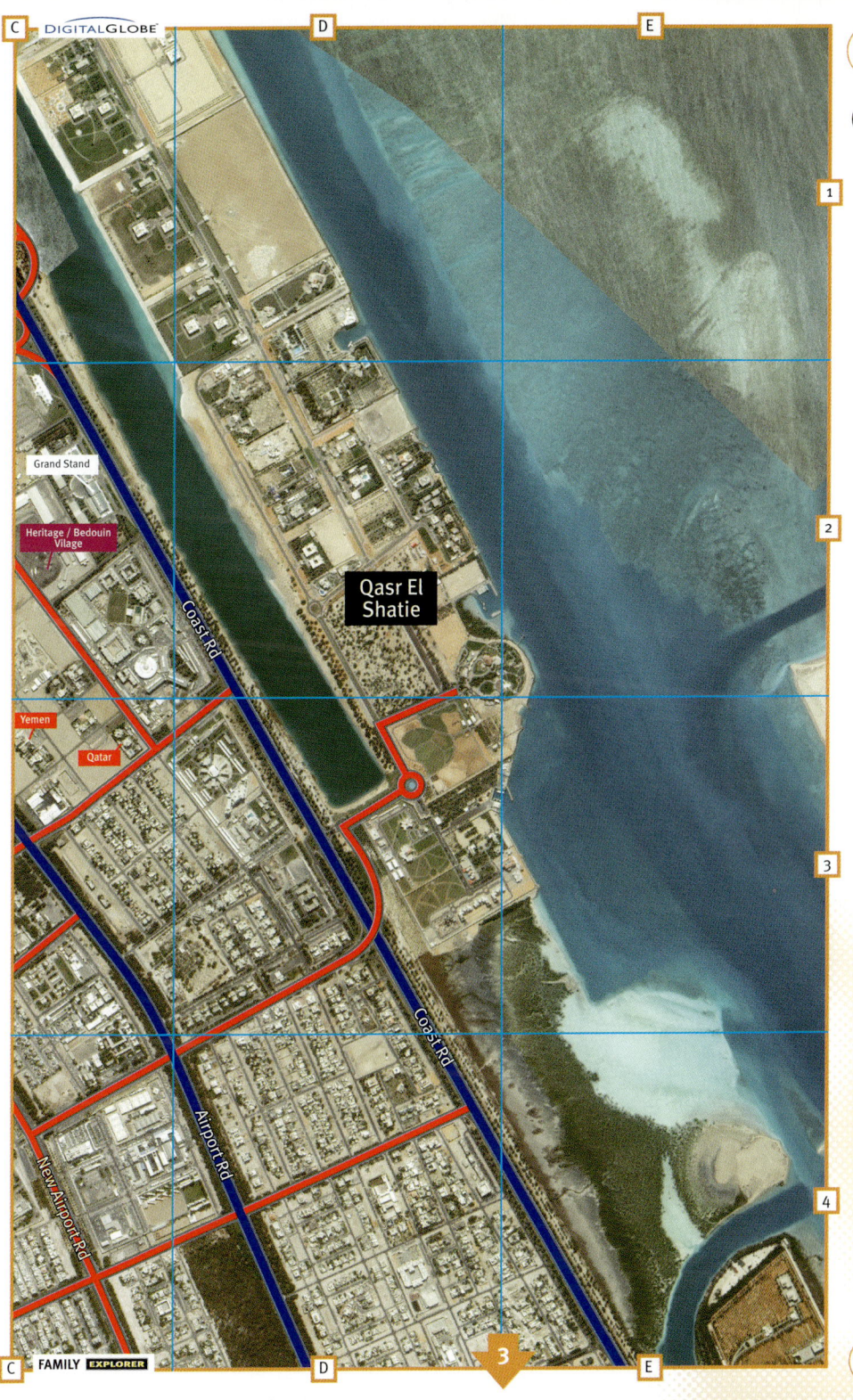

Grand Stand
Heritage / Bedouin Village
Yemen
Qatar
Coast Rd
Coast Rd
Airport Rd
New Airport Rd

Abu Dhabi — Maps

209

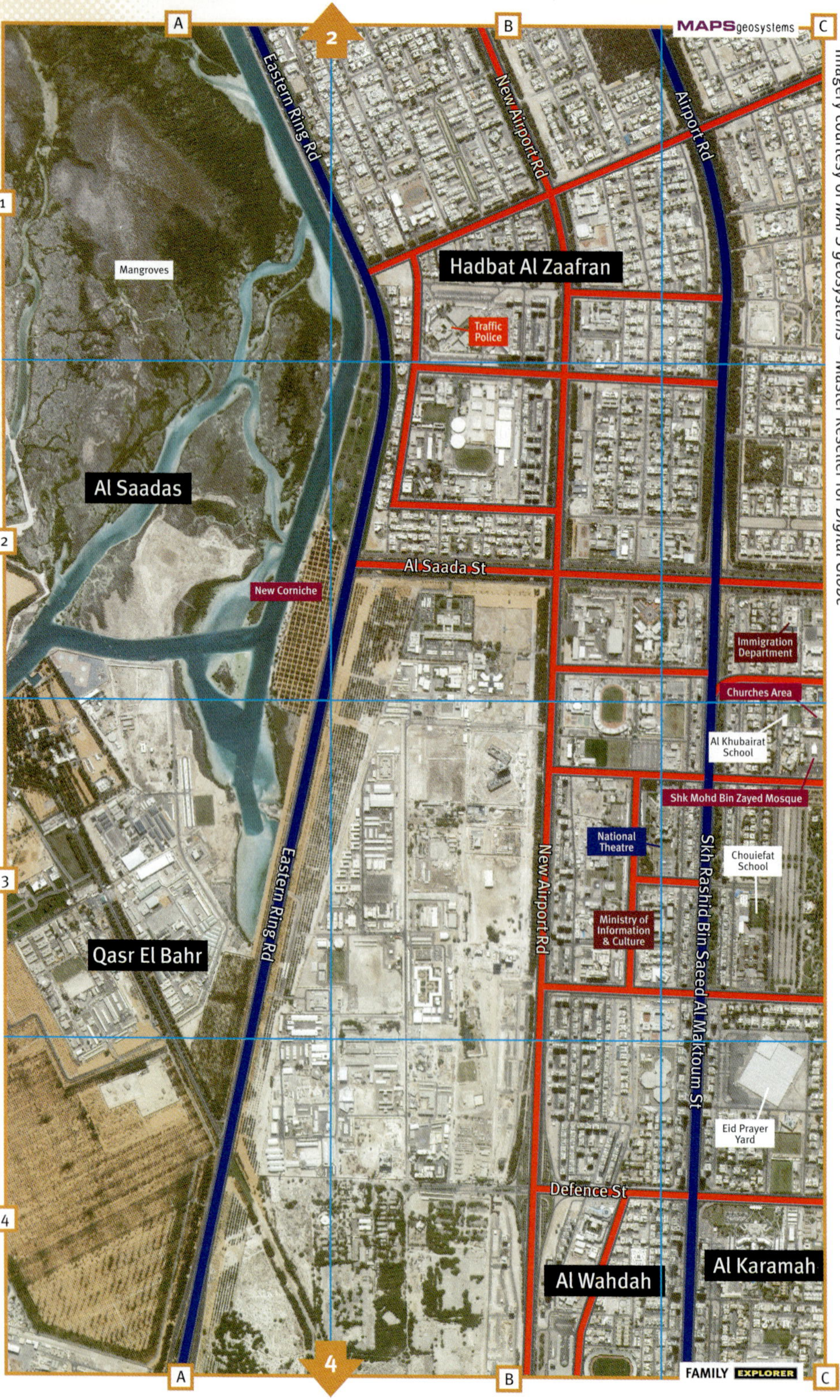

Imagery courtesy of *MAPS geosystems* – Master Reseller for *Digital Globe*

Abu Dhabi

Map 3

- Qasr El Shatie
- Coast Rd
- Al Mushrif
- Saeed Bin Tahnoon St
- Oman
- Korea
- Abu Dhabi Health & Fitness Club
- Race Track
- Abu Dhabi Golf & Equestrian Club
- Al Karamah St
- Khalifa Bin Shakhbout St
- Sultan Bin Zayed St
- Al Mushrif Childrens Garden
- Mohammed Bin Khalifa St
- Al Bateen
- Al Nahyan St
- Ministry of State
- Gulf Diagnostic Centre
- Delma St
- Al Rowdah

FAMILY EXPLORER

Maps

211

Abu Dhabi

4

Imagery courtesy of MAPS geosystems – Master Reseller for Digital Globe

- Qasr El Bahr
- Ministry of Labour
- Al Falah
- Al Meena
- Beach Rotana Hotel & Towers
- City Terminal Abu Dhabi Airport
- Abu Dhabi Mall
- Century Cinema
- Ninth St
- Abu Dhabi Marina & Yacht Club
- Al Diar Dana Hotel
- Le Meridien Hotel
- Post Office
- Mosque Gardens
- Abu Dhabi Tourist Club
- Al Salam Hospital
- The Club
- Power & Desalination Plant
- Al Meena
- Emirates Plaza Hotel
- Water & Electricity Club
- Al Diar Capitol Hotel
- Slaughterhouse & Livestock Market
- Meena St
- Corniche Hospital
- Fire Station
- Port Rd
- Customs Department
- Port Zayed
- Fish Market
- Dhow Harbour
- Al Meena Vegetable Market
- Al Dhafra
- Meena Souk
- Iranian Souk / Afghan Bazaar
- Kids Play / Toys 'R' Us / Ace Hardware

212

FAMILY EXPLORER

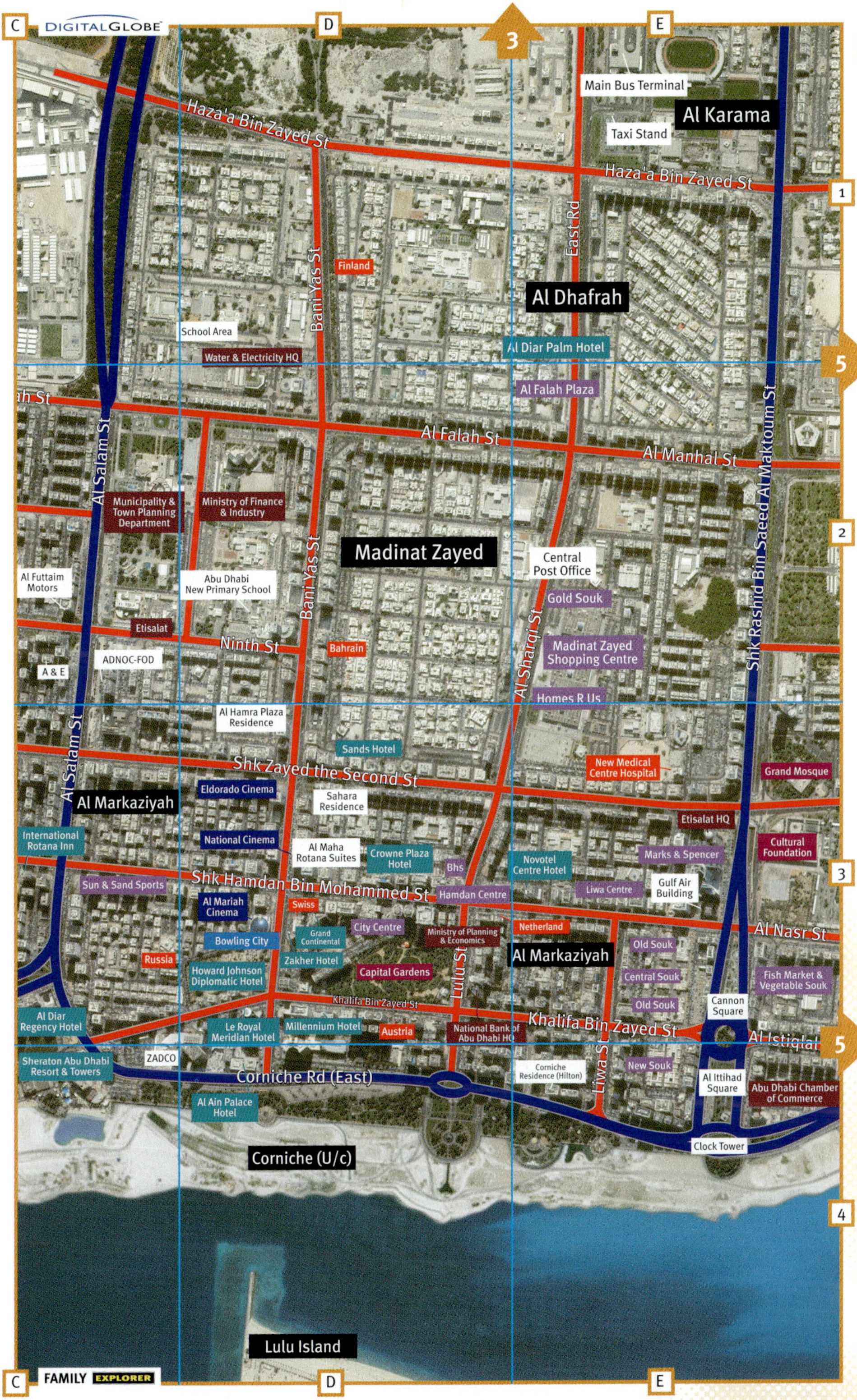

Abu Dhabi

Maps

Imagery courtesy of *MAPS geosystems* – Master Reseller for *Digital Globe*

Abu Dhabi

Maps

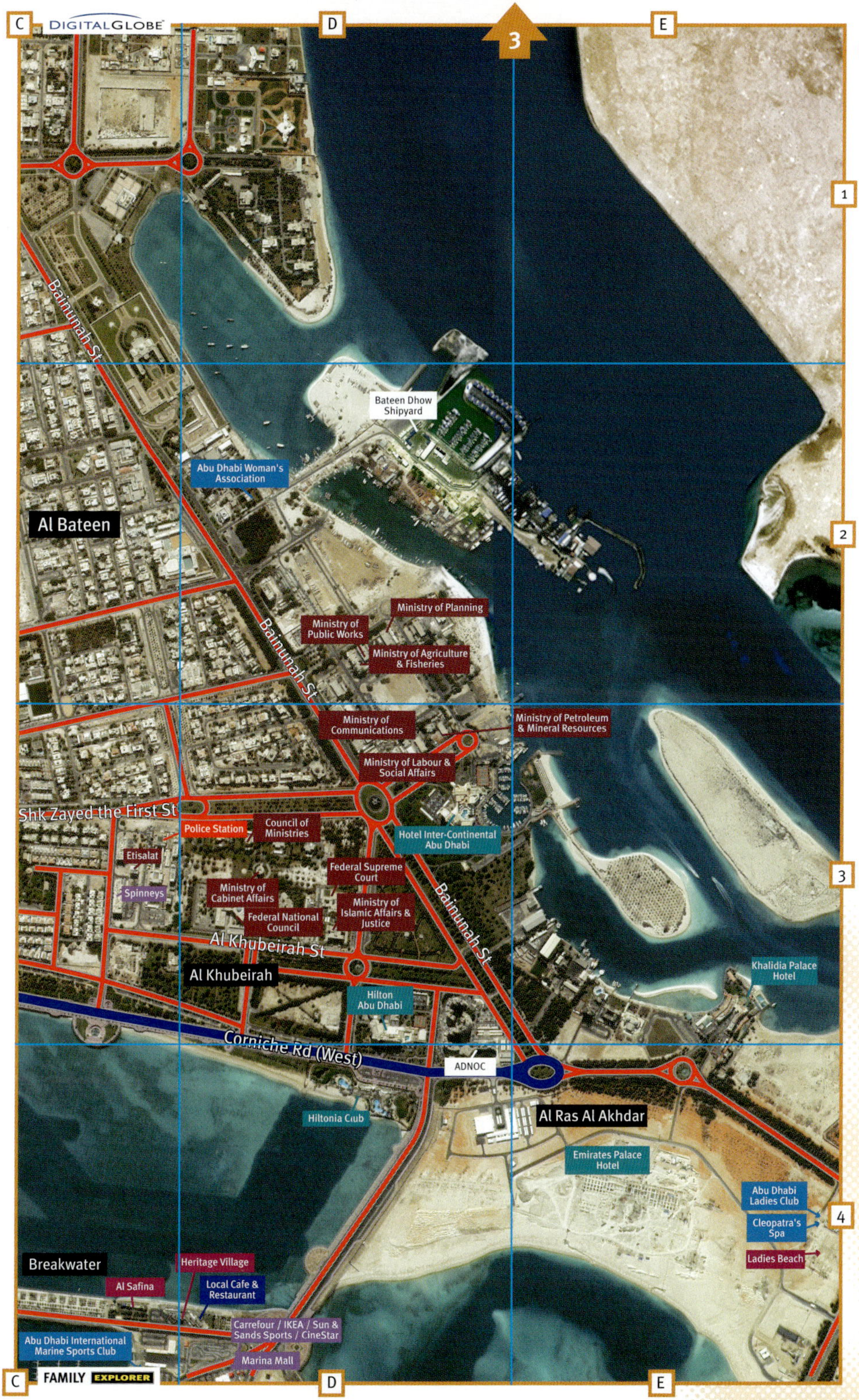

Abu Dhabi

Maps

Al Ain – Street Index

The following is a list of the main streets and hotel buildings in Al Ain, which are referenced on map pages 6 - 9. Many roads are longer than one grid reference, in which case the main grid references have been given.

Street	Map Ref
Abu Bakr Al Siddiq St	7-D3/D4
Abu Obaida Bin Al Jarrah St	7-D2
Al Ain R/A	7-C4; 9-C1
Al Ain St	9-C1
Al Asar St	see Al Athar St
Al Athar St	7-D1/E1
Al Baladiyya St	7-C2
Al Basra R/A	7-B3
Al Buraimi R/A	7-D3
Al Falah St	7-D2
Al Falaheya St	see Othman Bin Affan St
Al Forousiya St	see Khalifa Bin Zayed St
Al Gaba St	see Abu Bakr Al Siddiq St
Al Ghozlan Garden R/A	6-E4
Al Ghozlan R/A	8-D2
Al Hili R/A	7-D1
Al Hili St	see Mohammed Bin Khalifa St
Al Istraha R/A	7-E4
Al Ja'amah R/A	7-C3
Al Jamia St	7-B4/C4
Al Jimi R/A	7-C3
Al Khabisi R/A	7-B2
Al Khaleej Al Arabi St	6-B2/E2
Al Kharis R/A	7-D3
Al Khatem R/A	7-E4
Al Khatem St	see Khata Al Shinkle St
Al Mahad R/A	7-C4
Al Markahniya St	see Shakhboot Bin Sultan St
Al Mashatel R/A	7-E3
Al Masoudi R/A	7-C2
Al Mira St	see Al Salam St
Al Muraba R/A	7-D4
Al Muttarath R/A	7-C4
Al Nadi R/A	7-C4
Al Nakheel St	7-C2
Al Salam St	7-E4
Al Salama R/A	7-D4
Al Thakteet St	9-C1
Ali Bin Abi Taleb St	7-D3
Arah Al Jaw St	7-E1
Bani Yas St	7-C2/D1
Clock Tower R/A	7-D4
Eighth St	see Al Salam St (Eastern Corniche Rd)
Fourth St	see East Rd (New Airport Rd)
Hamdan Bin Mohammed St	7-B3
Hamdan Bin Zayed Al Awwal St	7-C3

Street	Map Ref
Hazah St	see Khalid Bin Sultan St
Hazzaa Bin Sultan St	6-E3; 9-A3
Hazzaa R/A	9-A1
Hospital R/A	7-C3
Khalid Bin Al Waleed St	7-B2/C2
Khalid Bin Sultan St	7-D4
Khalid St	see Sultan Bin Zayed Al Awwal St
Khalifa Bin Zayed Al Awwal St	7-C4
Khalifa Bin Zayed St	7-A4/B4; 8-D1/E1
Khata Al Shikle St	7-E4
Lotus R/A	7-D1
Lulu St (North)	see East Rd (New Airport Rd)
Mohammed Bin Khalifa St	7-C3/D2
Mubarak St	see Hamdan Bin Zayed Al Awwal St
Municipality R/A	7-C3
Municipality St	see Al Baladiyya St
Nahyan Al Awwal St	9-B2
Najda St	see Bani Yas St (Najda Rd) (East)
Old Airport Rd	see Maidan Al Ittihad (North)
Omar Bin Al Khattab St	7-E4
Othman Bin Affan St	7-E4
Oudh Alttoba St	see Ali Bin Abi Taleb St
Saeed Bin Tahnoon Al Awwal St	7-A3
Salahuddeen Al Ayyubi St	7-D4
Salana St	see Salahuddeen Al Ayyubi St
Second St	see Airport Rd (South)
Second St	see Maidan Al Ittihad (North)
Selmi St	see Hamdan Bin Mohammed St
Shakboot Bin Sultan St	7-A4/B3
Shk Zayed Bin Khalifa St	see Shakhboot Bin Sultan St
Silmi R/A	7-C3
Sixth St	see Bani Yas St (Najda Rd) (East)
Sultan Bin Zayed Al Awwal St	7-C4/D4
Tahnoon St	see Nahyan Al Awwal St
Tawam R/A	8-D1
Tawam St	8-E2
Thirtieth St	see Al Khaleej Al Arabi St (West)
Thirty Fourth St	see Bainona St (West)
Tourist Club Area	see Al Salam St (Corniche Rd)
Twenty Eighth St	see Khalifa Bin Shakbout St (West)
Twenty Fourth St	see Al Karamah St (West)
Twenty Second St	see Khalid Bin Al Waleed St (West)
Zakher R/A	9-A2
Zayed Al Awwal St	14-C3; 9-B1
Zayed Bin Sultan St	7-B4; 17-E1
Zoo R/A	9-B1

Al Ain Overview Map

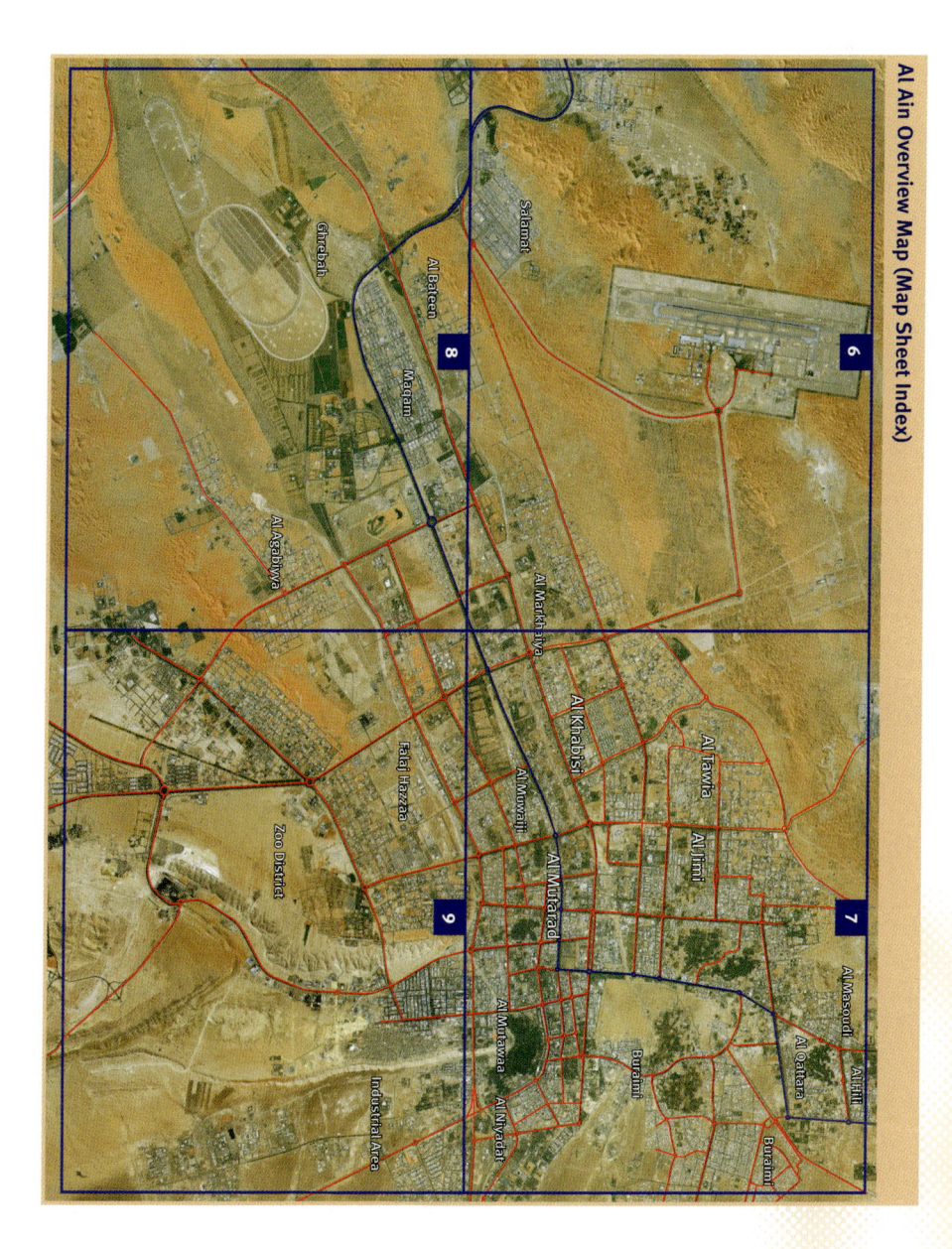

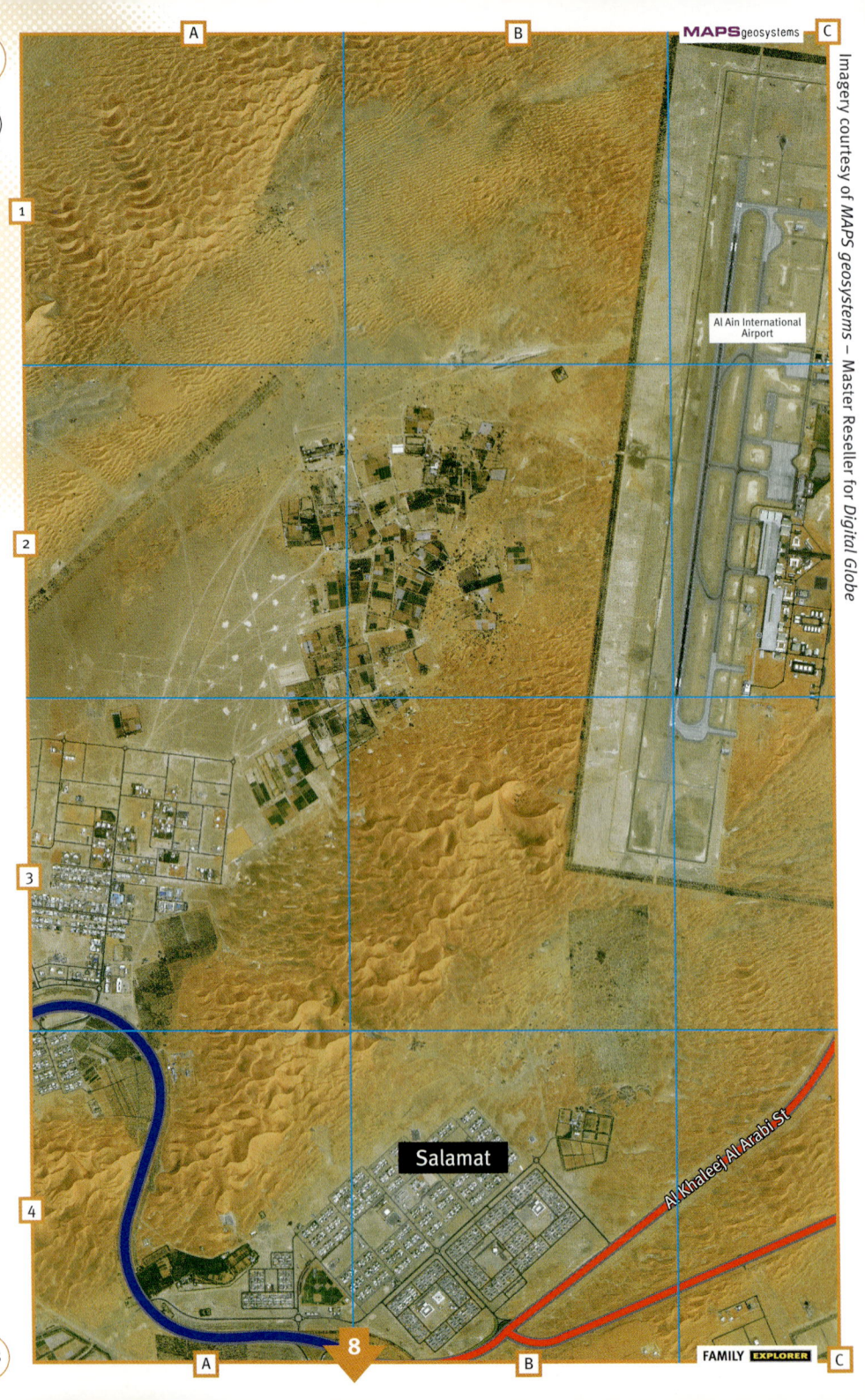

Al Ain

Al Ain International Airport

Salamat

Al Khaleej Al Arabi St

Imagery courtesy of MAPS geosystems – Master Reseller for Digital Globe

Hazza Bin Sultan St

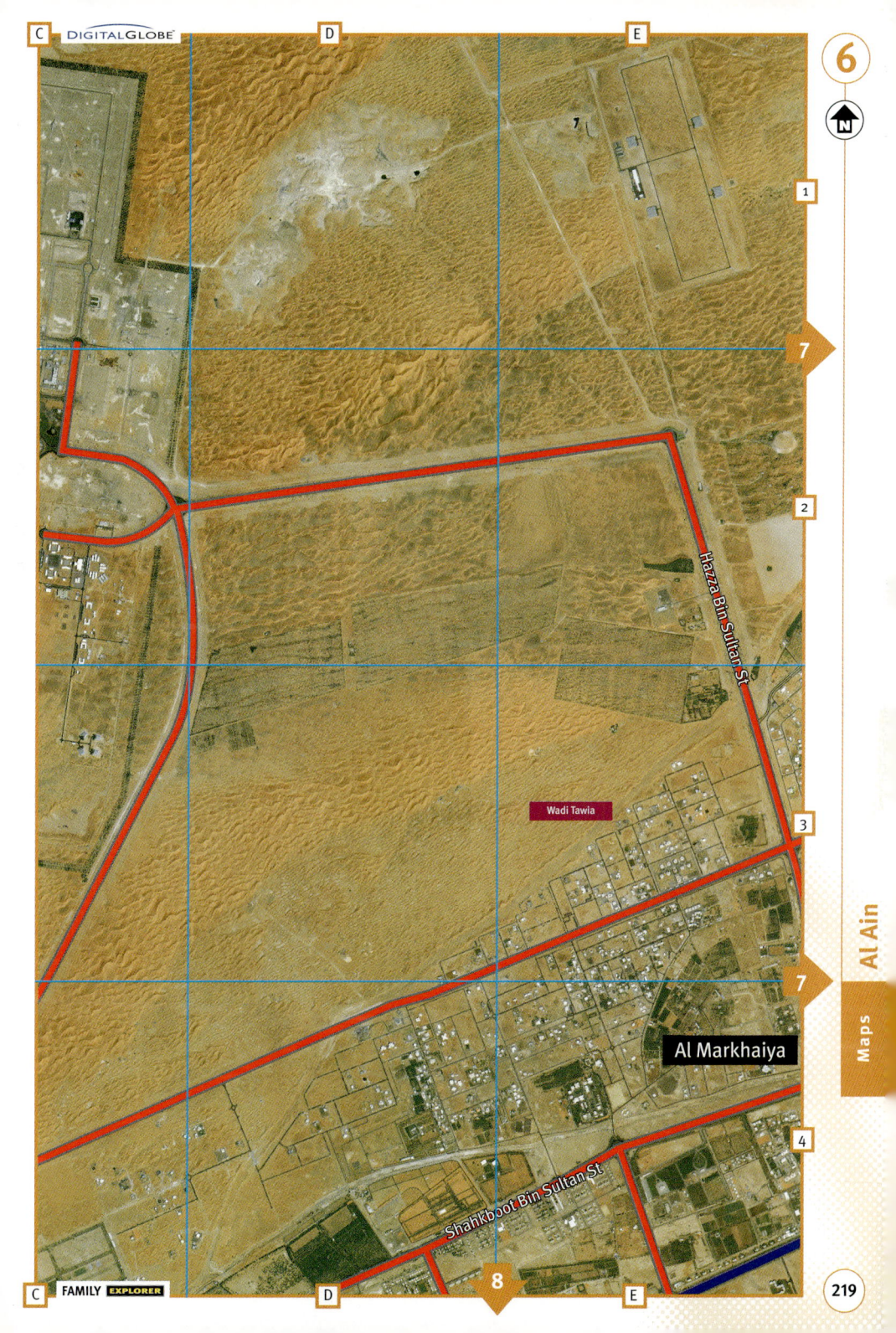

Wadi Tawia

Al Markhaiya

Shahkboot Bin Sultan St

Al Ain

Maps

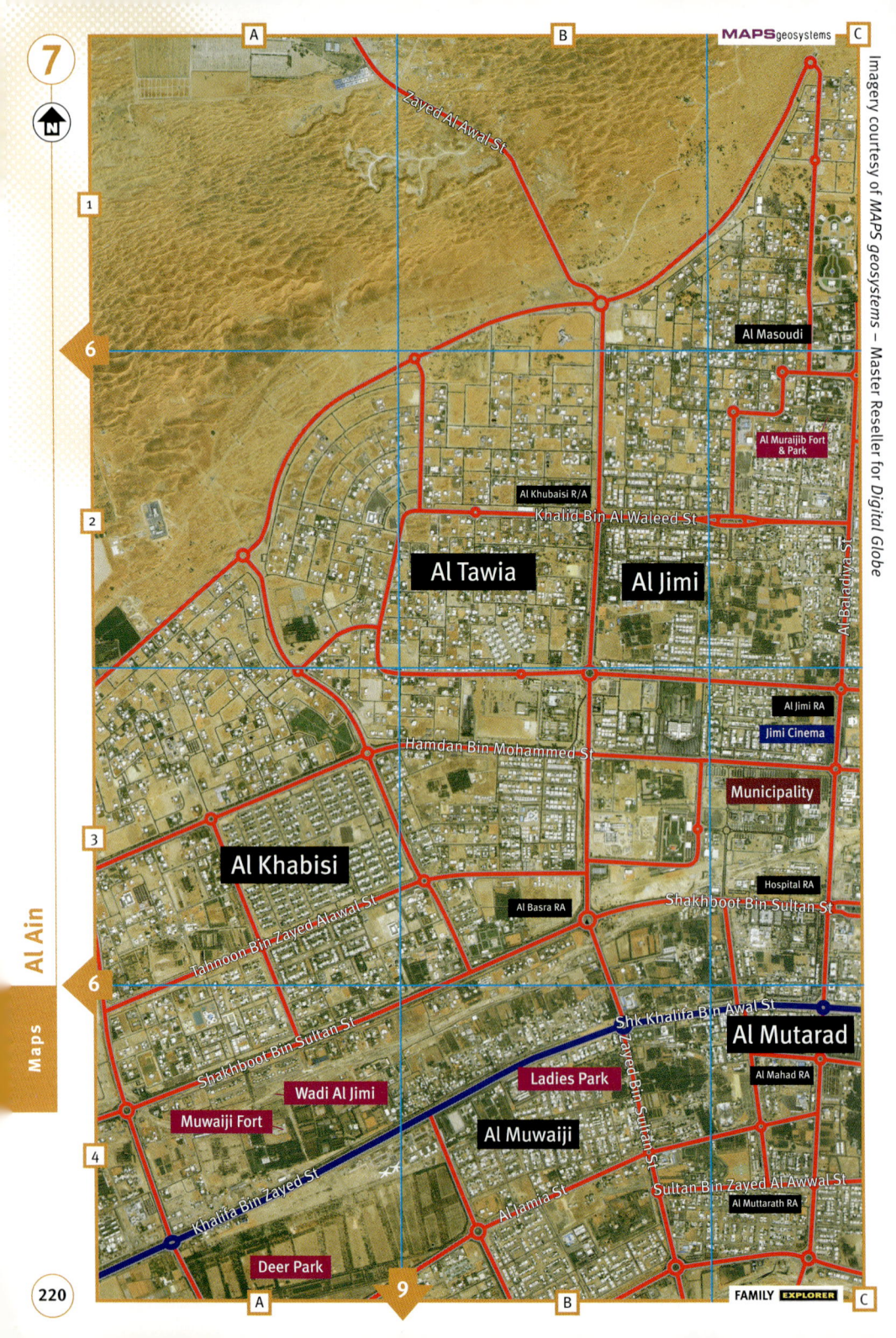

Al Ain

Imagery courtesy of MAPSgeosystems – Master Reseller for Digital Globe

- Zayed Al Awal St
- Al Masoudi
- Al Muraijib Fort & Park
- Al Khubaisi R/A
- Khalid Bin Al Waleed St
- Al Tawia
- Al Jimi
- Al Baladiya St
- Al Jimi RA
- Jimi Cinema
- Hamdan Bin Mohammed St
- Municipality
- Al Khabisi
- Al Basra RA
- Hospital RA
- Shakhboot Bin Sultan St
- Tahnoon Bin Zayed Alawal St
- Shk Khalifa Bin Awal St
- Al Mutarad
- Shakhboot Bin Sultan St
- Wadi Al Jimi
- Ladies Park
- Al Mahad RA
- Muwaiji Fort
- Al Muwaiji
- Zayed Bin Sultan St
- Khalifa Bin Zayed St
- Al Jamia St
- Sultan Bin Zayed Al Awwal St
- Al Muttarath RA
- Deer Park

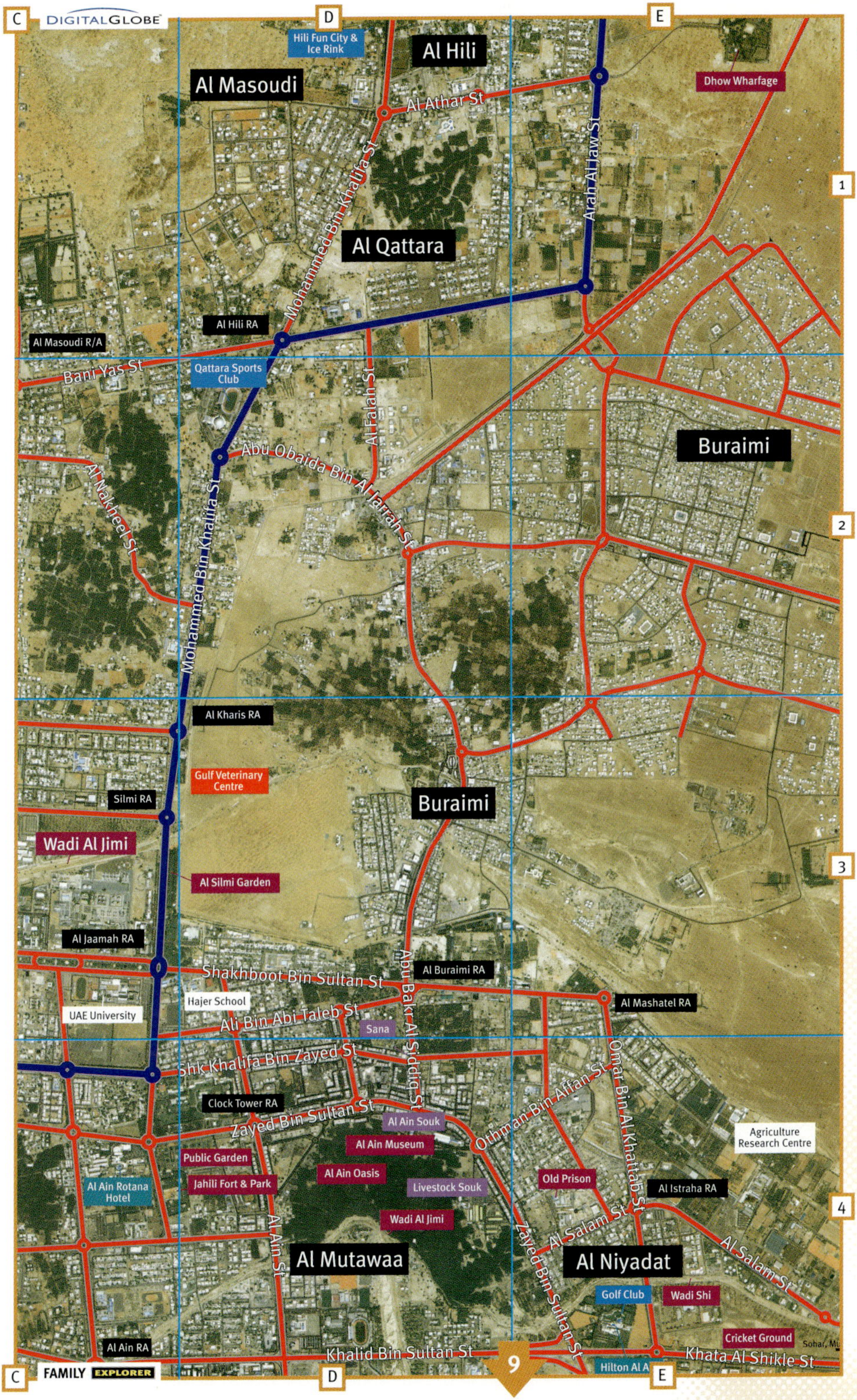
DIGITALGLOBE
C
D
E
1
2
3
4
Hili Fun City & Ice Rink
Al Hili
Al Masoudi
Dhow Wharfage
Al Athar St
Arah Al Jaw St
Al Qattara
Mohammed Bin Khalifa St
Al Hili RA
Al Masoudi R/A
Bani Yas St
Qattara Sports Club
Al Falah St
Abu Obaida Bin Al Jarrah St
Buraimi
Al Nakheel St
Al Kharis RA
Gulf Veterinary Centre
Silmi RA
Wadi Al Jimi
Al Silmi Garden
Al Jaamah RA
Al Buraimi RA
Shakhboot Bin Sultan St
Abu Bakr Al Siddiq St
Al Mashatel RA
Hajer School
UAE University
Ali Bin Abi Taleb St
Sana
Shk Khalifa Bin Zayed St
Omar Bin Al Khattab St
Othman Bin Affan St
Clock Tower RA
Zayed Bin Sultan St
Al Ain Souk
Agriculture Research Centre
Al Ain Museum
Public Garden
Al Ain Oasis
Livestock Souk
Old Prison
Al Istraha RA
Jahili Fort & Park
Al Ain Rotana Hotel
Wadi Al Jimi
Al Salam St
Al Ain St
Al Mutawaa
Zayed Bin Sultan St
Al Niyadat
Golf Club
Wadi Shi
Cricket Ground
Al Ain RA
Khalid Bin Sultan St
Khata Al Shikle St
9
FAMILY EXPLORER

Al Ain

Maps

Al Bateen

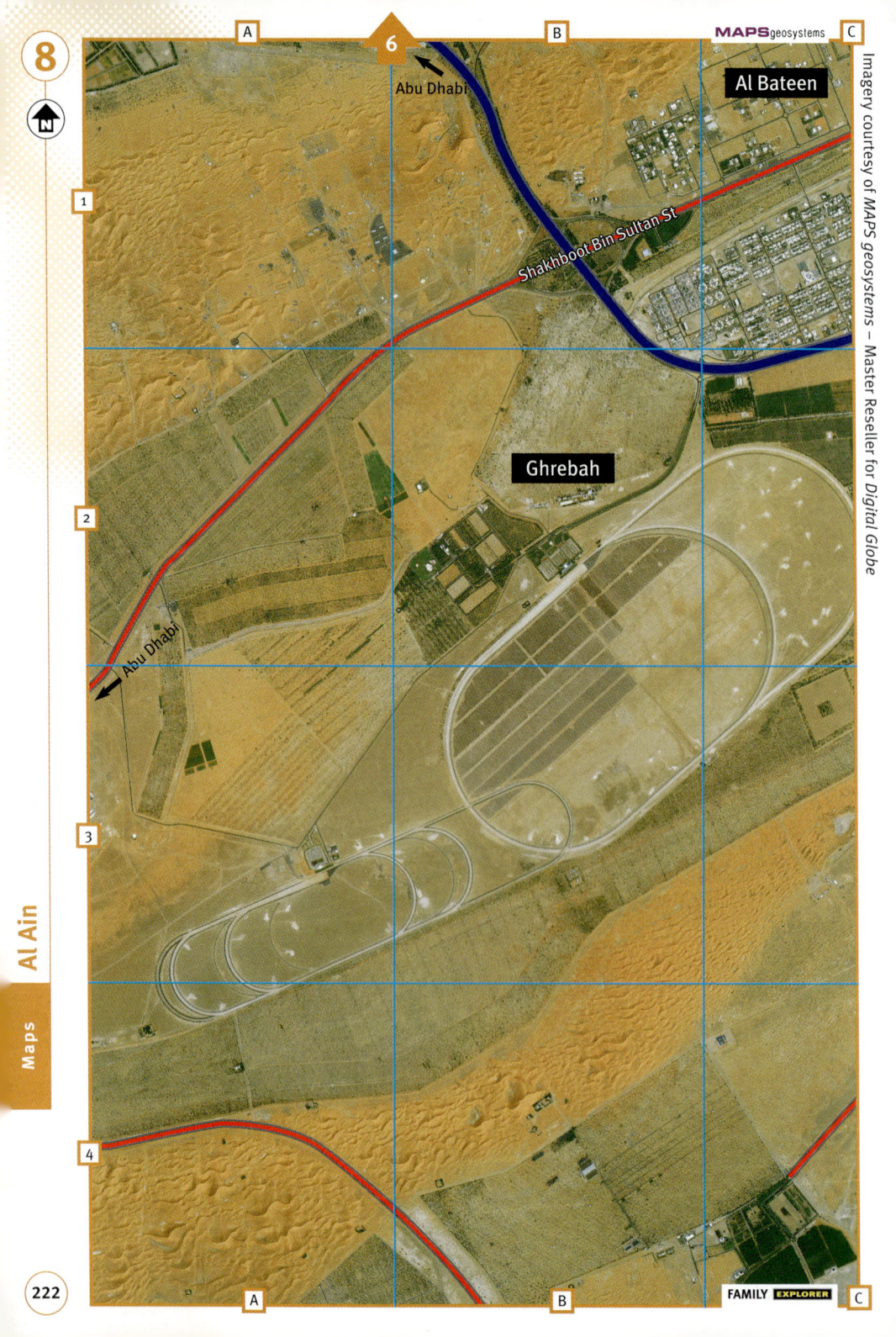

Abu Dhabi

Shakhboot Bin Sultan St

Ghrebah

Abu Dhabi

Al Ain

Imagery courtesy of MAPS geosystems – Master Reseller for Digital Globe

Maqam

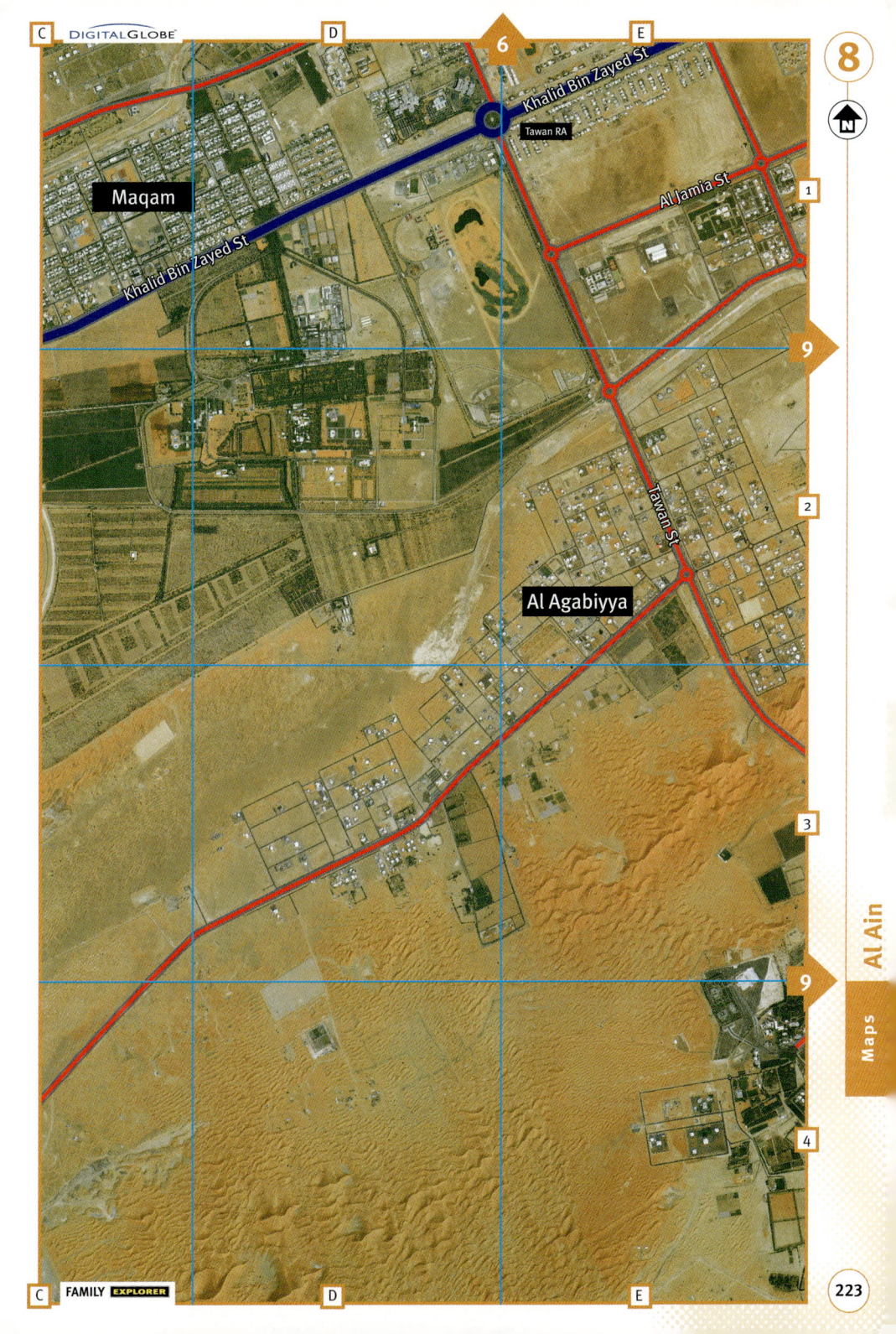

Khalid Bin Zayed St

Tawan RA

Al Jamia St

Tawan St

Al Agabiyya

Al Ain

Maps

223

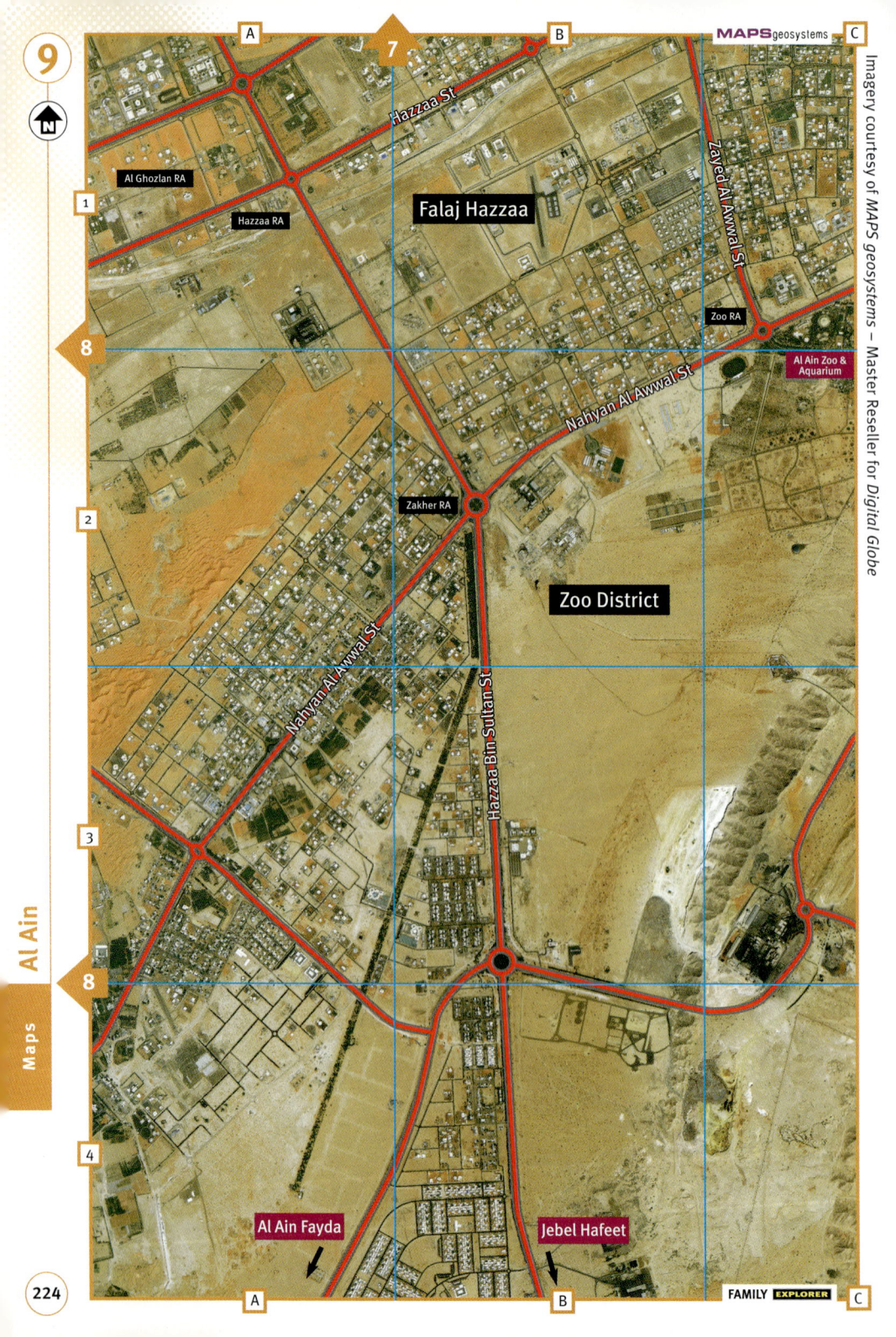

Al Ain

9

Falaj Hazzaa

- Al Ghozlan RA
- Hazzaa RA
- Hazzaa St
- Zayed Al Awwal St
- Zoo RA
- Al Ain Zoo & Aquarium
- Nahyan Al Awwal St
- Zakher RA

Zoo District

- Nahyan Al Awwal St
- Hazzaa Bin Sultan St

- Al Ain Fayda
- Jebel Hafeet

Imagery courtesy of *MAPS geosystems* – Master Reseller for *Digital Globe*

224 FAMILY EXPLORER

Industrial Area

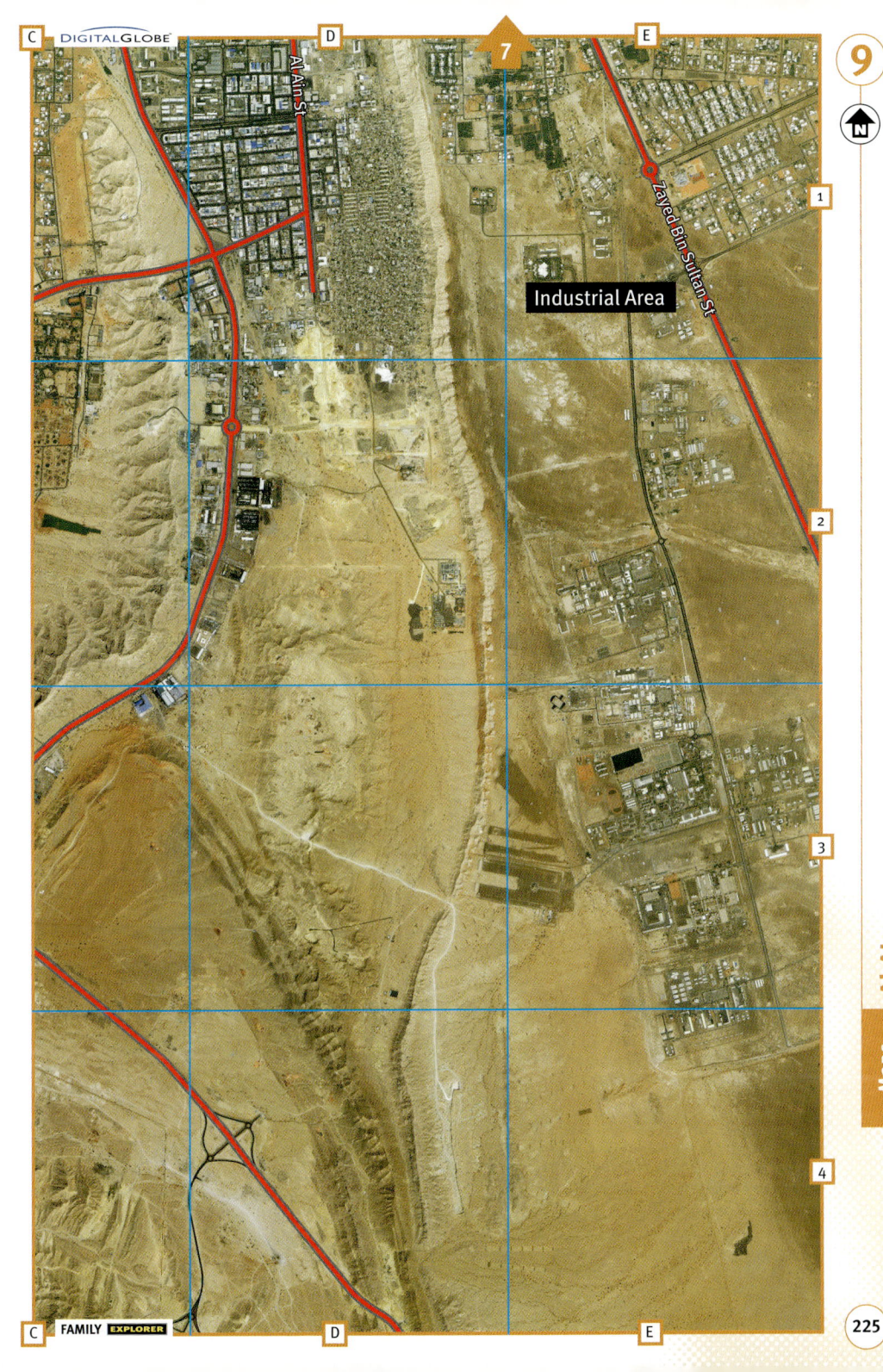

Dubai – Community & Street Index

The following is a list of the main streets in Dubai, which are referenced on the map pages 10-15. Many roads are longer than one grid reference, in which case the main grid reference has been given.

Community	Map Ref			Street	Map Ref		
Al Barsha	11-E3	Emirates Hill 1	11-C2	2nd Za'abeel Rd	15-B1	Al Rigga Rd	14-B3
Al Garhoud	15-D1	Emirates Hill 2	11-C3	Abu Hail Rd	14-E4	Al Satwa Rd	13-B2
Al Hamriya	14-E3	Hor Al Anz	14-D3	Airport Rd	15-D1	Al Sufouh Rd	11-D1
Al Jafilia	13-D2	Jaddaf	15-C2	Al Adhid Rd	13-D2	Al Wasl Rd	12-E1
Al Karama	13-E3	Jebel Ali FZ	11-B2	Al Diyafah Rd	13-C2	Beniyas Rd	14-B2
Al Mamzar		Jumeira	13-A1	Al Fahidi Rd	14-A1	Casablanca Rd	15-D1
Al Mankhool	13-E2	Jumeira 2	12-E1	Al Garhoud Rd	15-D1	Damascus Rd	15-E2
Al Quoz	13-D2	Jumeira 3	12-C1	Al Ittihad Rd	14-D4	Doha Rd	15-A1
Al Quoz Ind. 1	12-B3	Marsa Dubai	11-B1	Al Jumeira Rd	12-B2	Dubai - Al Ain Rd	17-A4
Al Quoz Ind. 3	12-B2	Mirdif	15-E4	Al Khaleej Rd	14-A1	Emirates Rd	11-B4
Al Qusais	15-E1	Oud Mehta	13-E4	Al Khail Rd	12-B4	Khalid Bin AlWaleed	
Al Safa 1	12-D2	Port Rashid	13-D1	Al Khawaneej Rd	15-E3	Rd	14-A2
Al Safa 2	12-C2	Port Saeed	14-B3	Al Maktoum Rd	14-B3	Muscat Rd	12-D2
Al Satwa	13-B2	Rashidiya	15-D3	Al Mankhool Rd	13-E2	Oud Mehta Rd	15-B1
Al Satwa East	13-B3	Shindagha	14-A1	Al Mateena Rd	14-C3	Rabat Rd	15-D4
Al Sufouh	11-E1/E2	Trade Centre 1	13-A3	Al Mina Rd	13-E1	Ras Al Khor Rd	15-b3
Al Tawar	15-E3	Trade Centre 2	13-B3	Al Muraqqabat Rd	14-C3	Riyadh Rd	15-C1
Al Wasl	12-E2	Umm Hurair 2	14-A4	Al Musallah Rd	14-A2	Salah Al Din Rd	14-D4
Bastakiya	14-A2	Umm Suqeim 1	12-C1	Al Naif Rd	14-B2	Sheikh Zayed Rd	13-B3
Bur Dubai	14-A2	Umm Suqeim 2	12-B1	Al Quds Rd	15-E1	Trade Centre Rd	13-D3
Deira	14-B1	Umm Suqeim 3	12-A1	Al Quta'eyat Rd	15-C1	Umm Hureir Rd	13-E4
Dubai Int. Airport	15-E1	Za'abeel	13-C4	Al Rasheed Rd	14-D3	Za'abeel Rd	13-E3

Dubai Address System

Dubai is in the process of completing a Comprehensive Addressing System that consists of two complementary number systems – the Route Numbering System and the Community, Street & Building Numbering System. The former helps an individual to develop and follow a simple series of directions for travelling from one area to another in Dubai; the latter helps a visitor to locate a particular building or house in the city.

Routes Numbering System

Various routes connecting Dubai to other emirates of the UAE, or to main cities within an emirate, are classified as 'Emirate-Routes' or 'E-Routes'. They comprise of two digit numbers on a falcon emblem as shown on the UAE Map. Routes connecting main communities within Dubai are designated as 'Dubai-Routes' or 'D-Routes'. They comprise of two digit numbers on a fort emblem. D-Routes parallel to the coast are even numbered, starting from D94 and decreasing as you move away from the coast. D-Routes perpendicular to the coast are odd numbered, starting from D53 and decreasing as you move away from the Abu Dhabi border.

Community, Street Numbering System

This system helps an individual to locate a particular building or house in Dubai. The emirate is divided into nine sectors.

Sectors 1, 2, 3, 4 and 6 represent urban areas.
Sector 5 represents Jebel Ali.
Sectors 7, 8 and 9 represent rural areas
Sectors are sub-divided into communities, which are bound by main roads. A three digit number identifies each community. The first is the number of the sector, while the following two digits denote the location of the community in relation to neighbouring communities in sequential order.

Buildings on the left hand side of the street have odd numbers, while those on the right hand side take even numbers. Again, building numbers increase as you move away from the city centre. The complete address of a building in Dubai is given as Community Number, Street Number and Building Number.

Dubai Overview Map (Map Sheet Index)

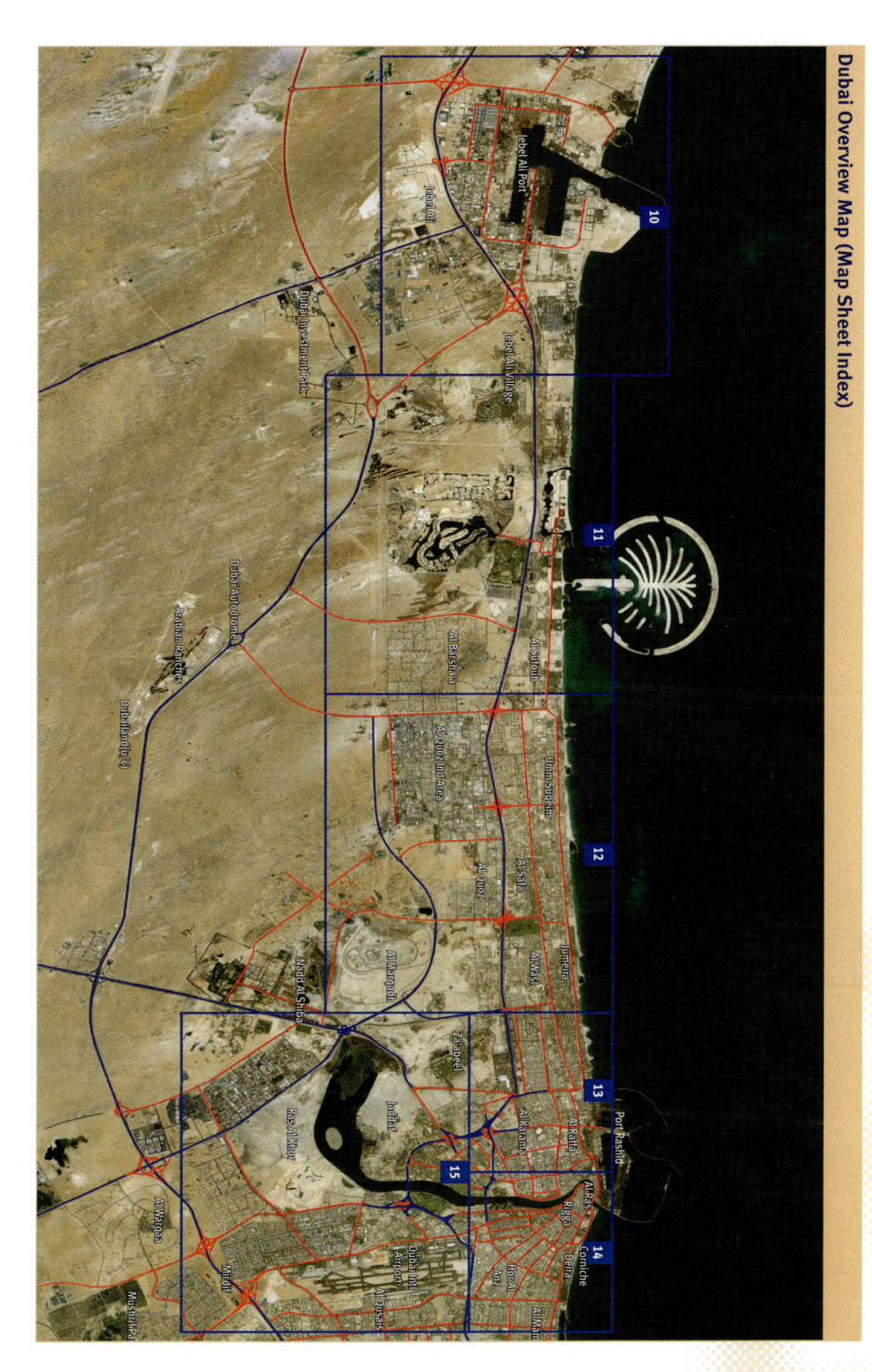

10

Palm, Jebel Ali (u/c)
Jebel Ali Beach
Jebel Ali Hotel & Golf Resort
Emirates Kart Club
Jebel Ali Shooting Club
Jebel Ali Free Zone
Interchange No-9
Interchange No-8
Sheikh Zayed Road

Imagery courtesy of *MAPS geosystems* – Master Reseller for *Digital Globe*

Dubai | Maps

228

Arabian Gulf

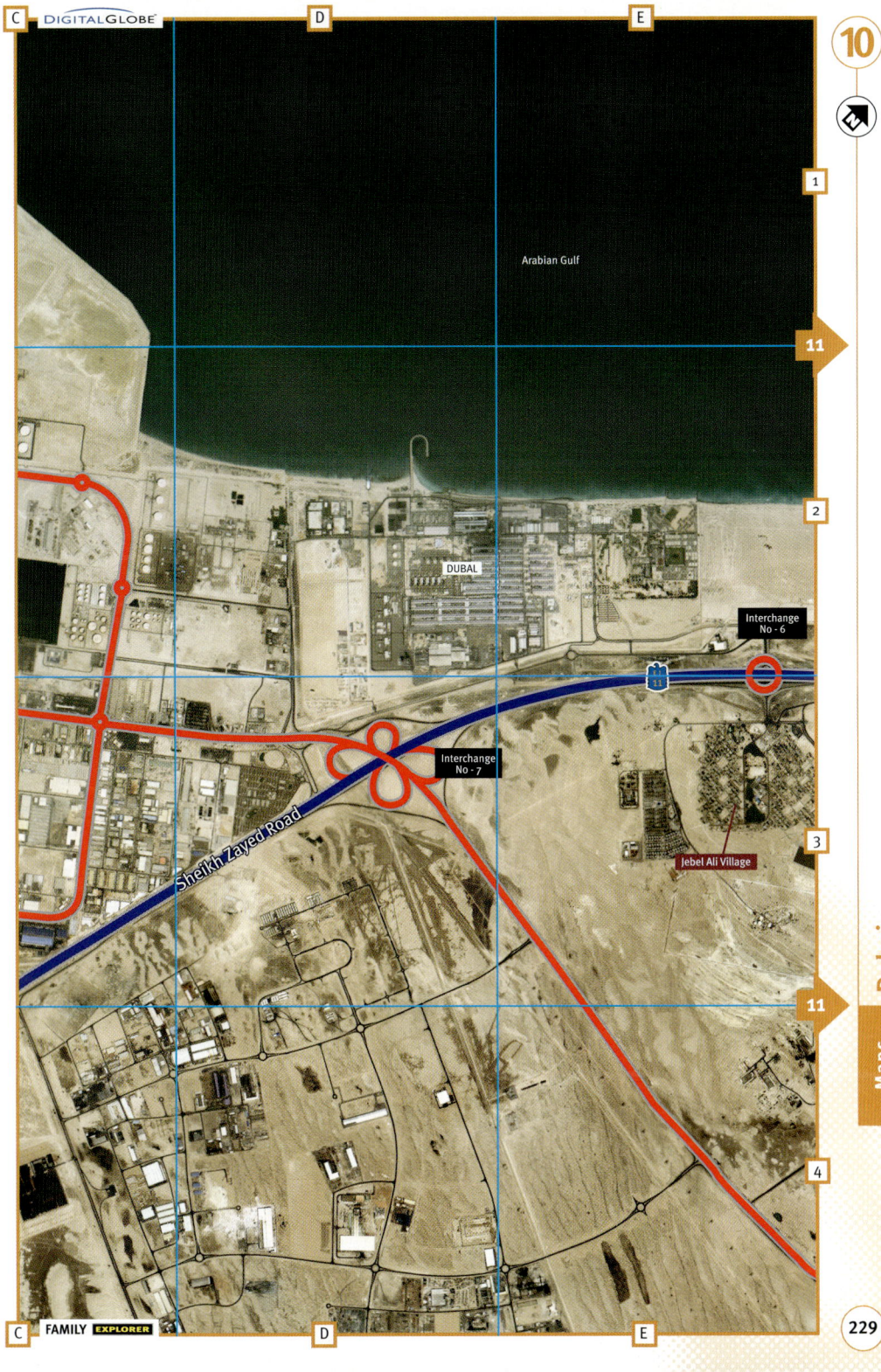

DUBAL

Interchange No - 6

Interchange No - 7

Jebel Ali Village

Sheikh Zayed Road

Dubai

Maps

229

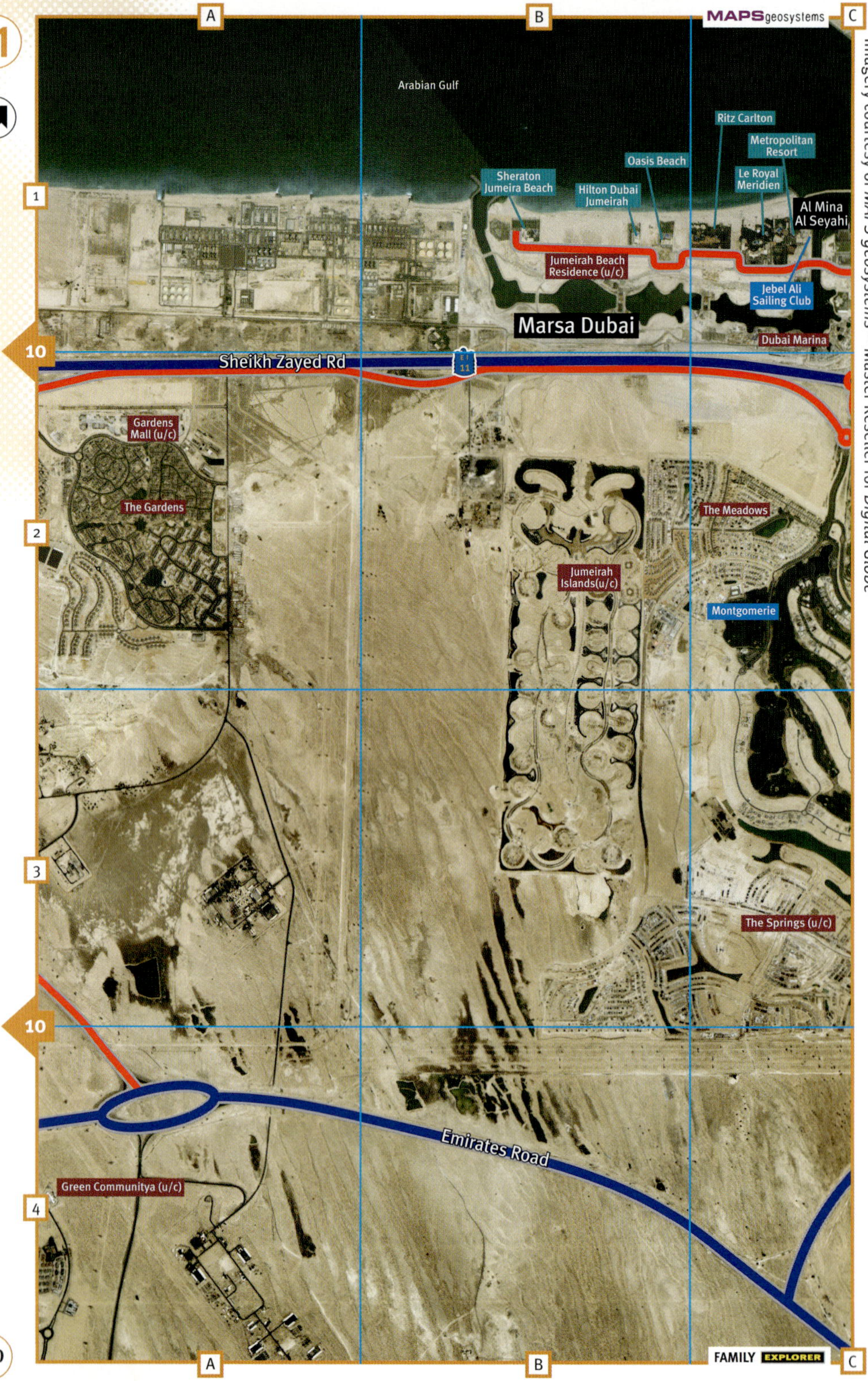

Imagery courtesy of *MAPS geosystems* – Master Reseller for *Digital Globe*

Dubai

Maps

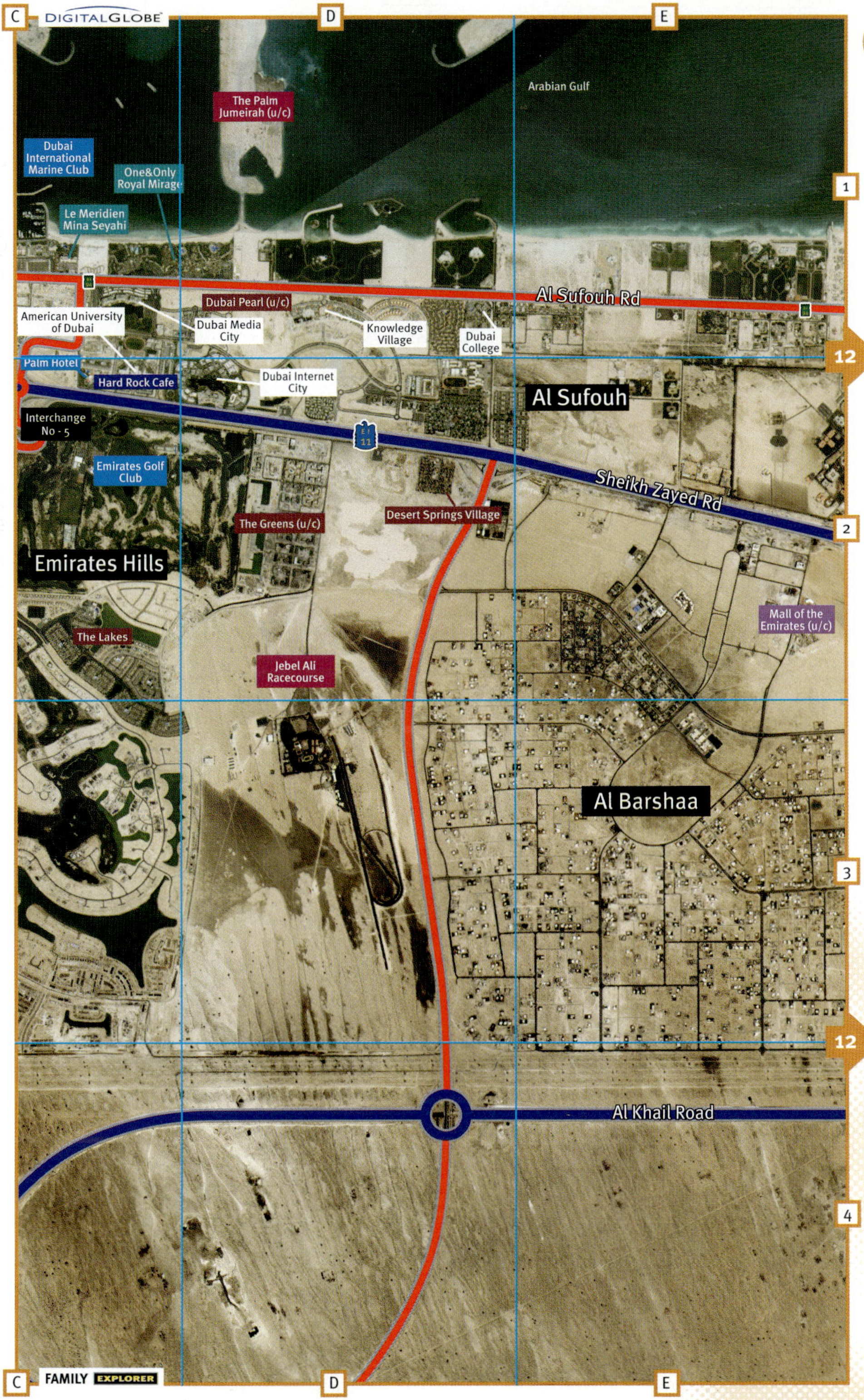
C
D
E
DIGITALGLOBE
Arabian Gulf
The Palm Jumeirah (u/c)
Dubai International Marine Club
One&Only Royal Mirage
Le Meridien Mina Seyahi
Al Sufouh Rd
Dubai Pearl (u/c)
American University of Dubai
Dubai Media City
Knowledge Village
Dubai College
Palm Hotel
Hard Rock Cafe
Dubai Internet City
Al Sufouh
Interchange No - 5
E 11
Emirates Golf Club
Sheikh Zayed Rd
Desert Springs Village
The Greens (u/c)
Emirates Hills
Mall of the Emirates (u/c)
The Lakes
Jebel Ali Racecourse
Al Barshaa
Al Khail Road
1
2
3
4
12
12
FAMILY EXPLORER

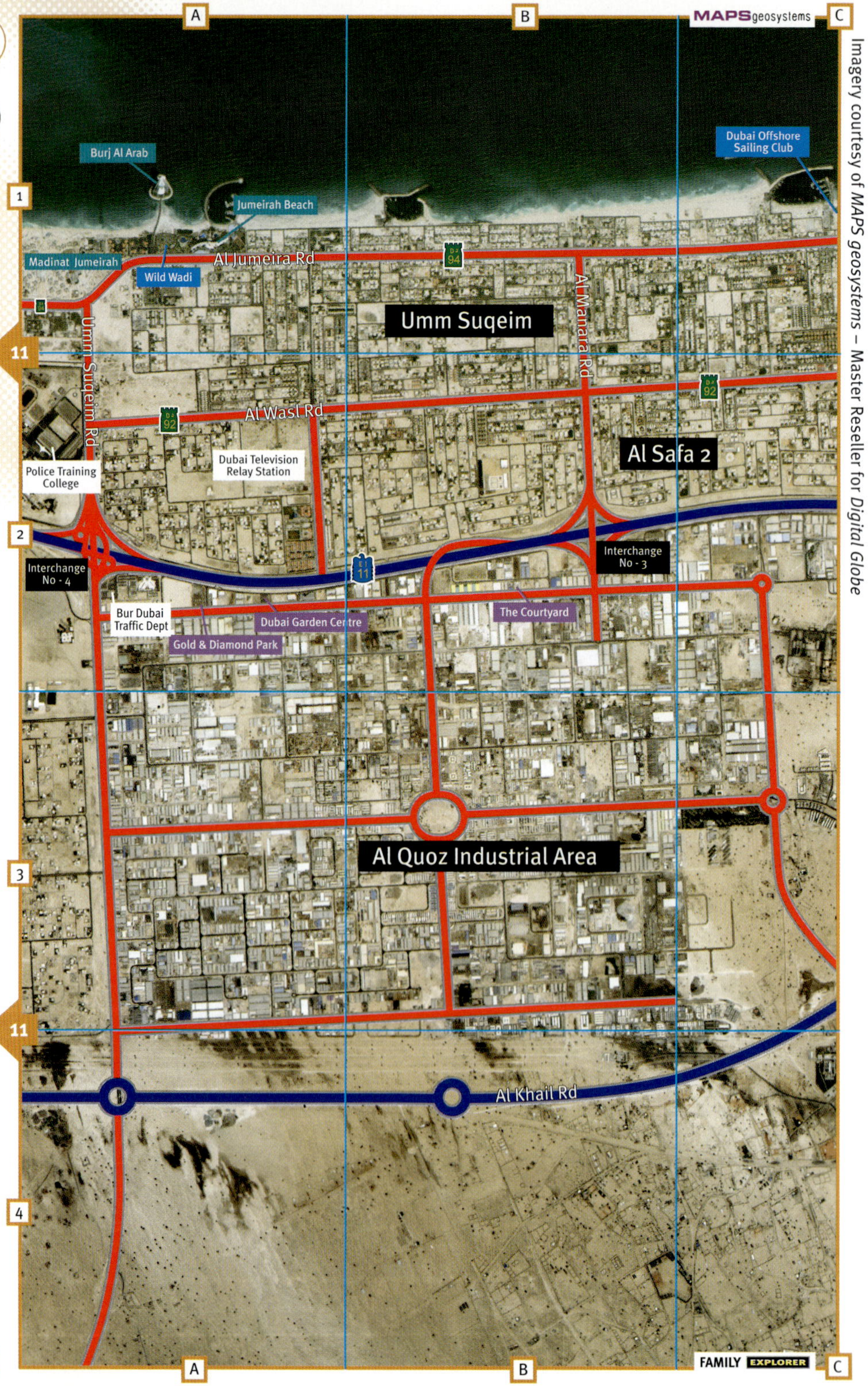
A
B
C
MAPSgeosystems
Imagery courtesy of MAPS geosystems – Master Reseller for Digital Globe
1
2
3
4
11
11
Burj Al Arab
Jumeirah Beach
Dubai Offshore Sailing Club
Madinat Jumeirah
Wild Wadi
Al Jumeira Rd
94
Umm Suqeim
Al Manara Rd
Umm Suqeim Rd
Al Wasl Rd
92
92
Al Safa 2
Police Training College
Dubai Television Relay Station
Interchange No - 4
Interchange No - 3
11
Bur Dubai Traffic Dept
Dubai Garden Centre
Gold & Diamond Park
The Courtyard
Al Quoz Industrial Area
Al Khail Rd
FAMILY EXPLORER

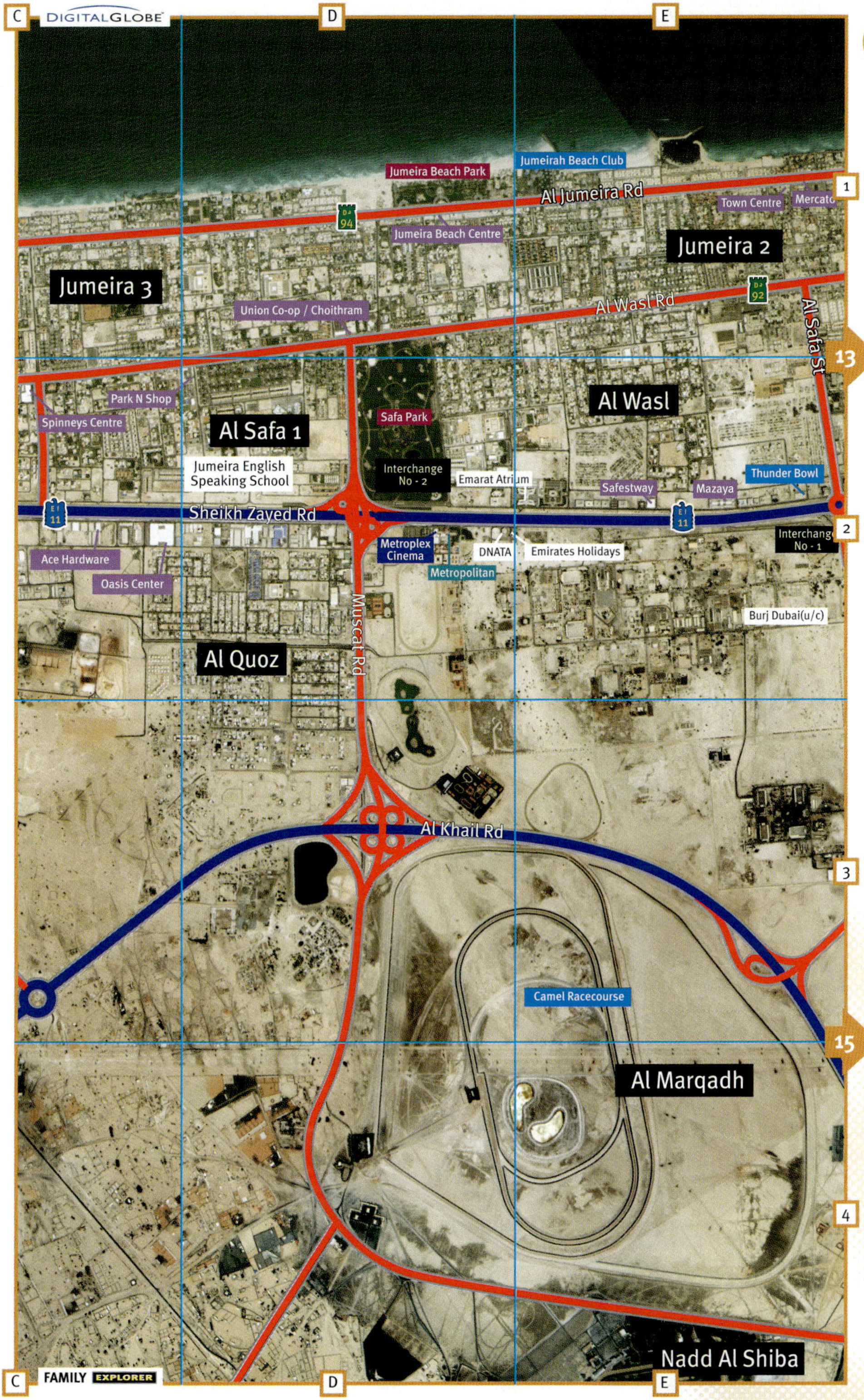
DIGITALGLOBE
C
D
E
1
2
3
4
13
15
Jumeira Beach Park
Jumeirah Beach Club
Al Jumeira Rd
Town Centre
Mercato
Jumeira Beach Centre
Jumeira 2
Jumeira 3
Union Co-op / Choithram
Al Wasl Rd
Al Safa St
Park N Shop
Spinneys Centre
Al Safa 1
Safa Park
Al Wasl
Jumeira English Speaking School
Interchange No - 2
Emarat Atrium
Safestway
Mazaya
Thunder Bowl
Sheikh Zayed Rd
Metroplex Cinema
DNATA
Emirates Holidays
Interchange No - 1
Metropolitan
Ace Hardware
Oasis Center
Burj Dubai(u/c)
Muscat Rd
Al Quoz
Al Khail Rd
Camel Racecourse
Al Marqadh
Nadd Al Shiba
FAMILY EXPLORER

Dubai

Maps

Dubai Map 13

Imagery courtesy of MAPS geosystems – Master Reseller for Digital Globe

Grid references: A, B, C (columns) / 1, 2, 3, 4 (rows)

Labels visible on map:

- Union House
- Dubai Marine
- Jumeira Beach Corniche
- Palm Strip
- Dubai International Art Centre
- Al Jumeira Rd
- Beach Centre
- Dubai Zoo
- Century Plaza
- Jumeirah Centre
- Magrudy's
- Jumeirah Plaza
- Jumeira Mosque
- Jumeira Rotana
- Dune Centre
- Jumeira
- Iranian Hospital
- American School
- Al Wasl Rd
- 'Plant Street'
- Al Satwa
- Al Satwa Rd
- Al Satwa
- Wafa
- Towers Rotana
- Kalantar
- Al Rostamani
- Doha
- Zabeel
- City Tower
- Trade Centre 1
- Al Durrah
- AP World Tower
- Fairmont
- Shk Ahmed
- Number One
- Oasis
- Al Salam
- Al Moosa
- Sahara
- Al Safa
- Crowne Plaza
- Shangri-La
- Sheikh Zayed Road
- Ibis
- Trade Centre 2
- Dubai International Conference Centre
- Dubai International Exhibition Centre
- Al Kawakeb
- 21st Century Tower
- Al Attar
- Oasis
- Al Ghadier
- Kendah House
- The Tower
- Capricorn
- Emirates Towers
- Dusit
- Dubai International Financial Centre (u/c)
- The Gate (u/c)
- Novotel
- Etisalat
- Al Murooj Complex (u/c)

Roads/Routes: 94, 92, 90, 11

234

FAMILY EXPLORER

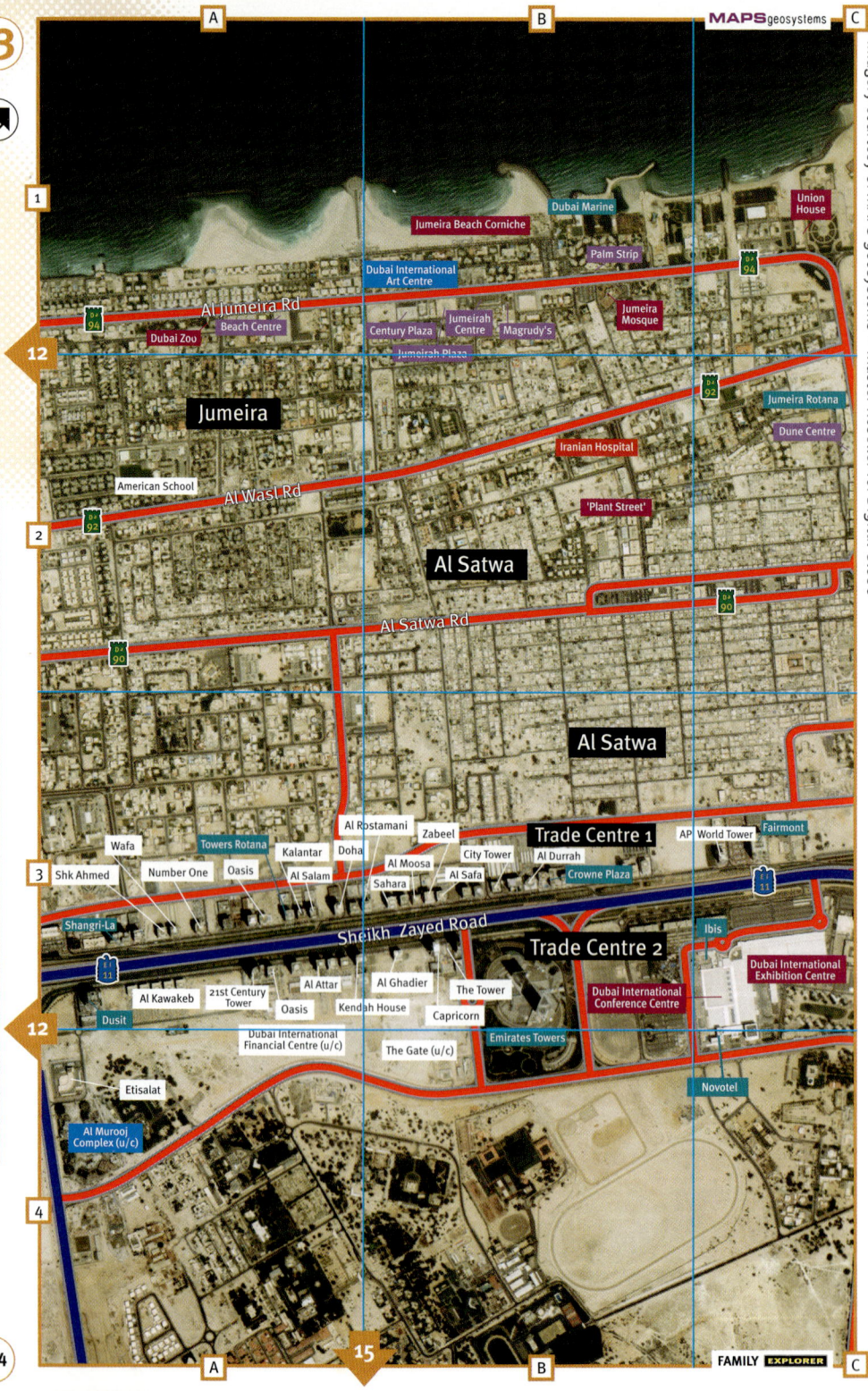

Port Rashid / Bur Dubai / Al Karama / Oud Metha

Port Rashid
- Dubai Ports & Customs Authority
- Dubai Port Police HQ
- Al Mina Road
- Khalid Bin Al Waleed Rd
- Capitol

Bur Dubai
- Al Mankhool Road
- Al Khaleej Centre
- Al Hana Centre
- Al Dhiyafah St

Al Jafilia

Al Mankhoul
- 'Golden Sands Area'
- Spinneys
- Trade Centre Rd
- Passport & Immigration Office
- Department Of Health & Medical Services
- Dubai Regional Police Headquarters
- Al Dhiyafah Rd
- Al Adhid Rd

Al Karama
- Dubai World Trade Centre
- World Trade Centre Hotel
- Za'abeel Park (u/c)
- Al Qutaeyat Rd
- Al Karama Shopping Centre
- Emirates Post
- Za'abeel Rd
- Zomorrodah
- Umm Hureir Rd

Za'abeel

Oud Metha
- Al Nasr Cinema
- Lamcy
- Al Nasr Leisureland
- Cyclone
- American Hospital

Dubai Maritime City (u/c)

FAMILY EXPLORER

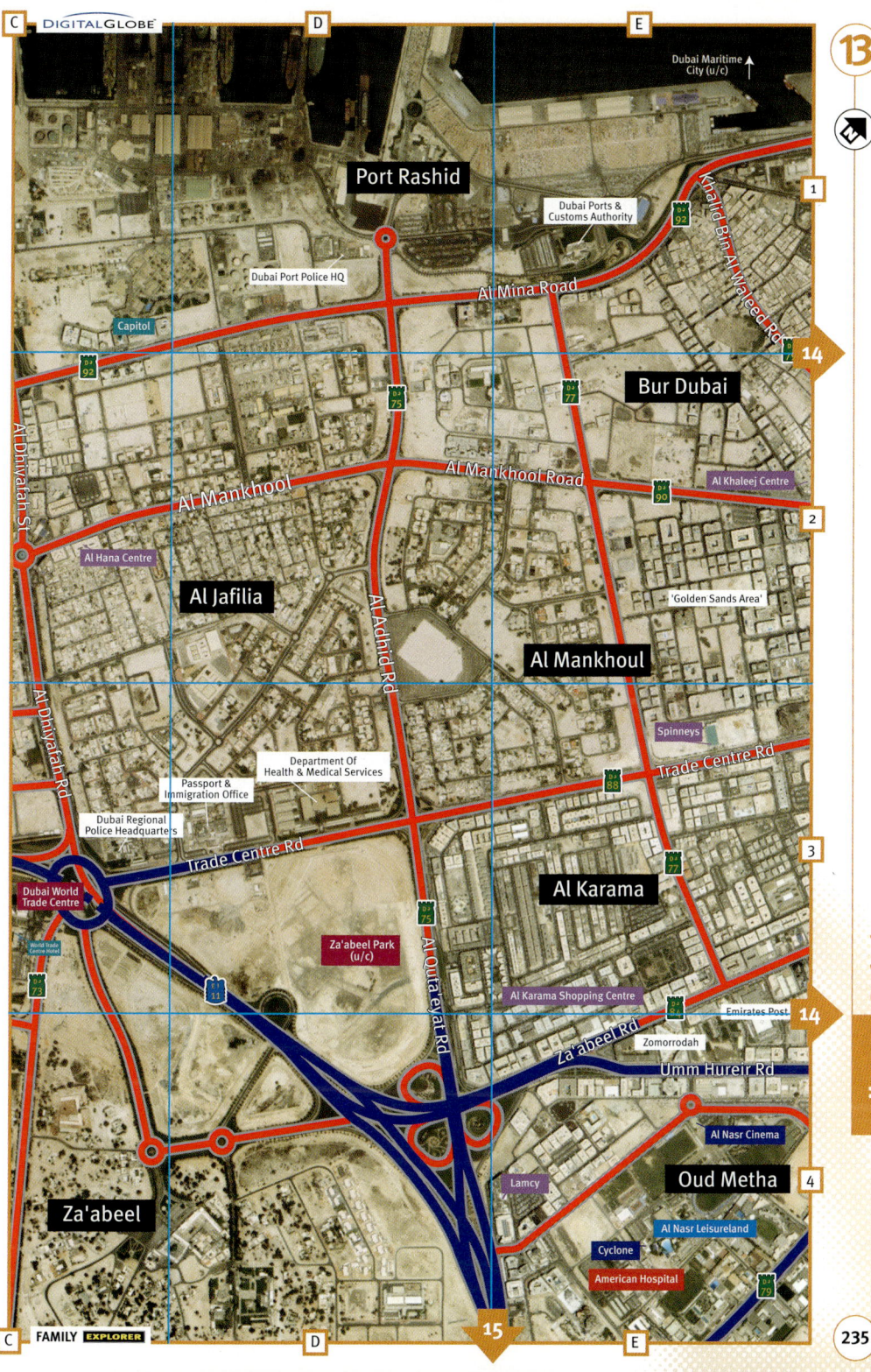

Dubai — Maps

235

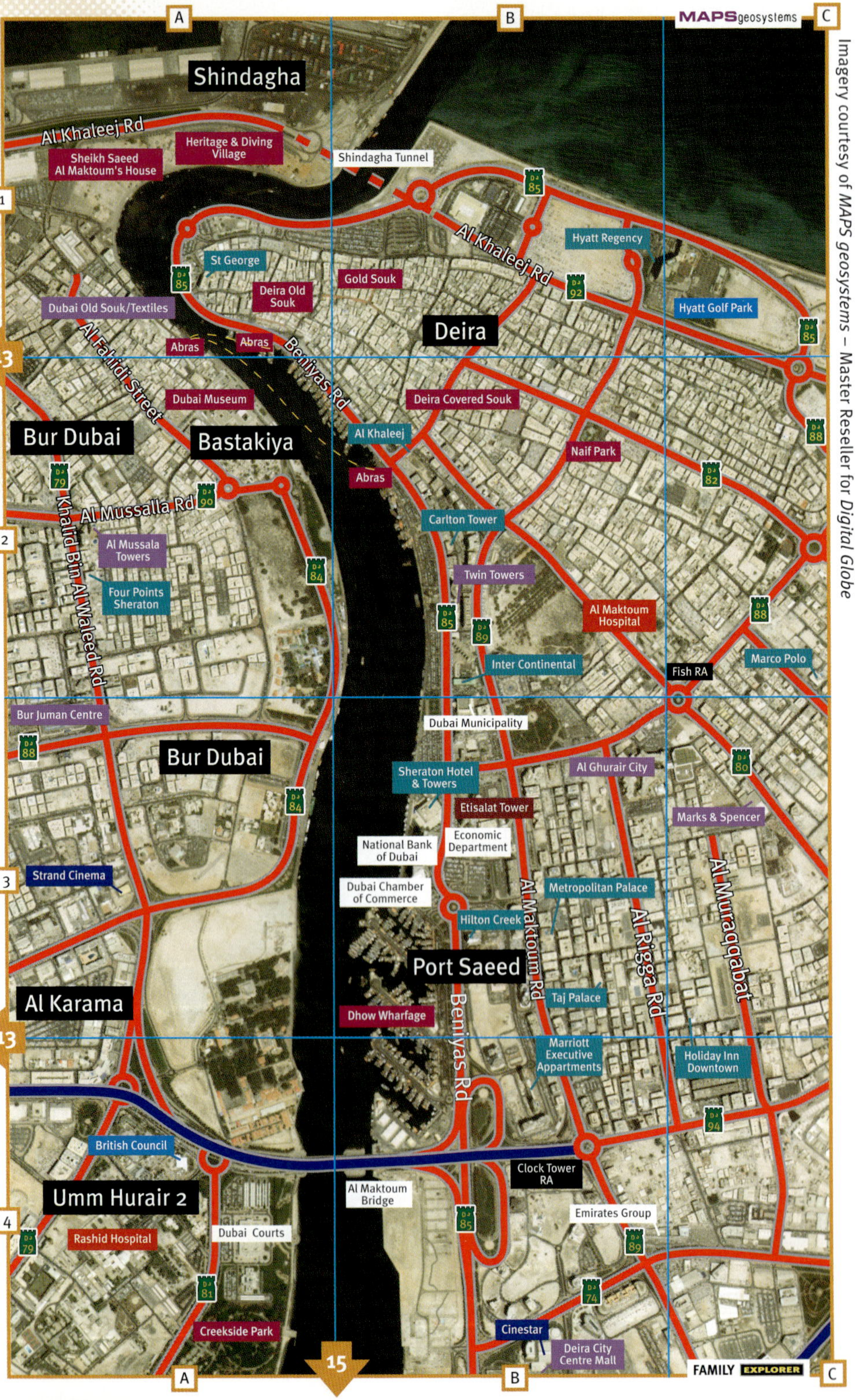
A
B
C
1
2
3
4
13
15
MAPSgeosystems
Shindagha
Al Khaleej Rd
Heritage & Diving Village
Sheikh Saeed Al Maktoum's House
Shindagha Tunnel
Hyatt Regency
St George
Gold Souk
Deira Old Souk
Dubai Old Souk/Textiles
Hyatt Golf Park
Deira
Abras
Beniyas Rd
Al Fahidi Street
Dubai Museum
Deira Covered Souk
Bur Dubai
Bastakiya
Al Khaleej
Naif Park
Al Mussalla Rd
Carlton Tower
Al Mussala Towers
Khalid Bin Al Waleed Rd
Twin Towers
Four Points Sheraton
Al Maktoum Hospital
Inter Continental
Marco Polo
Fish RA
Bur Juman Centre
Dubai Municipality
Sheraton Hotel & Towers
Al Ghurair City
Etisalat Tower
Marks & Spencer
National Bank of Dubai
Economic Department
Strand Cinema
Dubai Chamber of Commerce
Metropolitan Palace
Hilton Creek
Al Maktoum Rd
Al Rigga Rd
Al Muraqqabat
Port Saeed
Al Karama
Taj Palace
Dhow Wharfage
Marriott Executive Appartments
Holiday Inn Downtown
British Council
Clock Tower RA
Al Maktoum Bridge
Umm Hurair 2
Emirates Group
Dubai Courts
Rashid Hospital
Creekside Park
Cinestar
Deira City Centre Mall
FAMILY EXPLORER
Imagery courtesy of MAPS geosystems – Master Reseller for Digital Globe

Dubai

Maps

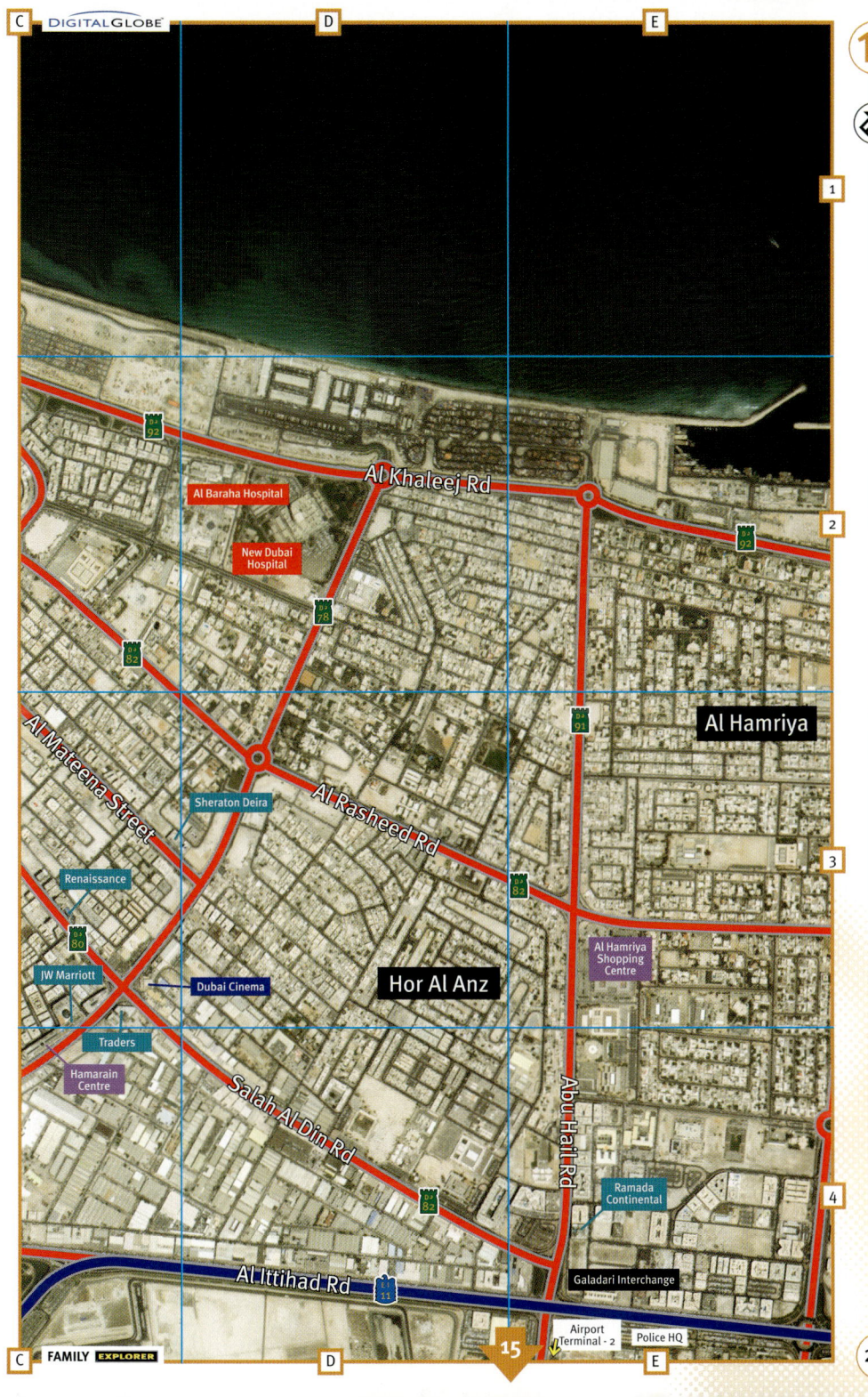

Dubai

Maps

- Al Baraha Hospital
- New Dubai Hospital
- Al Khaleej Rd
- Al Hamriya
- Al Mateena Street
- Sheraton Deira
- Al Rasheed Rd
- Renaissance
- JW Marriott
- Dubai Cinema
- Hor Al Anz
- Al Hamriya Shopping Centre
- Traders
- Hamarain Centre
- Salah Al Din Rd
- Abu Hail Rd
- Ramada Continental
- Al Ittihad Rd
- Galadari Interchange
- Airport Terminal - 2
- Police HQ

237

A
B
C
13
12
1
2
3
4
MAPSgeosystems
Doha Rd
E 44
Za'abeel
2nd Za'abeel Rd
Umm Hurair 2
Wafi City
Oud Metha Rd
Al Wasl Hospital
E 11
E 66
Al Wasl Club
Grand Cineplex
Grand Hyatt
Riyadh Rd
Al Qutaeyat Rd
Dubai Officers Club
Dubai Municipality Nursery
Jaddaf
Khor Dubai Wildlife Sanctuary
Bu Kidra / Country Club Int.
Dubai Exiles Rugby Club
Dubai Country Club
E 44
Dubai Polo Club
E 66
Dubai - Al Ain Rd
Ras Al Khor Rd
Ras Al Khor
Al Awir Industrial Area
FAMILY EXPLORER

Imagery courtesy of MAPS geosystems – Master Reseller for *Digital Globe*

Dubai

Maps

DIGITALGLOBE
C
D
14
E
Deira City Centre Mall
Dubai Police
Creekside Park
Dubai Creek Marina
Dubai Traffic Dept.
Childrens City
Cargo Village
Dubai Creek Golf & Yacht Club
Welcare Hospital
1
Wonderland
Aviation Club
Al Bustan Rotana
Airport Terminal 2
Al Boom Tourist Village
Dubai Tennis Stadium
Le Meridien Dubai
Dubai International Airport
Al Quds Rd
Airport Rd
Al Garhoud Bridge
Al Garhoud Complex
Airport Terminal 1
Jet Ski Area
Al Garhoud
Dhow Building Yard
Dubai Creek
Airport Free Zone
2
Al Khawaneej Rd
Tunnel(u/c)
Airport Expo Dubai
Festival City (u/c)
Bin Saugat Centre
Al Tawar
3
Nadd Shamma Park
Rashidiya
Nadd Shamma
Rashidiya Park
Rabat Rd
Nadd Al Hamar
4
Mirdif
Al Warqaa
C
FAMILY EXPLORER
D
E

Dubai

Maps

A-Z Index

#

7 Seas Divers **94**

A

A & E **28**
Abela Superstore **165**
Abu Dhabi Catamaran
  Association **108**
Abu Dhabi Cricket Council **93**
Abu Dhabi Down Netball
  League **106**
Abu Dhabi Dramatic
  Society (ADDS) **128**
Abu Dhabi Equestrian Club **99**
Abu Dhabi Falcons Ice
  Hockey **100**
Abu Dhabi Golf & Equestrian
  Club **97**
Abu Dhabi Golf and Equestrian
  Club **162**
Abu Dhabi Golf Club by
  Sheraton **97**
Abu Dhabi Grammar School **52**
Abu Dhabi Health & Fitness **86**
Abu Dhabi Health & Fitness
  Club **112, 121**
Abu Dhabi Hockey Club **99**
Abu Dhabi Ice Rink **158**
Abu Dhabi Mall **61**
Abu Dhabi Marina 'The Yacht
  Club' **119**
Abu Dhabi Mums **43, 68**
Abu Dhabi Municipality **12**
Abu Dhabi MX Club **104**
Abu Dhabi Nomads Club **96**
Abu Dhabi Rugby Football
  Club **107**
Abu Dhabi Sailing Club **108**
Abu Dhabi Squash League **110**
Abu Dhabi Striders **108**
Abu Dhabi Sub Aqua Club **93**
Abu Dhabi Tourist Club **88, 119**
Abu Dhabi Triathlon Club **114**
Abu Dhabi University **56**
Accessories for the Home **71**
Accidents **28**
...See Burns **37**
...See Marine Stings **36**
...See Snake Bites **36**
ACE Hardware **72**
ACI (Italian Cultural
  Association) **130**
Action Zone **83**
Active Sports **96, 113**
Activities **83**
Adams 0 - 10 **68**
Adventureland **84**
...See Advert **85**
Aeroplane **188**
Ajman Kempinski Hotel
  & Resort **141**
Ajman Museum **136**
AKM Music Centre **73**
Al Ain Flower Festival **23**
Al Ain Museum **136**
Al Ain Zoo & Aquarium **139**
Al Areesh **188**
Al Boom Diving **94, 110**
Al Boom Marine
...See Advert **79**

Al Boom Tourist Village **87**
Al Bustan Centre **62**
Al Bustan Palace
  InterContinental Muscat **144**
Al Diar Gulf Hotel & Resort **92**
Al Diar Jazira Beach
  Resort **121, 143**
Al Diar Siji Hotel **142**
Al Futtaim Centre **62**
Al Ghazal Golf Club **97**
Al Ghurair City **62**
Al Hamra Fort Hotel **92, 146**
Al Hamur Marine **75**
Al Hisn Kalba **137**
Al Jazira Diving Centre **93**
Al Jazira Hotel and
  Resort **91, 101, 118**
Al Khayal **188**
Al Khazzan Park **125**
Al Koufa **188**
Al Mamzar Beach Park **123**
Al Maqtaa Fort **135**
Al Mawakeb School **53**
Al Mushrief Children's
  Garden **124**
Al Nasr Fitness Centre **122**
Al Nasr Leisureland **152, 158**
Al Noor Centre, Dubai **57**
Al Noor Speech, Hearing
  & Development Centre **56**
Al Sawadi Resort **142**
Alliance Française **130-131**
Alternative Medicine **37**
American Arabian Gulf
  Squares **127**
American Community School
  of Abu Dhabi **52**
American Hospital
...See Advert **IFC**
American International
  School **52**
American Language
  Center **130**
American School of Dubai **53**
American University of
  Dubai **56**
Amusement Centres **83, 151**
Amusement Parks **86**
Annual Events **15, 22**
Antenatal **32**
Apollo **71**
Application Requirements **42**
Aquarius **71**
Arabian Adventures **172**
Arabia's Wildlife Centre **139**
Arabic **43**
...See Language **10**
...See Language Schools **130**
Archie's Library **131**
Argila **184**
Art Classes **126**
Art Shop **77**
Art
...See Art Shops **77**
Arty Parties **151**
Aviation Club,
  The **103, 113, 122**

B

Babes in Arms Dubai **153**
Baby Clothing **68**

Baby Equipment
...See Hire **68**
Baby Proofing **17**
...See Home Safety **72**
Baby Shop **66**
Baby Swimming **112**
Babycasa **66**
Babysitting **18**
...See Domestic
  Help/Maids/Housecleaners **20**
Ballet Centre, The **102, 128**
Balloon Lady,
  The **167-168, 170**
Baroudy's Sports Club **102**
Basketball **86**
Baskin Robbins **165-166**
Bastakiya **135**
Beach Centre, The **63**
Beach Clubs **119**
Beach Hut, The **91, 110**
Beachcombers **178**
Beaches **122, 161**
...See Beach Parks **123**
Beethoven Institute
  of Music **132**
Bella Vista **182**
Benetton **69**
Benihana **178, 182**
Berlitz **130**
Biella Caffé **188**
Biking Frontiers **104**
Birth Registration **35**
...See Registering a Birth **35**
Birth **32**
Birthday Cakes **165**
Birthday Parties **151**
...See Arty Parties **151**
...See Indoor Venues **151**
...See Out Of Town Parties **170**
...See Outdoor Venues **161**
...See Parties at Home **163**
...See Theme Parties **170**
...See Sporty Parties **162**
...See Party Survival Tips **151**
Bites **36**
Blue Dolphin **87, 109**
Blue Elephant **189**
Boarding - Sand **109**
Boarding Abroad **50**
Boardwalk, The **189**
Boat Charters **86**
Bodylines **121**
Book Worm **126**
Books Gallery **70**
Books **70**
Boulevard Gourmet, The **166**
Bowling **88, 152**
British Council Library **132**
British Council **130-131**
British Home Stores **68**
British School Al
  Khubairat, The **52**
British Therapy Service **57**
British University in Dubai **56**
Brownies **127**
Brush & Bisque It **152**
Bugs **22**
Burger King **157**
BurJuman Centre **63**
Burns **36**
Buses **12**
Business Hours **6**
Buying Property **16**

C

Cabs **12**
Cactus Cantina **189**
Café Ceramique **152, 194**
...See Advert **169**
Cafe Insignia **182**
Cafés **193**
Cambridge High School,
  Abu Dhabi **52**
Cambridge High School,
  Dubai **53**
Camel Racing **88**
Camping **90**
Canoeing **91**
Capital Gardens **124**
Caracalla Spa & Health
  Club **120**
Card Shop **168**
Carpe Diem **71**
Carrefour **78**
Cars **12**
...See Car Seats **14**
Carter's **182**
Cats **18**
...See Pets **17, 73**
Chemists **28**
Children's City **159**
Children's Clothes **68**
Children's Farm **139**
Children's Oasis Nursery **45**
...See Advert **38**
Childrens' Hairdressers **71**
Chili's Abu Dhabi **153, 156**
Chili's Dubai **184, 189**
...See Advert **187**
China White **189**
Chinese Pavilion **190**
Chiropractors **32**
Chriopodists **32**
Churches **11**
Cinemas **153**
Citrus **194**
City 2000 **84**
City Museums **135**
Cleopatra & Steiner
  Beauty Training Centre **56**
Climate **9**
Climbing **92**
Clinics - Well Woman &
  Well Man **37**
Clinics **29**
Club Joumana **98, 100, 121, 163**
Club Mina **120**
Club, The **119, 127, 131, 153**
Clubs & Associations **127**
Coastal Cruises **87**
Coco's **166, 190**
Coconut Bay **184**
Coffee Shops **193**
Colour 4 Kids **71**
Cosmetic Surgery **37**
Cottage Furniture **71**
Counselling **35**
Craft Corner **77, 126**
Crafts Shops **77**
Crafts **76**
Crazy Golf **92**
...See Mini Golf **103**
Creative Art Centre **72**
Creative Modern Center **126**
Creek Cruises **87**
Creekside Leisure **88**
...See Advert **89**

A-Z Index

C
Creekside Park **125**
Cricket **92**
Crystal Music Institute **133**
Cultural
  Foundation **126-127, 135**
Cultural Groups **11, 37**
Culture **9, 135**
Culture Shock **4**
Currency **9**
Curriculums **41**

D
Da Vinci's **190**
Daly Community Library **131**
Danat Dubai Cruises **88**
Dance Centre, The **128**
...See Advert **129**
Dance Classes **127**
Dar El Ilm School of
  Languages **131**
Darjeeling Cricket Club **93**
Darjeeling Hockey Club **99**
Debenhams **68**
Deira City Centre **63**
Dentists **30**
Dermatologists **32**
Descamps **66**
Desert
  Rangers **91, 104, 114, 172**
Dhow & Anchor **190**
Dhow Charters **86**
Discovery Centre **137, 159**
Diving **93**
Doctors **29**
Dog Show, The **23**
Dogs **18**
...See also Pets **17, 73**
Dome Café **194**
Domestic Help Agencies **20**
Domestic Help **20**
Domestic Services **18**
Don Corleone **191**
Doodles **160**
Dorothy Perkins **73**
Drama Groups **128**
Dreamland Aqua Park **116, 163**
Dress **10**
Drink Driving **15**
Driving **14**
Drs Nicolas & Asp
...See Advert **31**
Dubai Adventure Mums **43**
Dubai Aikido Club **103**
Dubai American Academy **53**
Dubai Charity Association **69**
Dubai College **127**
Dubai Community
  Health Centre **57**
Dubai Country
  Club **96-97, 113, 122, 134**
...See Advert **111**
Dubai Creek Golf & Yacht
  Club **97, 122**
Dubai Drama Group **128**
Dubai English Speaking
  School **54**
Dubai Exiles Rugby Club **107**
Dubai Health Authority **35**
Dubai International Art
  Centre **126, 134**
Dubai Junior Ice Hockey **100**
Dubai Karate Centre **103**
Dubai Kennels & Cattery **18**
...See Advert **19**
Dubai London Clinic
...See Advert **33**
Dubai Municipality **12**
Dubai Museum **135**
Dubai Music School **133**
Dubai Netball League **106**
Dubai Offshore Sailing
  Club **108, 123**
Dubai Palm Island **18**
Dubai Raft Race **23**
Dubai Road Runners **108**
Dubai Sandstorms Junior Ice
  Hockey Club **100**
Dubai Shopping
  Festival **15, 23**
Dubai Shopping Festival **61**
Dubai Special Needs Center **57**
Dubai Squash League **110**
Dubai Summer
  Surprises **15, 23, 61**
Dubai Summer Surprises **134**
Dubai Tennis
  Academy **113, 134**
Dubai Tennis Open **23**
Dubai Travel & Tourist
  Services **172**
Dubai Triathlon Club **114**
Dubai Water Sports
  Association **118**
Dubai Wind Band **133**
Dubai Youth Moto-Cross
  Club **104**
Dubai Zoo **139**
Dugym **98**
Dune Bashing **114**
Dune Buggy Riding **94**
Dyslexia Support Group **56**

E
Ear Problems **37**
Early Learning Centre **78**
Earnest Insurance Brokers
...See Advert **5**
Eauzone **191**
Education **41**
Electricity **21**
Elle **68**
ELS Language Center **130**
Elves & Fairies **77, 127**
Emaar Properties **16**
Emergencies **28**
...See Burns **37**
...See Marine Stings **36**
...See Snake Bites **36**
...See Menigitis **37**
Emirates Aviation College **56**
Emirates British Nursery **46**
Emirates Golf Club **98**
Emirates Hobbies Ass. Art
  and Crafts **127**
Emirates International
  School **54**
Emirates Karting Centre **158**
Emirates Parent Plus
...See Advert **173**
Emirates Riding Centre **99, 162**
Emirates Sports Centre **102**
Emirates Sports Stores **75**
Emirates Trading
  Establishment **77**

F
Emirta Horse Requirements **75**
Encounter Zone **84**
English College Dubai **54**
E-sports **113**
E-sports Football Academy **96**
Estithmaar **16**
ExpatRegister
...See Advert **13**
Expatriation **3**
ExpatWoman
...See Advert **13**

Falaj Daris Hotel **146**
Fantasy Kingdom **84**
Fast Food **157**
Fees – Schools **42**
Feline Friends **73**
Fiesta World Cafe **194**
First Aid **36**
First Steps Kindergarten
  & Primary School **45**
Fishing **95**
Fishmarket, The **185**
Flamingo Beach Resort **146**
Flash Floods **115**
Flavours **180**
Flying Elephant **167-168**
...See Advert **148**
Fontana **182**
Foodcourts **196**
Foodlands **185**
Football **95**
...See Ball Skills **74**
Foresight
...See Advert **24**
Formes **73**
Formula One Dubai **101, 159**
Foton World **83-84**
Fotouh Al Khair Centre **62**
French Bakery **166**
French Connection **166, 195**
Friday Brunch Abu Dhabi **178**
Friday Brunch Al Ain **180**
Friday Brunch Dubai **182**
Fruit & Garden Luna Park **86**
Fudd's Playland **156**
Fuddruckers
  Abu Dhabi **154, 185**
Fuddruckers Dubai **191**
Fujairah Aviation Centre **106**
Fujairah Heritage Village **136**
Fujairah Hilton **143**
Fujairah Museum **136**
Fun Corner **160**
Fun Island **159**
Fun Sports **101, 109, 118**
Fun World **83-84**
Future Centre **56**
Futurekids **134**

G
Galleria Ice Rink **158**
Games **78**
Gap **68**
Garden, The **178**
Gardenia **191**
Gardening **20**
Gemaco **71**
General Practitioners **29**
General Safety **36**
Gift Express **166**
Giggles English Nursery **45**
Go West **191**
Golden Boats **94**
Golden Dragon Kung Fu
  Institute **102**
Golden Falcon Karate
  Centre **103**
Golf House **75**
Golf **96**
...See Crazy Golf **92**
...See Mini Golf **103**
Gozo Garden **182**
Grand Hyatt Dubai
...See Advert **197**
Grand Hyatt Muscat **144**
Grand Stores **9**
Great British Day **23**
Great Expectations **73**
Guides **127**
Gulf Greetings **167-168**
Gulf Montessori Centre **57**
Gulf Montessori Nursery **46**
Gymboree Play & Music
  Abu Dhabi **132, 160**
Gymboree Play & Music
  Dubai **133, 160**
Gymnastics **98**
Gynaecologists **34**

H
Hairdressers – Kids **71**
Hard Rock Café Abu Dhabi **156**
Hard Rock Café Dubai **192**
Hardee's **157**
Hatta Dam **137**
Hatta Fort Hotel **103, 143**
Hatta Heritage Village **137**
Havana Cafe **194**
Health
...See Maternity **32**
...See Medical care **28**
...See Paediatricians **29**
Health & Sports Clubs **121**
Health Card **27**
Health Insurance **17**
Health Requirements **12**
Heat Waves **75**
Heritage & Diving
  Village **87, 135**
Heritage **135**
Hili Fun City & Ice Rink **86**
Hilton Abu Dhabi **140, 154**
Hilton Al Ain **141**
Hilton Baynunah Tower **154**
Hobby Centre **78**
Hockey **99**
Holiday Inn Muscat **144**
Holidays **15**
Home Centre **71**
Home Furnishings
  & Accessories **71**
Home Improvements **21**
Home Safety **72**
...See Baby Proofing the Home **17**
Homewares
...See Interior Design **72**
Horizon School **54**
Horse Riding **99**

A-Z

Horse World Trading 75
Hospitals 29
...See A & E 28
...See Maternity 32
...See Medical care 28
...See Paediatricians 29
Hotel InterContinental
  Abu Dhabi 141
Hotel InterContinental Al Ain 142
Hotel InterContinental
  Muscat 144
Housecleaners 20
Household Insurance 17
Housing 15, 16
Humpty Dumpty Nursery 45
Hyatt Golf Park 92, 103

I

Ice Hockey 100
Ice Skating 100, 158
IKEA 71, 195
Il Palazzo 185
Immunisations 35
In Disguise 170
...See Advert 171
In Touch Relocations
...See Advert x
India Palace 192
Insect Stings 36
Insects/Rodents 22
Insurance Brokers 17
Insurance Companies –
  Medical 27
Interior Design 72
International Community
  School 53
International Music Institute 132
International School of
  Choueifat Abu Dhabi 53
International School of
  Choueifat Dubai 54
Irish Village 192
Italian Cultural Association 130

J

Jamil Fashions 69
JC Penny 68
Jebel Ali Equestrian
  Club 100, 162
Jebel Ali Golf Resort & Spa 143
Jebel Ali Primary School 54
Jebel Ali Sailing
  Club 91, 109, 118, 162
Jellyfish 123
Jenny Rose 73
Jet Skiing 101
Johnny Rockets 192
Jumeira Beach Corniche 123
Jumeira Beach Park 124
Jumeirah Beach
  Club 103, 112, 120, 122
Jumeirah Beach Hotel 123
Jumeirah Centre 64
Jumeirah College 55
Jumeirah English
  Speaking School 55
Jumeirah Health &
  Beach Club, The 120
Jumeirah International
  Nursery School 46
Jumeirah Plaza 64
Jumeirah Primary School 55

K

K9 Friends 73
Karting 101, 158
KAS 71
Kennels
...See Dubai Kennels &
  Cattery Advert 19
Kentucky Fried Chicken 157
Keys 21
Khalidia Palace Hotel 141
Khalidiya Children's
  Garden 124
Khalifa International
  Bowling Centre 152
Khasab Hotel 143
Khasab Travel & Tours 87
Kids Clothes 68
Kids Play Abu Dhabi 160, 168
Kids Play Dubai 160, 168
Kids' Cottage 46
Kids' Hairdressers 71
Kids' Island Nursery 46
Kids' Village 47
Kite Flying 101
Kite Surfing 101
Knowledge Village 56
Kodak 9

L

La Brasserie 179
La Brioche 195
La Piazza 179
Ladies Art Group, The 126
Ladies Park 124
Ladybird Nursery 47
Lamcy Plaza 64
Language 10
...See Arabic 43
...See Education 40
Language Schools 130
Laundry 20
Le Belvedere 180
Le Meridien
  Abu Dhabi 141, 154
Le Studio Mystique 74
Leisure Games Centre 101, 158
LG InSportz 93, 96, 114, 134, 161
Libraries 131
Lime Tree Café 195
Little Land Montessori 47
Liwa Resthouse 144
Local Media 8
Locks 21
Lodge, The 183
Lou Lou Al Dougongs 160

M

MacKenzie Associates 72
...See Advert 145
Madinat Jumeirah 65
Magazines 8
Magic Planet 84
Magrudy's
...See Book Shop 70, 168

...See Shoe Shop 69
...See Shopping Mall 64
Maids 20
Maintenance 21
Malls 61
Manzil Centre for Challenged
  Individuals 57
Maps 200
Marina Gulf Trading 71
Marina Mall 62, 154
Marine Stings 35
Market Place, The 183
Marks & Spencer 68
Marks & Spencer Café 195
Martial Arts 102
Maternity 32
...See Hospitals 29
...See Maternity Clothes 73
...See Natural Child Birth 34
...See Obstetricians &
  Gynaecologists 34
...See Support Groups 37
Mazaya Centre 65
McDonald's 157
Media 8
Medical Care 26
Medical Institutions 28
...See Hospitals 29
...See General Practitioners 29
Medical Insurance 27
Medical Insurance
  Companies 28
Melody House Musical
  Instruments 73
Meningitis 37
...See Emergencies 28
Mental Health 35
Mercato 65
Mercure Al Falaj Hotel 144
Metropolitan Resort &
  Beach Club 120, 123
Mini Golf 103
...See Crazy Golf 92
Ministry of Agriculture &
  Fisheries 18
Ministry of Education 43
Ministry of Health Department
  of Preventive Medicine 35
Mirdif Mums 44
Miss J Café 165
Mister Baker 165-166
Money 9
Monsoon 68
Montgomerie Golf Club 98
More 196
Mother and baby groups
...See Toddler groups 44
Mothercare 66
Mothers and Miracles 44
Mother to Mother 44
Moto-Cross 104
Mountain Biking 104
Moving to the UAE 3
Multinational Education 41
Mummy & Me 68
Mums and Tots Group 43
Municipality hotline 95
Municipality
...See Ministry of Agriculture &
  Fisheries 18
...See Ministry of Education 43
...See Ministry of Health Department
  of Preventive Medicine 35
...See Public Parks and Recreation
  Section 90, 123
Museums 135, 159

...See Museums – City 135
...See Museums – Out of City 136
Mushrif Park 125
Music Lessons 132
Musical Instruments 73
Musical Youth Theatre, The
  Ballet Centre 128

N

Nad Al Sheba Club 183, 98
National Library 131
National Museum of
  Ras Al Khaimah 137
Natural Childbirth 34
...See Maternity 32
Net Tours 172
Netball 104
Newspapers 8
Next 68
Nihal Restaurant 186
Nina 192
North Star Expeditions LLC 142
Nurseries 44, 48

O

Oasis Beach Club 120
Oasis Centre 65
Oasis Chinese Restaurant 186
Obstetricians 34
Oceanic Hotel 110, 144
Offroad Emirates 172
Okaidi 68
Old Library, The 132
Organisers & Entertainers 167
Orient Tours 172
Oriental Karate & Kobudo
  Club 102
Orthodontists 30
Osteopaths 32
Ovo 68
Oxford School, The 55

P

P. J. O'Reillys 179
Pablosky 68
Paediatricians 29
Pagoda House 71
Paintballing 106, 161
Palace at One&Only
  Royal Mirage, The 142
Palm Beach Leisure Club 91
Palm, The 186
Palms Nursery School 47
Palms Resort 120
Panda Panda Chinese
  Restaurant 186
Papermoon 168
Park N Shop 166
Parks 124, 162
...See Beach Parks 123
Parties 151
Party Accessories 167
Party Food 165
Party Games 164
Paul Thuysbaert
  Photography 74

242

FAMILY EXPLORER

A-Z Index

Pavilion Dive Centre 94
Pavilion Marina &
  Sports Club, The 118
Pesticides 22
Pet Land 73
Pet Zone 73
Pets 17, 73
  ...See Bringing Your Pet
    into the UAE 18
  ...See K9 Friends 73
  ...See Dubai Kennels &
    Cattery Advert 19
Pharaoh's
  Club 92, 112, 114, 122, 156
Pharmacies 28
Phones 21
Photography 9, 74
Physios 32
Picnico General Trading 76
Pinkies 71
Pizza Hut 157
Pizzaland 157
Pizzeria Italiana 186
Pizzeria Uno Chicago Grill 193
Places of Worship 6, 11
Plaice, The 193
Plane Tours 106
Planet Hollywood 156, 183
  ...See Advert 155
Play Centres 106, 159
Plumbing 21
Polyglot Language Institute 131
Population 6
Portrait Photographer/Artist 74
Portrait Photography 74
Posters 170
Pre Flight Checks 106
Pre Schools 44, 48
Prémaman 69
Private Medical Insurance 27
Property Purchase 16
Property Rental 15
Psychiatry 35
Psychology 35
Public Garden 125
Public Parks and
  Recreation Section 90, 123
Pursuit Games 106, 161

R

Radisson SAS Muscat 146
Rainbow Steak House 186
Rainbows 127
Ramadan 8, 176
Rangers 127
Ras Al Khaimah Hotel 146
Rashid Paediatric
  Therapy Centre 57
Rashidiya Park 125
Recreational Gymnastics
  Club 98
Recycling 21
Reebok Fitkids 99
Regent School 55
Registering a Birth 21
  ...See Birth 32
Religion 6, 11
Relocation 16
Rent a Crib, Dubai 68
Renting Property 15
Reset 68
Restaurant Taxes 177

Restaurants
  ...See Abu Dhabi 184
  ...See Dubai 188
Riding for the Disabled
  Association of Dubai 57
Ritz-Carlton 120, 142
Road Safety 14
Rock Bottom Café 179
Rollerblading 107
Rosebuds 179
Rotana Junior Golf League 97
Roundabouts 14
Royal Mirage 142
Royal Music Academy 132
Royal Orchid, The 179
Rubbish Disposal 21
Rugby 7s 15
Rugby 107
Running 107

S

Safa Kindergarten Nursery
  School 47
Safa Park 86, 125
Safe Play 160
Safety 8, 36
Sailing 108
Sam Tours 87
Sand Boarding 109
Sand Skiing 109
Sandra Metaxa 74
Sandy Beach Motel 143
Schools 50
  ...See Acceptance 41
  ...See At a Glance 48
  ...See Curriculum 41
  ...See Fees 42
  ...See Hours 41
  ...See Starting Age 41
  ...See Uniforms 48
Scouts Association (British
  Groups Abroad) 127
Scuba 2000 110
Scuba Diving 93
Scuba Dubai 94, 110
Scuba Dubai Shop 76
Scubatec 94
Sea World 193
Secondhand Clothes 69
Security 8
Sesame Street Private
  Nursery 45
Seven Seas Divers 94
Sevilo's 180
Shadows 12
Sharjah Archaeological
  Museum 138
Sharjah Desert park 138
Sharjah Fort (Al Hisn) 138
Sharjah Heritage Museum 138
Sharjah Natural History
  Museum 138
Sharjah Science Museum 138
Sheikh Saeed Al Maktoum's
  House 87
Sheraton Abu Dhabi Resort &
  Towers 141, 154
Sheraton Jumeirah 123
Sheraton Oman Hotel 146
Shk Mohammed Centre for
  Cultural Understanding 136
  ...See Advert IBC

Shoe City 69
Shoe Mart 69
Shopping Malls 61
Shopping 61
Showcase Antiques 71
Sinbads Club 156
Skiing – Sand 109
Skyline Health Club 121
Small Steps Nursery School 47
Small World Nursery 47
Snake Bites 36
Snorkelling 109
Social Hours 6
Social Groups 11, 37
Sohar Beach Hotel 146
Souk Madinat Jumeirah 65
Special Needs 56
Specialist, The
  ...See Advert 7
Speed Limits 15
Spice Island 183
Spinneys 65, 167
SplashLand 116, 163
Sporting Goods 74
Sports 83
Sports United 134
Sporty Parties 162
Squash 110
St Andrews Playgroup 43
St. Mary's Catholic School 55
Stationery 70
Stepping Stones Nursery 45
Steve & Mary Smith
  Photography 74
Stings 36
Studio Al Aroosa 74
Studio R 68
Subway 158
Summer Camps 133
Sun & Sand Sports 75
Sun Protection 124
Sunburn 36
Sunshine Tours 172
Super Kids Nursery 50
SuperSports 114
Support Groups 11, 37
Swimming 112

T

Tap Dancing 128
Tavern 180
Taxes 177
Taxis 12
Teachers 41
Telecommunications 21
Television 21
Tender Love and Care 50
Tennis 113
Terry Fox Run 23
Tertiary Education 55
TGI Friday's Abu Dhabi 154
TGI Friday's Dubai 156, 193
Thai Chi 193
THE One Abu Dhabi & Dubai 72
THE One Café Abu Dhabi 194
The Warehouse 71
Theme Parties 170
Thomsun Music 73
Thunder Bowl 153
Tiny Home Montessori 50
Toby's Jungle Adventure 160
Toddler Groups 43

Tour Operators 140
Town Centre 65
Toy Town 83
Toys 76
Toys & Games 78
Toys 'R' Us Abu Dhabi 78, 168
Toys 'R' Us Dubai 78, 170
Travel Agents 140
Travel Insurance 12
Trekking 114
Triathlon 114

U

UAE English Soccer School
  of Excellence FZ-LLC 96, 163
UAE Golf Association 98
UAE kite surfing
  association 102
Umm Suqeim Park 126
Undercover Mums 133
Uniforms - Schools 48
University of Southern
  Queensland in Dubai 56
University of Wollongong 56

V

Visas 11, 140
Vocal Studio 133

W

Wadi Bashing 114
Wafi City 135
Wafi Mall 66
Walks 115
Wasco White Star 78
Water Parks 116, 163
Water Skiing 116
Water Sports 118
Weekend Breaks 140
Well Woman & Well Man 37
West One 196
Westwood 68
Wheels Trading 76
Wild Wadi Water Park 116, 163
  ...See Advert 117
Windsurfing 118
Wolfi's Bike Shop 76
Wonder Sea Fish 73
WonderLand Theme &
  Water Park 86
Woolworths 68

Y

Yellow Brick Road Nursery 50
Yoga 118
Young Leaders & Rangers 127

Z

Zak Electronics &
  Musical Instruments 73
Zoos 139

FAMILY EXPLORER   243

Notes

Notes

Notes